Computer Organization and Programming: VAX-11

Computer Organization
and Programming: VAX-11

Souhail El-Asfouri
Olin Johnson
Willis K. King
University of Houston

ADDISON-WESLEY PUBLISHING COMPANY
Reading, Massachusetts • Menlo Park, California
London • Amsterdam • Don Mills, Ontario • Sydney

This book is in the
Addison-Wesley series in Computer Science
MICHAEL A. HARRISON
CONSULTING EDITOR

VAX/RMS is a trademark of Digital Equipment Corporation.

Library of Congress Cataloging in Publication Data

El-Asfouri, Souhail.
  Computer organization and programming: VAX-11.

  Bibliography: p.
  Includes index.
  1. VAX-11 (Computer)—Programming.   I. Johnson, Olin.
II. King, Willis K.   III. Title.
QA76.8.V37E4   1984   001.64′2   83-3699
ISBN 0-201-10425-3

ISBN 0-201-10425-3
ABCDEFGHIJ-MA-89876543

Dedicated to our parents and families

Preface

THIS BOOK is designed for a one-semester course in basic computer organization and assembly language programming. It generally follows the guidelines for the course designated CS-3, Introduction to Computer Systems, as specified in the ACM Curriculum 78. The Digital Equipment Corporation's VAX-11 System is used as a running example throughout the text. Prerequisites should include a course in computer programming in a higher-level language such as FORTRAN, Pascal, or PL/I.

This book leads the students step by step, from understanding the primitive actions a computer can perform, to writing nontrivial programs in assembly language. Good programming practices, such as top-down design and modular and structural construction of programs, are emphasized. A student will not be able to assimilate the material presented in the book unless he or she has adequate opportunity to practice what he or she learns on a computer. In order to get the students on the machine as early as possible, only a small subset of the instructions, addressing modes, and data types are introduced in the beginning chapters. Discussions on the more advanced addressing modes and data types are delayed until later on. Other instructions are explained as they are used in programming examples.

The VAX-11 is used not only because of its popularity, particularly among computer science departments, but also because of its state-of-the-art architecture, the richness of its addressing modes, and its well-designed instruction set. Reasonable care has been exercised, however, so that every important concept is first introduced in machine-independent generality, followed by specific implementation examples using the VAX-11. The text uses DEC terminology in the VAX-11 examples; when this terminology varies from the norm of the industry, however, the differences are pinpointed. We believe that the student will be able to learn and use other computer systems at the assembly language level very quickly after studying this text.

The use of system input/output (I/O) macros is demonstrated very early in the book, in somewhat of a "cookbook" manner. We encourage our students to use these macros to perform the input/output operations. This frees them from dependence on a higher-level language for I/O operations. Further, it gives them some insight into the problems involving these operations in general and prepares them for learning the details presented in the last chapter of the book. The treatment of I/O is a compromise between the use of a higher-level language that completely obscures the real action taken by the computer, and the use of privileged I/O hardware instructions. Such instructions give the student complete control of the machine, which is an unaffordable luxury for most computer science departments.

Several appendixes are included to make the book as self-contained as possible. Appendix A presents a thorough discussion of number representations and their conversion from one system to another. It also covers basic binary arithmetic and logic operations. Subsequent appendixes teach the students the use of the terminal, the basics of the editor and the debugger, and so on. They should be handy for students trying to enter and debug programs on a terminal. Obviously, the appendixes cannot cover every detail of the VAX-11 assembly language. We recommend the following publications as references, all published by the manufacturer of the machine:

1. *VAX Architecture Handbook*
2. *VAX-11 MACRO Language Reference Manual AA-D032D-TE*
3. *VAX-11 MACRO User's Guide AA-D033D-TE*

The organization of the book is as follows:

Chapter 1 gives an overview of the assembly language and its position among different levels of programming languages.

Chapter 2 introduces basic computer organization and its operations. It also discusses basic data types and machine instruction formats.

Chapters 3 and 4 describe the basics of assembly language. Chapter 3 introduces the concepts and terminology in general, and Chapter 4 describes the specifics using the DEC VAX-11 MACRO as an example.

Chapter 5 begins where Chapter 4 leaves off, with a systematic discussion of the addressing modes available on the VAX-11.

Chapter 6 presents a general discussion of subroutines and their implementation on the VAX-11.

Chapter 7 shows the structure of a two-pass assembler and gives examples of object code generation by the VAX-11 MACRO Assembler. This is followed by a discussion of the linker and the loader.

Chapter 8 discusses macros, including conditional assembly and repeat blocks.

Chapter 9 extends the discussion of data types. It describes floating point and various forms of decimal number representations, as well as the "edit" instruction provided on the VAX-11 system.

Chapter 10 shows input/output programming at the assembly language level.

At the University of Houston, the material in this book is covered in a four-credit-hour course in one fifteen-week semester at the sophomore level. This includes three hours of lectures and three hours of laboratory class each week. Students are required to write five to six programs to complete the course. We also consider the book appropriate for self-study by professional people who have access to a VAX-11 system.

Depending on local conditions and teaching philosophy, the instructor may choose to reorder the presentation of the materials. Some may prefer to teach Chapter 7 (on the Assembler) after a discussion of the macros and the more advanced data types (Chapters 8 and 9); others may want to move the topic up and present it immediately after Chapter 4 (on VAX-11 assembly language). Chapter 7 is sufficiently independent to allow such movement without much difficulty. In our own experience, we find it necessary to cover the materials presented in Appendix A ("Number Representations and Arithmetic") in some detail at the beginning of the semester. Others, however, may want to go to the assembly language of the VAX-11 as early as possible and consequently may even skip parts of Chapter 2. For schools that are on a quarter system and courses that concentrate on VAX-11 assembly language programming only, the instructor may elect to cover only Sections 2.2, 2.3, and 2.5 of Chapter 2; to select parts of Chapters 7, 8, and 9 within the time constraint; and to skip Chapter 10 altogether.

Houston, Texas   S.E., O.J., W.K.K.
August 1983

Contents

Chapter 1

Introduction

THE FIRST electronic computer was built in the mid-1940s. Since then, in less than forty years, we have witnessed an unprecedented development of this marvelous machine. Today, the computer is ubiquitous in our society. Many people may use computers without even realizing that they are doing so. When a person looks at a digital watch, cooks a meal with a microwave oven, or uses a bank card at an automatic bank teller, he or she is using a computer. Other people recognize that the computer can be directed to solve their particular problems. They learn programming languages such as BASIC, FORTRAN, COBOL, or Pascal to enable them to communicate with computers. Still others want to have deeper understanding of computers and how they operate. This book is intended for this last group of people. It gives them a first look at the internal workings of the computer.

The first requirement for gaining in-depth understanding of computers and their operations is to have a good knowledge of the language of the machine. This chapter is a step in that direction. Section 1.1 introduces the language of the machine. Then a closely related language, assembly language, is introduced. As we shall see, it is far easier to work with the symbolic assembly language than with the numeric machine language. Yet understanding assembly language is comparable to understanding machine language in its usefulness for examining the internal workings of the computer.

Because of different design preferences by computer manufacturers, as well as different intended applications, every computer has its own machine language or, equivalently, its own assembly language. In other words, there are as many assembly languages as there are types of computers. Hence, an assembly language program is written for a particular type of computer. (Contrast this with a higher-level language program, which may be run, possibly with some modifications, on any computer that supports the language.) Thus programming in assembly language requires intimate knowledge of the particular computer to be programmed. In this book we use the VAX-11 computer system and its assembly language for illustration, although every attempt is made to point out common features among assembly languages. A VAX-like assembly language is introduced in Section 1.2 and is used to show an example of an assembly language program. The program is then shown in VAX-11 assembly language.

Assembly language has uses beyond understanding computers. Section 1.3 details some of the reasons for learning assembly language. For efficient use of a computer system, the computer hardware must be supplemented with special software. Section 1.4 is a brief introduction to that software. The chapter concludes with an overview of the VAX-11 family of computers.

1.1 Machine and Assembly Languages

The objective of this section is to answer the question: What are machine and assembly languages? We begin by looking briefly at what a higher-level language program goes through before it can be executed by the computer hardware. We assume that the reader is familiar to some extent with a higher-level language such as FORTRAN, Pascal, or PL/I.

Program Translation

Conventional computers cannot directly execute the English-like statements of a higher-level language program. Such programs must first be translated into a language that the computer comprehends. This language is called *machine language.*

A program that is written in a higher-level language is commonly referred to as the *source program;* the translated program, which is in machine language, is called the *object program.* The translation of a higher-level language (HLL) program is performed by a program called the *compiler.* The compiler reads the HLL source program, much as any other program reads data, and generates the machine language object program. Thus the source program is the input (data) to the compiler, and the object program is the output. This relation is depicted pictorially as follows:

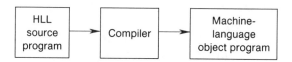

Note that during the translation phase, the compiler is the program that is being executed by the computer hardware, *not* the user's source program. Later, after the object program is completely generated, the user's program in its new form can be executed.

Machine Language

We now look at the nature of machine language or, equivalently, at object programs. Although different computers have different machine languages, as mentioned earlier, there are certain features that are common to most of them. The following characteristics are shared by all conventional computers.

The computer hardware can execute only basic instructions, such as *add, subtract, compare, branch,* and the like. Thus the object program consists of basic instructions that correspond to the statements in the source program. The computer identifies each instruction by a code called the *operation code, or op code* for short. The code is often represented in numeric form. For example, 65 is one of the VAX op codes for *add,* and 81 is one of the op codes for *compare.* The instructions in the object program are represented by their op codes.

Some instructions require operands (data) to be operated on. The operands would have to be specified to the hardware together with the operation. Operands in a computer system are stored in storage (or memory) locations where every location is identified by a unique number called its *address.* When an operation that requires operands is presented to the hardware for execution, the address of the locations at which the operands are to be found and the address of a location to hold the result are also specified.

The format of an instruction and its operand specifiers might look like this:

```
65    20,30,40
```

which means *add* 20,30,40. This instructs the computer hardware to add the operands at memory locations 20 and 30 (that is, to add the *contents* of these two locations) and to store the result in memory location 40. Figure 1.1 shows the memory locations referenced before and after executing the foregoing instruction. The question marks (?) in location 40 indicate that the initial contents of this location are not significant since they will be overwritten by the result of the instruction.

Another characteristic of conventional computers is that they comprise electronic devices that can be in only one of two states at any time; these states are represented by 0 and 1. Thus the computer hardware can process only information in binary, and all information presented to the hardware for processing consists of strings of

Contents	Address		Contents	Address
106	20		106	20
. . .	. . .		. . .	. . .
−54	30		−54	30
. . .	. . .		. . .	. . .
???	40		052	40

(a) before	(b) after

Figure 1.1 Contents of memory before and after executing the instruction *add* 20, 30, 40

0s and 1s. Note that numbers in Figure 1.1 are shown in decimal for clarity; inside the computer, however, the contents of the memory locations—as well as the op code of the instruction and the addresses in the instruction—will be represented in the two states 0 and 1. For example, the instruction

```
65    20,30,40
```

might be represented inside the computer by

```
1000001    010100 011110 101000
```

In summary, an object (machine language) program is a sequence of basic instructions, with the instructions and the operands encoded in binary.

Assembly Language

In the early days of computers, programmers wrote programs in machine language; that is, they manually supplied the binary encodings of their programs. Needless to say, programming in machine language is extremely tedious and error-prone. Because of these difficulties, programmers later used symbols to describe operations and specify operands. For example, they would use the *mnemonics* A and S to represent the *add* and the *subtract* instructions, instead of the op codes of the instructions. Similarly, they would use symbolic names instead of numeric addresses to refer to memory locations. For example, they would write

```
A    X,Y,Z
```

instead of something like

1000001   010100 011110 101000

where X, Y, Z refer to memory locations 010100, 011110, 101000.

When machine instructions are specified by using symbolic names, they are called *assembly instructions. Assembly language* is simply machine language in symbolic form.

As with a higher-level language program, an assembly language program must be translated into machine language before it can be executed. A program called the *assembler* performs the translation. Like the compiler, the assembler reads an assembly language source program as data and generates its equivalent machine language object program. This is depicted pictorially as follows:

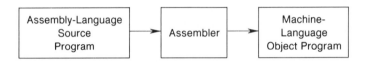

The time period during which an assembly language program is being translated is called *assembly time*. The actual translation process is called *assembly*. The time period during which the user's program (in its *object* form) is executed is called *run time*, or *execution time*. During this time the program (data and instructions) resides in the main memory of the computer.

As in higher-level languages, an assembly language program consists of a sequence of executable statements as well as declaration statements. An executable statement requests that an operation be performed at execution time. Whereas an executable statement in a higher-level language may be translated into several machine instructions, an executable statement in assembly language is translated into only one machine instruction.

As in some higher-level languages, such as Pascal, most assembly languages require that every variable used in the program be explicitly declared. Declaration statements are used to define variables so that memory locations are reserved for the variables, and the locations may be initialized to specific values. The size of the memory location reserved for a variable depends on the data type of the variable. Many assembly languages support several data types, (for example, integers with different ranges, reals with single and double precision, and so on). In such languages the type of the variable is specified in the declaration statement, so that the required amount of storage is reserved for it.

For declaring variables, two types of declaration statements in assembly languages are (1) those that are used to reserve *and* initialize memory locations to particular values, and (2) those that are used to reserve memory locations without initializing them.[1] The name of the variable declared will be the symbolic name of the memory reserved for the variable. When a scalar variable is declared, a memory location is reserved for it and is assigned the name of the variable. Thus the program can refer to the memory location by the variable name. For an array variable, a number of consecutive memory locations, equal to the size of the array, are reserved. The first location reserved is given the name of the array; the other locations can then be referenced as offsets from the beginning of the array. Examples on declaring variables are presented in the next section.

1.2 An Assembly Language Program

In this section we first present a higher-level language program that performs a simple function. Then we write an equivalent assembly language program that performs the same function.

The program is to read a set of five integer numbers, find the average of the numbers, and then print the average. Assume there are ten such sets.

In FORTRAN, the program (with the format statements ignored) may be coded as follows:

```
C       THIS PROGRAM READS A SET OF INTEGER NUMBERS, FIND THEIR
C       AVERAGE, AND THEN PRINT THE AVERAGE. EVERY SET CONSISTS
C       OF FIVE NUMBERS, AND THERE ARE TEN SETS TO BE PROCESSED
C
        INTEGER SIZE,SETS,SUM,AVG,N,J
        DIMENSION LIST(5)
        SIZE= 5
        SETS= 10
        N= 1
        DO WHILE (N.LE.SETS)
            DO 10 J=1,SIZE
                READ(5,100) LIST(J)
     10     CONTINUE
            SUM=0
            DO 20 J= 1,SIZE
                SUM= SUM+LIST(J)
     20     CONTINUE
            AVG= SUM/SIZE
            WRITE(6,200)AVG
            N= N+1
        END DO
        STOP
        END
```

---

[1] Some computer systems initialize uninitialized locations to zeroes; others initialize them to different values. In any case, as a good programming practice, uninitialized variables should be explicitly assigned values in the program before they are used.

In Pascal, the program might look like this:

```
{THIS PROGRAM READS A SET OF INTEGER NUMBERS, FIND THEIR
 AVERAGE, AND THEN PRINT THE AVERAGE. EVERY SET CONSISTS
 OF FIVE NUMBERS, AND THERE ARE TEN SETS TO BE PROCESSED
}
PROGRAM FINDAVERAGE(INPUT,OUTPUT);
CONST
   SIZE= 5;
   SETS= 10;

TYPE
   INDEX= 1..SIZE;
   INTARRAY= ARRAY[INDEX] OF INTEGER;

VAR
   SUM,AVG: INTEGER;
   N: 1..SETS;
   LIST: INTARRAY;
   J: INDEX;

BEGIN
   N:= 1;
   WHILE N <= SETS DO
      BEGIN
         FOR J:= 1 TO SIZE DO
            READ(LIST[J]);
         SUM:= 0;
         FOR J:= 1 TO SIZE DO
            SUM:= SUM+LIST[J];
         AVG:= SUM DIV SIZE;
         WRITELN(AVG);
         N:= N+1
      END
END.
```

As noted in the previous section, every variable name in a program actually refers to a memory location. The content of the location is the value of the variable. For the foregoing program, assuming that all values are in the same range, the section of memory reserved for the variables is shown in Figure 1.2. Both the addresses and the contents of the locations are shown in decimal. Values of variables that change in the program are shown as question marks (?). The program is assumed to be loaded (placed) in memory starting at address 0. We have also arbitrarily placed the constants and variables in memory before the instructions.

We now write an assembly language program that performs the same function as in the HLL programs. For this, we introduce a VAX-like assembly language with enough statements to enable us to write the program. The statements introduced are representative of statements found in most assembly languages. Only one integer data type is introduced, and in the rest of this section we assume all scalar variables and each element of an array variable to be of this data type.

Many assembly languages allow different data types for an integer

Contents	Address	Symbolic Name
05	0	SIZE
10	1	SETS
??	2	SUM
??	3	AVG
??	4	N
??	5	LIST
??	6	LIST+1
??	7	LIST+2
??	8	LIST+3
??	9	LIST+4
??	10	J

Figure 1.2 Memory reserved for program constants and variables

number depending on the range of the integer. One such data type is the *byte*. A byte is simply a memory location that can store a signed integer, usually in the range −128 to +127 decimal.

The general format of the declaration statement for defining a variable in our language is:

label   BYTE   *i*

This statement reserves one byte of storage and initializes it to the integer *i*. The statement may be preceded by a symbolic name, *label*. The label is the name of the reserved byte or, equivalently, the name of the variable whose value resides in the byte. For example, the statement

SETS   BYTE   5

initializes the reserved byte to 5 and assigns the byte the symbolic name SETS. The program can then refer to this byte by the name SETS.

The declaration statement for reserving a block of bytes for an array variable has the general format:

label   BLKB   *n*

This statement reserves *n* consecutive bytes in memory. The name assigned to the first byte is *label,* so the program can refer to this byte by *label.* The second byte reserved by BLKB can be referred to in the program by *label*+1, and the *n*th byte by *label*+*n*−1. For example, an array variable, LIST, of size 5 can be declared by

```
LIST    BLKB    5
```

This statement reserves 5 bytes where the first can be referenced by LIST, the second by LIST+1, the third by LIST+2, and so on. Note that if we assume that the five reserved bytes are initialized to zeroes, the foregoing statement is equivalent to

```
LIST        BYTE        0
            BYTE        0
            BYTE        0
            BYTE        0
            BYTE        0
```

Obviously, the BLKB declaration is more practical and more elegant.

We now introduce some assembly instructions that perform arithmetic, comparison, and branching. The instructions, the operands required, and the function of each instruction are as follows:

```
ADD    X,Y,Z    ADD the contents of byte X to the
                contents of byte Y and store the result
                in byte Z

DIV    X,Y,Z    DIVide the contents of byte Y by the
                contents of byte X and store the result
                in byte Z

MOV    X,Y      Copy the contents of byte X into byte Y

CMP    X,Y      CoMPare the contents of bytes X and
                Y and set some indicators in the hardware
                according to the result of the comparison

BGEQ   label    Branch on Greater or EQual to "label".
                This instruction tests the comparison
                indicators and if they indicate that the
                first quantity compared is greater than
                or equal to the second then a branch takes
                place to the statement whose label is
                specified; otherwise execution continues
                following the branch instruction

INC    X        INCrement the contents of byte X by 1 and
                store the result in X
```

With the foregoing set of instruction and declaration statements, we are almost ready to write an assembly language program for the example described previously. One thing is missing, however. We need a mechanism for inputting data from and outputting results to input and output devices. Input and output in a computer system are very complex processes. Reading or writing a set of values could require hundreds of machine instructions. Therefore, we assume the existence of input and output routines that can be called from the assembly program (much as the READ and WRITE routines are called from a higher-level language program). We call these routines IN and OUT and assume the following formats and functions for them:

```
IN    label,n    INput n data values and store them
                 into n consecutive bytes starting
                 at byte "label", one value per byte

OUT   label,n    OUTput n values from n consecutive
                 bytes in memory starting at byte
                 "label", one value per byte
```

To return to the example, an assembly language program that implements the specifications in the example is shown in Figure 1.3. The first three lines in the program that start with an asterisk (*) and the text next to each statement are comments. The END statement simply indicates the end of the program.

```
* THIS PROGRAM READS A SET OF INTEGER NUMBERS, FIND THEIR
* AVERAGE, AND THEN PRINT THE AVERAGE. EVERY SET CONSISTS
* OF FIVE NUMBERS, AND THERE ARE TEN SETS TO BE PROCESSED
*
SIZE    BYTE    5                   SIZE OF SET
SETS    BYTE    10                  NUMBER OF SETS
SUM     BLKB    1                   VARIABLE TO HOLD SUM OF SET ELEMENTS
AVG     BLKB    1                   VARIABLE TO HOLD AVERAGE
N       BYTE    1                   LOOP COUNTER FOR NUMBER OF SETS PROCESSED
LIST    BLKB    5                   STORAGE AREA FOR ELEMENTS OF SET

MORE    IN      LIST,5              INPUT THE 5 ELEMENTS OF SET
        MOV     LIST,SUM            FIRST ELEMENT INTO SUM
        ADD     LIST+1,SUM,SUM      ADD FIRST TWO ELEMENTS
        ADD     LIST+2,SUM,SUM      ADD THIRD ELEMENT
        ADD     LIST+3,SUM,SUM      ADD FOURTH ELEMENT
        ADD     LIST+4,SUM,SUM      ADD FIFTH ELEMENT
        DIV     SIZE,SUM,AVG        COMPUTE AVERAGE = SUM/SIZE
        OUT     AVG,1               OUTPUT AVERAGE
        INC     N                   INCREMENT LOOP COUNTER
        CMP     SETS,N              HAVE ALL SETS BEEN PROCESSED?
        BGEQ    MORE                NO: CONTINUE WITH NEXT SET
        END                         YES: END OF PROGRAM
```

Figure 1.3 An assembly language program

Note that, unlike the HLL programs presented earlier, the assembly language program in Figure 1.3 does not index through the elements of the array in a loop to sum them. Rather, it sums the elements in a straight-line code (that is, a sequence of ADD statements), which, of course, is impractical for large arrays. This is not a deficiency of assembly language, but indexing requires additional concepts that will be developed later.

Some observations about the foregoing program, and assembly language programming in general, are in order:

1. The BLKB statement, rather than the BYTE statement, is used to reserve one byte of storage for each of the variables SUM and AVG. The BYTE statement should be used when the initial contents of the byte to be reserved are known.
2. Every assembly statement is documented with a comment next to it. This should serve as a model for every assembly language program, where nearly every statement in the program should be documented.
3. Labels used for variable names in declaration statements, as well as labels of executable statements, should be as descriptive as possible. For example, labels such as SIZE, AVG, SUM, should be used, rather than A1, A2, A3.
4. Storage areas for variables should be grouped in a single place, not mixed with executable code. Although assembly languages allow mixing declaration statements with executable statements, the beginner should avoid such mixing.

The reader, of course, must be eager to see a real VAX-11 assembly program as soon as possible. We now accommodate by reprogramming the foregoing example exactly as required by the VAX-11 assembler MACRO, which we will study in detail in Chapter 4. There are some pedagogical problems in doing so. We have not yet studied the syntax of this particular assembler. We have not explained the information units of the VAX-11. We certainly don't know how to call subprograms (needed to perform input and output), and we don't even know the instruction set. Hence, the reader must be patient and accept, for the present, a sketchy explanation of the program that follows. First, MACRO labels must be followed by a colon, and MACRO comments must be preceded by a semicolon. Second, directives (as opposed to executable machine instructions) all start with a period. Thus the directive BYTE is written .BYTE in MACRO. Third, instructions such as ADD must be suffixed with a B if one is adding bytes and must also be suffixed with the numeral 3 if there are three operands. Thus ADDB3 A,B,C means add the byte

```
; THIS PROGRAM READS A SET OF INTEGER NUMBERS, FIND THEIR
; AVERAGE, AND THEN PRINT THE AVERAGE. EVERY SET CONSISTS
; OF FIVE NUMBERS, AND THERE ARE TEN SETS TO BE PROCESSED
;
SIZE:   .BYTE    5                  ;SIZE OF SET
SETS:   .BYTE    10                 ;NUMBER OF SETS
SUM:    .BLKB    1                  ;VARIABLE TO HOLD SUM OF SET ELEMENTS
AVG:    .BLKB    1                  ;VARIABLE TO HOLD AVERAGE
N:      .BYTE    1                  ;LOOP COUNTER FOR NUMBER OF SETS PROCESSED
LIST:   .BLKB    5                  ;STORAGE AREA FOR ELEMENTS OF SET
;
        .ENTRY   FINDAVERAGE,0      ;BEGIN EXECUTION
MORE:
;CALL TO AN INPUT ROUTINE WHICH READS THE FIVE ELEMENTS OF SET
        MOVB     LIST,SUM           ;FIRST ELEMENT INTO SUM
        ADDB3    LIST+1,SUM,SUM     ;ADD FIRST TWO ELEMENTS
        ADDB3    LIST+2,SUM,SUM     ;ADD THIRD ELEMENT
        ADDB3    LIST+3,SUM,SUM     ;ADD FOURTH ELEMENT
        ADDB3    LIST+4,SUM,SUM     ;ADD FIFTH ELEMENT
        DIVB3    SIZE,SUM,AVG       ;COMPUTE AVERAGE = SUM/SIZE
;CALL TO AN OUTPUT ROUTINE WHICH OUTPUTS THE AVERAGE
        INCB     N                  ;INCREMENT LOOP COUNTER
        CMPB     SETS,N             ;HAVE ALL SETS BEEN PROCESSED?
        BGEQ     MORE               ;NO: CONTINUE WITH NEXT SET
        .END     FINDAVERAGE        ;YES: END OF PROGRAM
```

Figure 1.4   A VAX-11 assembly language program

at address A to the byte at address B, and store the resulting byte in address C.

With this brief explanation, we exhibit a complete VAX-11 program (except for input and output) in Figure 1.4. If the reader is still not completely comfortable with all aspects of the program, there is no need to worry at this point. The directive .ENTRY, for example, which appears at the beginning of the executable part of the program with two operands, can be ignored for the present. If the reader has a VAX-11 terminal available, Appendix B can be used to enter the program in Figure 1.4 and assemble it. It cannot be run, however, unless input and output subprograms are supplied.

Now that we have looked at the nature of assembly language, we next look at why we should learn or use assembly language.

1.3 Why Assembly Language?

As noted earlier, in the beginning there was machine language. Assembly language followed because of the difficulty of programming in machine language. Although assembly language greatly simplifies programming, most programmers still find programming in assembly language tedious and error-prone compared with using higher-level languages. Why, then, should we learn or use assembly language?

Before listing some of the reasons for learning and using assembly language, we must mention that some opponents of programming in assembly language may offer counterarguments. Nevertheless, many computer scientists find these reasons valid, at least for the near future.

1. It is imperative that the computer scientist have a clear understanding of how a computer functions. Such understanding is also important to the high-level language programmer—if not for the sheer knowledge, then to help him or her design programs that use the computer more effectively. To have a clear understanding of conventional computers and how they work, one should have good knowledge of machine language or, equivalently, assembly language. After all, a computer executes a machine language program to perform a certain task.
2. There are certain functions on many computer systems that are still in the domain of assembly language—for example, the operation of physical input and output devices, and the transfer of control of the computer from one job to another in a multiprogramming system. Although there are attempts to use higher-level languages for such functions, assembly language still prevails in these instances.
3. In principle, an assembly language program is more efficient than its higher-level language counterpart. This is so because compilers, in general, tend to generate less optimal code than the code of a carefully handwritten assembly language program. Therefore, in applications in which saving memory storage and execution time is of primary importance, assembly language may be advantageous.

The foregoing reasons should not be interpreted as a plea for writing all programs in assembly language. They mean only that assembly language can be used to add to the capabilities of higher-level languages. Since most higher-level languages allow the user to write subroutines in assembly language, a programmer can, through judicious choices, combine the advantages of both higher-level and assembly languages. For instance, the programmer can write those parts of a program that are machine-dependent or that execute very frequently as subroutines in assembly language, and the rest of the program in a higher-level language.

1.4 Operating Systems

The term *operating system,* which we will have occasion to refer to in later chapters, refers to a large collection of program modules whose purpose is to manage the hardware components of a computer as well as the information (programs and data) stored in a computer. The operating system provides a hospitable interface between the user and the computer. It hides the complexities of the hardware and simplifies its use.

In order to introduce operating systems and establish the need for them, consider a computer installation that is shared by several users simultaneously. The users either may enter the programs into the system interactively from a terminal or may submit them to run in batch, perhaps as a deck of punched cards. In a system with a single *central processing unit* (CPU),[2] only one program can be executing at any one time, although several programs may exist in the system at the same time. Obviously, a decision must be made about which program is to be executed next. Should it be the program that has been waiting the longest, or the one that is the shortest, or the one with the highest priority? Maybe, to satisfy all users, the system will execute a program for a certain period of time and then, if not finished, put the program at the end of a waiting queue, choose another program from the waiting queue, execute the latter program for a certain period of time, and so on. (Many computer systems, particularly larger ones, do this to serve a large number of users per unit of time and to give the illusion of executing several programs simultaneously. Such systems are called *multiprogramming systems.*) Deciding which program is to be executed next and managing and keeping track of programs are tasks performed by the operating system.

To illustrate further the need for an operating system, consider the input and output (I/O) devices. These devices operate under the control of the computer. A set of instructions (I/O routines) must be executed by the computer in order for the device to perform a certain task, such as reading or printing a line. All users of a computer system need to perform input and output. Instead of having every user write his or her own I/O routines (often a complex task beyond the capability of most users), a set of I/O routines is provided as part of the operating system. These routines can be shared by all users who call them to perform a certain task.

A modern operating system provides many other services in a computer system. To cite a few examples:

1. It allows the interactive user to log on the system and keeps the unauthorized user away.
2. It manages the user's program and data files on secondary storage, keeps track of where they are located, and protects them from being accessed by other users.

---

[2] The CPU is the hardware unit responsible for executing machine instructions. Chapter 2 presents this unit in detail.

3. It prints helpful error messages that may occur during the execution of a program.
4. It performs the functions of accounting and keeping track of the amount of resources a program uses, such as CPU time, number of lines printed, length of time spent on an interactive terminal, and the like.

The operating system is normally provided by the computer manufacturer. With the operating system, various language compilers, assemblers, and other utility programs, such as editors and debuggers, are also provided.

1.5 The VAX-11 Family of Computers

The VAX-11 is a digital computer manufactured by Digital Equipment Corporation (DEC or DIGITAL). The VAX-11 comes in various models with common characteristics and properties, hence the term family of computers. The first model of the VAX-11 family, the VAX-11/780, was introduced in 1977. Other models were introduced later: the VAX-11/750 in 1980, the VAX-11/782 in 1981, and the VAX-11/730 in 1982. The four models are shown in Figures 1.5–1.8.

The VAX machine extends the capabilities of Digital's earlier family of computers, the PDP-11. The PDP-11 family has been very popular since the early 1970s, and the VAX-11 has come to share this popularity in the 1980s. One of the major extensions to the PDP-11 is the VAX machine's capability to address a larger memory space—hence the name VAX, for *Virtual Address eXtension*. The term *virtual* means that the computer can run a program whose size is much greater than the physical main memory of the computer. The system creates the illusion of a very large memory, called *virtual memory*. For example, the VAX-11/780 supports a maximum of about 12 million bytes of physical main memory, yet a user's program can be up to 1 billion bytes. This feat is accomplished by the operating system with assistance from the hardware.

The various VAX-11 models differ in speed, size, and cost. According to data provided by the manufacturer, and taking the VAX-11/780 model as a standard, the VAX-11/782 delivers about 60 percent more processing power (speed) at about a 40 percent increase in cost. The VAX-11/782 is actually a dual-processor system (two VAX-11/780 processors) sharing the same main memory and I/O devices. At the lower end of the VAX-11 family, the VAX-11/750 is smaller than the VAX-11/780, with 60 percent of its processing power at approximately half the price. The VAX-11/730 is currently the smallest model, with about 30 percent of the performance

Figure 1.5   The VAX-11/780

Figure 1.6   The VAX-11/750

Figure 1.7   The VAX-11/782

Figure 1.8   The VAX-11/730

of the VAX-11/780 at about one-quarter the price.

The aforementioned differences result from the use of different amounts of hardware, as well as hardware of different speeds, in the various models. All the VAX-11 models, however, are designed to be *compatible* with each other. That is, they have the same architecture and execute the same machine and assembly languages. Furthermore, a program (in any language) that runs on any model can be run on any other model.

The VAX-11 family is also designed to support running programs written for the PDP-11 computers. Digital refers to this capability as *compatibility mode*. This compatibility, however, is not 100 percent as it is among the VAX-11 models. That is, the PDP-11 programs might have to be modified in order to be run on a VAX-11.

For all the VAX-11 models, Digital supplies one operating system, the VAX/VMS (for *Virtual Memory System*). VMS is a multiprogramming operating system. It allows one to enter and execute programs interactively from a terminal. It also allows one to submit programs to run in batch. Appendix B introduces some of the commands for interacting with the VMS operating system.

This concludes our introductory presentation of assembly language, operating systems, and the VAX-11 computer family. Most of the concepts presented in this chapter will be elaborated on in later chapters.

1.6 Summary

This chapter introduced the basic concepts of machine language and assembly language. We saw that each different computer architecture has its own machine language and its related assembly language. Thus there are as many assembly languages as there are types of computers. Programming in assembly language requires intimate knowledge of the particular computer to be programmed. In this book we use the VAX-11 computer system and its assembly language for illustration, although every attempt is made to point out common features among assembly languages. In order to fix the notion of assembly language in our minds, we examined multiple versions of a simple task programmed in FORTRAN; in Pascal; in a hypothetical, simplified assembly language; and finally in VAX-11 MACRO assembly language. We also reviewed some of the reasons for learning assembly language and presented a brief overview of the basic software environment or operating system in which assembly programs and other user programs reside. The chapter concluded with an overview of the VAX-11 family of computers.

EXERCISES

1. Define the following:
   - **a.** Source program
   - **b.** object program
   - **c.** machine language
   - **d.** assembly language
   - **e.** assembly time
   - **f.** run time

2. **a.** What is a compiler? What is its function?
   b. What is an assembler? What is its function?
   c. Which do you expect to be more difficult to write, a compiler or an assembler? Why?

In Exercises 3 through 6, use the generalized assembly language of this chapter. You may also introduce basic instructions of your own, provided that you clearly define these instructions. Declare all variables you need in each program. Assume that all variables are integers and that each occupies one byte.

3. Translate the following FORTRAN statements into assembly language.

```
X= B**2-4*A*C
IF (X.LT.0) X=-X
```

4. Translate the following program segment into assembly language:

Program Segment in FORTRAN	Program Segment in Pascal
N= 0	N:= 0;
10 N= N+1	10: N:= N+1;
I= I-N**2	I:= I-N**2;
K= 5*I+K/N-1	K:= 5*I+K DIV N-1;
IF (K.LT.0) GO TO 20	IF K >= 0 THEN
IF (N.GT.10) GO TO 10	IF N > 10 THEN GOTO 10
20 CONTINUE	ELSE

5. Write a segment of an assembly program that evaluates the expression $B^2 - 4AC$ and sets a flag to -1, 0, or $+1$ depending on whether the value of the expression is negative, zero, or positive.

6. A program is to read a set of five numbers and print out the maximum number in the set. Assume there are ten such sets. Write an assembly language program that performs this function. (Use the IN and OUT routines of this chapter for input and output.) You may assume each set of numbers occupies one data line, or you may assume each number occupies one line. Assume that the IN statement reads one line at a time.

7. Input, edit, and assemble the MACRO program given in Figure 1.4. Use Appendix B as your guide to using the terminal.

Chapter 2

Hardware Organization

THIS CHAPTER examines the major hardware components of a computer system, their functions, and the interaction between them. The purpose of the discussion is to give the reader an understanding of how instructions are executed by the hardware, not how to design the machine. The discussion is sufficiently general to cover most computers, but Digital Equipment's VAX-11 is used as a running example.

Although different models of computers differ in their construction details, their basic organizations are quite similar. Indeed, most

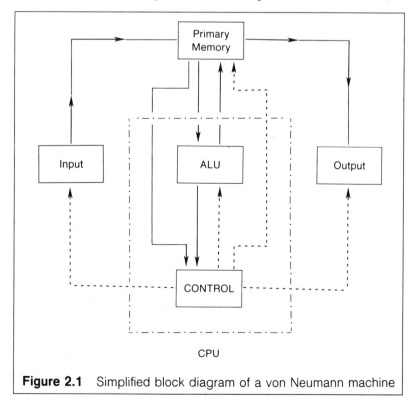

Figure 2.1 Simplified block diagram of a von Neumann machine

of today's computers are evolved from a classical model known as the *von Neumann organization* or the *von Neuman machine*. John von Neumann (1903–1957) was a mathematician who contributed much to the development of this basic organization. Figure 2.1 is a simplified block diagram of the von Neumann machine, which remains a good representation of most contemporary computers.

The major components of a computer are:

1. Primary memory.
2. Arithmetic and logic unit (ALU).
3. Control unit.
4. Input/output unit (I/O).

The ALU and the control unit are often considered as a single unit called the *central processing unit* (CPU). Instructions and data are stored in the primary memory. The CPU gets the instructions from the memory in a prescribed order and interprets them one at a time. In doing so, it fetches data from the memory and returns the results to the memory. The input/output unit serves as an interface between the computer and its external world. Originally, the term I/O referred to the devices that convert the electrical signals representing information internal to the computer to forms suitable for human users, and vice versa. Among the more popular I/O devices are keyboard and CRT (cathode ray tube) terminals, hard-copy printers, card readers, and graph plotters. Now the term has been generalized to refer to any devices connected to a computer that supply and/or receive data from it. In particular, it includes mass storage devices such as magnetic disks and tape drives.

Figure 2.1 shows how these components are interconnected. The solid lines in the diagram illustrate the data paths. The broken lines are the control paths along which control signals are sent from the control unit to the rest of the system.

2.1 Primary Memory

The *primary memory* is a storage device in which both instructions and data for a program are stored and from which they are fetched during the execution of the program. In modern computers, primary memories are usually built with semiconductor circuits. These devices are very fast; they can perform a fetch or store operation in a fraction of a microsecond (1 millionth of a second or 1 μs). They also operate in a random-access mode, which means that the access time of the memory is independent of the location of the item of information in memory. The word *primary* is used to distinguish this memory (also called the *main memory*) from other memories, called *secondary memories*. The latter are usually much larger in capacity and orders of magnitude slower in operation speed. We will discuss secondary memories in Section 2.7.

One can visualize the primary memory as a collection of a large number of cells, each of which holds the value of either a 0 or a 1. In other words, each cell can store a binary digit—*bit* for short. This collection of cells is organized into units of equal size called *memory words*. The information stored in a memory word can be moved into or out of the memory in one memory operation. Each memory word is assigned an identification number called the *memory address* by which the contents of the memory are referenced. Addresses are usually integers from 0 to 2^n-1, where 2^n is the number of words in the memory. Thus we can, for example, store the value 25 in memory location 12034; later, if we fetch the contents of memory at location 12034, we will obtain the bit string 00 . . . 011001. 11001 is the binary representation of 25, and the number of leading zeroes depends on the size of the memory word.

Figure 2.2 shows a simplified block diagram of the organization of a memory. The memory consists of 2^n words, each with w bits. In practice, w varies from 8 to 64, and n varies from 12 to 24, giving us memory sizes ranging from 4,096 words of 8 bits each to over 1 million words of 64 bits each. Modern computer systems often provide the user with a very large address space for his program independent of the actual size of the physical memory. Such memory systems are known as *virtual memories*. A user of a virtual memory system has an almost unlimited amount of primary memory space at his disposal. His program is actually stored in a large but slow secondary memory, typically a magnetic disk or drum. Only the portion that is currently being executed by the CPU resides in the primary memory. When new portions of the program are needed, they are transferred into the primary memory. The portions that are no longer active are then moved back to the secondary memory. This whole operation is monitored and controlled by the operating system. The transfer of program segments between the two memories is practically invisible to the user.

Although the principles of operation of virtual memory are beyond the scope of this book, one should be aware that the VAX-11 uses a virtual memory system. Each VAX-11 program has an address space of over 1 billion bytes, although the physical size of the primary memory cannot exceed 2^{23} (≈ 8 million) bytes. As in most virtual memory systems, the primary memory of the VAX-11 is divided into portions of equal length called *page frames*. All programs and data segments are also divided into portions of the same length called *pages*. (On the VAX-11 a page is 512 bytes.) All pages are kept on the disk. When any information on a page is needed by

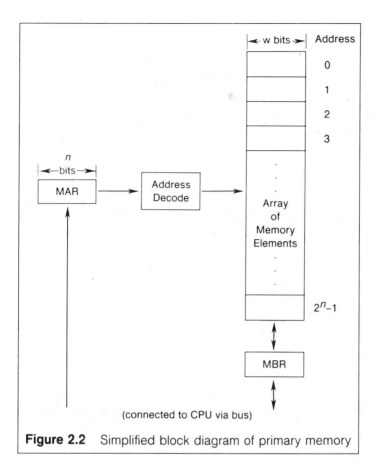

Figure 2.2 Simplified block diagram of primary memory

the CPU, that page will be loaded (copied) from the disk into an available page frame in the main memory. If no page frame is free, then the operating system will select one of the pages residing in main memory to be removed from the main memory to make room for the incoming page. Because of this mechanism for removing a page when a page frame is needed, the size of a program can exceed the size of the main memory.

Two special storage devices called *registers* are employed to help the memory operation. They are the *memory address register* (MAR) and the *memory buffer register* (MBR). The MAR is used to hold the address of the memory location to be accessed. The content of that register is fed into a memory address decoding circuit to select the proper memory location. The MBR is used to receive data read out of the memory (in the case of a fetch operation) or to store the data before they are transferred into the memory (in the case of a store operation).

The speed of the computer is significantly influenced by the speed of its primary memory. The operating characteristics of the memory are therefore quite important to the users. In describing a memory, besides its capacity (how many words and how many bits per word), one is usually interested in the *memory access time,* the *memory cycle time,* and the *memory bandwidth.* The memory access time is the time between the initiation of a fetch operation and the arrival of the data in the MBR. The memory cycle time is the minimum time delay required between the initiation of two memory operations. For semiconductor memories, the cycle time is usually only slightly longer than the access time. This is not true for magnetic core memories, the type of memory most common in older computers. With core memories, the cycle time is normally about double the access time. The memory bandwidth is defined as the maximum amount of information (in bits) that the memory unit can input or output in unit time. It is equal to the memory word length divided by the memory cycle time; for example, a memory with word length of 32 bits and cycle time of 1 μs will have a memory bandwidth of 32 million bits/second.

2.2 Information Units

Although the memory is constructed to allow a fixed number of bits to be accessed every memory cycle, the number of bits necessary to represent the data varies with the data type. Normally a number of basic information units are defined in a computer system to accommodate various data types used in the system. Some computers are built in such a way that the memory word length coincides with the information unit that holds an instruction or an item of the most frequently used data type. Such machines are knows as *word-addressable* or *word-oriented* machines. The Control Data Cyber 170 series (60 bits/word), as well as the Honeywell 60 series and the UNIVAC 1100 series (both 36 bits/word), computers are all systems of this type.

   Other computers, however, are designed to allow the user to access information units of various length directly, regardless of the size of the memory word. Although a memory operation will still transfer a whole memory word between the addressed memory location and the MBR, only the information unit specified by the instruction will be transferred between the MBR and the central processing unit. Whenever the information unit cannot be contained in one memory word, additional memory cycles will be initiated automatically. In practice, this involves providing each small basic information unit with an address; all larger information units are expressed as multiples of this basic unit. For example, most of the computers manufactured by IBM, DEC, and Data General, among others, use the *byte* as a basic information unit. Such machines are known as *byte-addressable* or *byte-oriented* machines.

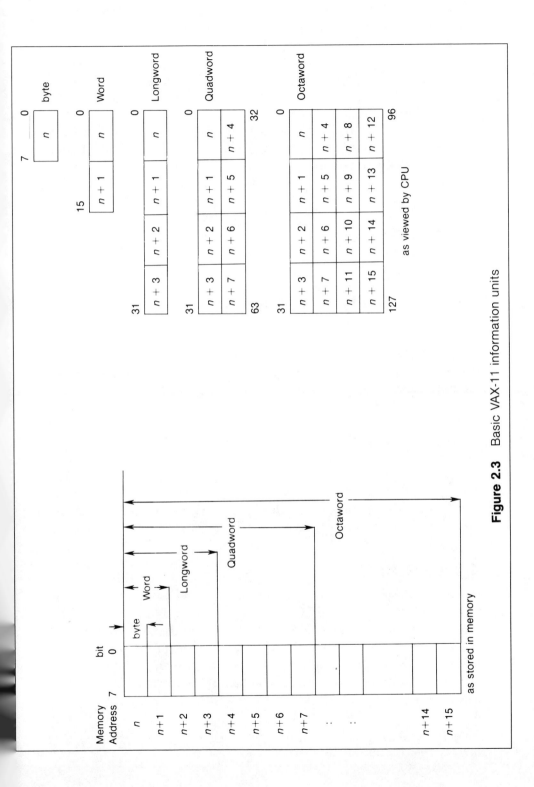

Figure 2.3 Basic VAX-11 information units

A byte is originally defined as the number of bits required to code a symbol of the basic character set. Today, however, all the byte-oriented computers use an eight-bit byte. Beyond this, every manufacturer has its own convention in specifying other information units. IBM, for example defines a *half word* as being equal to 2 bytes (16 bits), a *word* as equal to 4 bytes (32 bits), and a *double word* as equal to 8 bytes (64 bits).[1]

In the VAX-11 a *word* consists of 2 bytes (16 bits); a *longword* of 4 bytes (32 bits), a *quadword* of 8 bytes (64 bits), and an *octaword* of 16 bytes (128 bits). Figure 2.3 shows a diagram of these basic VAX-11 information units. With the exception of the byte itself, each unit is formed by a sequence of contiguous bytes in the memory. The address of the unit is the same as that of the lowest-order byte of the group. The individual bits within an information unit are numbered consecutively, starting with 0 for the rightmost bit. In other words, a longword with the address n consists of the bytes with addresses $n, n+1, n+2,$ and $n+3$. Bit 0 of byte n is bit 0 (LSB, the least significant bit) of the longword n, and bit 7 of byte $n+3$ is bit 31 (MSB, the most significant bit) of the longword n.

Although a byte is, in practice, the smallest addressable information unit, a group of 4 bits (half a byte) is often referred to as a *nibble*. It can be used to store a hexadecimal digit.

In some byte-oriented machines, the address of an information unit that is larger than a byte must be a value divisible by the length of the information unit (in bytes). That is, if a word is 4 bytes in length, then the beginning address of a word must be a multiple of 4. Such a restriction is known as *boundary alignment*. The IBM System/370 enforces such a restriction, whereas the VAX-11 does not. If an information unit in the VAX-11 is not boundary-aligned, however, it might take the computer longer to fetch the item.

2.3 Basic Data Types

In the previous section we introduced the concept of information units that are bit strings of fixed lengths. By assigning different interpretations to the bits of these units, we can define different data types. In this section we will introduce two of the most basic data types needed to enable us to write some programs: integers and characters. A more complete discussion of data types will be given in Chapter 9.

---

[1]Here the word *word* is an information unit, to be distinguished from a *memory word* as defined in the previous section.

Integers

Since computers are built with binary elements (elements that can assume two stable states), the most straightforward way of representing integers is by using the binary number system. In general, we can use n bits to represent 2^n different numbers. (For a comprehensive discussion of number representations, refer to Appendix A.) Depending on the applications, we may be interested in the natural numbers or the integers; therefore, most computers give us both the unsigned and signed number representations. In the VAX-11 the 2's complement format is adopted to represent signed numbers. An integer can be stored as a byte, a word, a longword, a quadword, or an octaword. Since each size provides a different range for the integer represented, the user may choose the right size for his or her particular application, thus gaining more efficient use of the memory. Table 2.1 shows the range of representation for each of the sizes.

Characters and Character Strings

To represent nonnumeric data, codes are used. Since n bits can provide 2^n different combinations, the size of the codeword depends on the size of the character set to be represented. For business data processing, algebraic and symbolic computation, and text processing, it is often necessary to represent the decimal digits and the alphabet of a natural language, as well as standard punctuation marks and basic mathematical symbols. The two most commonly used internal computer codes today are the American Standard Code for Information Interchange (ASCII) and the Extended Binary Coded Decimal Interchange Code (EBCDIC) (Table 2.2; also see Appendix D).

The ASCII code was originally designed as a 7-bit code; since most computers use an 8-bit byte as a basic information unit, however, a leading 0 is often attached to the codeword to fill the space. Today the 8-bit ASCII code is a de facto standard.

Table 2.1 VAX-11 Integer Representations

Data Type	Size	Range (decimal)	
Integer		Signed	Unsigned
Byte	8 bits	−128 to + 127	0 to 255
Word	16 bits	−32,768 to + 32,767	0 to 65,535
Longword	32 bits	-2^{31} to $+ 2^{31} - 1$	0 to $2^{32} - 1$
Quadword	64 bits	-2^{63} to $+ 2^{63} - 1$	0 to $2^{64} - 1$
Octaword	128 bits	-2^{127} to $+ 2^{127} - 1$	0 to $2^{128} - 1$

Table 2.2 Example of Some Character Codes

Character	BCD code	EBCDIC code	ASCII code
blank	110 000	0100 0000	0010 0000
.	011 011	0100 1011	0010 1110
(	111 100	0100 1101	0010 1000
+	010 000	0100 1110	0010 1011
$	101 011	0101 1011	0010 0100
*	101 100	0101 1100	0010 1010
)	011 100	0101 1101	0010 1001
−	100 000	0110 0000	0010 1101
/	110 001	0110 0001	0010 1111
.	111 011	0110 1011	0010 1100
,	001 100	0111 1101	0010 0111
=	001 011	0111 1110	0011 1101
A	010 001	1100 0001	0100 0001
B	010 010	1100 0010	0100 0010
C	010 011	1100 0011	0100 0011
D	010 100	1100 0100	0100 0100
E	010 101	1100 0101	0100 0101
F	010 110	1100 0110	0100 0110
G	010 111	1100 0111	0100 0111
H	011 000	1100 1000	0100 1000
I	011 001	1100 1001	0100 1001
J	100 001	1101 0001	0100 1010
K	100 010	1101 0010	0100 1011
L	100 011	1101 0011	0100 1100
M	100 100	1101 0100	0100 1101
N	100 101	1101 0101	0100 1110
O	100 110	1101 0110	0100 1111
P	100 111	1101 0111	0101 0000
Q	101 000	1101 1000	0101 0001
R	101 001	1101 1001	0101 0010
S	110 010	1110 0010	0101 0011
T	110 011	1110 0011	0101 0100
U	110 100	1110 0100	0101 0101
V	110 101	1110 0101	0101 0110
W	110 110	1110 0110	0101 0111
X	110 111	1110 0111	0101 1000
Y	111 000	1110 1000	0101 1001
Z	111 001	1110 1001	0101 1010
0	000 000	1111 0000	0011 0000
1	000 001	1111 0001	0011 0001
2	000 010	1111 0010	0011 0010
3	000 011	1111 0011	0011 0011
4	000 100	1111 0100	0011 0100
5	000 101	1111 0101	0011 0101
6	000 110	1111 0110	0011 0110
7	000 111	1111 0111	0011 0111
8	001 000	1111 1000	0011 1000
9	001 001	1111 1001	0011 1001

Some manufacturers make use of the availability of this extra bit to perform some error checking. They set the eighth bit to such a value that the total number of 1-bits in every codeword is always odd (or always even). This property, called *parity*, can be used to detect some transmission errors when data are moved from one place to another. If one of the bits is altered during transmission, the total number of 1-bits received will no longer be odd (even). Thus by checking the parity at the receiving end, one can detect single errors.

The EBCDIC was adopted by IBM in 1964 to replace a 6-bit code called the binary coded decimal (BCD) code that was then standard. As shown in Table 2.2, the original BCD code has representations for only 48 symbols. Even today, however, some computer manufacturers still use the BCD code as the internal code in their products, although they have extended the character set to 64.

The VAX-11 uses the ASCII code to represent characters. All data interchanges between the CPU and the input/output devices, such as the terminal or the line printer, are carried out using the ASCII code, regardless of how these data are represented inside the CPU.

There are many other data types beyond the two discussed so far. The two introduced here will allow us to demonstrate many of the operating features of the computer as well as many programming techniques. It should be kept in mind, however, that for more sophisticated or specialized applications, suitably designed data types will facilitate solution of problems. Data representation has a direct effect on the complexity of the algorithm and the efficiency of program execution. Therefore, it is important to understand the nature of data and the possible ways of representing them before starting to design an algorithm or write a program. Other VAX-11 data types will be discussed in Chapter 9.

2.4 Central Processing Unit (CPU)

The central processing unit (CPU) is the unit in which all the actual data operations take place. Instructions and data are fetched from the primary memory to the CPU, where the instructions are decoded and interpreted. Depending on the computer, the structure of the CPU can be relatively simple or very complicated. It is this part of the machine, more than any other, that distinguishes one computer from another. The major components in the CPU can be identified as:

1. The control unit.
2. The arithmetic and logic unit.
3. The registers.

The Control Unit

The control unit is the "brain" of the computer system. It is this unit that examines the instructions and issues the signals to the rest of the system to direct and regulate all its operations. The control unit also monitors and receives signals from other parts of the system. It is important for the control unit to know if any component of the system is not functioning properly. It is also often necessary for the control unit to find out the result of an operation (for example, if the result of an addition is positive, negative, equal to zero, or out of range), on the basis of which it can select a proper course of action.

When a computer is running, the control unit continuously performs a basic instruction execution cycle. This cycle can be summarized as follows:

1. Determine the memory address of the next instruction.
2. Fetch the instruction.
3. Decode the instruction.
4. Determine the memory address of the operand.
5. Fetch the operand. (Steps 4 and 5 may be skipped or repeated as often as necessary to obtain all the operands.)
6. Perform the operation.
7. Determine the memory address of the result.
8. Store the result in memory. (Steps 7 and 8 are omitted if the result is not stored back into memory immediately.)
9. Go back to step 1.

Figure 2.4 shows the basic instruction execution cycle in the form of a flow diagram.

The Arithmetic and Logic Unit (ALU)

The arithmetic and logic unit is the device that receives data and manipulates them. Basic arithmetic operations, such as ADD or SUBTRACT, and logic operations, such as AND, OR, or COMPLEMENT, take place here. The major components of this unit usually include a binary adder and a shifter. The binary adder accepts two binary numbers as inputs and produces a binary sum as its output. Most of the adders in the ALU can also perform certain logic operations, such as AND, OR, and COMPLEMENT. With such capabilities, the adder can perform subtraction by complementing the subtrahend and then performing an addition. (For a detailed discussion of 1's and 2's complement arithmetic, see Appendix A.) The shifter can move all the data bits it contains a specified number of posi-

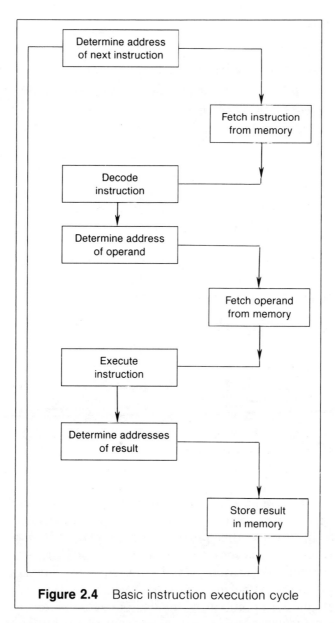

Figure 2.4 Basic instruction execution cycle

tions to the left or right. Coupled with the binary adder, it can be used to perform multiplication by repeated addition and shift. Similarly, division can also be realized by repeated subtraction and shift.

Of course, the adder and the shifter are not the only devices that can be found in the ALU. Larger computers usually include more hardware devices in the ALU to increase system performance. Hardware multipliers are commonly found in large computer systems. Some very high performance machines even include dedicated devices to perform some specific mathematic functions, such as division or square roots.

Registers

A number of storage elements are employed in the CPU to hold information needed during the execution of a sequence of instructions. These storage elements, known as *registers*, are different from the primary memory in that they are built with higher-speed circuits, at a higher cost per circuit, to match the operating speed of the ALU. The number of registers in a CPU varies from computer to computer. Some of them are used for specific purposes, whereas others may be for multiple or general purposes. In most CPUs, for example, there is a special-purpose register called the *instruction register* (IR) that holds the operation code of the instruction currently being executed. This register is usually not accessible to the programmer.

Most CPUs also use a special register, the *processor status register* (PSR), to store, among other things, the conditions of the processor after the execution of each instruction. Another special-purpose register is used to store the address of the current instruction. Since instructions are written and stored sequentially in the primary memory, the next instruction to be executed is normally the one stored in the locations immediately following the current instruction. To facilitate the fetching of the next instruction, the contents of this register are advanced (incremented) to the address of the next sequential instruction during the execution of the current instruction. Therefore, this register is often built in the form of a counter— hence the name *program counter* (PC).

There are registers whose contents are used during the decoding of an instruction to modify the operand address specified in the instruction to form an *effective address*, which is the location of the operand for this particular execution of the instruction. Registers used specifically for this purpose are known as *index registers*. There are also one or more registers into which the output of the ALU is normally deposited. If only one such register is used, it is usually given the name *accumulator* (ACC).

In many modern computers, instead of each register being designated for a specific purpose, a group of registers is provided to serve many of the aforementioned functions. Such registers are known as *general registers*. The VAX-11 has such an organization. In the VAX-11, in addition to the instruction register and the processor status register, sixteen general registers are provided in the CPU for data storage and addressing. Twelve of the sixteen are named R0 to R11, respectively. Three of the remaining four are given special names to emphasize their particular functions in connection with certain instructions to be discussed in Chapter 6. The sixteenth register, called PC, is reserved to work as the program counter. As will be shown later, this method of using a general register to serve as a program counter provides the machine with additional ways of addressing operands.

The Condition Codes

As mentioned in the previous section, a processor status register is often used to store important information about the processor as it executes a program. One type of information kept in the PSR is known as the *condition codes*. The condition codes reflect the result of a computer operation and are updated after the completion of every instruction. On the basis of this information, the programmer will decide what subsequent action to take. The most frequently used conditions are:

1. The result is equal to zero.
2. The result is negative.
3. The result is greater than zero.
4. The result is out of range (overflow).

In the VAX-11, the PSR is known as the PSL (for *processor status longword*). The lower-order half of the PSL, called PSW (for *processor status word*), contains two fields: the condition codes and the trap enable flags.[2] As illustrated in the following diagram, the rightmost four bits of the PSW are used to store the condition codes. They are:

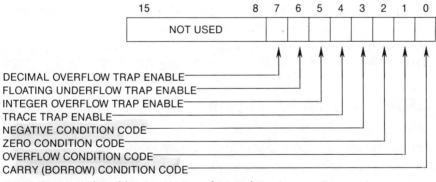

SOURCE: Reproduced by permission of Digital Equipment Corporation.

The N bit—the negative condition code: This bit is set to 1 if the result of an instruction is negative and set to 0 if it is positive or zero.

---

[2] The trap enable flags are outside the scope of this book.

The Z bit—the zero condition code: This bit is set to 1 if the result of an instruction is equal to zero and set to 0 otherwise.

The V bit—the overflow condition code: This bit is set to 1 if the result of an arithmetic operation is too large to be represented in the intended available space; it is set to 0 otherwise.

The C bit—the carry condition code: This bit is set to 1 if the result of certain arithmetic operations produces a carry out of, or borrow into, the most significant bit; it is set to 0 otherwise.[3]

The meanings of the overflow bit and carry bit are often confusing to the beginner. When two numbers of the same sign are added together, the result may be out of range and cause an overflow. This, however, may or may not generate a carry in the most significant digit. It depends on whether the two operands are both negative or positive. On the other hand, when two numbers of unlike signs are added together, there will never be an overflow; yet a carry in the most significant bit may be generated. (See Appendix A for a complete treatment.)

Note that many instructions have no effect on the C bit and that some instructions (most notably all the branch instructions) have no effect on any of the condition codes.[4] The status of the condition bits will remain unchanged when these instructions are executed.

Figure 2.5 shows a simplified block diagram of a VAX-11 computer system. The CPU, the primary memory, and the I/O devices are all interconnected via a central *bus*, which is a communication link through which information is transmitted. The CPU is also connected to a *console*. The console is the operator's interface to the CPU. Using the console terminal, the operator can start or stop the system, monitor the system operation, and run diagnostics.

2.5 Instruction Execution

Now that we have some knowledge of the memory and CPU organization, we are ready to examine the execution of instructions in more detail. Remember that both instructions and operands are stored in the primary memory. Let us assume that an instruction called ADD LONGWORDS 3 OPERAND (abbreviated ADDL3) is

---

[3] The carry condition code is used mainly for the implementation of multiple precision arithmetic and is meaningful only when used with unsigned binary numbers.

[4] That does not include those instructions that combine an arithmetic operation with a branch (see Chapter 5).

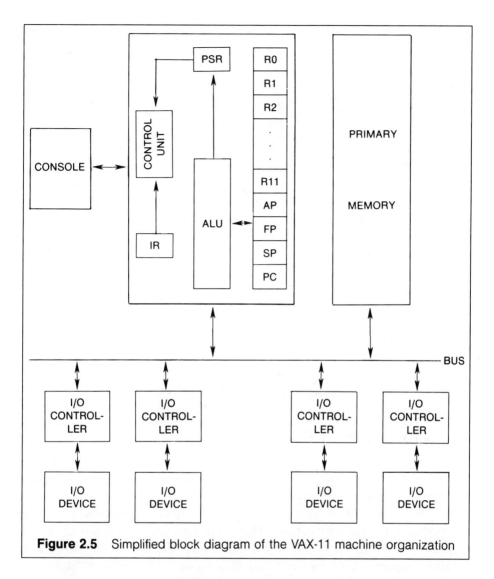

Figure 2.5 Simplified block diagram of the VAX-11 machine organization

stored at location 100. The instruction must also specify where the operands are and where the result will be stored. We shall assume that two 32-bit integers (longwords) are stored in the memory in locations 1000 and 1004, respectively. The instruction will cause the two operands be added together and the sum stored at memory location 1008, replacing the contents originally stored there. Symbolically, we may write the instruction as follows:

```
ADDL3     1000, 1004, 1008
```

The string ADDL3 tells us three things. First, the ADD tells us that this is an addition operation. Second, the letter L reminds us that the operands are 32-bit longwords. Finally, the suffix 3 indicates that the operation involves three operands. The numbers 1000, 1004, 1008 simply tell us where the operands are in the primary memory.

At the start of the execution cycle of this instruction, the program counter must contain the value 100; that is, it must point at the address at which the next instruction is to be fetched. The contents of the program counter (PC) are first sent to the MAR; then a memory read (fetch) operation is initiated. When the instruction reaches the MBR, the control unit will generate signals to affect the transfer of the contents in the MBR to the instruction register (IR). The control unit, after decoding the instruction, will send the address 1000 to the MAR and start another memory read operation. The operand obtained will be sent to the ALU, and the address 1004 will be sent to the MAR. When the second operand is read out and received in the ALU, the control unit will issue the *start add* signal. The sum generated will be sent to the MBR and the address 1008 transferred to the MAR. Finally, a memory write (store) operation will be initiated.

The specification of this instruction in this particular case on the VAX-11 takes 10 bytes, as we will see later. The PC will have advanced to 110 by the completion of the instruction. At this point the CPU is ready to repeat the instruction fetch and execute cycle by getting its next instruction at memory location 110.

2.6 Instruction Format

Just as numbers and characters are represented inside the computer by bit strings, so are the instructions encoded. From the previous section it is obvious that the computer will perform properly only when all the information necessary to carry out the instruction is specified in the instruction. This includes the specification of the type of operation, the data format, the locations of the operands, and the destination of the result. Using the foregoing example, the computer is "told" to carry out an ADDition operation using two 32-bit binary integers (Longwords) as operands. The character string ADDL3 is relatively easy for us to understand: ADD is for add; and the single letter L, in context, gives a clear picture of the data type to be used. One might question the necessity to include the digit 3 in the string. After all, everyone knows that an addition requires two operands and produces a result. As we shall see, however, some computers, including the VAX-11, have another add instruction that involves only two memory locations. Therefore, it is necessary to add the digit here. Of course, if a computer were to use only one type of add instruction and one form to represent an integer, then no specification other than the operation itself would be necessary.

This shorthand representation of an instruction is known as a *mnemonic.* It gives the programmer an economical and convenient way of describing the operation he or she intends to use. To the computer, however, even this character string is too long. It will take up 5 bytes when encoded in ASCII or EBCDIC code. When the computer is expecting the specification of an operation, all that is required is for it to recognize the members of an instruction set defined for it. The size of the set varies but is often less than 200. Therefore, in most cases, an 8-bit code is adequate to specify all the operations. The bit positions occupied by this code in an instruction are called the *op code field.*

There are currently over 300 instructions defined in the VAX-11. To circumvent the problem of trying to insert over 300 values in a space that can hold only 256, the VAX-11 uses a modified format for operation specification. The first byte of a VAX-11 instruction is always used as the operation code field. For example, the hexadecimal value C1 is the actual code for the instruction ADDL3. If, however, the first byte were to contain the value FD or FF (hex), then the second byte of the instruction would also be interpreted as part of the op code. There are currently about 60 such expanded instructions.

Next the computer needs to know where to fetch the operands and where to deposit the result. In principle, for a binary operation such as ADD (and most arithmetic and logic operations are binary operations), three addresses are required. Specifying all three addresses makes the instruction very long, however, especially since the size of the primary memory is now often quite large and each address will need a correspondingly long address field. Therefore, conventions have been adopted that eliminate one or more addresses in the instruction. Essentially, the omitted address(es) become implied in that the computer "knows" where they are.

Since the way an instruction is specified has direct implications on the structure of the CPU, the complexity of the control unit, and the efficiency of the program execution, it has been a popular subject for study and debate. In earlier days, when assembly language programming was more widely used, instruction format was used to classify computers. There were three-address machines, single-address machines, and so on, depending on how many addresses a given computer specified in its instructions for binary operations. Of course, binary operations are not the only type of operations. Some operations require only one operand (unary operations); some, such as the HALT instruction, may not use any operand at all. Thus even in a three-address machine there will be instructions that specify fewer than three addresses.

Today the structure of the CPU is more complicated and the control logic more sophisticated. It is not unusual for a computer to employ an assortment of instruction formats, none of which is considered the predominant one. One can, however, still identify the three-address, two-address, one-address and zero-address instruction formats.

The *three-address instruction format* intuitively appears the most logical form of instruction representation. For most arithmetic and logic operations, such as ADD, SUBTRACT, AND, and OR, the addresses identify the locations of the operands (sometimes also known as the *sources*) and the result (the *destination*). For example, for an operation of the type

$$C = A \; op \; B$$

where *op* can be ADD, SUBTRACT, and so on, we could have

```
ADD    A,B,C
SUB    A,B,C    for SUBTRACT
AND    A,B,C    for logical AND
```

where A, B, and C represent addresses of memory locations.

In the VAX-11, an example of a three-address instruction is the now familiar

```
ADDL3    A,B,C
```

If we designate the location of one of the source operands to serve as the location of the destination, we can reduce by one the number of addresses specified in an instruction. Thus we obtain the *two-address instruction format.* To perform the same function

$$C = A + B$$

the two-address instruction format will yield the following instruction sequence

```
MOVE    A,C
ADD     B,C
```

where the MOVE instruction simply transfers data from location A to C.

In the VAX-11, an example of a two-address instruction is

```
ADDL2    A,B
```

Note the suffix 2 instead of the 3 used in the previous example.

If the CPU uses one designated register (the accumulator) for the storage of the result as well as the source of one of the operands, we have the *one-address instruction format.* This was the most popular instruction format used in the early computers. The addition operation must now be coded this way:

```
LOAD        A
ADD         B
STORE       C
```

where the LOAD instruction transfers the contents in location A to the accumulator; the ADD instruction adds the content from location B to that in the accumulator and returns the sum to the accumulator; and the STORE instruction transfers the contents in the accumulator to memory location C.

In order to use a *zero-address instruction format,* all addresses have to be implied. This is accomplished by the use of a special storage device in the CPU called the *stack* or the *push-down.* The stack can be viewed as a column of registers, one on top of the other. All the neighboring registers are connected together. Only the topmost register is accessible to the CPU. When data are deposited into the stack, each item will be placed at the top. Before this is done, all data currently in the stack will be moved down from one register to the next. The effect is similar to that of placing a tray on the top of an automatic tray stacker in a cafeteria. Conversely, if data are taken out of the stack, the item in the topmost register will be fetched. In this case all the data remaining in the stack will move up one level. Data are taken out of the stack in the reverse order from that in which they are entered. Therefore, another name for the stack is *LIFO* (last in, first out).

With the help of such a device and with the understanding that the ALU will always fetch the necessary operands from the stack, perform the operation, and return the result to the stack, no addresses would be needed in the instruction specification. Of course, data to be manipulated must first be inserted into the stack, and later the result must be moved back to the memory. Special one-address instructions have been defined to achieve such data transfers (they are known as PUSH and POP instructions, respectively). Again, using our ADD example, the following sequence of instructions will be needed:

```
PUSH        A
PUSH        B
ADD
POP         C
```

It should be apparent by now that the same job requires different sequences of instructions when different instruction formats are used. It is not clear, however, which instruction format is the best. The answer is complicated and controversial. One way to measure the quality of an instruction set is to determine the program size that is required to perform a certain job, as well as the execution speed in terms of memory cycles to complete the job. Even such criteria, however, are difficult to apply in practice. The measurement depends greatly on the nature of the job as well as on other features of the computer not discussed here. It appears that contemporary designers, given the opportunity, tend to include many instruction formats in their instruction set.

We should note in closing that the VAX-11 has zero-address through six-address instructions. The general format of a VAX-11 instruction is as follows. It consists of 1 or 2 bytes for the operation code (op code), followed by 0 to 6 *operand specifiers*.

op code (1 or 2 bytes)
operand specifier 1
operand specifier 2
⋮
operand specifier *n*

An operand specifier occupies one or more bytes. It contains the information needed to locate the operand. The first byte of an operand specifier always has the format:

```
  7     4 3     0
 ┌───────┬───────┐
 │   M   │   R   │
 └───────┴───────┘
```

It consists of two 4-bit fields. The M field, called the *mode specifier,* is used to specify an addressing mode; the R field is used to specify a general register. The purposes of these fields will be explained in Chapter 5. Here it is sufficient to note that one can deduce from these fields the length of the operand specifier.

In executing an instruction, the VAX control unit examines the first byte of the instruction. This tells the control unit how many operand specifiers are required. (In the case of those instructions that have 2-byte op codes, the second byte also needs to be examined to determine the number of operand specifiers.) The first byte of each operand specifier in turn tells the control unit its own length. By examining the instruction one byte at a time, the control unit will always know exactly how far to go to fetch the whole instruction.

2.7 Input/Output System

Input/output devices are used to allow communication between the computer and the external world. We can divide I/O devices into two major categories: those that serve as an interface between the machine and human beings, and those that have a large storage capacity and are used as a secondary memory. Of course, with proper interfacing, computers can communicate with practically any device imaginable; in other words, any device can potentially be converted into an I/O device. Also, recently it has become popular to let computers communicate among themselves. In this book, however, we will concentrate only on the two most common categories of I/O devices just mentioned.

The binary signals inside the computer are not directly suitable for human use. The operating speed of the CPU and the primary memory is so high that it is uneconomical (if not impossible) to let human beings communicate directly with the computer. Output devices such as the line printer and the cathode ray tube (CRT) display transform the information sent from the computer into a form much more familiar to the user. The cardreader and the terminal keyboard, as input devices, serve the reverse purpose. These devices are character-oriented and work at relatively low speeds. In the VAX-11, for example, all information transmitted between those devices and the primary memory is in the form of ASCII-coded character strings. Transmission is at a maximum rate of less than 2,000 characters per second.

If one considers the speed of the CPU in terms of the amount of data it can process in unit time, the size of the primary memory is rather limited. Modern computer systems use devices that have a very large storage capacity (on the order of hundreds of millions of bytes) as backup devices to store information not immediately needed by the CPU. These devices are known as *secondary memories*. The most common are magnetic disks, magnetic tapes, and magnetic drums. These devices have capacities two to four orders of magnitude larger than that of the primary memory and cost two to four orders of magnitude less on a per byte basis. Their access time,

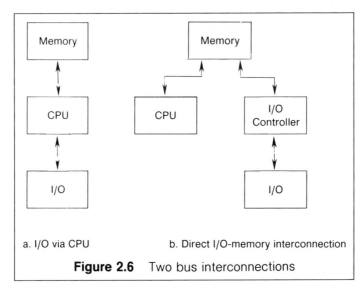

a. I/O via CPU   b. Direct I/O-memory interconnection

Figure 2.6   Two bus interconnections

however, is also four to six orders of magnitude larger than that of the primary memory.

The CPU, the primary memory, and the I/O devices are interconnected by communication lines called *buses*. A bus consists of a group of transmission lines that include the address, the control, and the data lines. All devices that are attached to a bus can send information to one another. The address lines specify the receiving device; the control lines specify the function to be performed, and the data lines carry the data to the destination. Different computer systems use different bus configurations. In the past the memory was usually connected to the CPU by one bus, and the I/O devices were connected to the CPU by another bus. Thus all I/O data would have to go through the CPU. More recently developed systems usually allow direct transfer of data between the primary memory and the I/O devices without the involvement of the CPU, regardless of whether it is a single-bus or a multibus system (see Figure 2.6). This *direct memory access* (DMA) feature relieves the CPU from handling the I/O data transfer but imposes an extra burden on the I/O controllers, which are the interfaces between the I/O devices and the bus.

2.8 Summary

The major components of a computer are the memory unit, the arithmetic and logic unit (ALU), the control unit, and the input/output (I/O) unit. When a program is ready to run, its instructions and data are first placed in the memory. The control unit then fetches the instructions out one at a time, following a predetermined sequence. Each instruction is examined by the control unit to determine its type and the operands it uses. When necessary, the control unit initiates memory operations to fetch data from the memory to the ALU. When all the operands are gathered, the control unit orders the ALU to perform the operation. Any result produced is deposited in a storage device as specified by the instruction. The next instruction in sequence is then fetched, and the cycle repeats itself.

Different types of computers use different sets of instructions and different ways to specify the operand addresses. Over the years, many instruction formats have been developed. Generally, they can be classified by the number of addresses each instruction specifies. The most common are the three-address, two-address, one-address, and zero-address instruction formats. The VAX-11 has a large instruction set and employs a variety of instruction formats.

EXERCISES

1. A memory unit has a word size of 36 bits and cycle time of 250 ns (1 nanosecond $= 10^{-9}$ sec). What is the bandwidth of the memory?

2. How many bits are necessary to represent the address of a memory with
   a. 16,384 locations?
   b. 131,070 locations?
   c. 4,294,967,296 locations?

3. The Greek alphabet consists of twenty-four letters. Suppose a programming language uses Greek and octal number representations and no other symbols. How many bits are required to code a basic symbol in this language?

4. Encode the following character strings in ASCII code:

FOUR SCORE AND SEVEN YEARS =
87 YEARS (OR 31,776 DAYS)

5. A decimal number (may or may not include sign) is represented in ASCII code. Each character is stored in a memory location in a computer. The computer performs arithmetic operation in binary using 2's complement arithmetic. Design an algorithm to be implemented on the computer that converts the number to its 2's complement representation. Verify your algorithm by using the following numbers as test cases (by carrying out the steps on paper).
   a. 1982
   b. −39
   c. +256

6. Write programs using 3, 2, 1, and 0 address instruction formats to evaluate the following expression:

$$f = (a-b)/(c+d*e)$$

Assume each of the variables $a, b, c, \ldots$ is stored in a different memory location. Only the contents of memory location f may be changed. You may use additional memory locations for temporary storage.

7. How will the condition codes be set on a VAX-11 computer after each of the following operations?
   a. $A + B$
   b. $A - B$
   c. $A + C$
   d. $A - C$
   e. $B + C$

   where

   A = 01011011
   B = 10100101
   C = 00110110

   All data are limited to a byte in size.

Chapter 3

Assembly Language Fundamentals

RECALL from Chapter 1 that assembly language is a symbolic representation of machine language. Whereas a machine language program consists of bit patterns, an assembly language program consists of alphanumeric names. The names describe operations to be performed, as well as storage locations and registers to be operated on.

This chapter introduces the basic elements of assembly language. The concepts introduced are common to assembly languages in general. The next chapter will be oriented specifically toward the VAX-11 assembly language and will give many examples for topics introduced in this chapter. This chapter uses the VAX-like assembly language used in Chapter 1 for examples.

3.1 Format of Assembly Statements

An assembly language program consists of a collection of statements. An assembly statement is usually entered on one line (or punched on one card). The set of rules that specifies the physical form of a statement is called the *format* of the statement. An assembly statement may consist of as many as four fields: the *label*, the *operator*, the *operand*, and the *comment* fields. The general format of a statement is:

Label   Operator   Operand   Comment

For example:

```
LOOP    MOV    SUM,TEMP    SAVE SUM
```

Some assemblers require that the fields start in particular columns. Such assemblers are said to require the statements to be in *fixed format.* Other assemblers allow *free format,* wherein the fields can be separated by one or more blanks or, occasionally, by special symbols. In the following, we describe each of the four fields of an assembly statement.

Label Field

A label is a user-defined symbol that is used as the name of a memory location. The name may then be used by other statements to refer to that memory location, instead of the numerical machine address of the location.

A label on a statement is needed only when the statement is referred to elsewhere in the program. If a label is not needed in a statement, then the label field should be left blank.

Operator Field

The operator (or operation) field contains a symbolic name of an operation. The operation specifies an action to be performed by the computer either at assembly time or at run time, depending on the type of operation.

An operation may be one of three types:

1. A mnemonic of a machine language instruction (such as DIV, MOV, or INC).
2. A directive to the assembler (such as BYTE, or BLKB).
3. A macro call.

The first two types are described in detail in Section 3.2. The third type is also described briefly in Section 3.2, but a full treatment of macros and macro calls is given in Chapter 8.

Operand Field

The operand field contains information needed by the operator. The information specifies operand(s) to be operated on by the operator. An operand may be specified in a number of ways. In a declaration statement, the operand may be specified as a value. For example,

```
LIST    BLKB    10
        BYTE    5
```

For an instruction, the operand may be specified by specifying the memory location at which the operand resides or is to reside. For example, TEN and N in the following contain the operands

```
TEN    BYTE   10
N      BYTE   0
          .
          .
          .
       ADD   TEN,N,N
```

If the operand is contained in a register or is to be stored in a register, then the register name is specified. Register names are usually of the form Rn, where n is the register number. Thus, for example, R6 in the following statement contains an operand

```
       MOV   R6,TEMP
```

The number of operands required in a statement is determined by the operator. For example, if DIV is an operator that divides two operands by each other and stores the result in a third operand, then it requires three operands:

```
       DIV   A,R2,R3
```

As another example, if INC is an operator that increments an operand by one and replaces that operand by the result, then it requires only one operand:

```
       INC   A
```

Symbolic addresses for operands are not limited to single symbols. Most assemblers allow some arithmetic expressions for the addresses in the operand field. For example,

```
       INC   A+1
```

means increment the contents of the next address after A. As another example,

```
       INC   2*A+1
```

means increment the contents of the address computed as twice the address of A plus 1. Addresses in these forms are called *address expressions*.

Comment Field

The comment field contains a description of the function of the statement. Although the comment field does not affect the execution of the program, nearly every statement in an assembly program should have a comment. The comment should not be a reiteration of the statement; rather, it should explain the intent of the statement or describe the reason for the statement. For example, the comments in the following statements do not add to clarity:

```
INC    R1              INCREMENT REGISTER R1 BY 1
DIV    SIZE,SUM,AVG     DIVIDE CONTENTS OF LOCATION
                       SUM BY SIZE AND STORE IN AVG
```

If in the foregoing R1 is used as a loop counter, SUM contains the cumulative sum of a set of numbers, and SIZE is the number of elements in the set, then comments like these would be more helpful:

```
INC    R1              INCREMENT LOOP COUNTER
DIV    SIZE,SUM,AVG     COMPUTE AVERAGE = SUM/SIZE
```

Writing good comments is an art that can be developed with practice. It may not be an easy task, but it is well worth the effort. Comments make the debugging and maintenance of a program much easier. Proper comments help the programmer remember what the program does when he or she reads it at a later time. They are also indispensable to other persons reading the program.

3.2 Types of Statements

A statement's type is determined by the operator in the statement's operator field. As mentioned in the previous section, an operator may be: (1) a directive to the assembler, (2) a mnemonic of an instruction, or (3) a macro call. These are the three types of statements that may occur in an assembly program.

Assembly Directives

Assembly directives perform such functions as declaring variables used in a program and designating the beginning and end of the program. Directives are commands to the assembler; their actions are performed during assembly time, not during run time. For example, consider the BYTE directive in the statement

```
N    BYTE    5
```

This causes the assembler to store in a byte the binary equivalent of 5. The byte will be given the symbolic name N. This is done at assembly time, and the directive will have no further effect.

Because directives do not perform any actions at run time, they are also referred to as *pseudo-operations,* or *pseudo-ops.*

Recall from Chapter 1 that directives that are used for declaring variables are of two types. The first type is used when certain variables (or constants) are to be initialized to known values; storage locations will be reserved and initialized to the data specified in the directive statement. The second type is used to reserve a block of consecutive memory locations without initializing the locations to any particular values.

Directive statements that are used to reserve and initialize memory locations have this general format:

name   directive   value$_1$, value$_2$, . . . , value$_n$

The name of the first location to be reserved appears in the label field, and the directive in the operator field. Value$_1$, value$_2$, . . . , value$_n$ in the operand field are the values to which the reserved locations are initialized. For example, assuming that our BYTE directive can reserve and initialize a number of 8-bit bytes, the statement

```
TABLE   BYTE   5,-10,0
```

requests reserving three bytes, with the first byte having the symbolic name TABLE. The initial contents of the bytes are the binary equivalents of the values specified:

00000101	TABLE
11110110	TABLE + 1
00000000	TABLE + 2

Directive statements that are used to reserve a block of memory locations have this format:

name   directive   size

The *name* of the first location to be reserved appears in the label field, the *directive* in the operator field, and the amount of storage to be reserved (*size*) in the operand field. For example, our BLKB directive has the following format:

At assembly time, the assembler will reserve five consecutive bytes, with the first byte having the symbolic name ARRAY:

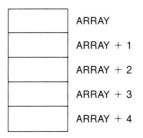

The memory locations following the first byte are not given individual names in the program. They can, however, be referenced as offsets from a label defined in the program. In the foregoing example, consecutive bytes can be referenced as offsets from ARRAY by the symbolic address expressions ARRAY+1, ARRAY+2, ARRAY+3, and ARRAY+4, respectively.

On machines that support several data types, different directives are provided for the various types. For example, on the VAX-11, the directives WORD and LONG are used to reserve and initialize words and longwords. Similarly, the directives BLKW and BLKL are used to reserve blocks of words and blocks of longwords. Furthermore, in addition to directives that reserve and initialize memory locations, there are directives that perform control functions at assembly time. We shall describe these directives in the next chapter.

Executable Instructions

Unlike an assembler directive that specifies an operation to be performed at assembly time, an instruction specifies an operation to be performed during the actual execution of the program—that is, at run time. Thus an instruction is a command to the computer hardware to perform a certain action.

As we have seen, an instruction is coded in an assembly language program by a *mnemonic*, which is the symbolic name of the instruction. At assembly time the mnemonic of an instruction is simply translated by the assembler into its *op code*, and no further action is caused by the mnemonic during this time. Later, at run time, the hardware decodes (or interprets) this op code and performs the corresponding operation. Thus the action requested by an instruction is performed only when the program is run—at run time or execution time.

Although different computer manufacturers supply different instructions for their computers, the instruction sets of most computers can be divided into the following broad categories:

1. Data transfer instructions.
2. Arithmetic instructions.
3. Comparison instructions.
4. Branch instructions.
5. Shift instructions.
6. Logical instructions.
7. Input/output instructions.

In the following sections we present the characteristic of these categories.

Data Transfer Instructions

These instructions simply perform the function of moving data between memory locations, between memory locations and registers, and between registers. Typical data transfer instructions are *load, store,* and *move.* The instructions *load* and *store* usually indicate moving data from memory to a register, and moving data from a register to memory, respectively. For example,

```
LOAD    A,R5    Copy contents of location A into
                R5.
STORE   R5,A    Copy contents of R5 into location
                A.
```

Some machines that have *load* and *store* instructions also have a *move* instruction to copy data from a memory location into another. For example,

```
MOVE    A,B    Copy contents of A into B.
```

Other machines have a single instruction to perform all the aforementioned types of data transfer. For example, the VAX-11 uses only the *move* instruction to:

```
MOVE    A,R5    Copy contents of A into R5.
MOVE    R5,A    Copy contents of R5 into A.
MOVE    A,B     Copy contents of A into B.
```

The first operand, referred to as the *source*, is copied into the second, referred to as the *destination*.

Arithmetic Instructions

This category includes such instructions as *add, subtract, multiply, divide, decrement,* and *increment.* Arithmetic instructions operate on operands contained in memory locations or registers. The result of an arithmetic instruction is stored in a memory location or a register, the destination.

The binary operations *add, subtract, multiply,* and *divide* require two operands and a third operand for the destination. As seen in Chapter 2, the two operands and the destination may or may not all be specified explicitly in the statement; that is, one or more of them may be implied. *Decrement* and *increment* require a single operand, which is decreased or increased by one.

Subtract and *divide,* being noncommutative operations, might work differently in different computers. For example, in some computers the instruction

```
SUBTRACT    R5,A
```

means subtract the contents of A from the contents of R5, whereas in others it means subtract the contents of R5 from the contents of A. The destination might be A or R5, also depending on the particular computer.

Clearly, decrementing or incrementing can be performed by an *add* or a *subtract* instruction. For example, assuming that ONE is a memory location that contains 1, the instruction

```
ADD    ONE,R2
```

is equivalent to *increment* R2, and

```
SUBTRACT    ONE,R2
```

is equivalent to *decrement* R2. Many machines, however, provide *decrement* and *increment* instructions since they execute faster than *add* and *subtract* (for example, no operand fetch from memory location ONE) and are shorter (that is, they occupy less memory space). The saving in time and space could be very significant when one considers the frequent need to increment and decrement by one in a typical computer program.

On some machines the destination of an arithmetic instruction cannot be a memory location; that is, the destination must be a register. Thus instructions such as

```
ADD     A,B
DIVIDE  R1,B
```

where B is a memory location destination, are not allowed. Those machines are said not to allow *memory-to-memory* or *register-to-memory* arithmetic instructions. Such machines usually have *load* and *store* instructions to implement instructions effectively, as in the foregoing. For example, to add the contents of A and B and store the result in B, one can do this:

```
LOAD    B,R2    Copy B into R2.
ADD     A,R2    Add A to R2 and store in R2.
STORE   R2,B    Copy R2 into B.
```

The terms *register-to-register, register-to-memory, memory-to-register,* and *memory-to-memory* are used to describe what source and what destination a machine supports for its instructions.

Comparison Instructions

These instructions do not involve data movement and do not manipulate data. Their sole purpose is to examine or compare the contents of memory locations and registers, and set the condition codes (CCs) in the CPU. The CCs will be set or reset depending on the result of the comparison. Comparison instructions are usually used to determine which segment of a program to execute. Therefore, they are usually followed by conditional branch instructions to decide on branching.

Typical comparison instructions are *compare* and *test*. The *compare* instruction compares two operands; the comparison is performed by effectively subtracting one operand from the other and setting the condition codes according to the result. The result of the subtraction is not preserved, and the two operands are not altered in any way. The *test* instruction tests an operand for a positive, negative, or zero value, and sets the condition codes accordingly. The operand is not altered.

Note that the *test* instruction is equivalent to the *compare* instruction with one of the operands being zero. For example, assume that in a *compare* instruction the second operand is subtracted from the first. Then, if ZERO is a memory location that contains 0, the instruction

```
COMPARE    R2,ZERO
```

is equivalent to

```
TEST    R2
```

test, however, is faster and shorter.

It must be mentioned that the comparison instructions are not the only instructions that affect the condition codes. For instance, arithmetic and data transfer instructions also set or reset the CCs according to the value that is stored into the destination.

Branch Instructions

Branch instructions affect the flow of control in a computer program; that is, they can alter the sequential order of executing program instructions. A branch statement specifies in its operand field an address that should be the address of an instruction. This will be the next instruction to be executed if the branch takes place. In some machines branch instructions are called *transfer* or *jump* instructions.

Branch instructions are of two types: *conditional* and *unconditional*.

CONDITIONAL BRANCH INSTRUCTIONS These instructions specify a condition to be inspected at the time of execution of the branch instruction. If the condition is met, then execution continues at the address specified in the branch statement; otherwise, execution continues at the statement following the branch statement.

Typical conditional branch instructions are *branch on equal zero, branch on greater than zero, branch on less than zero, branch on greater or equal zero,* and *branch on less or equal zero.* The condition specified in the instruction is inspected for a true or false value by testing the CCs.

Conditional branch instructions are used when one of two segments of a program must be chosen for continuing the execution. The choice is usually based on the condition of the result of the most recently performed instruction that affects the CCs. Recall that the CCs are set or reset by comparison, arithmetic, data transfer, and other instructions. Therefore, whereas a comparison instruction is almost always followed by a branch instruction, a branch instruction is not necessarily preceded by a comparison instruction.

UNCONDITIONAL BRANCH INSTRUCTIONS These instructions cause a branch without testing any condition. The branch is to an instruction whose address is specified in the operand field of the unconditional branch statement. An unconditional branch is equivalent to the GOTO statement in higher-level languages.

There is another type of branch instructions, that of *branch to subroutine.* This type is similar to the unconditional branch in that a branch is taken unconditionally to the address (beginning address of the subroutine) specified in the branch statement. The branch, however, takes place "with the intent to return." That is, after the subroutine is executed, execution will continue at the instruction following the branch statement. The mechanism for branching to and returning from a subroutine will be presented in Chapter 6.

Shift Instructions

These instructions operate on an operand by shifting the individual bits of the operand one or more places, left or right, as specified by the instruction. Depending on the direction of the shift, the leftmost or rightmost bits being vacated are filled with 0s or 1s, depending on the instruction. The bits that are shifted out are either lost or preserved, also depending on the instructions of the particular machine. Typical shift instructions are *shift left* and *shift right.* The number of places for the shifting is either implied by the instruction or specified by an operand. In some machines the direction of the shift is also implied by an operand.

As an example, assume that the instruction SHL shifts left the contents of a storage location one place and feeds a 0 in the rightmost vacated bit. If a location N contains the number

| 00110101 | N |

then after executing the statement

        SHL   N

N will contain

| 01101010 | N |

Shift instructions can be used when an operand is to be multiplied or divided by a number that is a power of 2. *Shift* instructions in these cases are preferred over *multiply* or *divide,* for they are more efficient. Shifting an operand left once and feeding 0 in the rightmost bit of the operand is equivalent to multiplying the operand by 2. Shifting an operand right once and feeding 0 in the leftmost bit has the effect of dividing the number by 2. The division, however, is equivalent to integer division. Care must be taken with negative numbers: the idiosyncrasies of the particular machine should be studied to determine the effects of these instructions.

Logical Instructions

Logical instructions implement Boolean operations such as *and, or,* and *xor (exclusive or)* (see Appendix A). These operations are binary operations; thus, as with arithmetic instructions, they require two operands and a third for the destination. As an example, assume that two memory locations, A and B, contain the binary numbers:

```
+----------+
| 00110101 | A
+----------+
```

```
+----------+
| 00001111 | B
+----------+
```

then after executing the instruction

```
AND     A,B
```

location B will contain

```
+----------+
| 00000101 | B
+----------+
```

Input/Output (I/O) Instructions

These instructions perform the function of moving data between main memory (or the CPU) and the input/output devices (such as terminals, printers, and disks). I/O instructions are capable of moving a single character at a time (for character-oriented I/O devices like terminals), or a group of characters (for other I/O devices like disks). Some computers have special instructions whose sole purpose is to perform I/O. Other computers do not have special instructions for I/O. Instead the registers of the I/O devices are treated like the CPU registers or like memory locations, and data transfer instructions are used to perform I/O. The VAX-11 is an example of the latter.

The mnemonics and the operation of I/O instructions, and I/O programming in general, differ vastly from one machine to another. Therefore, we shall defer the detailed treatment of I/O until Chapter 10. Section 4.3, however, describes how to perform simple I/O operations on the VAX-11.

Macros

A *macro* assigns a name to a sequence of assembly statements, called the *body* of the macro. In this respect a macro is similar to a function or to a procedure in a higher-level language. Usually, a sequence of statements is defined as a macro when the sequence is needed frequently in the program. By specifying a sequence of statements as a macro, the programmer need not enter the sequence at the sites at which the statements are needed in the program. Instead, the programmer supplies the name of the macro in a statement at every site at which he wishes the sequence to be inserted; then, at assembly time, the assembler inserts the macro sequence at the sites specified, saving the programmer work. The assembler is said to *expand* the macro name into the macro body.

A statement that invokes a macro is referred to as a *macro call* or a *macro instruction*. The name of the macro appears in the operator field, and the operand field may specify arguments that would correspond to parameters defined in the macro. A macro call can optionally have a label and a comment.

Macros are normally used in large programs by experienced assembly language programmers; therefore, we defer treating macros in depth until Chapter 8.

3.3 Summary

Machine language instructions are represented in alphanumeric symbols in an assembly language program. An assembler is used to translate these symbols back into the binary-coded form of machine instructions, which is the only representation "understood" by the computer. To facilitate the translation, each assembler prescribes a specific input format to be followed by the programmer. Although the rules may vary in detail between different assemblers, the general formats are quite similar. Usually, an assembly statement occupies one line and consists of up to four fields: the label field, the operator field, the operand field, and the comment field.

There are three types of assembly language statements. First, the *directives* or *pseudo-operations* are commands to the assembler to perform certain functions during assembly time. Second, the *executable instructions* are machine instructions to be carried out by the computer at run time. Finally, the *macros* are sequences of statements that are inserted at every place where a macro name is invoked in the program.

EXERCISES

1. Consider a machine wherein the destination of an arithmetic instruction cannot be a memory location. Assume that the machine has LOAD and STORE instructions that function as described in Section 3.2. Write a segment of a program for this machine that copies a block of 5 bytes that starts at address A into another block starting at address B.

In the following exercises, use the instructions of this chapter. You may introduce mnemonics of your own choosing for the various instructions. Assume that all integers have a range of a byte.

2. Two locations, FIRST and SECOND, contain two integer numbers. Write a program that finds the larger of the two numbers and stores it in location MAX.

3. Write a program that finds the absolute value of an integer number contained in location NUM and stores it in location ABS.

4. Write a program that adds the numbers one through 15 inclusive and stores the result in location SUM. Your program may not create the list of numbers in memory.

5. Write a program that computes the factorial of the number five (5!) and stores the result in location FACT.

6. The Fibonacci sequence is defined by:

$$F(0) = 0$$
$$F(1) = 1$$
$$F(i) = F(i-1)+F(i-2) \qquad (i \geq 2)$$

Write a program that computes $F(10)$ and stores it in location FIB.

7. Write a program that computes X^N ($X > 0$, $N \geq 0$).

8. Multiplication of two integers can be performed by repeated addition. Write a program that multiplies any two integers by repeated addition. Each of the two numbers may be positive, negative, or zero.

9. Division of two integers may be performed by repeated subtraction. Write a program that performs integer division of two integers by repeated subtraction. Assume both numbers to be positive.

Chapter 4

Introduction to the VAX-11 MACRO Language

FOR COMMERCIAL reasons, and because a manufacturer may provide a number of different assemblers for the same computer, the assemblers are often given individual names. The assembler for the VAX-11 computer is called MACRO, and the VAX-11 assembly language is referred to as the MACRO language.[1]

This chapter introduces a simple subset of the MACRO language. Although only subsets of the instructions and directives are introduced, enough is presented to enable us to write nontrivial MACRO programs. Toward the end of the chapter a simple method is provided for performing input and output directly from a VAX-11 assembly language program.

4.1 Format of a MACRO Statement

A MACRO statement has the general format:

   Label: Operator   Operand   ;Comment

where the label, if present, must end with a colon (:), and the comment field must start with a semicolon (;). The operator and operand fields must be separated by at least one blank or horizontal tab character. Although the fields may start in any column, it is recommended that the fields be formatted to start in particular columns. Such consistent formatting greatly improves readability. Digital recommends that the fields begin in the following columns:

---

[1] The name MACRO is not to be confused with the general term *macro* discussed in the previous chapter. In this book, if the entire word is capitalized, we mean the MACRO language or the MACRO assembler.

Field	Column
Label	1
Operator	9
Operand	17
Comment	41

These starting columns are chosen because the horizontal tabs on a terminal are usually set every eight columns.

A statement may be continued on several lines. The hyphen (-) is used for continuation and is placed at the end of the line to be continued. Following the hyphen a comment may appear on that line. As an example,

```
label:    operator    operand1,operand2,-    ;comment
                      operand3,-             ;comment
                      operand4
```

Continuation, of course, should be used only if the statement is too long or for clarity.

A label or any other user-defined symbol in a MACRO statement must conform to the following rules:

1. It may consist of letters and digits, underscores(__), dollar signs ($), and periods (.); no other characters may be used.
2. The first character may not be a digit.
3. It can be up to thirty-one characters long.
4. It cannot be one of the register names R0, R1, . . . , R12, AP, FP, SP, or PC.

AP (argument pointer), FP (frame pointer), and SP (stack pointer) are the names of registers R12, R13, and R14, respectively. These registers are used for special purposes, as will be seen in Chapter 6 on subroutines. PC is the program counter, register R15. Note that register R12 can be referenced as either R12 or AP. Registers R13, R14, and R15, however, are known to the MACRO assembler by the names FP, SP, and PC only. That is, if the symbols R13, R14, R15 appear in a program, they are considered to be user-defined symbols.

In addition, it is recommended that the dollar sign ($) not be used as the first character of a user-defined name. This is to ensure that a user-defined symbol does not conflict with names defined internally by the VAX operating system that start with a dollar sign.

If a label is more than seven characters long, it is recommended that it be placed on a line by itself so that the operator field can start in column 9 on the next line. In this case the hyphen (-) is not

```
;THIS PROGRAM MULTIPLIES EACH ELEMENT OF AN ARRAY, LIST,
;BY A CONSTANT.
;
;CONSTANTS AND VARIABLES
;
CONSTANT=4                            ;CONSTANT OF MULTIPLICATION
LIST:   .BYTE 1,2,3,4,5               ;ARRAY OF SIZE 5 BYTES
SIZE:   .BYTE SIZE-LIST               ;ARRAY SIZE
;
;EXECUTABLE CODE
;
        .ENTRY SCALE_ARRAY,0          ;BEGIN EXECUTION
        CLRB    R5                    ;R5 IS A LOOP COUNTER
        MOVAB   LIST,R6               ;POINT TO 1ST ELEMENT OF LIST
LOOP:   MULB    #CONSTANT,(R6)        ;MULTIPLY ITH ELEM BY CONSTANT
        INCL    R6                    ;POINT TO NEXT ELEMENT OF LIST
        INCB    R5                    ;INCREMENT LOOP COUNTER
        CMPB    SIZE,R5               ;ALL ELEMENTS PROCESSED?
        BGTR    LOOP                  ; NO: CONTINUE
        $EXIT_S                       ; YES: TERMINATE PROGRAM
        .END    SCALE_ARRAY           ;END OF PROGRAM
```

Figure 4.1   An assembly language program

needed following the label to indicate continuation. Finally, a comment can appear on a line by itself, in which case the first nonblank character on the line must be a semicolon (;).

Figure 4.1 shows an example of a MACRO program, and Figure 4.2 shows the *listing* of the program. The listing is produced by the assembler, and it shows the source code together with the equivalent object code. The figures are intended to show what a MACRO program and its listing look like. The elements of the program and the listing will be explained in the sequel.

4.2 Simple MACRO Directives

As we already know, directives perform such functions as reserving memory space for the variables in the program, initializing memory locations to certain values, designating the beginning and end of a program, and instructing the assembler to do certain control functions at assembly time. In this section we look at a simple subset of the VAX-11 MACRO Assembler directives. The format of the directive is given first, followed by the function of the directive and an example. The operands of the directives are given in forms that are commonly used by beginners. Note that every directive is preceded by a period (.), which is part of the directive syntax. The period is used by the MACRO Assembler to distinguish between directives and instruction mnemonics.[2] Unless otherwise specified, all numbers are assumed by the MACRO Assembler to be decimal.

---

[2] Requiring a period before a directive, a colon after a label, and a semicolon before a comment is simply to aid MACRO in the translation process.

```
                                    1  ;THIS PROGRAM MULTIPLIES EACH ELEMENT OF AN ARRAY, LIST,
0000                                2  ;BY A CONSTANT.
0000                                3  ;
0000                                4  ;CONSTANTS AND VARIABLES
0000                                5  ;
0000         00000004               6  CONSTANT=4           ;CONSTANT OF MULTIPLICATION
0000   05 04 03 02 01               7  LIST:  .BYTE 1,2,3,4,5    ;ARRAY OF SIZE 5 BYTES
0005               05               8  SIZE:  .BYTE SIZE-LIST    ;ARRAY SIZE
0006                                9  ;
0006                               10  ;EXECUTABLE CODE
0006                               11  ;
0006         0000                  12         .ENTRY SCALE__ARRAY,0   ;BEGIN EXECUTION
0008         55 94                 13         CLRB   R5            ;R5 IS A LOOP COUNTER
000A   F3 AF 9E                    14         MOVAB  LIST,R6       ;POINT TO 1ST ELEMENT OF LIST
000E   66 04 84                    15  LOOP:  MULB   #CONSTANT,(R6) ;MULTIPLY ITH ELEM BY CONSTANT
0011         56 D6                 16         INCL   R6            ;POINT TO NEXT ELEMENT OF LIST
0013         55 96                 17         INCB   R5            ;INCREMENT LOOP COUNTER
0015   55 ED AF 91                 18         CMPB   SIZE,R5       ;ALL ELEMENTS PROCESSED?
0019         F3 14                 19         BGTR   LOOP          ; NO: CONTINUE
001B                               20         $EXIT_S             ; YES: TERMINATE PROGRAM
0024                               21         .END   SCALE__ARRAY  ;END OF PROGRAM
```

Figure 4.2 Listing for program of Figure 4.1

Data Storage Directives

Data storage directives are used for reserving storage when the initial values of the storage locations to be reserved are known. In the following, we look at directives that reserve and initialize bytes (.BYTE), words (.WORD), longwords (.LONG), quadwords (.QUAD), and octawords (.OCTA). These directives accept integer values only, and one or the other is used depending on the range of the integer. (See Table 2.1 for the various ranges.)

The .BYTE Directive

FORMAT

    label: .BYTE   value$_1$, value$_2$, . . . , value$_n$

FUNCTION Reserve consecutive bytes in memory and initialize them to the binary equivalents of value$_1$, value$_2$, . . . , value$_n$ one value to a byte. Assign the address of the first reserved byte to the symbolic address in the label field.

EXAMPLE The statements

    LIST: .BYTE   35,-60,5
    COUNT: .BYTE   10

will result in storing, in 4 consecutive bytes, the binary equivalents of the specified values in the operand field. Assuming the 4 bytes start at memory address 200, the contents of the 4 bytes in hexadecimal would be:

Contents (Hex)	Address	Symbolic Address
23	200	LIST
C4	201	
05	202	
0A	203	COUNT

Note that the second value in the list (at address 201) may be referenced in the program either by the symbolic address expression LIST+1 or by COUNT−2. Similarly, the value at address 203 may be referenced by the symbolic address LIST+3.

The fact that a memory location can be referenced by an offset from a symbolic address is very useful. It is also the source of one of the most common errors in programming, however. If, for example, the programmer's intention is for LIST to be an array of three elements only, but as a result of an error the program refers to a fourth element of LIST as LIST+3, there may be no indication of this error (this is also true in many higher-level languages). Sometimes, however, such an error (fortunately) may cause side effects, such as referencing a location outside the memory area reserved for the program. Since most computer systems protect programs in memory from one another, such errors can be caught at run time. The system then displays a run-time error message to this effect.[3]

The .WORD Directive

FORMAT

    label: .WORD   value$_1$, value$_2$, . . . , value$_n$

FUNCTION Reserve consecutive words in memory and initialize them to the binary equivalents of value$_1$, value$_2$, . . . , value$_n$, one value to a word. Assign the address of the first reserved word to the symbolic address in the label field.

EXAMPLE The statements

    NUM: .WORD   346
    VALUES: .WORD   5,-346,0

will result in storing, in four consecutive words, the binary equivalent of the specified values in the operand field. Assuming the four words start at memory address 210, the contents of the four words in hexadecimal would be:

Contents (Hex)	Address	Symbolic Address
015A	210	NUM
0005	212	VALUES
FEA6	214	
0000	216	

Note that location 210 contains 5A, 211 contains 01, 212 contains 05, 213 contains 00, and so on. This is consistent with the VAX-11 convention in numbering bytes from *right* to *left*.

Recall from Chapter 2 that the address of a word is the address of the lower (right) byte in the word. This implies that, in the foregoing, label NUM is equated to address 210, and VALUES is equated to

---

[3]VMS refers to this type of error as *access violation*. It is perhaps the most common run-time error, occurring whenever the user's program attempts to access a location that should not be accessed.

212. Therefore, the word at address 214 is referenced symbolically in the program as VALUES+2, *not* VALUES+1. Similarly, the word at address 216 is referenced as VALUES+4.

The .LONG Directive

FORMAT

    label: .LONG   value₁, value₂, . . . , valueₙ

FUNCTION This is the same as for the .WORD directive except that consecutive longwords (4 bytes) are reserved and initialized. Note that the longwords reserved, starting with the first one, have the symbolic addresses "label," "label+4," "label+8," and so on.

The .QUAD and .OCTA Directives

FORMATS

    label: .QUAD   value
    label: .OCTA   value

FUNCTION Reserve one quadword (octaword) and initialize it to the specified value. These directives differ from the previous ones in that they accept only one value in the operand field (they do not accept a list of values). In addition, the value specified may not have a negative sign.

The foregoing directives can also be used to store ASCII characters. This is done by specifying the ASCII code equivalents of the characters as operands. For example, the three characters ABC can be stored in three bytes by

    .BYTE   65,66,67

Another way to store characters is by using directives specifically designed for this purpose. In MACRO terminology, these directives are called ASCII character storage directives. Two of these directives are .ASCII and .ASCIC, which we present next.

The .ASCII Directive

FORMAT

    label: .ASCII   dstringd

The *d*s around the string are delimiters and can be any printable characters except the blank, tab, equal sign (=), semicolon (;), and left angle bracket (<). The delimiters around a string must match. The string may contain any ASCII character except the null, the carriage return, the form feed, and the chosen delimiter character.

FUNCTION Store in consecutive bytes the ASCII representation of the characters of the string, one character to a byte. Assign the address of the first byte to the symbolic name in the label field.

EXAMPLE The statement

```
STRING:    .ASCII    /INPUT DATA/
```

stores in 10 consecutive bytes the ASCII representation of the 10 characters INPUT DATA. Thus, if STRING starts at address 300, for example, then the contents of the 10 bytes would be:

Contents (Hex)	Address	Symbolic Address
49	300	STRING
4E	301	
50	302	
55	303	
54	304	
20	305	
44	306	
41	307	
54	308	
41	309	

The .ASCIC Directive

FORMAT

```
label:    .ASCIC    dstringd
```

FUNCTION Same as .ASCII except it inserts the number of characters in the string in the first byte reserved (the count byte).

EXAMPLE

```
STRING:    .ASCIC    'INPUT DATA'
```

This has the same effect as

```
STRING:    .BYTE    10
           .ASCII    'INPUT DATA'
```

There is another storage directive, .ADDRESS, that is used to store addresses instead of data values. This directive is useful in certain situations as we will see later.

The .ADDRESS Directive

FORMAT

label: .ADDRESS $symbol_1$, $symbol_2$, . . . , $symbol_n$

FUNCTION   Reserve consecutive longwords in memory and store in them the *addresses* of $symbol_1$, $symbol_2$, . . . , $symbol_n$, one address to a longword. Assign the address of the first reserved longword to the symbolic address in the label field.

EXAMPLE   The statement

TABLE: .ADDRESS   NUM,VALUES

will result in storing, in two consecutive longwords, the addresses of NUM and VALUES. Assuming the two longwords start at memory address 250, and that NUM and VALUES are as defined previously by the .WORD directives, the contents of the two longwords would be:

Contents (Hex)	Address	Symbolic Address
00000210	250	TABLE
00000212	254	

Equivalently, the .LONG directive can be used to reserve long-words and store addresses. For example, the statement

TABLE: .LONG   NUM,VALUES

is equivalent to

TABLE: .ADDRESS   NUM,VALUES

The use of .ADDRESS is recommended for storing addresses, however, since it is more indicative

It must be emphasized that in the foregoing .LONG statement, the addresses of NUM and VALUES—*not* the contents of the locations at these addresses—are stored in the reserved longwords. This is true whenever a label is specified in the operand field of a data storage directive. Since an address in the VAX-11 is 32 bits, it might not make sense to specify a label in the operand field of some storage directive statements, particularly .BYTE and .WORD. Specifying an expression that has labels in it might make sense, however, and is sometimes useful. For example, in the following segment of code, the byte at SIZE will contain the number of bytes reserved for the list.

```
LIST:       .BYTE 0,5,10,15,20      ;A LIST OF NUMBERS
SIZE:       .BYTE SIZE-LIST         ;SIZE OF THE LIST
```

The expression (SIZE − LIST) is evaluated as the difference between the addresses of SIZE and LIST, which is 5. This may be preferred over declaring SIZE as

```
SIZE:       .BYTE    5
```

because one can add more numbers to LIST without changing the declaration of SIZE.

Block Storage Allocation Directives

Block storage allocation directives are used for reserving storage for variables whose values are unknown at the start of the program. The MACRO Assembler reserves storage as specified by these directives and initializes the reserved locations to all 0 bits. In the following, we look at directives that reserve a block of bytes (.BLKB), words (.BLKW), longwords (.BLKL), quadwords (.BLKQ), and octawords (.BLKO).

The .BLKB Directive

FORMAT

```
label:    .BLKB    size
```

FUNCTION   Reserve a block of consecutive bytes of the specified size. Assign the address of the first reserved byte to the symbolic name in the label field.

EXAMPLE   The statements

```
ARRAY:    .BLKB    10
TABLE:    .BLKB    5
```

reserve a block of 10 consecutive bytes in memory, with the address of the first byte named ARRAY. The second byte can be referred to as ARRAY+1, the third byte as ARRAY+2, and so on. Immediately following this block, a block of 5 consecutive bytes is reserved, with the address of the first byte named TABLE.

The .BLKW, .BLKL, .BLKQ, and .BLKO Directives

FORMATS

```
label:    .BLKW    size
label:    .BLKL    size
label:    .BLKQ    size
label:    .BLKO    size
```

FUNCTION   Same as .BLKB except for reserving a block of consecutive words, longwords, quadwords, and octawords. The total number of bytes reserved is equal to the size specified times the number of bytes in the data type. For example, the statement

```
LIST:    .BLKL    10
```

reserves a block of 40 consecutive bytes (10 longwords) in memory. The symbolic address of the first byte reserved is LIST. Note that .BLKB can be used equivalently in place of any of the foregoing directives; depending on the application, however, it may be more indicative to use these other directives.

The .BLKA Directive

FORMAT

```
label:    .BLKA    size
```

FUNCTION   Same as .BLKL; but the use of .BLKA is recommended for reserving a block of addresses because it adds to the clarity of the program.

The directives of this section are summarized in Table 4.1.

Entry Point and End Directives

The *entry point* of a program is the address of the first instruction to be executed in the program. The entry point of a MACRO program is specified by the .ENTRY directive, whose format is

```
.ENTRY    program-name,0
```

where program-name is a user-defined symbol. This symbolic address is used by the operating system to determine where program execution should begin. The function of the zero (0) following the

Table 4.1 Storage Directives

	Directive	Operand(s)	Function
label:	.BYTE	list of values	Store values specified in consecutive bytes starting at address *label*.
label:	.WORD	list of values	Store values in consecutive words.
label:	.LONG	list of values	Store values in consecutive longwords.
label:	.QUAD	value	Store value specified in one quadword.
label:	.OCTA	value	Store value specified in one octaword.
label:	.ADDRESS	list of symbols	Store the addresses of the specified symbols in consecutive longwords starting at *label*.
label:	.BLKB	size	Reserve a consecutive block of bytes of the size specified starting at address *label*.
label:	.BLKW	size	Reserve a consecutive block of words of the size specified.
label:	.BLKL	size	Reserve a consecutive block of longwords of the size specified.
label:	.BLKQ	size	Reserve a consecutive block of quadwords of the size specified.
label:	.BLKO	size	Reserve a consecutive block of octawords of the size specified.
label:	.BLKA	size	Reserve a consecutive block of longwords of the size specified.
label:	.ASCII	*d*string*d*	Store the ASCII codes of the characters in the string in consecutive bytes starting at address *label*.
label:	.ASCIC	*d*string*d*	Store the number of characters in the string in byte at *label*, followed by the ASCII codes of the characters.

program-name will be clarified in Chapter 6 on subroutines.

The entry point of a MACRO program can also be defined by the directive .WORD, as follows:

```
program-name:    .WORD    0
```

.ENTRY is recommended for readability, however.

The end of a MACRO program must also be specified to the assembler. This is done by the .END directive, whose format is

```
.END    program-name
```

The program-name following the .END must be the same name defined by the .ENTRY directive. The .ENTRY statement can have a label, in which case the label will be equated to the program-name; the .END statement can then specify either name.

```
⎰ Data storage,
⎱ block storage, and      ⎱
⎱ ASCII storage directives ⎰

.ENTRY program-name,0

{ Instructions }

$EXIT_S
.END      program-name
```

Figure 4.3   General format of a MACRO program

The .END directive terminates the source program; no text should occur beyond this point. If any text occurs beyond the .END statement, the assembler ignores the additional text.

The general format of a MACRO program is shown in Figure 4.3. In the figure, $EXIT__S is a call to a system macro; it is used by the VMS operating system to properly terminate a program.

4.3 Direct Assignment Statement

A *direct assignment statement* simply assigns a symbolic name to a value. The general format of a direct assignment statement is:

    name = expression

where the name is a user-defined symbol. For example, the statements

```
LENGTH = 10
N = 20
TWO = 2
```

equate the names to the specified values. The names can then be used in place of the value, thus providing more readability and generality.

Like a directive statement, the effect of a direct assignment statement is performed at assembly time, not at run time. Unlike the case of a directive statement, however, the assembler does not reserve any storage for symbols defined in direct assignment statements; it merely substitutes the value of the symbol when the symbol is encountered in the program. For example,

```
LENGTH = 10
TABLE:    .BLKB    LENGTH
```

is equivalent to

```
TABLE:    .BLKB    10
```

Note the advantage of using a direct assignment statement: if LENGTH is used several times in the program, then if the value of LENGTH is to be changed from one run to another, the first form is superior in that only one modification would be needed. In addition, assignment statements increase the readability of the program and provide better programming style.

It is important to understand the difference between a symbol that is defined in a direct assignment statement and one that is defined as a label:

A symbol defined in a direct assignment statement will have the value assigned to it in the statement independent of the position of the statement in the program.

A label is an address of a memory location; the address depends on the position of the label in the program.

Unlike a label, a symbol defined in a direct assignment statement may be redefined anywhere in the program. For example, if N is defined in a program by

```
N = 20
```

it can be followed later by

```
N = N+10
```

after which N becomes 30. Similarly, N can also be redefined later as

```
N = LENGTH+N
```

An expression used in a direct assignment statement can contain only symbols that have been previously defined in the program. Furthermore, an expression is evaluated from left to right with no operator precedence rules. However, angle brackets (<>) can be used to change the order of evaluation. For example, the statements

```
LENGTH = 10
N = 5+4*LENGTH
```

result in a value of 90 for N, whereas

```
LENGTH = 10
N = 5+<4*LENGTH>
```

result in a value of 45 for N. Finally, an expression can contain any of the arithmetic operators +, −, *, and /.

4.4 Simple VAX-11 Instructions

The VAX-11 computer has over three hundred instructions. In this section we present a subset of these instructions that is often used by beginning assembly language programmers. We begin by introducing some of the common characteristics of the VAX-11 instruction set.

Many of the instruction mnemonics on the VAX-11 are formed by combining a generic name as a prefix and a data type as a suffix. The generic name is the name of an operation (for example, ADD, MOV, INC). The data type is the type of the operands in the operand field, such as byte(B), word(W), or longword(L). For example, the MOV instruction can appear in any of the following mnemonics:

```
MOVB    Move Byte
MOVW    Move Word
MOVL    Move Longword
```

One instruction or the other is used depending on what is to be moved. For example, given the declarations

```
A:    .BYTE  28
B:    .BYTE  -15
C:    .WORD  -157
X:    .BLKB  1
Y:    .BLKB  1
Z:    .BLKW  1
```

if A, B, C are to be copied into X, Y, Z, then the following instructions can be used:

```
MOVB    A,X
MOVB    B,Y
MOVW    C,Z
```

Note that copying can also be done by the two instructions

```
MOVW    A,X
MOVW    C,Z
```

where the first MOVW copies bytes A and B into bytes X and Y, respectively. The first method is preferred in this example for readability, however.

It is very important to observe that, in the foregoing example, even though A is declared as a byte, it can be operated on by a word instruction. This is true regardless of the numeric address of A. (This is a consequence of the fact that the VAX-11 does not enforce a boundary alignment restriction; see Section 2.2.) In general, in the VAX-11, the context of an operand is determined by the instruction, not by how the operand is declared in the program. Thus, for example, the instruction

```
MOVL    A,X
```

will copy the four bytes starting at address A into the four bytes starting at address X.

To illustrate further, assume that A, B, C, X, Y, and Z are declared as in the foregoing. The instruction

```
ADDL    A,X
```

adds the longword at A (that is, the four bytes starting at A taken as a single longword number) to the longword at X, and stores the result in the longword at X. (Determining the contents of the longword at A is left as an exercise.)

The VAX-11 allows some arithmetic and logic instructions to have two or three operands. The number of operands is appended to the instruction; the MACRO Assembler, however, permits dropping the suffix 2. Thus, for example, the ADD instruction can appear in the following forms:

```
ADDB2    (or ADDB)
ADDB3
ADDW2    (or ADDW)
ADDW3
ADDL2    (or ADDL)
ADDL3
```

For two- and three-operand instructions, the last operand is the destination. For example, in the instruction

```
ADDW2    A,B
```

B is the second source operand as well as the destination, whereas in the instruction

C is the destination.

Finally, we mention that the VAX-11 allows register-to-register, register-to-memory, memory-to-register, and memory-to-memory instructions (see Section 3.2 for definitions of these terms).

Now we divide a simple subset of the VAX-11 instructions into categories as presented in Section 3.2. For every category, a list of instructions under that category is given. The characters of the instruction name that are capitalized are part of the mnemonic. The data types and the number of operands that the instruction can have are shown next to the instruction. The abbreviations B, W, L, Q, and O stand for byte, word, longword, quadword, and octaword, respectively. Following every category, a table is given showing the mnemonics, the operands required by the instruction, and the effect of the instruction. The tables use the following notations:

src	source
dst	destination
disp	displacement
(x)	contents of memory location whose address is x
Rn	contents of register Rn
←	quantity on left of arrow is replaced by quantity on right of arrow

Data Transfer Instructions

The following table summarizes some of the data transfer instructions available on the VAX-11.

Instruction	Data Type	No. of Operands
MOVe		2
CLeaR	B,W,L,Q,O	1
MOVe Address		2
Move NEGative	B,W,L	2

A data transfer instruction moves an operand from a source to a destination and sets the condition codes (CCs). The CCs are set according to the value moved into the destination (Appendix C shows how the CCs are affected.)

The general formats of the data transfer instructions are shown in Table 4.2. The MOV instruction simply copies the contents of the source into the destination. The CLR instruction transfers all 0 bits into the destination. The MNEG instruction moves the 2's comple-

Table 4.2 Data Transfer Instructions

Mnemonic	Operand(s)	Effect	Name of Instruction
CLRB	dst	(dst)← 0	Clear byte
CLRW	dst	(dst)← 0	Clear word
CLRL	dst	(dst)← 0	Clear long
CLRQ	dst	(dst)← 0	Clear quad
CLRO	dst	(dst)← 0	Clear octa
MNEGB	src,dst	(dst)← −(src)	Move negated byte
MNEGW	src,dst	(dst)← −(src)	Move negated word
MNEGL	src,dst	(dst)← −(src)	Move negated long
MOVAB	src,dst	(dst)← src	Move address of byte
MOVAW	src,dst	(dst)← src	Move address of word
MOVAL	src,dst	(dst)← src	Move address of long
MOVAQ	src,dst	(dst)← src	Move address of quad
MOVAO	src,dst	(dst)← src	Move address of octa
MOVB	src,dst	(dst)←(src)	Move byte
MOVW	src,dst	(dst)←(src)	Move word
MOVL	src,dst	(dst)←(src)	Move long
MOVQ	src,dst	(dst)←(src)	Move quad
MOVO	src,dst	(dst)←(src)	Move octa

Note: Octaword instructions may not be fully supported in some VAX installations.

ment of the source into the destination. For MOV and MNEG, the source and the destination are both of the same data type, which is specified by the instruction. For the CLR instruction, the source is also the destination and is of the type specified by the instruction.

The source and destination of a data transfer instruction can be memory locations or registers. When a register is specified, then, depending on the instruction, part of the register, all of the register, or multiple registers are affected, as follows:

Recall from Chapter 2 that a register, R*n,* in the VAX-11 is 32 bits, or 4 bytes, which can be viewed as

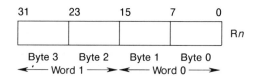

Byte instructions operate on the rightmost byte (byte 0) of the specified register (the other bytes are not affected).

Word instructions operate on the rightmost word (word 0) of the register.

Longword instructions operate on the 4 bytes of the register.

Quadword instructions operate on the specified register and the adjacent higher-order register concatenated as follows:

63	32	31	0
R(n+1)		Rn	

Thus quadword instructions operate on a pair of registers. For example:

Effect

```
CLRQ   R3        R4 ← 0, R3 ← 0
MOVQ   R2, R7    R8 ← R3, R7 ← R2
```

Octaword instructions operate on the specified register and the three adjacent higher-order registers concatenated as follows:

127	96	95	64	63	32	31	0
R(n+3)		R(n+2)		R(n+1)		Rn	

Thus octaword instructions operate on four registers. For example:

Effect

```
CLRO   R3       R6←0, R5←0, R4←0, R3←0
MOVO   R2,R7    R10←R5, R9←R4, R8←R3, R7←R2
```

Care must be taken with quadword and octaword instructions so that they do not affect registers AP, FP, SP, and PC (that is, R12, R13, R14, R15), since these are used for special purposes.

Whereas the MOV instruction moves the *contents* of a source operand into a destination, the MOVe Address (MOVA) instruction moves the *address* (32 bits) of a source operand into a destination. The source of a MOVA instruction is the address of a byte, word, longword, quadword, or octaword. The destination is always a longword memory location or a register. To illustrate, assume that NUM is declared as

```
NUM:   .WORD   47
```

The instruction

```
MOVW   NUM,R6
```

moves the contents of the word at NUM (the value 47) into the right 2 bytes of R6. The instruction

```
MOVAW    NUM,R6
```

moves the address of word NUM into R6. Figure 4.4 shows the results of the MOVW and MOVAW.

Note that the following segment of code also moves the address of NUM into R6:

```
NUM:    .WORD   47
NUM_ADDR:
        .ADDRESS NUM
        .
        .
        .
        MOVL    NUM_ADDR,R6
```

MOVAW NUM,R6 is clearer and shorter, however.

Whether B, W, L, Q, or O is specified with MOVA, the result is always a 32-bit address moved into the destination. Thus, for example, the statements

```
MOVAW    NUM,R6
```

and

```
MOVAQ    NUM,R6
```

have exactly the same effect, regardless of how the label NUM is declared. If NUM is declared as a word, however, then the MOVAW is more readable. Furthermore, specifying B, W, L, Q, or O becomes important in some contexts that will be presented in Chapter 5.

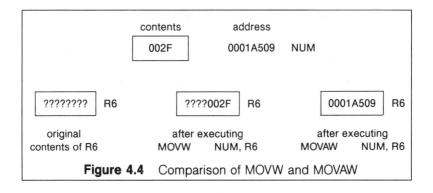

Figure 4.4   Comparison of MOVW and MOVAW

Arithmetic Instructions

The most commonly used arithmetic instructions are summarized in the following table:

Instruction	Data Type	No. of Operands
ADD		
SUBtract	B,W,L	2 or 3
MULtiply		
DIVide		
DECrement	B,W,L	1
INCrement		

These instructions perform arithmetic operations and set the condition codes (CCs). The CCs are set according to the result of the operation (Appendix C shows how the CCs are affected). Note that arithmetic instructions do not operate on quadwords or octa-words.

The general format of the arithmetic instructions are shown in Table 4.3. The source and destination of these instructions can be memory locations or registers. When a register is specified, then part of the register or all of the register is used depending on the instruction, in a similar manner to the data transfer instructions. Note that the SUB instruction subtracts the first operand from the second, and the DIV instruction divides the second operand by the first.

It must be emphasized that an arithmetic instruction affects the specified destination only, regardless of the range of the result. Thus, when the result of an instruction overflows, only part of the result (the low-order bits) is stored in the destination. To illustrate, assume the following declarations:

```
A:    .BYTE   53
B:    .BYTE   12
```

The instruction

```
MULB3    A,B,R5
```

results in the number 124 (7C hex) to be stored in byte 0 of register R5; the rest of R5 is not affected:

```
??????7C   R5
```

Table 4.3 Arithmetic Instructions

Mnemonic	Operand(s)	Effect	Name of Instruction
ADDB	src,dst	(dst)←(dst)+(src)	Add byte 2-operand
ADDB3	src1,src2,dst	(dst)←(src2)+(src1)	Add byte 3-operand
ADDW	src,dst	(dst)←(dst)+(src)	Add word 2-operand
ADDW3	src1,src2,dst	(dst)←(src2)+(src1)	Add word 3-operand
ADDL	src,dst	(dst)←(dst)+(src)	Add long 2-operand
ADDL3	src1,src2,dst	(dst)←(src2)+(src1)	Add long 3-operand
DECB	dst	(dst)←(dst)−1	Decrement byte
DECW	dst	(dst)←(dst)−1	Decrement word
DECL	dst	(dst)←(dst)−1	Decrement long
DIVB	src,dst	(dst)←(dst)/(src)	Divide byte 2-operand
DIVB3	src1,src2,dst	(dst)←(src2)/(src1)	Divide byte 3-operand
DIVW	src,dst	(dst)←(dst)/(src)	Divide word 2-operand
DIVW3	src1,src2,dst	(dst)←(src2)/(src1)	Divide word 3-operand
DIVL	src,dst	(dst)←(dst)/(src)	Divide long 2-operand
DIVL3	src1,src2,dst	(dst)←(src2)/(src1)	Divide long 3-operand
EDIV	src1,src2, dst1,dst2	(dst1)←(src2)/(src1) (dst2)←remainder	Extended divide
EMUL	src1,src2, src3,dst	(dst)←(src2)·(src1) +(src3)	Extended multiply
INCB	dst	(dst)←(dst)+1	Increment byte
INCW	dst	(dst)←(dst)+1	Increment word
INCL	dst	(dst)←(dst)+1	Increment long
MULB	src,dst	(dst)←(dst)·(src)	Multiply byte 2-operand
MULB3	src1,src2,dst	(dst)←(src2)·(src1)	Multiply byte 3-operand
MULW	src,dst	(dst)←(dst)·(src)	Multiply word 2-operand
MULW3	src1,src2,dst	(dst)←(src2)·(src1)	Multiply word 3-operand
MULL	src,dst	(dst)←(dst)·(src)	Multiply long 2-operand
MULL3	src1,src2,dst	(dst)←(src2)·(src1)	Multiply long 3-operand
SUBB	src,dst	(dst)←(dst)−(src)	Subtract byte 2-operand
SUBB3	src1,src2,dst	(dst)←(src2)−(src1)	Subtract byte 3-operand
SUBW	src,dst	(dst)←(dst)−(src)	Subtract word 2-operand
SUBW3	src1,src2,dst	(dst)←(src2)−(src1)	Subtract word 3-operand
SUBL	src,dst	(dst)←(dst)−(src)	Subtract long 2-operand
SUBL3	src1,src2,dst	(dst)←(src2)−(src1)	Subtract long 3-operand

If the correct result, 636 (27C hex, which requires a word), is to be stored in R5, then something like this can be used:

```
CLRW    R2        R2 becomes = ????0000
CLRW    R3        R3 becomes = ????0000
MOVB    A,R2      R2 becomes = ????0035
MOVB    B,R3      R3 becomes = ????000C
MULW3   R2,R3,R5  R5 becomes = ????027C
```

On occasion, the remainder of a division is needed. The DIVide instruction on byte, word, and longword performs integer division only; the remainder is not preserved. If the remainder is needed, then the instruction EDIV (Extended DIVide) must be used. EDIV has the format.

```
EDIV    divisor, dividend, quotient, remainder
```

where the dividend is a quadword (8 bytes) and each of the divisor, quotient, and remainder is a longword (4 bytes). The following example illustrates the use of EDIV.

Assume that the following declarations are made in a program:

```
A:    .QUAD    858
B:    .LONG    12
C:    .BLKL    1
D:    .BLKL    1
```

where it is desired to divide the number in quadword A by the number in longword B to obtain the quotient and the remainder. The EDIV instruction can be used to perform this as follows:

```
EDIV    B,A,C,D
```

The contents of memory (depicted as an array of longwords) before and after executing EDIV are shown in Figure 4.5.

Had B, C, D been declared as in Figure 4.5, but A declared as

```
A:    .WORD    858
```

the EDIV instruction would not produce the correct result; the dividend must be in a quadword. Something like this can be done:

```
CLRQ    R2
MOVW    A,R2
EDIV    B,R2,C,D
```

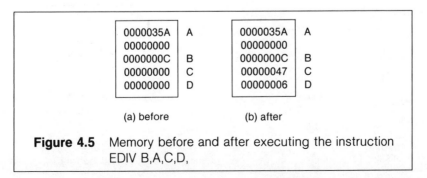

(a) before   (b) after

Figure 4.5   Memory before and after executing the instruction EDIV B,A,C,D,

We note in passing that there is also the Extended MULtiply (EMUL) instruction, which is capable of multiplying two 32-bit operands by each other, giving a 64-bit product. (Contrast this with the integer MULtiply instruction, which is capable of giving at most a 32-bit product.) EMUL also provides for an additional operand to be added to the 64-bit product. The general format of the EMUL instruction is

EMUL   multiplier, multiplicand, addend, product

where the product operand is a quadword, and each of the multiplier, mutiplicand, and addend is a longword. The instruction multiplies the first two operands by each other, producing a 64-bit result; adds the third operand to this result; and stores the final result in the fourth operand.

Comparison Instructions

Instruction	Data Type	No. of Operands
CoMPare	B,W,L	2
TeST	B,W,L	1

These instructions do not affect their operands in any way; they merely set the condition codes according to the result of the comparison.

Table 4.4 shows the general formats of the comparison instructions. The CMP instruction determines whether the first operand is greater than, equal to, or less than the second operand. The comparison is performed by subtracting the second operand from the first operand and setting the condition codes according to the result. The result of the subtraction is not preserved, and the two operands are not altered in any way.

The operands of a CMP instruction are compared as signed integers. That is, the leftmost bit of each of the two operands is looked

Table 4.4   Comparison Instructions

Mnemonic	Operand(s)	Effect	Name of Instruction
CMPB	src1,src2	(src1)-(src2), and	Compare byte
CMPW	src1,src2	set the CCs	Compare word
CMPL	src1,src2	accordingly	Compare longword
TSTB	src	Test src and	Test byte
TSTW	src	set N or Z	Test word
TSTL	src	accordingly	Test longword

at as a sign bit. (Recall that negative numbers are represented inside the VAX in 2's complement.) To illustrate, assuming that the contents of registers R2 and R3 are:

| A051C200 | R2 |

| 00020000 | R3 |

CMPL	R2,R3	finds R2 less than R3
CMPW	R2,R3	finds word 0 of R2 less than word 0 of R3
CMPB	R2,R3	finds byte 0 of R2 equal to byte 0 of R3

The TST instruction determines whether the operand is negative, zero, or positive. For example, assuming R2 and R3 are as shown previously:

TSTL	R2	finds a negative operand
TSTL	R3	finds a positive operand
TSTW	R3	finds a zero operand
TSTW	R2	finds a negative operand

As we already know, the result of comparing (or testing) operands is indicated in the CCs. The CCs are then examined by conditional branch instructions to decide on branching, as we will see next.

Branch Instructions

There are over forty conditional and unconditional branch instructions in the VAX-11. Some of these instructions are shown in Table 4.5.

Among the conditional branch instructions are:

BEQL	Branch on EQual
BGEQ	Branch on Greater or EQual
BGTR	Branch on GreaTeR
BLEQ	Branch on Less or EQual
BLSS	Branch on LeSS than
BNEQ	Branch on Not EQual

These instructions require a single operand, called the *displacement* in VAX terminology.[4] The operand is a label of an instruction

---

[4] The reason for the term *displacement* will be made clear in Chapter 5.

Table 4.5 Branch instructions

Conditional Branch Instructions

Mnemonic	Operand	CCs Checked	Name of Instruction
BEQL	disp	Z=1	Branch on equal
BGEQ	disp	N=0	Branch on greater or equal
BGTR	disp	N=0 and Z=0	Branch on greater
BLEQ	disp	N=1 or Z=1	Branch on less or equal
BLSS	disp	N=1	Branch on less
BNEQ	disp	Z=0	Branch on not equal

Unconditional Branch Instructions

Mnemonic	Operand	Name of Instruction
BRB	disp	Branch with byte displacement
BRW	disp	Branch with word displacement
JMP	address	Jump

Other Branch Instructions

Mnemonic	Operand(s)	Name of Instruction
BLBC	src,disp	Branch on low bit clear
BLBS	src,disp	Branch on low bit set

to be branched to if the condition is met. The condition is checked for by examining the CCs.

As an example, assume that three different segments of codes in a program are to be executed depending on whether a variable A is greater than, equal to, or less than a variable B. Assuming that A and B are bytes, the following segment of code performs this function:

```
          CMPB    A,B
          BGTR    POSITIVE
          BEQL    ZERO

NEGATIVE: .
          .       }  code to be executed if A < B
          .

POSITIVE: .
          .       }  code to be executed if A > B
          .

ZERO:     .
          .       }  code to be executed if A = B
          .
```

The result of the CMPB A,B is indicated by the CCs as follows:

N	Z	
0	0	if A > B
0	1	if A = B
1	0	if A < B

Either BGTR will find N=Z=0 and branches to label POSITIVE, or BEQL will find Z=1 and branches to label ZERO, or execution continues at label NEGATIVE. (Label NEGATIVE is not needed in the program, but it improves readability.) Note that the BGTR instruction does not alter the CCs; hence, BEQL finds the same values in the CCs set by the CMPB instruction. None of the branch instructions presented in this section alter the CCs.

As another example, consider the following segment of code.

```
        DECL    R5
        BEQL    EXIT
        ADDL    A,R6
          .
          .
          .
EXIT:   INCL    R2
```

The instruction DECL decrements the contents of register R5 by 1 and sets the condition codes according to the result stored in R5. Next the instruction BEQL inspects the condition code Z, and if it is 1 (that is, the result of DECL R5 was zero), then execution continues at the instruction whose (symbolic) address is EXIT; otherwise, Z is 0, and execution continues at ADDL A,R6.

A conditional branch instruction can branch to an instruction that is about 127 bytes away. The branch can be in either direction; that is, the instruction to be branched to can be before or after the branch instruction. If the branch target is further than 127 bytes, an out-of-range error message will be generated by the assembler. The programmer, therefore, should estimate the "distance" between the branch instruction and the branch target. (As an estimate, assume every instruction to occupy 6 bytes; in Chapter 5 we see how to determine the exact length of an instruction.) If a branch outside this range is needed, then changes in the logic of the program are required, as we will see shortly.

Sometimes a branch in a program must be taken regardless of the result of a prior instruction. In such cases, unconditional branch instructions are used. These instructions perform a branch to a specified instruction without testing any condition codes. Two of these instructions are

    BRB   BRanch with Byte displacement
    BRW   BRanch with Word displacement

BRB allows a branch within 127 bytes in either direction. BRW allows a branch within 32,767 bytes. There is a third unconditional branch instruction

    JMP   JuMP

that allows branching (or jumping) to within (2^{31-1}) bytes—that is, to anywhere in the program. Each of these three instructions requires a single operand that specifies the address of an instruction to be branched to. BRB and BRW must specify this address as a label. JMP can specify the address as a label or by other addressing modes, as we will see in Chapter 5.

Because the conditional branch instructions and the BRB instruction allow for branching within 127 bytes only, the BRW or JMP instruction should be used when it is desired to branch outside this range. This requires changes in the logic of a program. To illustrate, assume that the instruction at address EXIT in the previous example is more than 127 bytes beyond the BEQL instruction, so that BEQL cannot reach it. We would then recode the foregoing segment of code as follows:

```
              DECL    R5
              BNEQ    CONTINUE
              BRW     EXIT
    CONTINUE: ADDL    A,R6
                  .
                  .
                  .

    EXIT:     INCL    R2
```

Two additional branch instructions that do not test the condition codes are

        BLBC   Branch on Low Bit Clear
        BLBS   Branch on Low Bit Set

These instructions require two operands: the first is a source operand, and the second is a label of an instruction. The BLBC (BLBS) inspects the rightmost bit of the source operand. If this bit is zero (one) then a branch takes place; otherwise execution continues at the next instruction. For example, the instruction

```
BLBC    R5, DONE
```

causes a branch to the instruction whose address is DONE if the rightmost bit of R5 is 0 (for example, R5 contains an even number). BLBC and BLBS allow branching to within 127 bytes only.

This concludes our introduction of the simple VAX-11 instructions. Now we present examples of MACRO programs that use some of the instructions presented.

Example:

```
;THIS PROGRAM FINDS THE MAXIMUM OF TWO NUMBERS CONTAINED
;IN TWO LONGWORDS.
;
FIRST:  .BLKL   1               ;FIRST NUMBER
SECOND: .BLKL   1               ;SECOND NUMBER
MAX:    .BLKL   1               ;MAXIMUM OF THE TWO NUMBERS
;
        .ENTRY  MAXIMUM,0
        CMPL    FIRST,SECOND    ;IS FIRST NUMBER>SECOND?
        BGTR    GREATER         ;YES
        MOVL    SECOND,MAX      ;NO: SECOND NUMBER IS MAXIMUM
        BRB     EXIT            ;
GREATER:MOVL    FIRST,MAX       ;FIRST NUMBER IS MAXIMUM
EXIT:   $EXIT_S
        .END    MAXIMUM
```

Example:

```
;THIS PROGRAM FINDS THE ABSOLUTE VALUE OF AN INTEGER NUMBER
;CONTAINED IN A WORD
;
NUMBER: .BLKW   1               ;THE NUMBER
ABS:    .BLKW   1               ;ABSOLUTE VALUE OF NUMBER
;
        .ENTRY  ABSOLUTE,0
        MOVW    NUMBER,R2       ;IS NUMBER >=0?
        BGEQ    POSITIVE        ;YES
        MNEGW   R2,R2           ;NO: NEGATE NUMBER
POSITIVE:
        MOVW    R2,ABS          ;ABSOLUTE VALUE IS IN R2
        $EXIT_S
        .END    ABSOLUTE
```

Example:

```
;THIS PROGRAM EVALUATES THE EXPRESSION B**2-4*A*C AND SETS A
;FLAG TO -1, 0, OR +1 DEPENDING ON WHETHER THE VALUE OF THE
;EXPRESSION IS NEGATIVE, ZERO, OR POSITIVE. ALL VALUES ARE
;ASSUMED TO HAVE A RANGE OF A BYTE.
;
A:          .BLKB   1
B:          .BLKB   1
C:          .BLKB   1
FLAG:       .BLKB   1
ONE:        .BYTE   1
MINUS_ONE:
            .BYTE   -1
FOUR:       .BYTE   4
;
            .ENTRY  SET_FLAG,0
            MULB3   B,B,R2              ;COMPUTE B**2
            MULB3   A,C,R3              ;COMPUTE A*C
            MULB    FOUR,R3             ;COMPUTE 4*A*C
            SUBB    R3,R2               ;COMPUTE B**2-4*A*C
            BGTR    POSITIVE            ;IS NUMBER > 0?
            BEQL    ZERO                ;NO: IS NUMBER=0?
NEGATIVE:
            MOVB    MINUS_ONE,FLAG      ;   NO: SET FLAG TO -1 AND
            BRB     EXIT                ;         EXIT PROGRAM
ZERO:       CLRB    FLAG                ;   YES: SET FLAG TO 0 AND
            BRB     EXIT                ;         EXIT PROGRAM
POSITIVE:
            MOVB    ONE,FLAG            ;YES: SET FLAG TO 1
EXIT:       $EXIT_S
            .END    SET_FLAG
```

The foregoing program examples are complete MACRO programs that may be assembled, linked, and run (see Appendix B). They do not perform any input or output, however. If it is desired to "see" them run, the debugger can be used to deposit values in the variables of the programs and then examine the contents of the results (see Appendix E).

4.5 Simple VAX-11 MACRO Addressing

Addressing refers to specifying locations of operands in instructions. There are many techniques for specifying this information; the techniques are referred to in assembly language as *addressing modes.* We will examine four of the addressing modes here: the *direct mode,* the *register mode,* the *immediate mode,* and the *register deferred mode.*

The first two modes are the ones that we have been using for illustrations. In the *direct mode* a memory location is specified in the instruction; the operand is the contents of the memory location.[5] Usually, the location is specified by its symbolic name. As examples, the following instructions use the direct mode.

Effect

```
MOVB    A,B      (B) ← (A)
CLRL    Y        (Y) ← 0
INCW    X        (X) ← (X) + 1
SUBB3   A,B,C    (C) ← (B) − (A)
```

In the register mode, a register is specified in the instruction; the content of the specified register is the operand. As examples, each of the following instructions specifies a register mode for at least one of the operands.

Effect

```
MOVL    R3,R5     R5  ← R3
ADDW    R6,R7     R7  ← R7 + R6
DECL    R5        R5  ← R5 − 1
DIVB3   A,R7,R4   R4  ← R7 / (A)
MOVL    A,R5      R5  ← (A)
MULL3   A,R6,B    (B) ← R6 * (A)
```

In the *immediate mode* the operand itself, not the address of the operand, is specified in the instruction.[6] The immediate operand is preceded by the number sign (#) to denote immediate addressing. For example, to add the value 2 to the contents of register R6, one can specify the value 2 in the instruction as *immediate* as follows:

```
ADDL    #2,R6
```

This instruction has the same effect on R6 as

```
TWO:    .LONG   2
        .
        .
        .
ADDL    TWO,R6
```

---

[5] This mode is called *relative* mode in the VAX-11, although the term *direct* is the standard. The reason for the term *relative* will become apparent in Chapter 5.

[6] On the VAX-11 this mode is called the *literal* mode or the *immediate* mode, depending on the value specified. The reason for this will be shown in the next chapter. Immediate mode is the standard terminology used by most computer manufacturers.

but it is more convenient to use the immediate mode in this instance. Furthermore, the immediate mode is faster since it does not require a memory access to location TWO.

As other examples, the following instructions use the immediate mode:

Effect

MOVL	#1,R5	R5 ← 1
MOVW	#5,A	(A) ← 5
MULW	#2,R6	R6 ← R6 * 2
MULB3	#2,A,C	(C) ← (A) * 2

The *register deferred mode* specifies the *address* of the operand in a register.[7] Thus the content of the register is the memory address of the operand, rather than the operand itself. Obviously, the register must first be loaded with the address of the desired location before it is used; the register is said to be *pointing* to that memory location. To denote this mode, the register name is enclosed by parenthesis. As an example, the statement

        INCB   (R2)

increments the contents of the byte whose address is contained in R2. Thus if, prior to executing the INCB instruction, R2 and the byte pointed to by R2 are as shown

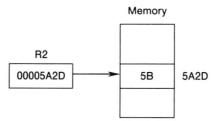

then after execution, R2 and the byte will be as follows:

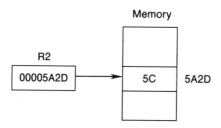

---

[7] The term *deferred* is an invention of DEC; the term *indirect* is commonly used by other manufacturers.

The register deferred mode is very useful in referencing successive locations in a block of memory, such as an array. This is shown in the following example.

Example: Multiply every element of an array, LIST, by a constant, say 4.

```
;THIS PROGRAM MULTIPLIES EACH ELEMENT OF AN ARRAY, LIST,
;BY A CONSTANT.
;
;CONSTANTS AND VARIABLES
;
CONSTANT=4                        ;CONSTANT OF MULTIPLICATION
LIST:    .BYTE 1,2,3,4,5          ;ARRAY OF SIZE 5 BYTES
SIZE:    .BYTE SIZE-LIST          ;ARRAY SIZE
;
;EXECUTABLE CODE
;
         .ENTRY SCALE_ARRAY,0     ;BEGIN EXECUTION
         CLRB    R5               ;R5 IS A LOOP COUNTER
         MOVAB   LIST,R6          ;POINT TO 1ST ELEMENT OF LIST
LOOP:    MULB    #CONSTANT,(R6)   ;MULTIPLY ITH ELEM BY CONSTANT
         INCL    R6               ;POINT TO NEXT ELEMENT OF LIST
         INCB    R5               ;INCREMENT LOOP COUNTER
         CMPB    SIZE,R5          ;ALL ELEMENTS PROCESSED?
         BGTR    LOOP             ; NO: CONTINUE
         $EXIT_S                  ; YES: TERMINATE PROGRAM
         .END    SCALE_ARRAY      ;END OF PROGRAM
```

In the foregoing program, register R5 keeps track of the number of elements (number of bytes) that have been processed. Register R6 is a pointer to the elements of the array. Initially, R6 is made to point to the first byte of the array, at LIST; the contents of this byte are multiplied by the constant, and the result replaces the initial contents. Then, in a loop, R6 is incremented by one in every iteration to make it point to successive bytes in the array, and the multiplication is performed on every byte. Note that, if the elements of the array were of a different data type than a byte, R6 would have to be incremented by the size of the data type in bytes.

As a final example in this section, we write a program that sorts an array of integers, in ascending order, using bubble sort. The algorithm for bubble sort is shown in Figure 4.6. The equivalent Pascal program is shown in Figure 4.7. Figure 4.8 shows the MACRO program with comments explaining the program. It is assumed that a number of elements have been read into the array, A, and the number of elements read in is stored in the byte at SIZE. Later we present a program that performs this input function.

4.6 Simple Input/Output

One way to perform input and output (I/O) in assembly language on the VAX-11 is to call subroutines written in a higher-level lan-

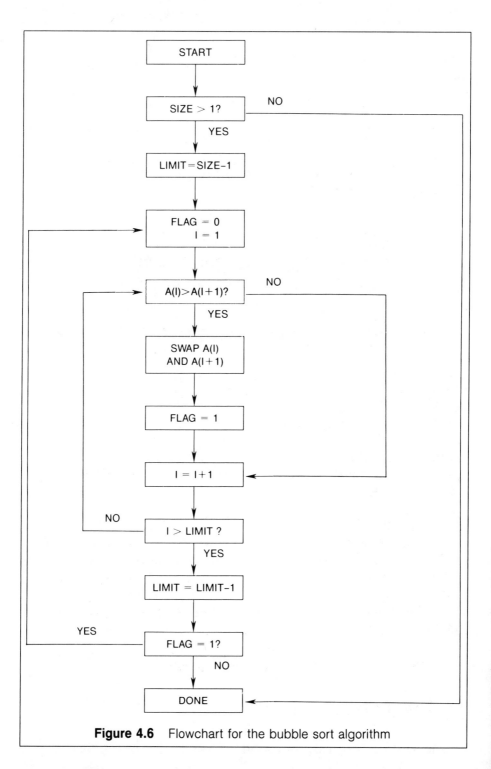

Figure 4.6 Flowchart for the bubble sort algorithm

```
            IF SIZE > 1 THEN
               BEGIN
                  LIMIT:=SIZE-1;
                  REPEAT
                     FLAG:=0;
                     FOR I:=1 TO LIMIT DO
                        BEGIN
                           IF A[I] > A[I+1] THEN
                              BEGIN
                                 TEMP:=A[I];
                                 A[I]:=A[I+1];
                                 A[I+1]:=TEMP;
                                 FLAG:=1
                              END
                        END;
                     LIMIT:=LIMIT-1
                  UNTIL FLAG=0
               END
```

Figure 4.7 Pascal program for the bubble sort algorithm

```
;THIS PROGRAM SORTS AN ARRAY OF INTEGERS IN ASCENDING ORDER USING
;BUBBLE SORT
;
;ASSUMPTIONS:
;      - THERE IS A MAXIMUM OF 100 ELEMENTS IN THE ARRAY
;      - THE ELEMENTS OF THE ARRAY ARE IN THE RANGE OF A WORD
;
;CONSTANTS AND VARIABLES:
MAX_SIZE  = 100                    ;MAXIMUM SIZE OF ARRAY
A:        .BLKW   MAX_SIZE         ;ARRAY TO HOLD BINARY INTEGERS
SIZE:     .BLKB   1                ;ACTUAL NUMBER OF ELEMENTS IN ARRAY
LIMIT:    .BLKB   1                ;UPPER LIMIT ON NUMEBR OF ITERATIONS
FLAG:     .BLKB   1                ;FLAG TO INDICATE END OF SORTING
TEMP:     .BLKW   1                ;A TEMPORARY
;                                  ;
          .ENTRY  BUBBLE_SORT,0    ;
          CMPB    SIZE,#1          ;IS NUMBER OF ELEMENTS <= 1?
          BLEQ    SORT_COMPLETED   ; YES: NO SORTING NEEDED
START_SORT:                        ; NO: START SORTING
          SUBB3   #1,SIZE,LIMIT    ;SIZE-1 IS MAX NUMBER OF ITERATIONS
OUTER:    CLRB    FLAG             ;ASSUME ARRAY IS SORTED
          MOVAW   A,R10            ;R10 POINTS TO 1ST ELEMENT
          ADDL3   #2,R10,R11       ;R11 POINTS TO 2ND ELEMENT
          CLRB    R1               ;R1 IS INNER LOOP COUNTER
INNER:    INCB    R1               ;
          CMPB    R1,LIMIT         ;HAVE ALL ELEMENTS BEEN COMPARED?
          BGTR    EXIT             ; YES
          CMPW    (R10),(R11)      ;IS ITH ELEMENT >I+1ST ELEMENT?
          BLEQ    NEXT_ELEMENT     ;NO: LEAVE ELEMENT AS IS
          MOVW    (R10),TEMP       ;YES: SWAP ELEMENTS
          MOVW    (R11),(R10)      ;
          MOVW    TEMP,(R11)       ;
          MOVB    #1,FLAG          ;SET FLAG=1: SORTING NOT COMPLETE
NEXT_ELEMENT:                      ;
          ADDL    #2,R10           ; UPDATE POINTERS TO
          ADDL    #2,R11           ;...ARRAY ELEMENTS, AND
          BRB     INNER            ;...CONTINUE COMPARING
;
EXIT:     DECB    LIMIT            ;DECREMENT NUMBER OF ITERATIONS
          TSTB    FLAG             ;WERE ANY ELEMENTS SWAPPED IN
                                   ;...PREVIOUS ITERATION?
          BNEQ    OUTER            ;YES: NEED MORE ITERATIONS
SORT_COMPLETED:                    ;NO: ARRAY IS NOW SORTED
          $EXIT_S
          .END    BUBBLE_SORT
```

Figure 4.8 MACRO program for the bubble sort algorithm

guage such as FORTRAN or Pascal.[8] These subroutines would contain READ and WRITE statements that in turn call system I/O routines that perform the actual input and output. These I/O routines are part of the operating system and can be called directly from the assembly language program.

There are several methods for calling system I/O routines under the VAX-11 VMS operating system; the methods differ in simplicity and flexibility. In the following we look at one of these methods that is provided by the VAX VMS Record Management System (RMS). The treatment is rather elementary, and some of it is presented like a recipe. Chapter 10 provides a more detailed explanation.

Before performing calls to read or write routines, the programmer must prepare certain facilities. These facilities include declaration of input and output files, the amount of data to be input or output, and storage areas to hold the input and output data.

Declaration of Files

Before we consider declaring input and output files in an assembly language program, we shall first introduce the notions of *file* and *record*.

A *file* is an organized collection of related data grouped in individual elements called *records*. Thus, when a program is entered interactively from a terminal, the collection of lines entered constitutes a file, and each line (terminated by a carriage return) a record. Similarly, a deck of punched cards is a file, and each individual card is a record.

When a deck of cards is read by a computer system, a copy of the program is usually preserved on disk (or some other secondary storage device) for later processing of the program. Similarly, a program that is entered from a terminal is copied on disk. The area that a program occupies on disk is referred to as a *disk file*. Every disk file is given a name by means of which the user can refer to it. The name of the file is established at the time the file is created. (For creating disk files and editing them under the VAX-11 VMS Operating System, refer to Appendix B.)

A disk file can be used to hold data to be read by a program (input file). (An input data file is created in the same way as a program file.) A disk file can also be used to hold the output generated by a program (output file). (An output file need not be created prior to

---

[8] See Appendix F for calling FORTRAN and Pascal routines from MACRO.

running the program; rather, if requested, it can be created by the program during its execution.)

Every file to be used for input or output by an assembly language program must be declared in the program. A file is declared by specifying a *file access block* (FAB) that describes the particular file. The FAB of a file specifies the file's name (FNM) and the file's attributes. The FAB of a file is established by a call to a system macro (routine) called $FAB (Note: All system macro names in the MACRO language start with the dollar sign.) The format of the call is

```
label:   $FAB   FNM=file-spec,attributes
```

As an example, suppose that an input file, called INFILE.DAT, is to be read. The file can be simply declared in the program by

```
INFAB:   $FAB   FNM=<INFILE.DAT>
```

In its simplest form, INFILE.DAT does not require any attribute specification. An output file—say, OUTFILE.DAT, can similarly be declared by

```
OUTFAB:   $FAB   FNM=<OUTFILE.DAT>,RAT=CR
```

where RAT stands for Record ATribute, and CR specifies a Carriage Return (and a line feed) after every output line.

Every FAB must have associated with it one or more *record access blocks* (RAB). The RAB specifies the FAB to be associated with, the storage area to be used for input or output, and the size in bytes of each record (or line) to be input or output. The RAB is established by a call to a system macro called $RAB. The format of the call is:

```
label:   $RAB   FAB=fab_label, storage area, record attributes
```

For example, the RAB associated with INFAB can be established by the macro call

```
INRAB:   $RAB   FAB=INFAB,UBF=input_buffer,USZ=record_size
```

where input_buffer is a user-defined symbol that is the starting address of a memory area that will receive the input record on an input operation. The parameter USZ specifies the maximum size of the input record in bytes. Similarly, the RAB associated with OUT-FAB can be declared by

```
OUTRAB:    $RAB    FAB=OUTFAB,RBF=output_buffer,RSZ=record_size
```

where output_buffer is a user-defined symbol that is the starting
address of a memory area whose contents should be the output
record on an output operation. The parameter RSZ specifies the size
of an output record in bytes. Note that the buffer address and the
size parameters for input are UBF and USZ, whereas the corresponding output parameters are RBF and RSZ. The calls to the system macros $FAB and $RAB should be placed at the very beginning
of the program.

The following example illustrates declaring:

An input file, INFILE.DAT, with a maximum record size of 80 bytes.

An output file, OUTFILE.DAT, with a record size of 80 bytes.

An input buffer, INBUF, of size 80.

An output buffer, OUTBUF, of size 80.

```
INFAB:   $FAB    FNM=<INFILE.DAT>        ;DECLARE INPUT FILE
INRAB:   $RAB    FAB=INFAB,-             ;ASSOCIATE RAB WITH FAB
                 UBF=INBUF,-             ;ADDRESS OF INPUT BUFFER
                 USZ=80                  ;MAX SIZE OF INPUT RECORD
OUTFAB:  $FAB    FNM=<OUTFILE.DAT>,-     ;DECLARE OUTPUT FILE
                 RAT=CR                  ;ADVANCE TO NEXT LINE AFTER
                                         ;...EVERY OUTPUT OPERATION
OUTRAB:  $RAB    FAB=OUTFAB,-            ;ASSOCIATE RAB WITH FAB
                 RBF=OUTBUF,-            ;ADDRESS OF OUTPUT BUFFER
                 RSZ=80                  ;SIZE OF OUTPUT RECORD
;
INBUF:   .BLKB   80                      ;INPUT BUFFER
OUTBUF:  .BLKB   80                      ;OUTPUT BUFFER
```

I/O Routines

Input

Input from a file can be performed by calling the system macro
$GET with the format

```
label:    $GET    RAB=label of input RAB
```

$GET reads the next record from the input file associated with the
specified RAB. The record obtained will be the next string of characters in the input file. The characters will be coded in ASCII and
stored in consecutive bytes, one byte per character, starting at the
address specified by parameter UBF of the RAB. For example,

```
$GET    RAB=INRAB
```

gets the next record from the input file INFILE.DAT. The end of the record is indicated by the carriage return (ret) character (the carriage return character is not stored as part of the record). If the record contains more characters than specified by the USZ parameter of INRAB, an error code (even number in register R0) is returned by $GET, but the input buffer will contain the first USZ characters of the record. If the record obtained has fewer characters than specified by the USZ parameter of the RAB, then the rest of the buffer will remain unchanged.

To illustrate, assume that the next record in INFILE.DAT (declared as previously) is the string of characters:

```
-84 +609
```

Then the macro call

```
$GET    RAB=INRAB
```

stores in input buffer, INBUF, the values shown below in hexadecimal

INBUF+79   INBUF

| ?? | ?? | ... | ?? | ?? | 39 | 30 | 36 | 2B | 20 | 34 | 38 | 2D |

Now assume that the next record in INFILE.DAT is the string

```
56 -24
```

Then a following call

```
$GET RAB=INRAB
```

will alter only the first six bytes of INBUF:

INBUF+79   INBUF

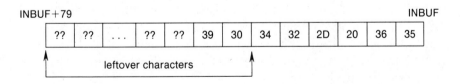

| ?? | ?? | ... | ?? | ?? | 39 | 30 | 34 | 32 | 2D | 20 | 36 | 35 |

leftover characters

One way to avoid the problem of leftover characters is to clear the input buffer to all zeroes (that is, to ASCII NUL) before every input operation. In this way the input buffer can be searched for the first byte that contains 0 to determine the end of the input record.

Output

Output to a file can be performed by calling the system macro $PUT with the format

    label: $PUT   RAB=label of output RAB

$PUT writes in the output file associated with the specified RAB a record of the size specified by the RSZ parameter of the RAB. The record will be written from consecutive bytes starting at the address specified by the RBF parameter of the RAB. For example,

        $PUT   RAB=OUTRAB

puts the record whose address is specified by the RBF parameter of the RAB in OUTFILE.DAT. The record written will be the characters that correspond to the ASCII codes stored in the bytes of the output buffer. The ASCII code 00 (NUL) does not have any effect on the output. Thus, for example, if a record of size 24 bytes contains

$i+11$ i Byte

41	0A	0D	31	00	00	31	2D	58	00	41	56

$i+23$ $i+12$ Byte

00	00	00	00	59	4C	42	4D	45	53	53	00

it will be printed as

    VAX-11
    ASSEMBLY

Note that the NUL character can be used conveniently to fill in the extra bytes of an output buffer when the number of characters to be printed is smaller than the size specified by the RSZ parameter of the output RAB.

Before reading from an input file, the file should be opened (made ready). This is done by calling the system macro $OPEN. Also, since an FAB can have more than one RAB associated with it, a particular RAB should be connected to the file. This is done by calling the system macro $CONNECT. For the previous example, before performing

        $GET   RAB=INRAB

one should perform

```
        $OPEN      FAB=INFAB
        $CONNECT   RAB=INRAB
```

Similarly, before one calls $PUT, the output file should be created and the RAB associated with the FAB of the output file connected. For example, before performing

```
        $PUT    RAB=OUTRAB
```

one should perform

```
        $CREATE    FAB=OUTFAB
        $CONNECT   RAB=OUTRAB
```

When the files are no longer needed, they should be closed. This is done by calling the $CLOSE macro, as in:

```
        $CLOSE    FAB=INFAB
        $CLOSE    FAB=OUTFAB
```

Every I/O routine returns a success code (odd number) or an error code (even number) in register R0. Therefore, to insure the absence of errors, R0 should be inspected after every call to a system routine. Particularly after $GET, R0 should be inspected to determine the end of the input file; at end of file, $GET returns an even code in R0. Inspecting the code is normally done with the BLBC or the BLBS instruction.

The following example is a complete MACRO program that reads a set of records from an input file and writes the records as they are read in. The program terminates when an end of file is encountered in the input file. For simplicity and clarity, we do not check R0 following every call to an I/O routine (except $GET). Also, we do not clear the input buffer before every call to $GET.

```
   INFAB:   $FAB    FNM=<INFILE.DAT>       ;DECLARE INPUT FILE
   INRAB:   $RAB    FAB=INFAB,-            ;ASSOCIATE RAB WITH FAB
                    UBF=INBUF,-            ;ADDRESS OF INPUT BUFFER
                    USZ=BUFSIZE            ;SIZE OF INPUT BUFFER
   OUTFAB:  $FAB    FNM=<OUTFILE.DAT>,-    ;DECLARE OUTPUT FILE
                    RAT=CR                 ;ADVANCE TO NEXT LINE AFTER
                                           ;...EVERY OUTPUT OPERATION
   OUTRAB:  $RAB    FAB=OUTFAB,-           ;ASSOCIATE RAB WITH FAB
                    RBF=OUTBUF,-           ;ADDRESS OF OUTPUT BUFFER
                    RSZ=BUFSIZE            ;SIZE OF OUTPUT BUFFER
   BUFSIZE = 80                            ;
   INBUF:   .BLKB   BUFSIZE                ;INPUT BUFFER
   OUTBUF:  .BLKB   BUFSIZE                ;OUTPUT BUFFER
   ;                                       ;
```

```
        .ENTRY   ECHO_CHECK,0           ;
        $OPEN    FAB=INFAB              ;READY INPUT FILE
        $CONNECT RAB=INRAB             ;CONNECT  INRAB TO INPUT FILE
        $CREATE  FAB=OUTFAB             ;CREATE OUTPUT FILE
        $CONNECT RAB=OUTRAB            ;CONNECT OUTRAB TO OUTPUT FILE
INPUT:  $GET     RAB=INRAB              ;READ NEXT RECORD
        BLBC     R0,EXIT                ;IF ERROR THEN EXIT
        MOVC3    #BUFSIZE,INBUF,OUTBUF  ;ELSE COPY INBUF INTO OUTBUF
        $PUT     RAB=OUTRAB             ;WRITE OUTPUT BUFFER
        BRB      INPUT                  ;CONTINUE
EXIT:   $CLOSE   FAB=INFAB              ;CLOSE INPUT FILE
        $CLOSE   FAB=OUTFAB             ;CLOSE OUTPUT FILE
        $EXIT_S                         ;TERMINATE PROGRAM
        .END     ECHO_CHECK             ;
```

The MOVC3 (MOVe Character 3 operands) instruction in the
above program has the general format

```
        MOVC3    length,A,B
```

The instruction copies a string of characters (or a block of bytes) of
the specified length from the source starting at address A into the
destination starting at B. The operand *length* is taken in the context
of a word (2 bytes); that is, if a register is specified as the first
operand, then the contents of word 0 of the register will be taken as
the length. If a memory address is specified, then the contents of
the word at that address will be taken as the length. The following
example illustrates the requirement of a word context.

Given the declarations

```
LENGTH:    .BYTE    5
FLAG:      .BYTE    1
             .

STRING1:   .BLKB    5
             .

STRING2:   .BLKB    5
```

The instruction

```
        MOVC3    LENGTH,STRING1,STRING2
```

moves a block of size

00000001	00000101
FLAG	LENGTH

261 bytes starting at address STRING1 into a block starting at STRING2. If only five bytes at STRING1 are to be moved into five bytes at STRING2, then one can do one of the following:

1. Use a register

```
CLRW    R2
MOVB    LENGTH,R2
MOVC3   R2,STRING1,STRING2
```

2. Declare LENGTH as a word

```
LENGTH:    .WORD    5
FLAG:      .BYTE    1
```

then

```
MOVC3    LENGTH,STRING1,STRING2
```

3. Use the immediate mode

```
MOVC3    #5,STRING1,STRING2
```

Care must be taken when using MOVC3, for after this instruction is executed, general registers R0 through R5 are affected as follows:

R0 = 0
R1 = address of byte just beyond source string
R2 = 0
R3 = address of byte just beyond destination string
R4 = 0
R5 = 0

Thus, if any of these registers is not to be destroyed by the MOVC3 instruction, it must be saved prior to the instruction and restored afterward.

Sometimes the user may not wish to read data from a disk file or direct output to a disk file. For example, an interactive user may wish to enter the data interactively from terminal and display the output on terminal. Similarly, a batch user may wish to supply the data with the deck and list the output on the printer. In these cases the VMS operating system associates the (default) file names SYS $INPUT and SYS$OUTPUT with the input and output files. For interactive users SYS$INPUT and SYS$OUTPUT are both equated to the user's terminal, and for batch users SYS$INPUT is normally the card reader and SYS$OUTPUT the printer. SYS$INPUT and SYS-$OUTPUT are declared in an assembly program in exactly the same way as disk files are declared—by calls to the system macro $FAB.

4.7 Program Example

In the rest of this chapter we write a MACRO program that reads an array of integers, sort the array in ascending order, and then print the sorted array. The integers are read in as ASCII strings, one string per record; then they are converted into their binary equivalents. After the binary array is sorted, its elements are converted to their ASCII equivalents and then printed one element per line. The program is shown in Figure 4.9.

The program is divided into a number of segments. We choose to divide it as follows:

1. Read the input file, one record at a time, and echo check it. As each record is read in, convert the numeric string in the record to its binary equivalent. Then read the next record and convert, and so on, until the end of file.
2. Sort the resulting array of binary integers in ascending order, using bubble sort. (This segment is exactly the same as the example program presented in Figure 4.8.)
3. Convert the binary integers in the sorted array to their ASCII equivalents, and output the sorted array.

```
;
;                        ****************
;                        *   SEGMENT 1   *
;                        ****************
;
;THIS SEGMENT DECLARES THE INPUT AND OUTPUT FILES AND PREPARES THEM
;FOR INPUT AND OUTPUT. AS EACH RECORD IS READ IN, IT IS ECHO CHECKED.
;THEN, THE CHARACTERS IN THE RECORD ARE SCANNED TO DETERMINE THE START
;AND END OF EVERY NUMBER. AS A STRING IS IDENTIFIED, IT IS CONVERTED
;TO BINARY AND STORED IN AN ARRAY. WHEN AN END OF FILE IS ENCOUNTERED,
;CONTROL IS TRANSFERRED TO SEGMENT 2 OF THE PROGRAM.
;
;        ASSUMPTIONS ABOUT INPUT RECORDS:
;
;        - MAXIMUM RECORD SIZE IS 80 CHARACTERS
;        - RECORD MAY HAVE AT MOST ONE NUMBER IN IT
;        - NUMBER MAY BE PRECEDED AND/OR FOLLOWED BY A NUMBER
;          OF BLANKS
;        - POSITIVE NUMBERS ARE NOT PRECEDED BY A PLUS (+) SIGN
;        - ALL NUMBERS ARE IN THE RANGE OF A WORD
;        - THERE IS A MAXIMUM OF 100 NUMBERS
;
;
INFAB:  $FAB    FNM=<INFILE.DAT>        ;DECLARE INPUT FILE
INRAB:  $RAB    FAB=INFAB,-            ;ASSOCIATE RAB WITH FAB
                UBF=INBUF,-            ;ADDRESS OF INPUT BUFFER
                USZ=BUFSIZE           ;SIZE OF INPUT BUFFER
OUTFAB: $FAB    FNM=<OUTFILE.DAT>,-    ;DECLARE OUTPUT FILE
                RAT=CR                ;ADVANCE TO NEXT LINE AFTER
                                      ;...EVERY OUTPUT OPERATION
```

(Continued)

```
OUTRAB: $RAB      FAB=OUTFAB,-            ;ASSOCIATE RAB WITH FAB
                  RBF=OUTBUF,-            ;ADDRESS OF OUTPUT BUFFER
                  RSZ=BUFSIZE            ;SIZE OF OUTPUT BUFFER
;                                        ;
;CONSTANTS AND VARIABLES                 ;
;                                        ;
BUFSIZE = 80                             ;
INBUF:  .BLKB     BUFSIZE               ;INPUT BUFFER
OUTBUF: .BLKB     BUFSIZE               ;OUTPUT BUFFER
;                                        ;
;                                        ;
MAX_SIZE = 100                           ;MAXIMUM SIZE OF ARRAY
A    : .BLKW      MAX_SIZE              ;ARRAY TO HOLD BINARY INTEGERS
SIZE:   .BLKB     1                     ;ACTUAL NUMBER OF ELEMENTS IN ARRAY
LIMIT:  .BLKB     1                     ;UPPER LIMIT ON NUMBER OF ITERATIONS
FLAG:   .BLKB     1                     ;FLAG TO INDICATE END OF SORTING
TEMP:   .BLKW     1                     ;A TEMPORARY
BLANK = ^A' '                           ;A BLANK CHARACTER
SIGN_FLAG:                               ;FLAG TO INDICATE SIGN OF
        .BLKB     1                     ;...A NUMBER
TEMPBUF:.BLKB     BUFSIZE               ;TEMPORARY BUFFER
;
;
;PREPARE INPUT AND OUTPUT FILES
;
        .ENTRY    CONVERT_AND_SORT,0     ;
        $OPEN     FAB=INFAB             ;READY INPUT FILE
        $CONNECT  RAB=INRAB             ;CONNECT   INRAB TO INPUT FILE
        $CREATE   FAB=OUTFAB            ;CREATE OUTPUT FILE
        $CONNECT  RAB=OUTRAB            ;CONNECT OUTRAB TO OUTPUT FILE
;
;INITIALIZATION
;
        CLRB      SIZE                  ;INITIALIZE NUMBER OF ELEMENTS TO 0
        MOVAW     A,R10                 ;POINT TO BEGINNING OF ARRAY
;
;BEFORE READING A RECORD, THE INPUT BUFFER WILL BE CLEARED TO ZEROES
;
CLEAR_AND_INPUT:
        MOVL      #BUFSIZE,R2           ;R2 IS LOOP COUNTER INTO INBUF
        MOVAB     INBUF,R9              ;POINT TO START OF INPUT BUFFER
CLEAR:  CLRB      (R9)                  ;
        INCL      R9                    ;POINT TO NEXT BYTE IN INBUF
        DECL      R2                    ;ALL BYTES CLEARED?
        BNEQ      CLEAR                 ; NO: CONTINUE CLEARING
;                                        ;
;READ A RECORD FROM INPUT FILE AND ECHO CHECK IT
;
INPUT:  $GET      RAB=INRAB             ;
        BLBS      R0,CONTINUE           ;IF NOT EOF THEN ECHO CHECK
        BRW       SORT                  ;...ELSE START SORTING
CONTINUE:                               ;
        MOVC3     #BUFSIZE,INBUF,OUTBUF ;
        $PUT      RAB=OUTRAB            ;ECHO CHECK
;
;SCAN INPUT RECORD UNTIL FIRST NON-BLANK CHARACTER, OR UNTIL END OF
;RECORD (I.E. UNTIL ASCII NUL IS ENCOUNTERED OR UNTIL ENTIRE RECORD
;IS SCANNED.) IF NOT END OF RECORD THEN START CONVERSION AND CONTINUE
;SCANNING THE DIGITS UNTIL THE FIRST BLANK OR UNTIL END OF RECORD.
;
        MOVAB     INBUF,R6              ;POINT TO BEGINNING OF INBUF
        MOVL      #BUFSIZE,R2           ;R2 IS LOOP COUNTER
SKIP_BLANKS:
        TSTB      (R6)                  ;IS CHAR ASCII NUL?
        BEQL      CLEAR_AND_INPUT       ; YES: BRANCH TO GET NEXT RECORD
        CMPB      #BLANK,(R6)           ; NO: IS CHAR A BLANK?
        BNEQ      START_OF_NUMBER       ;    NO: START CONVERSION
        DECL      R2                    ;    YES: END OF RECORD?
        BEQL      CLEAR_AND_INPUT       ;       YES
        INCL      R6                    ;       NO: POINT TO NEXT CHAR
        BRB       SKIP_BLANKS           ;       ...AND CONTINUE SCANNING
;
;BEGINNING OF NUMBER HAS BEEN FOUND. CHECK FIRST CHARACTER OF NUMBER
;FOR SIGN. THEN CONTINUE SCANNING THE DIGITS. AS EACH DIGIT IS
;ENCOUNTERED, CONVERT IT FROM ASCII TO BINARY AND ACCUMULATE WITH
;PREVIOUS DIGITS.
;
```

(Continued)

```
START_OF_NUMBER:
        CLRB    SIGN_FLAG               ;ASSUME NUMBER IS POSITIVE
        CMPB    #^A'-',(R6)             ;IS CHAR A MINUS SIGN?
        BNEQ    CONVERT                 ; NO: START THE CONVERSION
        MOVB    #1,SIGN_FLAG            ; YES: SET SIGN_FLAG
        INCL    R6                      ;
;                                       ;
;BEGIN CONVERTING THE NUMBER            ;
;                                       ;
CONVERT:CLRW    R0                      ;
        SUBB3   #^A'0',(R6),R0          ;CONVERT ASCII DIGIT TO BINARY
        ADDW    R0,(R10)                ;ACCUMULATE NUMBER IN ARRAY
        DECL    R2                      ;END OF RECORD?
        BEQL    CHECK_SIGN              ; YES
        INCL    R6                      ; NO: POINT TO NEXT CHAR IN INBUF
        TSTB    (R6)                    ;IS CHAR ASCII NUL?
        BEQL    CHECK_SIGN              ; YES: END OF NUMBER
        CMPB    #BLANK,(R6)             ; NO: IS CHAR A BLANK?
        BEQL    CHECK_SIGN              ;    YES: END OF NUMBER
        MULW    #10,(R10)               ;    NO: MULTIPLY ACCUMULATED NUMBER
        BRB     CONVERT                 ;    ...AND CONTINUE THE CONVERSION
;                                       ;
CHECK_SIGN:                             ;
        TSTB    SIGN_FLAG               ;IS NUMBER NEGATIVE?
        BEQL    NUMBER_POS              ; NO
        MNEGW   (R10),(R10)             ; YES: NEGATE NUMBER
NUMBER_POS:                             ;
        ADDW    #2,R10                  ;POINT TO NEXT ELEMENT IN ARRAY
        INCB    SIZE                    ;INCREMENT NUMBER OF ELEMENTS
        BRW     CLEAR_AND_INPUT         ;BRANCH TO INPUT NEXT RECORD


;                       *****************
;                       *   SEGMENT 2   *
;                       *****************
;
;THIS SEGMENT SORTS THE ARRAY OF BINARY INTEGERS, CONSTRUCTED IN
;SEGMENT 1, IN ASCENDING ORDER USING BUBBLE SORT. WHEN SORTING IS
;COMPLETED, CONTROL IS TRANSFERRED TO SEGMENT 3 OF THE PROGRAM.
;
;
SORT:   CMPB    SIZE,#1                 ;IS NUMBER OF ELEMENTS <= 1?
        BLEQ    SORT_COMPLETED          ; YES: NO SORTING NEEDED
START_SORT:                             ; NO: START SORTING
        SUBB3   #1,SIZE,LIMIT           ;SIZE-1 IS MAX NUMBER OF ITERATIONS
OUTER:  CLRB    FLAG                    ;ASSUME ARRAY IS SORTED
        MOVAW   A,R10                   ;R10 POINTS TO 1ST ELEMENT
        ADDL3   #2,R10,R11              ;R11 POINTS TO 2ND ELEMENT
        CLRB    R1                      ;R1 IS INNER LOOP COUNTER
INNER:  INCB    R1                      ;PROCEED THROUGH THE ELEMS OF ARRAY
        CMPB    R1,LIMIT                ;HAVE ALL ELEMENTS BEEN COMPARED?
        BGTR    EXIT                    ;YES
        CMPW    (R10),(R11)             ;IS ITH ELEMENT >I+1ST ELEMENT?
        BLEQ    NEXT_ELEMENT            ; NO: LEAVE ELEMENT AS IS
        MOVW    (R10),TEMP              ; YES: SWAP ELEMENTS
        MOVW    (R11),(R10)             ;
        MOVW    TEMP,(R11)              ;
        MOVB    #1,FLAG                 ;SET FLAG=1: SORTING NOT COMPLETE
NEXT_ELEMENT:                           ;
        ADDL    #2,R10                  ; NO: UPDATE POINTERS TO
        ADDL    #2,R11                  ;...ARRAY ELEMENTS, AND
        BRB     INNER                   ;...CONTINUE COMPARING
        DECB    LIMIT                   ;DECREMENT NUMBER OF ITERATIONS
        TSTB    FLAG                    ;WERE ANY ELEMENTS SWAPPED IN THE
                                        ;...PREVIOUS ITERATION?
        BNEQ    OUTER                   ; YES: NEED MORE ITERATIONS


;                       *****************
;                       *   SEGMENT 3   *
;                       *****************
;
;
;THIS SEGMENT CONVERTS THE BINARY INTEGERS IN THE SORTED ARRAY
;TO THEIR ASCII EQUIVALENTS AND OUTPUT THEM.
;A BINARY INTEGER IS CONVERTED TO ASCII BY SUCCESSIVELY DIVIDING
```

(Continued)

```
;THE INTEGER AND THE RESULTING QUOTIENTS BY DECIMAL 10.
;THE REMAINDERS ARE THEN MADE INTO ASCII CHARACTERS BY ADDING THE
;ASCII CODE OF DIGIT 0 TO EACH OF THEM.
;SINCE THE REMAINDERS ARE OBTAINED IN A REVERSE ORDER TO THE ORDER
;THEY SHOULD BE OUTPUT, THEY ARE FIRST STORED (IN THEIR ASCII FORM)
;IN A TEMPORARY BUFFER. THEN WHEN THE CONVERSION IS COMPLETE, THE
;TEMPORARY BUFFER IS COPIED IN A REVERSE ORDER INTO THE OUTPUT BUFFER.
;
;
SORT_COMPLETED:                         ;
        MOVB    SIZE,R3                 ;IS NUMBER OF ELEMENTS = 0?
        BEQL    EXIT                    ; YES: NOTHING TO OUTPUT
        MOVAW   A,R10                   ; NO: POINT TO FIRST ELEMENT
;                                       ;
;BEFORE WRITING A RECORD, THE OUTPUT BUFFER WILL BE CLEARED
;                                       ;
CLEAR_OUTBUF:                           ;
        MOVL    #BUFSIZE,R2             ;
        MOVAB   OUTBUF,R9               ;POINT TO OUTPUT BUFFER
CLEAR_OUT:                              ;
        CLRB    (R9)                    ;
        INCL    R9                      ;POINT TO NEXT BYTE IN OUTBUF
        DECL    R2                      ;ALL BYTES CLEARED?
        BNEQ    CLEAR_OUT               ; NO: CONTINUE CLEARING
;                                       ;
;BEGIN CONVERTING BINARY INTEGER AND STORE RESULTING ASCII CHARACTERS
;IN A TEMPORARY BUFFER. IF INTEGER IS NEGATIVE THEN SET FLAG AND OBTAIN
;MAGNITUDE.
;                                       ;
        CLRB    SIGN_FLAG               ;ASSUME NUMBER IS POSITIVE
        CLRQ    R4                      ;R5 AND R4 ARE USED FOR DIVIDEND
        MOVAB   TEMPBUF,R8              ;POINT TO TEMPORARY BUFFER
        MOVW    (R10),R4                ;GET DIVIDEND
        BGEQ    POSITIVE_NUM            ;IF DIVIDEND IS >=0, START CONVERSION
        MOVB    #1,SIGN_FLAG            ;...ELSE SET SIGN FLAG AND
        MNEGW   R4,R4                   ;...OBTAIN MAGNITUDE
;                                       ;
POSITIVE_NUM:                           ;
        MOVL    #1,R0                   ;R0 IS NUMBER OF DIGITS IN NUMBER
EXTRACT_CHAR:                           ;
        EDIV    #10,R4,R4,R6            ;GET QUOTIENT AND REMAINDER
        ADDB3   #^A'0',R6,(R8)          ;CONVERT REMAINDER TO ASCII
        TSTL    R4                      ;IS QUOTIENT 0?
        BEQL    TEMP_TO_OUTBUF          ; YES: END OF NUMBER
        INCL    R8                      ; NO: POINT TO NEXT BYTE IN TEMPBUF
        INCL    R0                      ;... AND INCREMENT NUMBER OF DIGITS
        BRB     EXTRACT_CHAR            ;
;                                       ;
;RESULTING ASCII STRING IS IN TEMPORARY BUFFER. MOVE IT TO OUTPUT BUFFER
;WITH A MINUS SIGN IF NUMBER IS NEGATIVE, THEN OUTPUT IT.
;                                       ;
TEMP_TO_OUTBUF:                         ;
        MOVAB   OUTBUF,R6               ;POINT TO OUTPUT BUFFER
        TSTB    SIGN_FLAG               ;IS NUMBER NEGATIVE?
        BEQL    COPY                    ; NO
        MOVB    #^A'-',(R6)             ; YES: PLACE A MINUS SIGN IN
                                        ;...FRONT OF NUMBER
        INCL    R6                      ;POINT TO SECOND BYTE IN OUTBUF
COPY:   MOVB    (R8),(R6)               ;COPY DIGIT FROM TEMPBUF INTO OUTBUF
        DECL    R0                      ;ALL DIGITS COPIED?
        BEQL    OUTPUT                  ; YES: READY TO OUTPUT NUMBER
        DECL    R8                      ; NO: MOVE TOWARD TOP OF TEMPBUF,
        INCL    R6                      ;...MOVE TOWARD BOTTOM OF OUTBUF
        BRB     COPY                    ;...AND CONTINUE COPYING
;                                       ;
;NUMBER IN ASCII CODE IS NOW IN OUTPUT BUFFER, READY TO BE OUTPUT.
;                                       ;
OUTPUT: $PUT    RAB=OUTRAB              ;OUTPUT NUMBER
        DECB    R3                      ;ENTIRE SORTED ARRAY PRINTED?
        BEQL    EXIT                    ; YES
        ADDL    #2,R10                  ; NO: POINT TO NEXT ELEMENT IN ARRAY
        BRW     CLEAR_OUTBUF            ;...AND REPEAT CONVERSION
EXIT:   $CLOSE  FAB=INFAB               ;CLOSE INPUT FILE
        $CLOSE  FAB=OUTFAB              ;CLOSE OUTPUT FILE
        $EXIT_S                         ;TERMINATE PROGRAM
        .END    CONVERT_AND_SORT        ;END OF ASSEMBLY
```

Figure 4.9 A program to read, sort, and print an array

Modifications and generalizations to the program in Figure 4.9 are left as exercises.

4.8 Summary

In this chapter the MACRO language is introduced. MACRO is the assembly language of the VAX-11 computer provided by the manufacturer. A subset of the most commonly used directives and instructions is presented. Additionally, four simple addressing modes are introduced. Together, they allow beginning students to write nontrivial assembly language programs. Finally, examples are given to show how input/output can be performed by using input/output macros of the VAX-11 VMS Operating System. For students who prefer to perform I/O using an HLL such as FORTRAN or Pascal, refer to Appendix F for detail.

EXERCISES

1. Give the range in hexadecimal of the signed integers that can be represented in a
   a. byte
   b. word
   c. longword

2. How many bytes are reserved by each of the following statements?

```
           .WORD      1000,-15,25,200
           .BYTE      0
           .BLKB      1
A:         .BLKL      4
B:         .BYTE      B-A
           .ADDRESS   A,B
N= 10
           .BYTE      5+2*N
           .BLKW      5+2*N
N= N+5
           .BLKB      N
           .ASCII     '-12.5'
           .ASCIC     /1/
```

3. What do the following declarations have in common?

   a. .ASCII   /NO/
   b. .BYTE   78,79
   c. .WORD   20302

(Hint: Look at the contents of the bytes reserved.)

4. Assume that *before* executing *each* of the following instructions, the registers and memory contain the values shown in hexadecimal. Show the contents of the memory locations and the registers affected *after* executing each of the following instructions.

		Address		Label
		5C0	61	
R6	000005C5	5C1	C4	B
		5C2	05	A
		5C3	00	
R7	001AC68E	5C4	00	
		5C5	FF	
		5C6	5B	
		5C7	00	
		5C8	DC	
		5C9		

a. ADDB   R6,R7
b. ADDW   (R6),R7
c. MOVW   #32,R7
d. MOVW   (R6),R7
e. MOVAB   B,R7
f. ADDB3   #5,R6,R7
g. INCW   (R6)
h. MOVQ   B-1,R6

5. Given the following declarations:

```
A:    .BYTE   63
B:    .BYTE   1
C:    .WORD   255
D:    .WORD   2
E:    .LONG   1024
```

What are the contents of the registers (or part of the registers) affected after executing each of the following instructions?

a. MOVB   C,R2
b. MOVW   A,R2
c. MOVAL   C,R2
d. MNEGB   C,R2
e. MNEGL   C,R2
f. ADDB3   A,C,R2
g. ADDW3   B,C,R2
h. ADDL3   A,D,R2
i. MULB3   A,D,R2
j. MULW3   A,D,R2
k. DIVB3   C,B,R2
l. EDIV   E,A,R2,R3

6. What is the effect of the instruction ADDW in each of the following program segments?

```
Segment 1          Segment 2
SIZE 500           SIZE 500
   .                  .
   .                  .
   .                  .
CLRW   A           CLRW   A
ADDW   #SIZE,A     ADDW   SIZE,A
```

7. It is desired to divide the number 15 by 4 to obtain the quotient and the remainder. Assume that the number 15 is contained in location X and the number 4 is contained in location Y, as declared in the following:

```
X:   .WORD   15
Y:   .WORD   4
```

Without altering these declarations, write a segment of a MACRO program that accomplishes the division. Show the declarations of any variables you might need in your program.

8. Write a segment of code that saves and restores registers R0 through R5 around the instruction MOVC3.

9. a. Consider the following declarations of two ASCII strings:

```
STRING:   .ASCIC   'CONCATENATE THIS STRING'
          .ASCIC   /TO THIS STRING/
BUFFER:   .BLKB    100
```

Without using MOVC3, show a segment of code that concatenates the two strings and stores them in memory starting at location BUFFER.
b. Repeat exercise 9a using MOVC3.
c. Modify the program so that it stores the length of the resulting string in the first byte of the buffer.

10. Write a MACRO program that multiplies the elements of an array, A, by five and adds the resulting array to another array, B. The final result is to be stored in array C. Assume each array is 10 words.

11. Write a complete MACRO program that adds the numbers 1 through 50 inclusive and stores the result in a variable SUM.

12. Modify the program in problem 11 to add only the even numbers between 1 and 50 inclusive.

13. Given a list of numbers of size *n*, write a program that finds the largest number and its position in the list.

14. Selection sort is a sorting method wherein the smallest element in a list is searched for and exchanged with the first element. Then the next smallest element is searched for and exchanged with the second element, and so on. Write a MACRO program that sorts a list using this method.

15. Two vectors V1 and V2, each of size n, are to be added. Write a MACRO program that adds the two vectors and stores the result in vector VSUM.

16. Write a MACRO program that computes the inner product of the two vectors in exercise 15 and stores the result in location PRODUCT.

The following exercises pertain to the program of Figure 4.9.

17. Modify the program to print headings before the echo-checked array and before the sorted array. Also, in the case of an empty array, print a message to that effect.

18. Modify segment 1 of the program to handle the case wherein a positive number may be preceded by a plus (+) sign.

19. Modify segment 3 of the program to print four elements of the sorted array per line.

20. Modify segment 1 of the program to handle the case wherein an input record may have more than one number in it. Assume that every two numbers in the record are separated by one or more blanks.

21. Modify segment 2 of the program to do the sorting by selection sort (see exercise 14).

22. Modify the program to handle numbers whose range is a longword.

Chapter 5

Addressing Modes

TO ACCESS a piece of data, it is necessary to specify its memory address. In Chapter 4 we discussed four basic addressing modes. In this chapter we shall systematically review those methods and examine new ones. We shall see how some addressing modes help make the coding of an algorithm easier, whereas others allow us to identify the operand location with fewer bits than a complete address needs, thereby shortening the instruction length. Still others enable us to locate operands whose exact addresses may not even be known when the program is written. In each case an addressing mode is designed to achieve one or more of the following objectives:

1. To make the instructions more powerful.
2. To make programming more convenient.
3. To make program execution more efficient.

Although some addressing modes are common to all computers, others are used in only a few computer systems. The VAX-11 has a larger than usual set of addressing modes. The terminology used in the VAX-11, however, varies somewhat from the norm. In this chapter we shall explain all these addressing modes and attempt to fit them into those that are more commonly known in the rest of the industry.

5.1 Basic Addressing Modes

In chapter 4 we discussed briefly the following basic addressing modes:

1. Direct addressing.
2. Immediate addressing.

3. Register addressing.
4. Register deferred addressing (indirect addressing).

Here we will examine these modes again in more detail.

Direct Addressing

By definition, an operand is accessed by direct addressing when its actual address is specified within the instruction. Generally, this can be done in two ways: (1) with a symbolic name representing the memory address, or less frequently (2) with an absolute numerical value.

Early computers had no addressing modes other than direct addressing. Absolute numerical addresses were often used in those days, since translators were generally not available and more sophisticated addressing schemes had not yet been invented. Moreover, the programmer had control over the entire machine when he ran his program. He could decide where every instruction and datum should reside. Today absolute numerical addressing is seldom used except in special situations, since a program usually has to share the primary memory with other programs, and the programmer has little control over where his program will be loaded in the memory.

Today, instead of absolute numerical value, the addresses of instructions and data of a program are normally expressed in terms of their displacements relative to the beginning of the program. For example, if A and B are labels representing locations 1000 and 1004, respectively, relative to the beginning of the program, then an instruction such as

```
ADD     A,B
```

is equivalent to

```
ADD     1000,1004
```

Now, if the program were to be loaded into the memory starting at location 5000, then the actual addresses of A and B would then be 6000 and 6004, respectively. Of course, if the loading address were 10000, then the actual addresses of A and B would be 11000 and 11004 respectively. In this case the addresses 1000 and 1004 are known as *relocatable addresses,* and the actual addresses used when the program is run are called *absolute addresses.* As indicated previously, absolute addressing is a form of direct addressing. In the MACRO language, absolute addressing is specified by

```
ADDL    @#1000,@#1004
```

Instructions using absolute addressing will always fetch their operands from the same memory location as specified, no matter where the program is loaded.

In the MACRO language, all operands that are assigned symbolic names can be addressed simply by using their names. For example:

```
ADDL    A,B
```

In this form it has the appearance of direct addressing, although, as we shall see later, in actual implementation the VAX-11 uses relative addressing.

Immediate Addressing

When the operand itself is included as part of the instruction, we have immediate addressing. Often when the programmer needs a constant in an instruction, instead of defining it by means of a directive, he can specify the value directly in the instruction. For example, one could implement the operation

$$(A) \leftarrow (A) + 10$$

by

```
TEN:    .LONG   10        ;define constant
        :

        :
        ADDL    TEN,A     ;(A) ← (A) + 10
        :
```

One may, however, find it easier simply to write

```
ADDL    #10,A
```

In this example, immediate addressing is specified using the MACRO convention. The constant, expressed in the form *"value,"* is known as a *literal* and is actually stored within the instruction. The value following the symbol # can be either a string of characters or a number expressed in one of the many recognized data representations. Table 5.1 summarizes the data representations used in MACRO.

Table 5.1 MACRO Symbols to Denote Data Representation

Symbol	Representation
^B	binary
^D	decimal
^O	octal
^X	hexadecimal
^A	ASCII
^F	floating point

Thus, for example, we can have

```
ADDL    # ^B10,A    ;for (A) ← (A) + 2
ADDL    # ^X10,A    ;for (A) ← (A) + 16
CMPB    # ^A';',A   ; compare char. ';' to (A)
```

The MACRO language further distinguishes two forms of immediate addressing depending on the amount of storage required to store the literal. In MACRO terminology, these two forms of immediate addressing are known as the *literal mode* and the *immediate mode.* In the case of the literal mode, the literal can only be a positive integer ranging from 0 to 63. (Strictly speaking, it can also be a short floating-point number; see Chapter 9 for details.) If the value of the number lies outside this range, or if it is a character string, then the immediate mode will be used. Depending on the value of the operand, the assembler normally determines which mode to use. If necessary, the programmer can specify the mode by placing the symbol

S^   (for literal mode)

or

I^   (for immediate mode)

preceding the #value string. Thus

```
MOVL    S^#6,R1
```

specifies the literal mode, whereas

```
MOVL    I^#6,R1
```

specifies the immediate mode for the source operand.

The general instruction format of the VAX-11 is shown in Section 2.5. As explained there, the first byte of an instruction contains the operation code (some instructions use 2-byte op codes). This is followed by zero to six operand specifiers, depending on the instruction. Each specifier occupies one or more bytes. The first byte of an operand specifier has the general format:

```
7    4 3    0
 ┌─────┬─────┐
 │  M  │  R  │
 └─────┴─────┘
```

The M field, called the *mode specifier,* specifies an addressing mode, whereas the R field addresses a general register.

The format of the operand specifier for the literal mode is an exception to the general format; it consists of a single byte having two leading zeroes followed by a 6-bit integer:

```
 ┌──────────────────┐
 │ 0 0 x x x x x x   │
 └──────────────────┘
```

The 6 bits marked *x* represent a number ranging from 0 to 63.

The immediate mode allows the programmer to specify an operand 1, 2, 4, or 8 bytes long, depending on the context of the instruction. In the following example,

```
MOVL    I^#6,R1
```

a longword containing the value 6 will be created and become part of the instruction. Details of the implementation of the immediate addressing mode will be presented in Section 5.2 under program counter addressing.

It should be apparent that if only a small positive constant is needed, the literal mode provides an economic way of specifying the operand. Study of actual programs shows that, in practice, most constants employed by the programmers are indeed small positive integers. Since the MACRO assembler will select the literal mode by default if the constant falls within range, there is really no need for the programmer to choose between the two modes when using immediate addressing.

Register Addressing

Strictly speaking, register addressing is a form of direct addressing since the addressed register contains the operand. It is treated as a different addressing mode, however, because of the advantages it provides. First, since the number of registers is usually small, only a few bits are needed to identify a register address completely. In the case of the VAX-11, only 4 bits are necessary to address the 16 registers. This provides coding economy. Second, since the registers are part of the CPU, fetching operands from the registers requires no memory cycle. This results in execution efficiency. Furthermore, the registers are normally given reserved names, making its addressing quite distinct and readable. In the VAX-11 the 16 registers are given the names R0, R1, ... R11, AP, FP, SP, and PC (AP can also be referred to as R12). In machine language, the registers are identified using 4 bits, with 0000 for R0, 0001 for R1, ... 1011 for R11, 1100 for AP, 1101 for FP, 1110 for SP, and 1111 for PC. This address is contained in the R field of the operand specifier. It should be pointed out, however, that PC could not be used as a register in the register addressing mode. Thus,

```
INCL    R7
MOVL    R3,SP
ADDL    AP,FP
```

are correct instructions using the register addressing mode,

```
MOVL    R0,PC
```

is not.

In the case of register addressing, the M field will have the value 5 (0101). The instruction

```
ADDL    R0,R1    ; R1 ← R0 + R1
```

will be assembled in machine language as follows:

23					0
5	1	5	0	C	0

The first byte (C0) is the op code; the 5 in the second byte indicates register addressing; and the 0 specifies register 0 for the source. Similarly, the value in the third byte (51) specifies register addressing and that R1 is used for the destination.

Indirect Addressing

In indirect addressing, the address specified in the operand field is actually a pointer. The content of the referenced location is the address of the operand. The register deferred mode described in Chapter 4 is really a special case of the indirect addressing mode wherein a register, rather than a memory location, is specified in the instruction. (The word *defer* is Digital Equipment Corporation's term to describe indirect addressing.) Let us again use the example

```
ADD    A,B
```

where A represents memory location 1000 and B memory location 1004. Further, let the number 2000 be stored in location 1000 and the number 1234 be stored in location 1004. After executing the instruction, one will find the sum 3234 in location 1004.

If the addressing mode is changed to that of indirect addressing,

```
ADD    A*,B*
```

where the symbol * is used to denote indirect addressing in many assembly languages—or using the MACRO language, in which the symbol @ is used to denote deferred addressing in general—we have

```
ADDL    @A,@B
```

The execution of this instruction can best be demonstrated with the help of Figure 5.1. The processor will first access location A (at location 1000) to fetch its contents and use that value as an address.

```
        memory location        contents

A:        00001000               00
          00001001               20
          00001002               00
          00001003               00
B:        00001004               34
          00001005               12
          00001006               00
          00001007               00
             :                    :
          00001234               25
          00001235               3C
          00001236               02
          00001237               00
             :                    :
          00002000               DB
          00002001               C3
          00002002               FD
          00002003               FF
             :                    :
```

Figure 5.1 Example of indirect addressing

In this case it will mean accessing location 2000 to get the first operand. Similarly, the processor will access location 1004, use its contents as an address, and fetch the operand at location 1234. The sum, which is equal to zero, is stored as a longword at location 1234.

Indirect addressing is not limited to the one case discussed so far. In fact, indirect addressing can be combined with most other addressing modes on the VAX-11 to provide ways of accessing data indirectly. Later we will discuss them individually in conjunction with the other addressing modes.

Indirect addressing is extremely useful for accessing data during subroutine calls, as we shall see in Chapter 6. It provides a means for referencing data whose addresses are unknown to the program using them, as is normally the case during subroutine execution. Indirect addressing is also a powerful means of simplifying the accessing of complex data structure. We will, however, present only an example to show how indirect addressing can help simplify programming even for a relatively simple problem.

Consider the evaluation of the expression:

$$SUM = \sum_{i=1}^{100} ARRAY\,[i].$$

The equivalent in Pascal statements would be:

```
SUM := 0;
FOR i := 1 TO 100 DO
     SUM := SUM + ARRAY[i];
```

Let the array of numbers, each a 32-bit integer, be stored in consecutive memory locations denoted by ARRAY, ARRAY+4, ARRAY+8, ... ARRAY+396. If only direct addressing were available, we may have the following program segment:

```
ARRAY:   .LONG   5
         .LONG   13
         .LONG   -17
           :
           :
N:       .LONG   100
SUM:     .BLKL   1
         CLRL    R5                ;R5 USED AS ACC.
         ADDL    ARRAY,R5          ;ADD 1ST ELEMENT
         ADDL    ARRAY+4,R5        ;ADD 2ND ELEMENT
           :
           :
         ADDL    ARRAY+396,R5      ;ADD 100TH ELEMENT
         MOVL    R5,SUM            ;STORE RESULT
```

One hundred ADD instructions would be used to implement the program in this manner. Using indirect addressing, however, we could have:

```
                 :
(same data definition)
                 :
          CLRL    R5                   ;R5 USED AS ACC
          MOVL    N,R6                 ;R6 AS COUNTER
          MOVAL   ARRAY,R4             ;ADDR. OF 1ST ELEM.
LOOP:     ADDL    (R4),R5              ;
          ADDL    #4,R4                ;ADDR. OF NEXT ELEM.
          DECL    R6                   ;UPDATE COUNTER
          BGTR    LOOP                 ;R6>0
          MOVL    R5,SUM               ;STORE RESULT
                 :
```

The program is much shorter but accomplishes the same task. In fact, this program is much more useful than the previous one. It can be used for the summation of arrays of practically any size without modifying the program proper. The only statements that need to be changed are the value of N and, perhaps, the name of the array. Later, using other addressing modes, we shall see still other ways of performing the same job.

5.2 Other Addressing Modes

Beyond the four basic addressing modes discussed previously, many other important addressing modes are available on the VAX-11. In this section we shall discuss them in detail.

Relative Addressing

For computers with a large addressing space, it it often uneconomical to address an operand by spelling out its full address. For example, it takes 32 bits to specify a memory address on the VAX-11. Taking advantage of the fact that the operands used in an instruction are often stored in locations not too far from the instruction itself and that the program counter (PC) in the CPU constantly keeps track of the address of the current instruction, it is easy for the machine to locate an operand by specifying its distance from the instruction. This type of addressing is known as *relative addressing*. In the VAX-11 the relative address is a signed number (that is, in 2's complement representation) called the *displacement*. It is added to the current value of the PC during instruction execution to form the actual address of the operand. This actual address of the operand is known as the *effective address*. When the effective address of the operand is between +127 and −128 bytes from the current value of the PC, only one byte is needed to specify the displacement. This is called *byte relative addressing*, and the code for the mode specifier is A (hex). The R field contains the value F (hex), signifying that the contents of PC are used as the *base address*. The first byte of the operand specifier will be:

Using a 2-byte relative address, we can specify any operand that is within ±32K (1K = 1,024) bytes from the instruction. This is called *word relative addressing*, and the code for the mode specifier is C (hex). When the operand is more than 32K bytes away from the instruction, a 32–bit displacement is used. This is called *longword relative addressing*. In this case the code for the mode specifier is E (hex). In summary, the object code of the operand specifier for relative addressing may take one of the following forms:

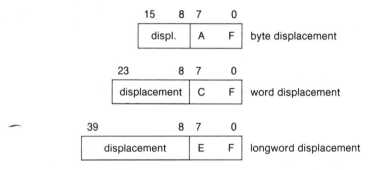

Since operands are seldom that far removed from the instructions that utilize them, one can see that the use of relative addressing shortens the length of the address field in the instruction and thus saves memory space.

Suppose we have the instruction

```
ADDL    A,B
```

Figure 5.2 shows the locations of the instructions and the operands. In this example, even without going through any detailed computation, we could see that the distance (in bytes) between the operand A and the instruction is greater than 128 but smaller than 32K. We conclude that a relative address field of 2 bytes is needed. In Chapter 2 it was pointed out that the contents of PC are incremented as the instructions are fetched and interpreted during a program execution. For byte-oriented machines such as the VAX-11, the PC is actually incremented as an instruction is scanned one byte at a time during decoding. The contents of the PC after the first displacement is fetched will be 2004 (hex). To obtain the effective address 1000 (hex), we need to subtract 1004 (hex) from the current value of PC. The radix complement representation of −1004 (hex) is EFFC (hex), which will be used as the displacement value in the instruction. Similarly, to obtain the effective address of B, we need a displacement that, when added to the updated contents of PC, will yield 1004 (hex). In this case PC is equal to 2007 (hex); as a result, the displacement should be −1003 (hex), which is EFFD (hex) in the radix complement representation. On the other hand, if operand B were located at 2080 (hex), then the distance between B and the updated content of PC would be less than 127, and one byte would be adequate to store the relative address. We have the updated contents of the PC equals 2006 (hex), and the displacement equals

$$2080 \text{ (hex)} - 2006 \text{ (hex)} = 7A \text{ (hex)}$$

This is shown in Figure 5.2 with the contents of memory locations 2004–2006 enclosed in parenthesis. Note that the M field (left nibble of location 2004) contains an A now instead of a C. Location

```
PC:        0 0 0 0 2 0 0 0 (Before instruction execution)


           memory loc.   cont

A:         00001000      00
           00001001      2C
           00001002      00
           00001003      00
B:         00001004      48
           00001005      12
           00001006      00
           00001007      00
              :           :

           00002000      CO ADDL
           00002001      CF                   00001000
           00002002      FC                  -00002004
           00002003      EF                   FFFFEFFC
           00002004      CF     (AF)
           00002005      FD     (7A)          00001004
           00002006      EF     (xx)         -00002007
           00002007      :                    FFFFEFFD
              :           :
(B:)       00002080      34                   00002080
           00002081      12                  -00002006
           00002082      00                   0000007A
           00002083      00
              :           :
```

Figure 5.2 Derivation of displacement for relative addressing

2006 will be the beginning byte of the next instruction. This is indicated in the diagram with the value *xx*.

If the operand is located very far from the instruction, then it is necessary to use a longword displacement. The instruction will become longer, but the relative address calculation follows along the same line.

All these computations might look rather formidable. Fortunately, the assembler actually performs the arithmetic and generates the displacement value. The programmer merely needs to specify the symbolic names.

In assembling an instruction using the relative mode, if the MACRO assembler encounters a symbol whose value is unknown (forward referencing), it will assume a range for the displacement (longword displacement in this case). If the programmer knows the displacement value, he can aid the assembler by specifying the range with the string B^, W^, or L^ inserted in front of the address to indicate byte, word, or longword, respectively. For example:

```
ADDL    B^X2080,L^X1000
```

or

```
ADDL    B^B,L^A
```

As mentioned in Section 5.1, indirect addressing can be combined with other addressing modes to give the programmer different ways of accessing data indirectly. We have, on the VAX-11, the *relative deferred addressing*. As with relative addressing, we also have three different ranges of displacement: the byte, word, and longword relative deferred modes. The code for the mode specifiers are B(hex), D (hex), and F (hex), respectively. Otherwise, the object code of the operand specifier is identical to that of the respective relative addressing.

Autoincrement and Autodecrement

In the previous section we saw that the contents of the memory location that stored the indirect address were incremented when we wanted to go to the next element of an array. Such operations occur so frequently that many computers provide special mechanisms to perform them. In the VAX-11 these are the autoincrement and autodecrement addressing modes. The addressing scheme is similar to that for the register deferred mode, except that the contents of the registers used are modified every time they are accessed. In the autodecrement mode the contents of the register are decremented *before* they are used as the operand address. In the autoincrement mode the contents of the register are incremented *after* they are used as the operand address.

To emphasize the moment at which the value in the register is changed, autodecrement is represented by $-(Rn)$ and autoincrement by $(Rn)+$. The amount to be incremented or decremented depends on the data type being addressed. This means that for a byte operand the contents of the register will be incremented (decremented) by 1, for a word operand by 2, for a longword operand by 4, and so on. To calculate the sum of 100 numbers, as in the example of the previous section, we could write:

```
          :
          MOVL    N,R0          ;INITIALIZAION
          CLRL    R5
          MOVAL   ARRAY,R6      ;ADDRESS IN R6
LOOP:     ADDL    (R6)+,R5      ;ADD/UPDATE POINTER
          DECL    R0            ;UPDATE COUNTER
          BGTR    LOOP          ;R0>0
          MOVL    R5,SUM        ;STORE SUM
          :
```

Here the contents of R6 will be incremented by 4, every time the ADDL instruction is executed.

In using these addressing modes, one should be very careful to understand the context of the instruction. For example, for an instruction such as

```
MOVW    (R1)+,(R7)+
```

when a word (2 bytes) is moved (copied) from one memory location to another, the contents of both R1 and R7 will be incremented by 2 after the foregoing instruction is executed. For an instruction such as

```
MOVAW   (R1)+,(R7)+
```

the situation is somewhat more complicated, however. The address of a word, which is 4 bytes long, is moved into a longword whose address is in R7. After the execution of this instruction, the value in R7 will be incremented by 4, whereas the value in R1 will be incremented by only 2. Had the foregoing instruction been MOVAB or MOVAL, R1 would be incremented by 1 or 4, respectively. The contents of R7, however, will be incremented by 4 in all these cases.

The mode specifier for autodecrement is 7 and for autoincrement 8. The operand specifier formats are respectively:

```
  7     4 3     0
 ┌──────┬───────┐
 │  7   │  Rn   │   autodecrement
 └──────┴───────┘

  7     4 3      0
 ┌──────┬───────┐
 │  8   │  Rn   │   autoincrement
 └──────┴───────┘
```

The VAX-11 also supports the *autoincrement deferred mode*. The syntax for autoincrement deferred mode is

    @(Rn)+

In this case the contents of Rn is the memory address in which the effective address of the operand is stored. For example, take the instruction

    ADDL   @(R3)+,R4

if before instruction execution, we have:

    R3:   0 0 0 0 2 0 0 0

    R4:   0 0 0 0 1 0 1 2

Memory Loc.	cont	
00001234	EE	00001012
00001235	2F	+00002FEE
00001236	00	00004000
00001237	00	
:	:	
00002000	34	
00002001	12	effective address
00002002	00	
00002003	00	
:	:	
00008000	C0	
00008001	93	instruction
00008002	54	

then after instruction execution, we have:

    R3:   0 0 0 0 2 0 0 4

    R4:   0 0 0 0 4 0 0 0

We note that in autoincrement deferred mode, since the contents of the register involved are used as an address, the value will always be increased by 4 every time the instruction is executed.

The mode specifier for autoincrement deferred addressing is 9. The operand specifier format is as follows:

```
7     4 3     0
┌──────┬──────┐
│  9   │  Rn  │
└──────┴──────┘
```

Index Mode

In index mode the effective address of an operand is derived by adding the contents of a designated register to a general operand address called the *base operand address*. In some computers, one or more special-purpose registers called *index registers* are employed specifically for the storage of index values, whereas others, such as the VAX-11, use the general registers for indexing. For example:

```
ADDB    ARRAY[R1],R2
```

is a MACRO instruction in which the first operand is accessed through index mode addressing. Figure 5.3 shows how the effective address is derived; another example of effective address calculation is shown in Figure 5.4, where the base operand address is specified in the autoincrement deferred mode. The code for the mode specifier of index mode is 4 (hex). The operand specifier consists of two or more bytes; the first byte specifies the index mode and the index register used, and the second byte (and if necessary the bytes following that) specifies the base operand address.

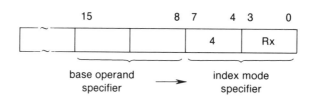

The index mode is designed for accessing an array of data. The base operand address points to the beginning of the array, whereas the value in the index register serves as a displacement to lead us to a particular element of the array. The register contents correspond to the array subscript.

In the VAX-11, since there are a number of defined data types and

```
       ADDB      ARRAY[R1],R2



       R1:       0 0 0 0 0 0 0 8

       R2:       0 0 0 0 0 0 3 B    (before inst. execution)
                 0 0 0 0 0 0 8 3    (after inst. execution)

       PC:       0 0 0 0 2 0 0 0    (where instr. is located)

                 memory loc.   cont
                                      ⎧ base
       ARRAY:    00001000      34    00001000 ⎨ operand addr.
                 00001001      12   +00000008—index value
                   :           :     00001008  effective addr.
                 00001008      48
                   :           :

                 00002000      80
                 00002001      41
                 00002002      CF
                 00002003      FB    00001000
                 00002004      EF   -00002005
                 00002005      xx    FFFFEFFB  displacement
                   :           :
```

Figure 5.3   Index mode addressing

the memory is byte-addressable, the interpretation of the index value is made a function of the instruction context (similar to autoincrement and autodecrement). Depending on whether the operand is a byte, word, longword, and so on, the contents of the index register are first multiplied by 1, 2, 4, and so on, respectively, before being added to the base operand address to form the effective address.

The invention of the index mode of addressing is considered one of the major advances in computer architecture. Previously, the only addressing mode available to the programmer was direct (absolute) addressing. It was very difficult to process large arrays of data, as in our previous example of adding 100 numbers. One either had to use 100 separate instructions or had to modify the instructions themselves during the program execution. This instruction modification was done by treating the instruction to be modified as data in the program. This practice was prone to error that could be not only very damaging but also difficult to debug. After the invention of index mode, this practice of instruction modification was soon discontinued. If we consider the programming problem discussed in the previous sections, then using index mode addressing we could have:

```
                    :
        (same data definition)
                    :

              CLRL    R5                   ;R5 AS ACC
              MOVL    N,R6                 ;R6 AS INDEX REG
              DECL    R6                   ;
       LOOP:  ADDL    ARRAY[R6],R5         ;ADD 100TH ELE.
              DECL    R6                   ;
              BGEQ    LOOP                 ;
              MOVL    R5,SUM               ;STORE RESULT
                    :
```

As in the case of indirect addressing, this program is much shorter than the one that uses direct addressing. By using another instruction that is available on the VAX-11, the program can be made even more compact:

```
                    :
              CLRL    R5
              CLRL    R6
       LOOP:  ADDL    ARRAY[R6],R5
              AOBLSS  N,R6,LOOP
              MOVL    R5,SUM
```

Here, AOBLSS is the mnemonic for the instruction Add One and Branch if Less than. Each time the instruction is executed, the second operand (contents of R6 in this case) is incremented by one and compared with the first operand (N). A branch is carried out if the second operand is smaller than the first.

It should be evident that the AOBLSS is essentially a combination of three VAX-11 instructions: INCx, CMPx, and BLSS. This is a popular sequence to implement loop control. Modern computer designers often try to design machine instructions that will efficiently carry out the commands of popular higher-level languages. AOBLSS is an example of such an attempt. As we see, both the Pascal FOR statement and the FORTRAN DO statement translates nicely to it.

The VAX-11 has three more instructions similar to AOBLSS, which are summarized in Table 5.2.

The syntax of the index mode addressing for the VAX-11 is in the form of

    B[Rx]

where Rx is one of the general registers other than PC, and B is the base operand address specifier. The base operand address can be specified with any one of the addressing modes except register mode, index mode, or the literal mode. The following are some examples of index mode addressing:

```
DECL  (R0)[R11]         ;REG DEFERRED INDEXED
CLRL  (R4)+[R5]         ;AUTOINCR. INDEXED
INCL  -(R6)[R3]         ;AUTODECR. INDEXED
MOVL  @(R11)+[R9],R1    ;AUTOINCR. DEFERRED INDEXED
CLRL  @#^X2000[R8]      ;ABSOLUTE INDEXED
DECW  B^6(R2)[R1]       ;DISPL. INDEXED
INCL  8(R0)[R7]         ;DISPL. DEFERRED INDEXED
```

Another restriction in index mode addressing is that the index register Rx cannot be a register that is used in the base operand address specifier and is modified during base operand address computation. For example, if the autoincrement or autodecrement mode is used in the base operand address specification, the same register could not be used for autoincrement (autodecrement) and as an index register at the same time. The following will lead to an unpredictable operand address

```
CLRL  (R5)+[R5]
INCL  -(R3)[R3]
MOVL  @ (R9)+[R9],R1
```

Therefore, it should never be used.

It should be emphasized that the base operand address is always

Table 5.2 Loop Control Instructions

Mnemonic	Operands	Effect	Name of Instruction
AOBLEQ	src1,src2,disp	(src2)←(src2) +1 if (src2)≤(src1) then PC←PC+disp	Add One and Branch on Less than or EQual
AOBLSS	src1,src2,disp	(src2)←(src2) +1 if (src2)<(src1) then PC←PC+disp	Add One and Branch on LeSS than
SOBGEQ	src,disp	(src)←(src)−1 if (src)≥0 then PC←PC+disp	Subtract One and Branch on Greater than or EQual
SOBGTR	src,disp	(src)←(src)−1 if (src)>0 then PC←PC+disp	Subtract One and Branch on GreateR than

Note: In addition to the four instructions listed in Table 5.2, there is another loop control instruction: Add Compare and Branch (ACBx). It has the format:

        ACBx   limit, incr, index, displacement

The operation of the instruction may be translated to the sequence: ADDx   incr,index; CMPx   limit,index;   and conditionally branch on index LEQ to limit (if incr GEQ 0) or GEQ to limit (if incr LSS 0) with word displacement. In a sense, it is a generalization of the instructions AOBLEQ and SOBGEQ.

completely evaluated before the index value is added to form the effective address. For example, consider the instruction

```
ADDL·    @(R7)+[R5],R0
```

Figure 5.4 illustrates this point.

As an example of indexed mode addressing, we rewrite the bubble sort program presented in Chapter 4 (see Figure 5.5)

Displacement Addressing

In relative addressing, we saw that a displacement was added to the contents of PC to form the effective address. If we specify in the R field any register other than the PC, an effective address can be formed in the same manner, except that in this case the contents of

---

If, before the execution of the instruction

```
  R0:    0 0 C B A 9 8 8
  R5:    0 0 0 0 0 0 0 3
  R7:    0 0 0 0 1 0 1 C
```

```
        memory loc.    cont
          00001000      C0
          00001001      45        instruction
          00001002      87
          00001003      50
             :          :

          0000101C      14
          0000101D      10        base operand
          0000101E      00        address            00001014
          0000101F      00        index value       +0000000C*
          00001020      78        eff. address       00001020
          00001021      56
          00001022      34              00345678
          00001023      00            +00CBA988
                                       01000000
```

Note that the index value 0000000C is obtained by multiplying the contents of the index register (R5) by 4 (longword). Then, after the execution of the instruction

```
  R0:    0 1 0 0 0 0 0 0
  R5:    0 0 0 0 0 0 0 3
  R7:    0 0 0 0 1 0 2 0
```

Figure 5.4   Autoincrement deferred indexed mode

```
;THIS PROGRAM SORTS AN ARRAY OF BINARY INTEGERS IN ASCENDING ORDER
;USING BUBBLE SORT.
;
;ASSUMPTIONS:
;       - THERE IS A MAXIMUM OF 100 ELEMENTS IN THE ARRAY
;       - THE ELEMENTS OF THE ARRAY ARE IN THE RANGE OF A WORD
;
;CONSTANTS AND VARIABLES:
MAX_SIZE = 100                          ;MAXIMUM SIZE OF ARRAY
A:       .BLKW   MAX_SIZE               ;ARRAY TO HOLD BINARY INTEGERS
SIZE:    .BLKB   1                      ;ACTUAL NUMBER OF ELEMENTS IN
                                        ;ARRAY
FLAG:    .BLKB   1                      ;FLAG TO INDICATE END OF
                                        ;SORTING
TEMP:    .BLKW   1                      ;A TEMPORARY
;                                       ;
         .ENTRY  BUBBLE_SORT,0          ;
         CMPB    #1,SIZE                ;IS NUMBER OF ELEMENTS <= 1?
         BGEQ    SORT_COMPLETED         ; YES: NO SORTING NEEDED
START_SORT:                             ;
         CLRL    R0                     ;
         SUBB3   #1,SIZE,R0             ;SIZE-1 IS MAX NUMBER OF
                                        ;ITERATIONS
OUTER:   CLRB    FLAG                   ;ASSUME ARRAY IS SORTED
         CLRL    R1                     ;R1 IS INNER LOOP COUNTER
         ADDL3   #1,R1,R2               ;R2 IS THE 2ND INDEX REG
INNER:   CMPW    A[R1],A[R2]            ;IS ITH ELEMENT >I+1ST
                                        ;ELEMENT?
         BLEQ    NEXT_ELEMENT           ;NO: LEAVE ELEMENT AS IS
         MOVW    A[R1],TEMP             ;YES: SWAP ELEMENTS
         MOVW    A[R2],A[R1]            ;
         MOVW    TEMP,A[R2]             ;
         MOVB    #1,FLAG                ;SET FLAG=1: SORTING NOT
                                        ;COMPLETE
NEXT_ELEMENT:                           ;
         INCL    R2                     ;UPDATE INDEX REG.
         AOBLSS  R0,R1,INNER            ;UPDATE INDEX CHECK LOOP
                                        ;COMPLETE
;CHECK FLAG TO DETERMINE IF ANY ELEMENTS WERE SWAPPED IN PRESENT
;ITERATION. IF NO ELEMENTS WERE SWAPPED THEN SORTING IS COMPLETED.
;                                       ;
CHECK_FLAG:                             ;
         DECL    R0                     ;
         TSTB    FLAG                   ;WERE ANY ELEMENTS SWAPPED?
         BNEQ    OUTER                  ; NO: ARRAY IS NOW SORTED
SORT_COMPLETED:                         ;
         $EXIT_S                        ;TERMINATE PROGRAM
         .END    BUBBLE_SORT
```

Figure 5.5   Bubble sort using index mode

the register specified will be used. This mode of addressing is called *displacement addressing*. In a sense, relative addressing is just a special case of the displacement addressing, where the value of the R field is F (hex). The effective address calculation for displacement addressing is more straightforward since the value in a register, unlike that in PC, remains unchanged during the instruction interpretation. The syntax of displacement addressing is

displacement(Rn)

where the displacement can be a constant, a symbol representing a constant, or a label. Rn can be any general register other than PC. For example, Figure 5.6 illustrates the displacement mode using the instruction

```
MOVW    ^X24(RI),R2
```

If, before the execution of the instruction,

R1:   0 0 0 0 1 2 3 4

R2:   0 0 0 0 0 0 0 0

```
memory loc.   cont
  00001258     00
  00001259     20
  0000125A     00
  0000125B     00
     :          :
  00002000     CD
  00002001     AB
     :          :
```

then after the execution of the instruction, the contents of R2 will be

R2:   0 0 0 0 2 0 0 0

Figure 5.6 Displacement mode

As in relative addressing mode, we may also have byte displacement, word displacement, and longword displacement.

The codes for the mode specifiers are the same as those for the corresponding relative addressing modes. The value in the R field is, of course, different. The operand specifier formats are as follows:

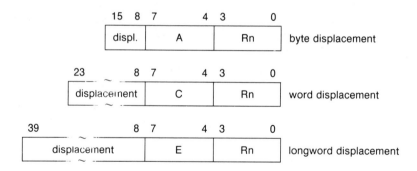

Additionally, the displacement mode can also be combined with the deferred mode to form *displacement deferred addressing mode.* The codes for the mode specifiers are the same as those for the corresponding relative deferred mode: B, D, and F for byte, word, and longword displacement, respectively. If the instruction in Figure 5.6 is changed to

```
MOVW    @X̂24(R1),R2
```

then, using the same memory and register contents as shown in Figure 5.6, the contents of R2 after the execution of the instruction will be

```
R2:    0 0 0 0 A B C D
```

Consider another example in which we combine the displacement deferred mode with the index mode:

```
ADDL    @X̂1C(R7)[R5],R0
```

If, before instruction execution, the contents of the registers are

```
R0:    0 0 C B A 9 8 8
R5:    0 0 0 0 0 0 0 3
R7:    0 0 0 0 1 0 0 0
```

then, using the same contents in memory locations 101C–1023 as shown in Figure 5.4, we will obtain the same sum in R0 (01000000). The contents of R7, however, will not be changed in this case (00001000).

When assembling an instruction using the displacement mode, if the MACRO assembler encounters a symbol whose value is unknown, it will assume a range for the displacement (word displacement in this case). If the actual distance turns out to be greater than the assumed range, the assembler will mark the instruction with an error indication. If the programmer knows the displacement value, he can help the assembler by specifying the range with the string B̂, Ŵ, or L̂ inserted in front of the address to indicate byte, word, or longword displacement, respectively.

Program Counter Addressing

We saw earlier that relative addressing is realized by using the contents of the PC as a reference point. We also understand that in the VAX-11, relative addressing is implemented by using the displacement addressing mode with PC as the base address register. This is an example of *program counter addressing*. There are other addressing modes which, when the PC is used, will produce meaningful desirable effects. Table 5.3 summarizes all such addressing modes.

As we see from Table 5.3, the immediate and absolute addressing modes are implemented through the use of autoincrement and autoincrement deferred mode, respectively. We can see how such desired effects are achieved if we examine the instruction decoding process. Consider the following instruction:

```
MOVW    Iˆ#X019B,R2
```

Its machine code is

```
52 01 9B 8F B0
```

In immediate addressing, after the CPU fetches the first byte of the operand specifier (8F), the PC will be pointing to the byte immediately following (9B). Now the autoincrement mode tells the CPU to use the contents of the register specified in the R field, which in this case is the PC, as the address from which the operand is fetched. Since the byte(s) following the mode specifier byte are the constant specified in the instruction, the correct operand is used. After the operand is fetched, the autoincrement mode advances the contents of the addressed register by the size of the operand, which means that the PC will be pointing to the next item to be processed.

In the case of absolute addressing, since the mode specifier indicates autoincrement deferred addressing, the control unit will use the contents of the longword following the mode specifier byte as the address of the operand, which is exactly what absolute addressing is. Again, the contents of PC will be incremented to the next byte once the current operand is fetched.

Table 5.3   PC Addressing

Mode	Name	Assembler Syntax	Operand Specifier Format
8	immediate	Iˆ# constant	const. (1-8 bytes) 8F
9	absolute	@ # address	address (4 bytes) 9F
A	byte relative	Bˆaddress	disp. (1 byte) AF
B	byte rel. def.	@Bˆaddress	disp. (1 byte) BF
C	word relative	Wˆaddress	disp. (2 bytes) CF
D	word rel. def.	@Wˆaddress	disp. (2 bytes) DF
E	longword rel.	Lˆaddress	disp. (4 bytes) EF
F	lgwd. rel. def.	@Lˆaddress	disp. (4 bytes) FF

Branch Addressing

For the group of branch instructions on the VAX-11, the address of the branch target is specified in a manner quite different from what we have seen so far. First, since there is only one way to specify the target address, no mode specifier byte is required or used. The method of addressing is similar to byte relative addressing or, in a few exceptional cases (such as BRW), to word relative addressing. In either case the symbolic target address will be used in the source program. In the corresponding machine code, a 1-byte (or 2-byte) displacement will be used:

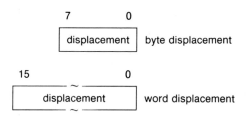

It should be pointed out that the jump (JMP) instruction is different from the branch instructions in that the addressing mode of the JMP instruction is not limited to the relative mode. One can use any addressing mode to specify the target location. As a result, one can branch to anywhere in his program using the JMP instruction. For example,

```
JMP   NEXT        ;branch to NEXT
JMP   @POINTER    ;target address stored
                  ;at location POINTER
JMP   (R6)        ;target address in R6
JMP   TABLE[R2]   ;target address at
                  ;TABLE+<4*(R2)>
```

5.3 Summary

All the addressing modes available on the VAX-11 are discussed in this chapter. The different addressing modes are designed to facilitate accessing data under different circumstances. They simplify the creation of some data structures and make the implementation of some algorithms easier. Examples presented in this and subsequent chapters attempt to demonstrate some of these cases. The key in learning assembly language programming, however, is practice. The more exercise one has, the better one will be in writing assembly language programs. Table 5.4 summarizes the VAX-11 addressing modes:

Table 5.4   Summary of VAX-11 Addressing Modes

Mode	Operand Specifier	Assembler Symbol	Indexable
Register	5 R*n*	Rn	no
Register deferred	6 R*n*	(Rn)	R*n*
Literal	00–3F	S^ # constant	no
Immediate	8 F	I^ # constant	no
Autoincrement	8 R*n*	(Rn) +	R*x*
Autoincrement deferred	9 R*n*	@ (Rn) +	R*x*
Autodecrement	7 R*n*	− (Rn)	R*x*
Index	4 R*n*	base-addr [Rn]	no
Displacement	A C R*n* E	B^ W^ displ. (Rn) L^	R*n*
Displacement deferred	B D R*n* F	B^ @W^ displ. (Rn) L^	R*n*
Relative	A C F E	B^ W^ address L^	R*n*
Relative deferred	B D F F	B^ @W^ address L^	R*n*
Absolute	9 F	@ # address	R*n*

Rn = 0 − E; Rx = 0 − E; n ≠ x

EXERCISES

1. Explain direct addressing and relative addressing. Why does the VAX-11 use relative addressing instead of direct addressing?

2. Explain immediate addressing and absolute addressing. How are these two addressing modes implemented on the VAX-11?

3. If the contents of registers R0, R1, R2, R3, and R4 and the contents of memory locations 1000 (hex)-1013 (hex) are as shown, what will their contents be after each of the following instructions is executed? Consider each case separately; that is, use the same data at the start of each instruction. Also, every instruction starts at location 2000 (hex).

```
R0:    00001000    R1:    00001010
R2:    FFFFEDB8    R3:    FFFFFEAB
R4:    00000002
```

Label	Memory Addr.	Contents
VAR1:	00001000	10
	00001001	10
	00001002	00
	00001003	00
	00001004	48
	00001005	12
	00001006	00
	00001007	00
VAR2:	00001008	FF
	00001009	EE
	0000100A	AA
	0000100B	00
	0000100C	22
	0000100D	44
	0000100E	88
	0000100F	FF
VAR3:	00001010	00
	00001011	10
	00001012	00
	00001013	00

a. ADDL   R0,R1
b. ADDL   (R1),(R0)
c. ADDL   R2,R3
d. ADDL   (R0),R3
e. MOVL   VAR2,R2
f. ADDL   VAR1+4,R2
g. SUBL   VAR3-4,R2
h. MOVAL   VAR2,(R0)
i. ADDL   #1,VAR2
j. ADDL   VAR3,VAR1
k. MOVAB   (R0)+,-(R1)
l. ADDL   VAR1[R4],R0
m. ADDL   ^X10(R0),(R0)
n. ADDL   @VAR1,VAR3
o. MOVB   (R0)+,(R0)+
p. MOVW   (R0)+,-(R0)
q. ADDB   ^X10(R0)[R4],R1
r. ADDL   ^X8(R0)[R4],R1
s. ADDW   @^X1165(R3)[R4],R1
t. ADDL   @^X1165(R3)[R4],R1

4. Assemble each of the instructions in Exercise 3 into a machine language instruction.

5. Examine the following MACRO statements and point out if there is any error in each:

a. ADDL   #3,PC
b. MOVL   R1,#10
c. INCL   R5[R6]
d. MOVB   #300,R2
e. BRB   (R0)
f. MOVL   (R5) [R5],R9

```
g. ADDL     #3(R4),R3
h. MOVL     (R5)+[R5],R11
i. MOVL     @-(R8),@(R8)+
j. MOVL  ,  #3[R5],3(R4)[R5]
```

6. Consider the following code segment in VAX-11 MACRO language:

```
            :
START:   DECL   R1
         BEQL   EXIT
         ADDL   #3,R2
            :
            :
EXIT:    MOVL   R2,A
            :
```

Supposing the instruction START is at location 1000 (hex) and the instruction EXIT at location 2000 (hex), point out any error the segment may
have. Write an equivalent segment of code that works correctly.

7. What are the contents of registers R6, R7, and R8 (in hex) and the condition codes *after* the execution of each of the following instructions:

```
           .ENTRY   BEGIN,0
ONE:       MOVL     #272,R6
TWO:       MOVL     #560,R7
THREE:     MULL3    R6,R7,R8
FOUR:      MOVW     R8,R7
FIVE:      MOVB     R8,R6
           $EXIT_S
           .END     BEGIN
```

8. Write a program in MACRO to find the number i such that $i^2 \leq N < (i+1)^2$,
where N is a given integer.

9. Write a program to count the number of times each letter of the alphabet
appears in a given sentence. Consider the sentence is stored in a buffer
BUFF that holds a maximum of 132 characters.

Chapter 6

Subroutines

ONE OF the most important lessons learned from experience in programming over the last thirty years is that a program should be organized and written in such a way that it is easy to understand and maintain. Maintaining a program involves activities such as improving and modifying it to accommodate the changing needs of users. One effective way to achieve the goal of maintainability and readability is to divide a problem into a number of subproblems and then program and test each subproblem individually. The programs for each subproblem are called *subroutines*. Each is simpler than the original program and therefore easier to construct and debug. Since each subroutine solves one well-defined portion of the original problem, it is also easier for people who read the program to follow the solution of the problem. Today, using subroutines as building blocks in the construction of programs is a widely accepted industry practice.

The subroutine was one of the most important concepts developed in the early days of computer science. Originally the idea was to save programmer time and effort by avoiding the repeated writing of the same sequence of instructions at various places in a program. Subroutines also saved precious memory space, since only one copy of the sequence of instructions was kept. For example, it might be necessary to compute the square root of numbers at different places in a program. Since the same sequence of instructions could be used to evaluate the square root of any positive real number, only one copy of the square-root-evaluating sequence need be written and kept in the memory. Although saving programmer effort and memory space are still valid reasons to construct subroutines in a program, the advantages of maintainability and readability provided by the subroutines are so overwhelming that instruction sequences are often made into subroutines even though they may be used no more than once in executing a program.

Because a subroutine can be called from many places within a program, it is impossible to know precisely the environment from which it was called. It is necessary to construct the subroutine in a manner that provides some mechanism for returning program control to the instruction immediately following the point of call once the subroutine finishes its execution. There should also be a well-defined interface—that is, a clear understanding between the calling program and the subroutine so that necessary parameters can be passed from one to the other. Once the subroutine is invoked, it should run independently of the calling program and should not affect the calling program in any way except for returning results, if any, when the execution is completed.

A subroutine so constructed has several advantages:

1. Since it can run independently, it can also be tested and debugged without involving other parts of the large program. It needs only a simple calling program, or driver, that supplies the input parameters and receives the results. This not only greatly simplifies debugging, but also facilitates the division of labor. A team of programmers can work together on a problem each developing one or more subroutines independently.

2. A subroutine is useful beyond a single program. Any subsequent program that needs the same function can use it without change. In fact, many standard mathematical functions are written as subroutines and made available to any user of the system.

3. The internal structure of a subroutine can be changed without affecting the calling program(s). Suppose that after a program has been used for some time, a better algorithm is discovered to evaluate a function. If the function is modularized as a subroutine, then the new code using the improved algorithm can be written to replace the old one. The calling programs are not disturbed in any way.

   In fact, this change need not be limited to replacing one subroutine by another. A subroutine can be replaced by a device that performs the same function. Hardware for performing floating-point arithmetic operations is one example.

4. Subroutines written in different programming languages can be incorporated into one program. This gives the user a means to code his algorithm using the most appropriate programming language. In fact, subroutines written in assembly language are often used in programs written in a high-level language such as FORTRAN to gain efficiency.

Subroutines are so useful that all computers today are designed with specific instructions to facilitate their implementation. The

VAX-11 provides two general forms of subroutine calls. In VAX-11 terminology, these are known as the *subroutine call* and the *procedure call*. Henceforth, we shall use these terms to distinguish between the two types of subroutine calls. We will use the generic term *subprogram* when there is no need to distinguish between the two.

6.1 Stacks

Before discussing the details of calling subprograms, we should take a closer look at the concept of the stack. In all contemporary computers this construct plays an important role in subprogram linking and interfacing.

As pointed out in Chapter 2, a stack is a storage device from which data can be accessed in a last in, first out manner. Because the cost of building such a device is high, stacks are usually simulated through programming as a data structure in the main memory. In the VAX-11 a stack is implemented with the help of a register and some stack-manipulating instructions. A block of contiguous memory locations in the main memory is reserved to simulate the column of registers of the stack. The convention used in the VAX-11 is such that the memory location with the highest address in the reserved block is considered the bottom of the stack, with the stack growing toward the memory location of lower addresses. The VAX-11 operating system VMS provides each user program with a stack called the *user stack*. One of the sixteen general registers, the *stack pointer* (SP) is used to keep track of the top of the stack—the *location* at which the last item of information pushed on the stack is stored. Originally, when the stack is empty, the SP is pointing to a memory location just beyond the bottom of the stack. As data are pushed in, the contents of the SP will be decremented so that the location pointed to by the updated SP is always the last item stored. Conversely, when the stack is popped, the data will be fetched from the location pointed to by the SP. The SP will then be incremented so that the next item on the stack will now be on the top of the stack. It is evident that instructions such as

```
MOVx    SOURCE,-(SP)          ;push SOURCE to stack
MOVx    (SP)+,DESTINATION     ;pop stack to DESTINATION
```

transfer data in or out of the stack and manage the stack pointer properly. The VAX-11, however, has several instructions specifically designed for manipulating the stack. Besides, as we shall see, the subprogram calls use the stack implicitly.

Table 6.1 shows the major stack manipulation instructions avail-

Table 6.1 Stack Manipulation Instructions

Mnemonic	Data types	Operation
PUSHAx	B,W,L,Q,O	−(SP)←src address
PUSHR	L	push ⎰ contents of register
POPR	L	pop ⎱ in/from stack
PUSHL	L	−(SP) ← src
POPL	L	dst ← (SP)+

able on the VAX-11. PUSHL deposits a longword into the stack, and PUSHAx deposits the address (also a longword) of an operand into the stack. Strictly speaking, the VAX-11 does not have an instruction for POPL; but the MACRO assembler allows the user to use such a mnemonic and automatically translates it to a "MOVL (SP)+,DES-TINATION" instruction.

The PUSHR and POPR instructions transfer a set of longwords between the stack and the general registers. The registers affected are specified in the operand field in the form of a mask. In the machine language instruction the mask is a 16-bit vector, with each bit representing a register in descending order from left to right. That is, the leftmost (MSB) bit of the vector representing PC, the second leftmost bit representing SP, and so on, and the rightmost bit R0. If a particular bit is set in the vector, a data transfer (push or pop) will occur between the stack and the register specified. In the MACRO assembly language, the bit vector can be specified in either of the following ways:

1. By naming the registers in a mask specification expression; for example:

```
PUSHR    #M<R1,R2,R7,R10,R11,SP>
POPR     #M<R0,R4,AP,FP>
```

2. By specifying the bit pattern directly using immediate addressing; for example:

```
PUSHR    #X4C86
POPR     #B0011000000010001
```

As the reader may have noticed, the two foregoing PUSHR (POPR) instructions push (pop) the same registers into (out of) the stack.

When executing the PUSHR instruction, the VAX-11 scans the mask from left to right and deposits into the stack the contents of the highest register first. The reverse is true when the POPR instruction is executed. This conforms to the operation characteristic of the stack. Using these two instructions, one can conveniently save and restore the contents of a set of registers. It should be pointed out, however, that the contents of PC will not be moved by the PUSHR or POPR instructions.

A programmer does not have to limit his use of the stack to the one provided by the system (the user stack). He can create his own stacks within his program by reserving blocks of contiguous memory for that purpose. Then, by using the autoincrement (autodecrement) addressing mode, he can manipulate his own stacks. For example:

```
NEWST:  .BLKL    100              ;RESERVE STACK SPACE
                 :
                 :
        MOVAL    NEWST+400,R8     ;SET R8 AS STACK POINTER
        MOVL     ITEM1,-(R8)      ;PUSH ITEM1 TO STACK
        MOVW     ITEM2,-(R8)      ;PUSH ITEM2 TO STACK
                 :
        MOVW     (R8)+,ITEM2      ;POP STACK TO RETRIEVE ITEM2
                 :
```

6.2 Subroutine Calls

The simplest way to call a subroutine in the VAX-11 is to use one of the two Branch to SuBroutine (BSB) instructions available. They are:

```
BSBB    Branch to Subroutine with Byte Displacement
BSBW    Branch to Subroutine with Word Displacement
```

As with the BRB (BRW) instruction, the BSBB (BSBW) transfers control to the target address, which is within a byte (word) displacement. The BSBB (BSBW) instruction also saves the contents of PC (which is pointing to the beginning byte of the next instruction of the calling program) in the user stack.

Additionally, there is also a Jump to SuBroutine instruction

```
JSB    Destination Address
```

which provides more general addressing capability for the branch target. In all cases, a Return from SuBroutine (RSB) instruction is used in the subroutine to return control to the calling program. The RSB instruction transfers the return address, which is previously pushed into the stack by the BSBx or JSB instruction, back to the PC.

The example in Figure 6.1 shows a subroutine call in which the subroutine is included as part of the main program. The subroutine is placed in front of the body of the main program together with the data definition. Another place one can put the subroutines is at the

```
;THIS IS AN EXAMPLE OF SUBROUTINE CALL; THE MAIN PROGRAM
;CALLS ON A SUBROUTINE TO COMPARE EACH ELEMENT IN TABLE3
;IN TURN WITH THE ELEMENTS IN TABLE1 UNTIL A MATCH IS FOUND,
;THEN THE SUBROUTINE IS CALLED AGAIN TO MATCH AN ELEMENT
;ELEM WITH MEMBERS OF TABLE2. IF BOTH SEARCHES ARE SUCCESS-
;FUL, A POSITIVE NUMBER WILL BE RETURNED IN R6, OTHERWISE
;R6 WILL CONTAIN THE VALUE -1. DATA I/O IS OMITTED.
;
SIZE1=10
SIZE2=100
SIZE3=20
TABLE1: .BLKW    SIZE1
TABLE2: .BLKW    SIZE2
TABLE3: .BLKW    SIZE3
ELEM:   .BLKW    1
;
; SUBROUTINE TO SEARCH A TABLE
;
;THIS IS A SUBROUTINE THAT SEARCHES THROUGH A TABLE OF
;ELEMENTS EACH 16 BITS LONG TO LOCATE A MATCH WITH A KEY.
;THE KEY IS STORED IN R4;
;THE BEGINNING ADDRESS OF THE TABLE IN R3;
;THE LENGTH OF THE TABLE IN R2.
;IF NO MATCH IS FOUND, R6 WILL BE SET TO -1 OTHERWISE
;R6 CONTAINS A POSITIVE NUMBER.
;
SEARCH: CLRL     R6
LOOP:   CMPW     (R3)[R6],R4        ;COMPARE NEXT ELEM.
        BEQL     FOUND
        INCL     R6                 ;UPDATE POINTER
        CMPL     R2,R6              ;END OF TABLE
        BGTR     LOOP
        MOVL     #-1,R6             ;NOT FOUND
FOUND:  RSB
;
;ENTRY POINT OF MAIN PROGRAM
;
        .ENTRY   MAIN,0             ;
        MOVL     #SIZE1,R2          ;LOAD PARAMETERS
        MOVAW    TABLE1,R3          ;FOR SUBROUTINE CALL
        CLRL     R5
NEXT:   MOVW     TABLE3[R5],R4      ;LOAD KEY
        BSBB     SEARCH             ;CALL SUBROUTINE
        CMPL     R6,#-1
        BNEQ     MATCH              ;FOUND MATCH
        INCL     R5
        CMPW     #SIZE3,R5
        BLEQ     EXIT               ;NO MATCH
        BRB      NEXT               ;TRY NEXT ELEMENT
MATCH:  MOVL     #SIZE2,R2          ;LOAD PARAMETERS
        MOVAW    TABLE2,R3          ;FOR SUBROUTINE CALL
        MOVW     ELEM,R4            ;USE ELEM AS KEY
        BSBW     SEARCH
EXIT:   $EXIT_S
        .END     MAIN
```

Figure 6.1 Example of a subroutine call

end of the main program, right after the $EXIT_S statement but before the .END directive.

One of the major advantages of using subprograms, however, is that subprograms can be written, assembled, and debugged independently. Figure 6.2 shows the same example except that the sub-

```
;THIS IS AN EXAMPLE OF SUBROUTINE CALL; THE MAIN PROGRAM
;CALLS ON A SUBROUTINE TO COMPARE EACH ELEMENT IN TABLE3
;WITH THE ELEMENTS IN TABLE1 UNTIL A MATCH IS FOUND, THEN
;THE SUBROUTINE IS CALLED AGAIN TO MATCH AN ELEMENT ELEM
;WITH MEMBERS OF TABLE2. IF BOTH SEARCHES ARE SUCCESSFUL,
;A POSITIVE NUMBER WILL BE RETURNED IN R6, OTHERWISE
;R6 WILL CONTAIN THE VALUE -1.
;
;
SIZE1=10
SIZE2=100
SIZE3=20
        .EXTERNAL-
                SEARCH                 ;SYMBOL NOT DEFINED LOCALLY
TABLE1: .BLKW   SIZE1
TABLE2: .BLKW   SIZE2
TABLE3: .BLKW   SIZE3
ELEM:   .BLKW   1
        .ENTRY  MAIN,0
        MOVL    #SIZE1,R2              ;LOAD PARAMETERS
        MOVAW   TABLE1,R3             ;FOR SUBROUTINE CALL
        CLRL    R5
NEXT:   MOVW    TABLE3[R5],R4         ;LOAD KEY
        BSBB    SEARCH                ;CALL SUBROUTINE
        CMPL    R6,#-1
        BNEQ    MATCH                 ;FOUND MATCH
        INCL    R5
        CMPW    #SIZE3,R5
        BLEQ    EXIT                  ;NO MATCH
        BRB     NEXT                  ;TRY NEXT ELEMENT
;
MATCH:  MOVL    #SIZE2,R2             ;LOAD PARAMETERS
        MOVAW   TABLE2,R3            ;FOR SUBROUTINE CALL
        MOVW    ELEM,R4              ;USE ELEM AS KEY
        BSBW    SEARCH
;
;
EXIT:   $EXIT_S
        .END    MAIN
;
;                                    (a)
;
;
; SUBROUTINE TO SEARCH A TABLE
;
;THIS IS A SUBROUTINE THAT SEARCHES THROUGH A TABLE OF
;ELEMENTS EACH 16 BITS LONG TO LOCATE A MATCH WITH A KEY.
;THE KEY IS STORED IN R4;
;THE BEGINNING ADDRESS OF THE TABLE IN R3;
;THE LENGTH OF THE TABLE IN R2.
;IF NO MATCH IS FOUND, R6 WILL BE SET TO -1 OTHERWISE
;R6 CONTAINS A POSITIVE NUMBER.
;
SEARCH::-                            ;GLOBAL LABEL
        CLRL    R6                   ;ENTRY POINT OF SUBR.
LOOP:   CMPW    (R3)[R6],R4          ;COMPARE NEXT ELEM.
        BEQL    FOUND
        INCL    R6                   ;UPDATE POINTER
        CMPL    R2,R6                ;END OF TABLE
        BGTR    LOOP
        MOVL    #-1,R6               ;NOT FOUND
FOUND:  RSB
;
        .END                   (b)
```

Figure 6.2 Example of a subroutine call with subroutine assembled separately: (a) main program; (b) subroutine

routine is separated from the main program. In fact, they are stored in separate files and assembled separately. Comparing Figure 6.2 with Figure 6.1, we see that a line is added in the main program:

```
.EXTERNAL-
          SEARCH
```

This directive tells the assembler or anyone else reading the program that the symbol SEARCH is not defined locally and that the linker should locate the item during linking time.[1] (The default mode of operation of the MACRO assembler is that any symbol that is not defined locally is assumed to be a global symbol; that is, it is defined somewhere else and made available to the program module referring to it. It is, therefore, normally not necessary to declare any symbol external; but most other assemblers do require the declaration of external symbols via a directive. The declaration does help alert the reader to the fact that other program module(s) are needed for the execution of the program at hand.)

In the subroutine of Figure 6.2, two modifications are made: first, an .END directive is added at the end of the subroutine to inform the assembler of the end of the program; second, the entry point of the subroutine—in this case the statement labeled SEARCH—is made *global* by the use of the double colon (::) following the word SEARCH. Most assemblers use a directive to declare all the symbols that are made available to other programs. The MACRO assembler also has such a directive: .GLOBAL. The manufacturer of VAX-11, however, encourages the use of the double colon (::), or, in the case of a direct assignment statement, the double equal sign (==). It should also be noted that the statement $EXIT_S is absent in the subroutine.

One important aspect of subroutine calls not discussed so far is the passing of parameters from the calling program to the called subroutine. Since both programs are using the same set of general registers, one simple way to transmit the parameters is to use those registers. As seen in the foregoing examples, registers R2, R3, and R4 are loaded with proper data before the BSBB(BSBW) instruction is executed. It should be noted, however, that although it is convenient to use the general registers for this purpose, the practice can also create problems. It is particularly important that information left in the registers by the calling program not be altered by the subroutine without the knowledge and consent of the calling program. The subroutine documentation should state which, if any, of the registers will be used by the subroutine (R2,

---

[1]For a discussion of the linker and linking, see Chapter 7.

R3, R4, and R6 in our example). If the contents of several registers need to be saved and restored, one can use the PUSHR and POPR instructions.

If the number of parameters needed exceeds the number of available registers, other ways of passing the parameters must be devised. One common method is to use indirect addressing. With this method, the addresses of the arguments will be stored immediately following the subroutine call instruction; for example:

The calling program:

```
ARG_1:  .LONG           1234
ARG_2:  .WORD           567
                :
ARG_N:  .BLKL           1
                :
        .ENTRY          MAIN,0
                :
        BSBW            N_ARG_SUBR
        .ADDRESS        ARG_1
        .ADDRESS        ARG_2
                :
        .ADDRESS        ARG_N    ;RESULT
        (next executable instr.)
                :
        .END
```

The subroutine:

```
TEMP_1: .BLKL   1
TEMP_2: .BLKW   1
             :
TEMP_N: .BLKL   1
N_ARG_SUBR::-
        POPL    R8                ;GET ARG POINTER
        MOVL    @(R8)+,TEMP_1     ;MOVE ARGUMENTS TO
        MOVW    @(R8)+,TEMP_2     ;LOCAL STORAGES
             :
        MOVL    TEMP_N,@(R8)+     ;MOVE RESULT BACK
        PUSHL   R8
        RSB
```

The BSBW instruction places the contents of PC into the user stack. When the BSBW instruction is executed, the address that is deposited on the top of the stack is the address immediately following the instruction. This, however, is the beginning byte of the address of ARG_1. As a result, the SP now points to the address of the memory location that contains the address of ARG_1. Because of this double-pointer idea, when the MOVL @(R8)+,TEMP_1, instruction is executed in the subroutine, the first argument is copied into TEMP_1, a local memory location of the subroutine. The autoincrement addressing mode advances the contents of R8 to the address of the next argument. This process is repeated until the last item of the argument list has been accessed. In the example, the subroutine places a result in location TEMP_N. R8 now points to the next executable instruction following the subroutine call. When we push the contents of R8 back to the user stack and then exit from the subroutine, control will be returned to the proper location of the calling program. It should be noted that R8 is chosen arbitrarily in the foregoing discussion.

The foregoing process is a very common technique. The reader is urged to go through the code using paper and pencil to be sure he understands each phase of the sequence.

6.3 Procedure Calls

The procedure call differs from the subroutine call in that it provides a uniform way to pass parameters and save the contents of the registers. It also automatically saves part of the processor status word (PSW) for the calling program. There are two instructions to invoke a procedure:

```
CALLG   arg-list,proc-name     ;call with general arg list
CALLS   arg-count,proc-name    ;call with stack arg list
```

The difference between the two calls lies in the way the parameters are stored and handled. In the former, the arg-list is the address of a data structure called the *argument list* that consists of the arguments to be passed to the procedure (see Figure 6.3a). In the latter, the number of arguments is specified in the call instruction itself. The arguments themselves are stored in the user stack by the calling program before the call.

The procedures are written in the format:

```
        :
        :
(data definition if necessary)
        :
        :
.ENTRY proc-name, ^M<Rx,Ry, . . . . . . .Rz>
        :
        :
(instructions)
        :
        :
RET
```

An alternative format is:

```
                :
                :
            (data definition if necessary)
                :
                :
proc-name:      .WORD   ^M<Rx,Ry, . . . . . . .Rz>
                :
                :
            (instructions)
                :
                :
            RET
```

where proc-name is the procedure name; and $\hat{}$M<Rx,Ry . . . . Rz> is a mask in which each x, y, or z is an integer between 2 and 11. In

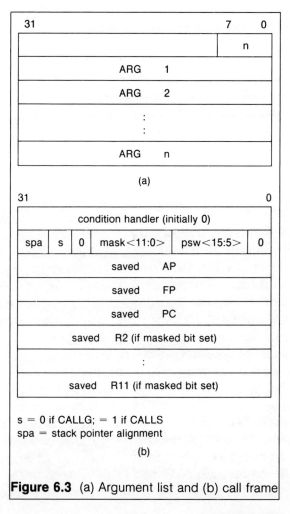

Figure 6.3 (a) Argument list and (b) call frame

other words, the mask can specify any number of the registers from R2 to R11. Whenever a register is named in the mask, it will be saved in the user stack. The VAX-11 designates R0 and R1 as the registers to be used to pass results back from the procedure to the calling program and does not allow the procedure to save the contents of R0 and R1. Therefore, the names of these two registers should never appear in the mask. If no register needs to be saved, a zero mask can be indicated by one of the following:

```
.ENTRY    proc-name,^M<>
.ENTRY    proc-name,0
```

Comparing these formats with those for a MACRO main program, as discussed in Chapter 4, the reader will notice that they are practically identical. In fact, a main program is treated as a procedure of the operating system and is invoked as one when the operating system is ready to run that program. The difference between the formats of a procedure and a main program are:

1. The main program uses a $EXIT_S macro to return control to the operating system, whereas a procedure uses RET to return control to the calling program.
2. The mask is equal to 0 for the main program but is usually some nonzero value for a procedure.

The VAX-11 employs several registers to facilitate the implementation of the procedure call: AP, FP, and SP.

The AP (for *argument pointer*) stores the beginning address of the argument list (Figure 6.3a). The argument list is an array of data, normally consisting of longwords. The first item on the list is a longword, the rightmost byte of which is used to specify the number of arguments in the list. This is followed by the arguments themselves or addresses pointing to the arguments. In the case of the CALLG instruction, the location of the argument list is specified in the instruction. In the case of the CALLS, the argument list is pushed into the user stack by the calling program.

The FP (for *frame pointer*) stores the beginning address of a data structure called the *call frame*. The call frame consists of an array of longwords that stores the contents of the registers specified by the mask as well as that of the AP, FP, PC, and part of the PSW before a procedure is entered. Figure 6.3b shows the details of a call frame.

Each time a procedure is called, a call frame will be created and stored in the user stack. The updated contents of SP will then be transferred to the FP before control is transferred to the procedure. When exiting from the procedure, the contents of the registers will be restored by popping the call frame out of the stack and returning its contents to the original registers.

RET is the mnemonic for the instruction RETurn from procedure. It restores the CPU to its original status just before the procedure call. Among other things, the RET instruction restores the AP, FP, PC, and other registers whose contents are saved in the call frame when the procedure is invoked. The condition codes (bits 0–3) in the PSW are reset to zero, and the rest of the PSW is restored.[2] In the process the call frame is eliminated, and the SP is pointing to the same location it did prior to the procedure call. Finally, if the procedure call is a CALLS, then the argument list, which is stored in the stack, is discarded.

Figure 6.4 shows an example of procedure call using the CALLG instruction; procedure SEARCH requires four arguments with the first, second, and fourth arguments being longwords and the third argument a word. In the main program the procedure is invoked in two places, each using a different argument list, as shown in Figure 6.4a. Although the third argument in the example requires only a word, it is nonetheless advisable to use a longword in the argument list. The reason for this will be apparent when we examine the CALLS instruction.

The VAX-11 executes the CALLS instruction as follows: it assumes the arguments are stored in the user stack with the first argument on the top of the stack. The first thing it does is to push the number of arguments supplied in the CALLS instruction into the stack to complete the argument list. It then transfers the contents of SP to a temporary storage location. Next the mask at the entry point of the procedure is examined, and the contents of the designated registers are saved in the stack, followed by the contents of PC, FP, and AP, along with the rest of the call frame, as shown in Figure 6.3. The contents of the updated SP are then sent to FP. The contents of SP previously saved in the temporary location (the beginning address of the argument list) are transferred to AP. Finally, control is transferred to the procedure at a location 2 bytes beyond the entry mask.

When returning from the CALLS call, the RET instruction automatically deletes the argument list from the stack by removing four times the number of bytes from the stack as the value indicated in the first longword of the argument list. In other words, VAX-11 assumes that every argument occupies a longword. Since normally one wants to build a procedure that could be called by both CALLG and CALLS, it is better to make every item in the argument list a longword.

---

[2]Actually, a fifth bit, the T (for trap) bit, is also cleared. The function of T, however, is outside the scope of this book.

Figure 6.5 shows how a procedure can be invoked by a CALLS instruction. The argument list is first pushed down into the user stack before CALLS is executed. Note that the last argument is pushed down first. Why? Procedure SEARCH in Figure 6.4b can be used here directly without any modification.

From the examples, it should be evident that when the argument list is fixed and known before the call, the CALLG instruction involves less overhead with respect to execution time. To use CALLS,

```
;THIS IS AN EXAMPLE OF PROCEDURE CALL WITH GENERAL
;ARGUMENT LIST. THE MAIN PROGRAM CALLS ON THE PROCEDURE
;SEARCH TO COMPARE EACH ELEMENT IN TABLE3 WITH THE
;ELEMENTS IN TABLE1 UNTIL A MATCH IS FOUND. THE PROCEDURE
;IS THEN CALLED AGAIN TO COMPARE AN ELEMENT ELEM WITH
;MEMBERS OF TABLE2. THE INPUT OF DATA IS OMITTED.


SIZE1=10
SIZE2=100
SIZE3=20
TABLE1:  .BLKW    SIZE1
TABLE2:  .BLKW    SIZE2
TABLE3:  .BLKW    SIZE3
ELEM:    .BLKW    1
RES:     .LONG    1
FLAG:    .LONG    1
PARMT:   .LONG    4
         .LONG    SIZE2
         .ADDRESS-
                  TABLE2
TMPLT:   .BLKL    1
         .ADDRESS-
                  RES
ARGLIST:
         .LONG    4
         .LONG    SIZE1
         .ADDRESS-
                  TABLE1
KEY:     .BLKL    1
         .ADDRESS-
                  FLAG
;
         .ENTRY   MAIN,^M<>
         CLRW     R5                  ;INITIALIZE
NEXT:    MOVW     TABLE3[R5],KEY      ;USE NEXT ELEMENT
         CALLG    ARGLIST,SEARCH
         CMPL     FLAG,#-1            ;MATCH?
         BNEQ     MATCH
         INCL     R5                  ;NO
         CMPW     #SIZE3,R5
         BLEQ     EXIT                ;FAILED
         BRB      NEXT                ;LOOP BACK
;
MATCH:   MOVW     ELEM,TMPLT          ;LOAD KEY
         CALLG    PARMT,SEARCH
EXIT:    $EXIT_S  R0
         .END     MAIN
;
```

(a)

```
;THIS IS A PROCEDURE THAT SEARCHES THROUGH A TABLE
;OF ELEMENTS EACH 16 BITS LONG TO FIND A MATCH WITH
;KEY. IT REQUIRES 4 ARGUMENTS: 1. LENGTH OF TABLE;
;2. BEGINNING ADDRESS OF TABLE; 3. KEY TO MATCH; 4.
;RESULT OF SEARCH. IF THE SEARCH FAILS THE RESULT
;WILL RETURN A VALUE OF -1 TO THE CALLING PROGRAM,
;OTHERWISE A POSITIVE INTEGER WILL BE RETURNED.
;
TAB_SZ=4
TAB_ADD=8
KEY=12
RESULT=16
;
          .ENTRY  SEARCH,^M<R2,R3,R4,R6>  ;SAVE REGISTERS
          MOVL    TAB_SZ(AP),R2      ;R2=SIZE
          MOVL    TAB_ADD(AP),R3     ;R3 POINTS TO TABLE
          MOVL    KEY(AP),R4         ;R4 =SEARCH VALUE
          CLRL    R6
LOOP:     CMPW    (R3)[R6],R4        ;COMPARE NEXT ELEM.
          BEQL    FOUND
          INCL    R6                 ;UPDATE POINTER
          CMPL    R2,R6              ;END OF TABLE?
          BGTR    LOOP
          MOVL    #-1,R6             ;NOT FOUND
FOUND:    MOVL    R6,@RESULT(AP)
          RET
;
          .END
```
(b)

Figure 6.4 Example of procedure call with general argument list: (a) main
program; (b) procedure

it is necessary to move the argument list into the stack before the
procedure is invoked. If the values of the arguments are computed
dynamically during the program execution time, however, the local
situation determines which is a better way to invoke the procedure.
Usually, it takes less time to move the arguments into the user stack
than to an argument list. Also, as we shall see in Section 6.5, CALLS
enables us to implement a recursive procedure in a natural and
efficient way.

6.4 Call-by-Reference and Call-by-Value

In Section 6.3 we examined the structure of the argument list in a
procedure call. We note that a parameter in the argument list can be
either an actual parameter value or a memory address at which the
parameter's value is stored. Furthermore, in the case of the procedure being invoked by CALLS, the argument list is destroyed when
control is returned to the calling program. A moment's reflection
will convince us that unless an address is used as a parameter, the
procedure could not pass a value back to the calling program. The
method of passing a parameter by its value is known as *call-by-*

```
;THIS IS AN EXAMPLE OF PROCEDURE CALL WITH STACK
;ARGUMENT LIST. THE MAIN PROGRAM CALLS ON THE PROCEDURE
;SEARCH TO COMPARE EACH ELEMENT IN TABLE3 WITH THE
;ELEMENTS IN TABLE1 UNTIL A MATCH IS FOUND. THE PROCEDURE
;IS THEN CALLED AGAIN TO COMPARE AN ELEMENT ELEM WITH
;MEMBERS OF TABLE2. THE INPUT OF DATA IS OMITTED.


SIZE1=10
SIZE2=100
SIZE3=20
TABLE1:  .BLKW    SIZE1
TABLE2:  .BLKW    SIZE2
TABLE3:  .BLKW    SIZE3
FLAG:    .LONG    1
RES:     .LONG    1
ELEM:    .BLKW    1
;
         .ENTRY   MAIN,^M<>
         CLRL     R5                      ;INITIALIZE
NEXT:    PUSHAL   FLAG                    ;LOAD ARGUMENTS
         PUSHL    TABLE3[R5]              ;INTO USER STACK
         PUSHAL   TABLE1                  ;TO BUILD
         PUSHL    #SIZE1                  ;ARGUMENT LIST
         CALLS    #4,SEARCH
         CMPL     FLAG,#-1                ;MATCH?
         BNEQ     MATCH
         AOBLEQ   #SIZE3,R5,EXIT          ;LOOP CONTROL
         BRB      NEXT                    ;LOOP BACK
;
MATCH:   PUSHAL   RES                     ;LOAD 2ND SET
         PUSHL    ELEM                    ;OF ARGUMENTS
         PUSHAL   TABLE2                  ;TO USER
         PUSHL    #SIZE2                  ;STACK
         CALLS    #4,SEARCH
EXIT:    $EXIT_S
         .END     MAIN
;
```

Figure 6.5 Example of CALLS procedure call

value; passing a parameter by its address is known as *call-by-refer-ence* or *call-by-address.*

Call-by-value has the advantage of straightforwardness in concept and implementation. Although it is limited by not being able to pass results back to the calling program, it has the advantage of being able to protect those parameters from being unknowingly changed by the procedure, thereby producing undesirable side effects. In dealing with a large array, however, call-by-value is inefficient since one has to move the entire array into the argument list. In such cases, call-by-reference is more appropriate.

The simple example shown in Figure 6.6 should illustrate these points. Suppose we have a procedure that evaluates the function RESULT = I^I (I to the power of I) where I is a positive integer and $I^I < 2^{31}$, as it is shown in Fig. 6.6.

```
;PROCEDURE POWER HAS TWO PARAMETERS:  I  AND RESULT;
;I  IS A NON-ZERO POSITIVE INTEGER
;RESULT  IS CALLED BY REFERENCE.
;THE VALUE OF RESULT WILL BE SET TO 0 IF I≤0
            .ENTRY   POWER,^M<R7,R8>
            MOVL     4(AP),R7          ;FETCH I
            BLEQ     EXIT              ;I ≤ 0
            MOVL     R7,R8
LOOP:       DECL     4(AP)             ;KEEP COUNT
            BEQL     OUT               ;DONE?
            MULL     R7,R8
            BRB      LOOP
EXIT:       MOVL     #0,R8             ;I ≤ 0
OUT:        MOVL     R8,@8(AP)         ;RETURN RESULT
            RET
            .END
```

Figure 6.6   Example of a procedure using call-by-value and call-by-reference

In the calling program, we have

```
            :
            :
    PUSHAL   RESULT
    PUSHL    I
    CALLS    #2,POWER
            :
            :
```

The value of I is passed to the procedure while the address of RESULT is supplied. After the execution of the procedure, the value of RESULT is passed back to the calling program; but the value of I in the calling program is not affected no matter what is done in the procedure. Now suppose we change the procedure so that I is also called by reference, as shown in Figure 6.7.

```
;PROCEDURE POWER HAS TWO PARAMETERS:  I  AND RESULT;
;BOTH ARE CALLED BY REFERENCE.
            .ENTRY   POWER,^M<R7,R8>
            MOVL     @4(AP),R7         ;FETCH I
            BLEQ     EXIT              ;I ≤ 0
            MOVL     R7,R8
LOOP:       DECL     @4(AP)            ;KEEP COUNT
            BEQL     OUT               ;DONE?
            MULL     R7,R8
            BRB      LOOP
EXIT:       MOVL     #0,R8             ;I ≤ 0
OUT:        MOVL     R8,@8(AP)         ;RETURN RESULT
            RET
            .END
```

Figure 6.7   Example of a procedure that causes side effect

In the calling program, we now have

```
          :
          :
PUSHAL    RESULT
PUSHAL    I
CALLS     #2,POWER
          :
```

The value of I in the calling program is reduced to 0 after the execution of the procedure. It should be apparent that if RESULT is changed to call-by-value, the computed value of RESULT in the procedure will not be transmitted to the calling program.

6.5 Recursive Procedure

A function is said to be defined recursively if it is defined in terms of itself in some way. A well-known example of such a definition is that of the function factorial (n), where n is a positive integer. We say that if $n = 0$, then

factorial $(0) = 1$

Otherwise,

factorial $(n) = n *$ factorial $(n - 1)$

By repeated application of the definition, we obtain

$$\begin{aligned} \text{factorial } (n) &= n * \text{factorial } (n - 1) \\ &= n * (n - 1) * \text{factorial } (n - 2) \\ &= \text{etc.} \end{aligned}$$

Eventually we will reach the point at which $n = 0$, and we can terminate this process. Then

factorial $(n) = n * (n - 1) * (n - 2) \ldots * 2 * 1 * 1$

as it should be.

A recursive procedure is one that calls itself. A recursive function can be evaluated by means of a recursive procedure. Some programming languages (such as FORTRAN), however, do not allow the use of recursive subprograms. Many computers lack the hardware to implement one conveniently. This is because they do not have the facilities to save the return addresses of the multiple calls simultaneously. The stack, however, with its last in, first out mechanism, is ideally suited to handle recursive calls.

As an example of a recursive procedure, let us consider the case of finding the greatest common factor (GCF) of two integers. We can find the GCF of two integers *a* and *b* by comparing the two numbers. If they are equal, then the GCF is the number itself. If not, then we subtract the smaller number from the larger one and then repeat the process by comparing the difference with the smaller of the two original numbers. Thus we can write

If $|a - b| = 0$ then GCF $(a,b) = a$
Else GCF (a,b) = GCF $(|a - b|$, smaller $<a,b>)$

In MACRO, we can construct a procedure GCF as follows:

```
        .ENTRY   GCF,^M<>
        CMPL     4(AP),8(AP)      ;COMPARE TWO OPERANDS
        BEQL     OUT              ;GCF FOUND
        BLSS     DIR
        SUBL     8(AP),4(AP)      ;1ST OP. LARGER
        BRB      RECUR
DIR:    SUBL     4(AP),8(AP)      ;2ND OP. LARGER
RECUR:  PUSHL    12(AP)           ;PUSH ARGUMENT LIST
        PUSHL    8(AP)            ;INTO STACK FOR
        PUSHL    4(AP)            ;RECURSIVE CALL
        CALLS    #3,GCF
        RET
OUT:    MOVL     4(AP),@12(AP)    ;RETURN RESULT
        RET
        .END
```

In the main program, we may have:

```
VAL1:   .LONG    60               ;1ST OPERAND
VAL2:   .LONG    24               ;2ND OPERAND
GCFAC:  .BLKL    1
        .ENTRY   MAIN,0
        PUSHAL   GCFAC            ;PUSH ARG. LIST
        PUSHL    VAL2             ;INTO STACK FOR
        PUSHL    VAL1             ;PROCEDURE CALL
        CALLS    #3,GCF
        $EXIT_S
        .END     MAIN
```

Before the procedure is entered in the main program, the top levels of the stack will look like this;

```
60
24
addr GCFAC
```

In the procedure, a subtraction will be executed; before the first recursive call is entered, the stack looks like this:

```
36
24
addr GCFAC
─────────
 call frame
 of MAIN
─────────
 3
60
24
addr GCFAC
```

In successive recursive calls, the stack will have the following configurations:

```
                                          12
                                          12
                                          addr GCFAC

                                          ─────────
                                           call frame
                                           of 2nd
                                           recursion
                      and                 ─────────
                                           3
12                                        12
24                                        24
addr GCFAC                                addr GCFAC

─────────                                 ─────────
 call frame                                call frame
 of 1st                                    of 1st
 recursion                                 recursion

─────────                                 ─────────
 3                                         3
36                                        36
24                                        24
addr GCFAC                                addr GCFAC

─────────                                 ─────────
 call frame                                call frame
 of MAIN                                   of MAIN

─────────                                 ─────────
 3                                         3
60                                        60
24                                        24
addr GCFAC                                addr GCFAC
```

The third time the procedure is reentered, the two operands are equal. The GCF is found, and the procedure will exit from one level of recursion to the next until it gets back to the main program.

6.6 Summary

Subprograms are instruction sequences that can be invoked from many different places in a program. When the execution of the instruction sequence is completed, program control will be returned to the point of invocation. Subprograms are normally self-contained and can be separately assembled. The use of subprograms facilitates modular programming, thereby improving the maintainability and readability of the program. It is also labor-saving, since only one copy of an instruction sequence needs to be created and kept when the same sequence is used in many places in a program. The drawback of a subprogram is in the overhead it incurs during execution time. The advantages of a subprogram so far outweigh its drawbacks, however, that the use of subprograms is encouraged.

The VAX-11 distinguishes two forms of subprograms: *subroutines* and *procedures*. The subroutines are invoked by one of the *branch* (*jump*) *to subroutine* instructions, which save the return address in the user's stack and transfer control to the entry point of the subroutine. Procedures are invoked by a *procedure call* instruction: CALLG or CALLS. There is a formal way of preserving the environment of the calling program at the point of call. A call frame is created in the user stack that saves the return address as well as part of the PSW and the contents of designated registers. There is also a prescribed format and method of passing the parameters. The parameters themselves may be call-by-value or call-by-address. A recursive procedure is one that calls itself. Recursive procedures can be implemented conveniently with the help of a stack.

EXERCISE

1. What are the reasons for writing subprograms?

2. In the VAX-11 the stack grows down; the top of the stack is in low memory and the bottom in high memory. Implement a stack that grows in the opposite direction.

3. What are the advantages and disadvantages of using the VAX-11 procedure calls, as opposed to subroutine calls?

4. Convert the bubble sort program shown in Chapter 4 (Figure 4.5) to (a) a subroutine and (b) a procedure. Document your program, indicating

clearly how the parameters are to be passed between the calling program and the subprogram.

5. Write a subroutine that converts a decimal number represented in ASCII code to its binary equivalent in 2's complement longword format. Do not use the registers to pass the parameters (cf. exercise 5, Chapter 2).

6. Write a procedure that scans a piece of text in English and enters the first occurrence of each word into a table. Also enter into the table the position of the word in the text.

7. Write a procedure to sort the table constructed in the previous problem in lexicographical order. (For this case, lexicographical order is defined as $,0,1 ... 9,a,b,c ... y,z.)

8. What is the difference between call-by-reference and call-by-value? Suppose a subprogram is required to evaluate the function

$$x := x + y$$

with x and y being the parameters. Discuss the ramifications if one or both parameters are called (a) by value and (b) by reference.

9. The Fibonacci sequence $F(0)$, $F(1)$, $F(2)$, ... can be defined recursively as follows:

$F(0) = 0$
$F(1) = 1$
$F(i) = F(i - 1) + F(i - 2)$ for $i \geq 2$

Write a recursive procedure to evaluate any Fibonacci number $F(j)$ of the sequence.

10. The "game of life" was developed by a mathematician named John Conway. The game consists of an $n \times n$ matrix of zeroes and ones. For instance, if $n = 7$, we might have:

```
1 0 1 0 1 0 1
0 1 0 1 0 1 0
0 0 1 0 1 0 0
0 0 0 1 0 0 0
0 0 1 0 1 0 0
0 1 0 1 0 1 0
1 0 1 0 1 0 1
```

Each coefficient of the matrix is thought of as a cell in which 1 means "alive" and 0 means "dead." The initial value of the matrix is called the *first generation*. The game involves creating a new generation from the old one. Each cell may or may not change values from one generation to the next. The algorithm for deciding is the following:

If a given cell is currently alive and two or three of its eight neighbors are alive, then it survives. Otherwise it dies.

If a given cell is currently dead and at least three of its neighbors are alive, then it is reborn. Otherwise it stays dead.

The neighbors of a given cell x are denoted by y in the following diagram:

yyy
yxy
yyy

If x is a corner cell or an edge cell, then its missing neighbors are to be treated as dead.

Write a program that implements the game of life. There are to be at least three subprograms: INPUT, LIFE, and OUTPUT. INPUT is to read in the value n and the first generation. OUTPUT is to echo-check the data and also write out each generation as it is computed with the proper heading.

The following initial generations may be used for test data:

```
1 1 1 1    1 1 1 1 1    0 0 0 0 0 0 0 0
1 1 1 1    0 0 0 0 0    0 1 1 1 1 1 1 0
1 1 1 1    1 1 1 1 1    0 1 0 0 0 0 1 0
1 1 1 1    0 0 0 0 0    0 1 0 0 0 0 1 0
           1 1 1 1 1    0 1 0 0 0 0 1 0
                        0 1 0 0 0 0 1 0
                        0 1 1 1 1 1 1 0
                        0 0 0 0 0 0 0 0
```

Chapter 7

Assemblers

FOR ITS execution, an assembly language program undergoes two distinct phases: *translation* and *execution*. During the translation phase the assembly program is translated into its machine language equivalent, and during the execution phase the computer hardware carries out the instructions requested by the program. This chapter examines in some detail the assembler that performs the translation.

The assembler program accepts as input an assembly source program and generates as output the object program equivalent of the source program. In many systems the object program is not in a form that is ready for execution (for example, there may be external symbols to be resolved); thus it must be processed further and made ready for execution. Once this is done, the program can be placed in main memory and given control of the computer, which starts its execution. The process of readying the program for execution is called *linking,* and the process of placing it in main memory is called *loading.* Toward the end of the chapter we look at linking and loading.

One of the main objectives of this chapter is to learn to read the object code generated by an assembler; such knowledge can greatly aid debugging. We will also discuss the design of an assembler. The reader should be able to write a simplified assembler for a small set of instructions and directives by the end of the chapter.

7.1 The Functions of an Assembler

The major function of an assembler is to generate the object code of an assembly source program. In the process, the assembler replaces symbolic names by numeric addresses, replaces instruction mnemonics by op codes, and translates constants into their binary equivalents. In addition, an assembler performs the following two functions:

1. It checks for syntactic errors in the source program and issues diagnostic messages.
2. Optionally, it produces a listing showing every statement in the source program, its relative location in the program, and the object code translation of the statement. (The object code is usually listed in hexadecimal or octal, depending on the particular assembler.) In addition, the listing contains diagnostic messages for any errors detected by the assembler.

A schematic showing an assembler, its input, and its outputs are shown in the following figure:

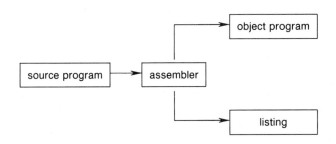

In the next section, we consider in some detail how an assembler generates object code. The treatment is directed mainly at byte-addressable machines, but the concepts apply to assemblers in general.

7.2 Object Code Generation

To generate the object code, the assembler reads the source program and scans it. Scanning proceeds sequentially, line by line; except for comments, every line is analyzed to identify basic elements such as keywords (or permanent symbols such as directives, instruction mnemonics, and register names); user-defined symbols; and numbers. The identification of these basic elements is called *lexical scanning.*

In identifying the basic elements, the assembler must isolate each element from its neighbors. Thus the beginning and end of each element must be determined. The elements are determined by scanning the source statements character by character, collecting the characters, and looking for delimiters such as blanks or commas. The operational details for identifying the basic elements involve conceptually simple string-processing techniques. Now we look at assembling the various fields of an assembly statement.

Assembling Comments

Comments do not affect the object code in any way; they are merely read by the assembler and copied into the listing file, if one is requested.

Assembling Directive Statements

The effect of a directive on the object program varies with the type of directive. Some directives have no effect on the object code. For example, the .END directive simply signifies to the assembler the end of the program. Storage directives, on the other hand, cause the assembler to generate object code signifying that memory locations are to be reserved for the variables specified. For example, a directive statement such as

```
.BYTE    9,-12
```

causes the assembler to write to the object file the binary equivalents of the numbers 9 and -12, where each number occupies one byte.[1] Assuming that this directive statement is the first statement in the program, the first two numbers in the object program will be:

Byte No.	Binary	Hex
0	00001001	09
1	11110100	F4

where the left-hand column shows the byte position relative to the beginning of the program.

As we will see, there is a one-to-one correspondence between the byte positions and the physical addresses that the object program occupies in memory during its execution. For this reason, the byte position is usually referred to as the *relative address,* or simply the *address.*

Now assume that the foregoing directive statement is immediately followed by

```
NUM:    .BLKW    3
        .WORD    200
```

These directives cause the assembler to reserve the next 8 bytes in the object program: the first 6 bytes for .BLKW 3 and the following 2

---

[1] The object program generated by the assembler is usually written to a file on a secondary storage device such as a disk. This file is commonly referred to as the *object file.*

bytes for WORD 200. The first 6 bytes will be initialized to values of the assembler's choosing (for example, 0s for the VAX-11 MACRO Assembler), and the next 2 bytes will be set to the binary equivalent of 200. Thus the first 10 bytes in the object program will contain the following values (the question marks indicate values that are unknown at the start of the program):

Address	Binary	Hex
0	00001001	09
1	11110100	F4
2	????????	??
3	????????	??
4	????????	??
5	????????	??
6	????????	??
7	????????	??
8	11001000	C8
9	00000000	00

Note that there is no indication in the object program that the symbolic name NUM is used in the source program. NUM, however, will be equated to the value 2, which is the address of the first byte that is reserved by the .BLKW directive. The assembler must somehow remember the symbolic name NUM and associate with it the address value 2 so that when NUM is referred to in the program, the assembler will have the necessary information to determine from where the operand is to be fetched. In general, the assembler must remember every user-defined symbol and its address. To do this, the assembler, as it scans the source program, enters every user-defined symbol it encounters in a table together with the address of the symbol. This table is called the *symbol table*. Section 7.4 will show in detail how the symbol table is constructed.

The address that a symbol represents is referred to as the *value* of the symbol. Note that this is in contrast to the "value of a symbol" in higher-level languages, where *value* refers to the contents of the memory location whose symbolic address is the symbol.

It must be mentioned that the addresses (or byte positions) referred to previously may or may not be the same as the physical addresses of the locations that an object program occupies in memory at execution time. If the program is loaded starting at physical address 0, then these addresses coincide with the physical addresses. If the program is loaded starting at some other physical location, say 1000, however, then an address in the foregoing corresponds to a physical address of 1000 plus the byte number. In either case there is a one-to-one correspondence between the byte numbers and the physical addresses. Therefore, the actual starting physical address need not be known at assembly time. (For clarity, it may be helpful to assume in this section that an object program will be loaded in memory starting at physical location 0.)

Assembling Instruction Statements

Whereas a higher-level language statement may be translated into a sequence of many machine language instructions, an assembly instruction generally translates into one machine instruction. Thus the machine instructions in the object code are generally in one-to-one correspondence with the assembly statements. The object code equivalent of an instruction statement consists of the op code of the instruction mnemonic and code that furnishes complete information about where operands are to be found at execution time.

The length of the object code generated for an instruction statement varies from one computer to another. On some computers it is the same for all instructions (for example, one word). On other computers it is the same for all instructions of the same type. On still others it varies depending on the addressing mode(s) used in the instruction statement. Usually, however, the size of the object code generated for a statement is a multiple of the byte or word size. In the following, we look at the object codes generated for the various entities that may appear in an instruction statement. The treatment is general, with no specific machine or assembler in mind.

Every instruction mnemonic must be represented by a unique op code. The size of the op code field in a given computer determines the maximum number of instructions for that computer. Usually all op codes are of the same size; on some computers, however, the size varies from one instruction to another.

The binary code generated for a register is the address assigned to that register. Thus the number of general-purpose registers (GPRs) in a machine determines the number of bits in the object code required to represent each register uniquely. For example, a machine with 16 GPRs requires 4 bits to specify any of the registers. In addition to the register number, the object code contains information about the addressing modes in which the register is used.

Symbolic names that appear in the operand field of an instruction statement are translated into numeric addresses. In its simplest form, the binary code of a symbolic name is the value of the name as entered in the symbol table at the time the symbol is encountered in the label field of a statement. Obviously, when the binary code of the symbolic name is the numeric address of the name, the number of bits in the object code required to represent the name uniquely will be equal to the length of the address in the machine.

For example, if a machine uses 32 bits to specify an address, then every name in the operand field will be assembled into a 32-bit binary code. Recall from Chapter 5 that this direct translation into a numeric address may be wasteful of memory space. For this reason, some machines translate a symbolic name into a displacement or an offset from some base register. Then the actual address is determined at execution time by adding the offset or displacement to the contents of the base register. Finally, in addition to the address, displacement, or offset, the object code of a symbol also contains information about the addressing mode used with the symbol.

7.3 Assembler Data Structures

Now we look at some of the important data structures that an assembler uses in the translation process. Four of these structures (which are used by almost every assembler) are the *op code table,* the *directive table,* the *symbol table,* and the *location counter.*

Symbol Table

As we saw earlier, the symbol table is used by the assembler to keep track of all user-defined symbols and their values. The table is built by the assembler as it scans the source program. The table contains every user-defined symbol encountered and the address of the symbol in the source program. It may also contain additional information that is needed by the linker for linking the program. (We will look at this information in Section 7.6.) A complete example that shows how a symbol table is built is given in Section 7.4 for a VAX-11 MACRO program.

Location Counter

To generate the symbol table, the assembler uses a pointer (a variable) called the *location counter* (LC). The location counter holds the address of the object code to be generated for the source statement that is currently being assembled. This counter is initially set to the starting address of the program (for example, 0). Then, for every statement, it is incremented by the size of the object code generated for that statement. Thus, at the end of assembling a statement, the contents of the LC will be the address of the object code of the next statement to be assembled. In other words, at the start of assembling a statement, the location counter points to the first byte that the object code of that statement will occupy. The location counter, then, determines the value of a symbol encountered in the label field of a statement. Thus a label is simply assigned the contents of the LC; this is the value that is entered in the symbol table for that symbol.

Note the similarity between the function of the LC and that of the program counter (PC): At the start of executing an instruction, the PC points to that instruction; at the start of assembling an instruction, the LC also points to that instruction. The location counter actually mimics the program counter.

Op Code Table

For generating the op codes of the instruction mnemonics, the assembler keeps an internal (predefined) table that lists every mnemonic and its op code. This table is called the *op code table*. The op code table is also used by the assembler to determine syntax errors and illegal instructions in the source program. The op code table may contain other information, such as the length of the instruction statement (for fixed-length statements), or the number of operands the instruction requires. Such information aids the assembler in the translation process. For example, the length of the statement can be used for updating the location counter, and the number of operands can be used to determine whether a statement has too few (or too many) operands. An op code table might look like this:

Mnemonic	Op Code	No. of Operands
ADDB2	80	2
ADDB3	81	3
ADDW2	A0	2
CLRL	D4	1
CMPL	D1	2
BGTR	14	1
MOVW	B0	2
INCL	D6	1
EDIV	7B	4

Directive Table

The *directive table* is also an internally predefined table that contains the name of every directive supported by the assembler. This table is searched by the assembler to determine the legality of a directive. For every directive in the table, the table might also contain the name (location) of a routine to be used for processing the directive. A possible directive table might look like this:

Directive	Address of Directive Routine
·BYTE	SUB_BYTE
·WORD	SUB_WORD
·BLKB	SUB_BLKB
·ASCII	SUB_ASCII

The periods (.) preceeding the directives in the foregoing table need not be stored; they are shown here for illustrative purposes only.

The following example shows a possible implementation of the directive table shown previously using MACRO. It also shows a segment of code that searches for a directive and branches to a corresponding routine to process the directive. The example neglects checking for an illegal directive.

Example:

Assuming that a directive has a maximum of six characters, the directive table can be implemented as follows:

```
DIRECTIVES:    .ASCII  'BYTE  '       ;THIS TABLE SHOWS 5
               .ASCII  'WORD  '       ;... DIRECTIVES WHERE
               .ASCII  'BLKB  '       ;... EVERY DIRECTIVE
               .ASCII  'ASCII '       ;... OCCUPIES 6 BYTES.
;
ROUTINE_ADDRESSES:
               .ADDRESS  SUB_BYTE,-   ;ADDRESSES OF
                         SUB_WORD,-   ; ... DIRECTIVE
                         SUB_BLKB,-   ; ... ROUTINES
                         SUB_ASCII,-
;
```

Suppose that a directive contained in a variable DIR is to be processed. The directive table will be searched first for the directive, and then a jump will be performed to the corresponding routine. This can be implemented as follows:

```
DIR:           .BLKB   6              ;DIRECTIVE TO BE
                                      ;... SEARCHED FOR
                  .
                  .
                  .
;
;SEARCH FOR DIRECTIVE IN DIRECTIVE TABLE
;
               CLRL    R7             ;R7 IS INDEX INTO TABLE
               MOVAL   DIRECTIVES,R6  ;POINT TO BEGINNING OF TABLE
SEARCH:        CMPC3   #6,(R6),DIR    ;DIRECTIVE FOUND?
               BEQL    FOUND          ; YES
```

```
                ADDL    #6,R6            ; NO: POINT TO NEXT DIRECTIVE
                INCL    R7               ;UPDATE INDEX INTO TABLE
                BRB     SEARCH           ;CONTINUE SEARCHING
;
;FIND ADDRESS OF CORRESPONDING ROUTINE THAT PROCESSES THE DIRECTIVE
;AND BRANCH TO IT
;
FOUND:          MOVAL   ROUTINE_ADDRESSES,R8
                MULL    #4,R7            ;R7 IS BYTE-INDEX INTO TABLE
                                         ;... OF ROUTINE ADDRESSES
                ADDL    R7,R8            ;POINT TO ADDRESS OF ROUTINE
                MOVL    (R8),R10         ;POINT TO ROUTINE
                JMP     (R10)            ;JUMP TO ROUTINE
                  .
                  .
                  .

;
SUB_BYTE:
                  .
                  . (routine to process .BYTE:
                  . scan operand field of directive,
                  . convert values found to binary,
                  . and write to object file. Increment
                  . LC by number of bytes written)
                  .

;
SUB_WORD:
                  .
                  . (routine to process .WORD:
                  .  similar to routine SUB_BYTE)
                  .

;
SUB_BLKB:
                  .
                  . (routine to process .BLKB:
                  . scan operand field and reserve
                  . in object file a number of
                  . bytes equal to value found.
                  . Increment LC by number of
                  . bytes reserved)
                  .

;
SUB_ASCII:
                  .
                  . (routine to process .ASCII:
                  . scan operand field and write
                  . ASCII equivalent of characters
                  . found to object file. Increment
                  . LC by number of bytes written)
                  .
```

The instruction CMPC3 (CoMPare Characters 3 operands) in the foregoing program segment has the general format:

```
CMPC3    length,A,B
```

The instruction compares two strings of characters (or two blocks of bytes) of the specified *length*, where the first string starts at address A and the second at address B, and sets the condition codes accordingly. The comparison is performed on a pair of bytes at a time, one from each string, starting at addresses A and B. The comparison proceeds until inequality is detected or until all the bytes of the strings have been examined. The condition codes are affected by the result of the last pair of bytes examined. Thus, following CMPC3 in the foregoing example, the instruction BEQL will cause a branch to FOUND only if all characters in both strings are exactly the same.

CMPC3 is similar to MOVC3 in that it affects registers R0 through R3 as follows:

1. If the two strings are equal, then R0 through R3 are affected in the same way as for MOVC3.
2. If the two strings are not equal, then:
   a. R0 contains the number of bytes remaining in either string at the time the comparison terminates, including the byte that terminated the comparison.
   b. R1 contains the address of the byte in the first string that terminated the comparison.
   c. R2 will always be equal to R0.
   d. R3 contains the address of the byte in the second string that terminated the comparison.

The operand *length* in CMPC3 is taken in the context of a word (2 bytes) in the same manner as the operand *length* of the MOVC3 instruction (see Section 4.6).

The foregoing program segment is a good example for illustrating a useful instruction on the VAX—that is, the CASE instruction.[2] Similar to the CASE statement in Pascal, the CASE instruction is used to select a segment of code to be executed based on the value of a certain variable.

The CASE instruction specifies three operands and a table of displacements that immediately follows the instruction:

```
        CASE    selector,base,limit

TABLE:  displacement 0

        displacement 1

        displacement 2

                .

                .

                .

        displacement n

OTHERWISE:
```

---

[2]The rest of this section may be skipped without loss of continuity.

The CASE instruction provides multiway branching depending on the values of the two operands: selector and base. The instruction is executed as follows:

The value of (selector − base) is used to select one of the displacements in the table. This displacement is added to the PC, which at the time of executing the CASE instruction will be pointing to the first displacement (displacement 0 at address TABLE in the example). The result of the addition is the address of the instruction to be branched to. In other words, CASE causes a branch to an instruction whose address is (TABLE + displacement i), where i is the value of (selector − base).

The limit operand is used to determine if the value of (selector − base) is in the range of the table of displacements. This operand is set to one less than the number of displacements. If the value of (selector − base) is greater than limit, then branching takes place to the instruction immediately following the table of displacements (at address OTHERWISE in this example).

Two additional things about the CASE instruction are:

1. There are three forms of CASE: CASEB, CASEW, and CASEL. The various forms determine the data type of the three operands, selector, base, and limit.
2. The displacements in the table of displacements are all word displacements. Thus branching can be at most to within 32,767 bytes from the CASE instruction in either direction.

Now we illustrate the use of the CASE instruction on the example program of searching the directive table. The segment of code that finds and branches to the corresponding routine that processes the directive can be replaced by the following segment:

```
;FIND ADDRESS OF CORRESPONDING ROUTINE THAT PROCESSES THE DIRECTIVE
;AND BRANCH TO IT
;
FOUND:      CASEL    R7,#0,#3
TABLE:      .WORD    SUB_BYTE-TABLE      ;IF R7=0, BRANCH TO SUB_BYTE
            .WORD    SUB_WORD-TABLE      ;IF R7=1, BRANCH TO SUB_WORD
            .WORD    SUB_BLKB-TABLE      ;IF R7=2, BRANCH TO SUB_BLKB
            .WORD    SUB_ASCII-TABLE     ;IF R7=3, BRANCH TO SUB_ASCII
OTHERWISE:
                 .
                 .
                 .
SUB_BYTE:
                 .
                 .
SUB_WORD:
                 .
                 .
```

```
SUB_BLKB:
            •
            •
SUB_ASCII:
            •
            •
            •
```

Note that CASEL, rather than CASEB or CASEW, is used in the foregoing program because register R7 is used as a longword in the original program. Note also that every displacement is formed as the difference between the address of the routine to be branched to and the starting address of the table of displacements. This is so because the destination address is computed as the sum of the displacement and the base address of the displacement table.

To the reader who knows Pascal, one difference between the CASE instruction and the CASE statement in Pascal should be noted. Whereas the Pascal CASE, after dispatching to a segment of code, returns control to the statement following the CASE statement, the CASE instruction does not. That is, after the CASE instruction dispatches to a segment of code, there is no automated way to return to the instruction following the CASE instruction.

7.4 The VAX-11 MACRO Assembler

In this section we look at the object code generated for a VAX-11 assembly program by the MACRO Assembler. The treatment is by no means complete because the actual workings of MACRO (and assemblers in general) are rather complex. Nevertheless, this introduction should give us a good insight into the assembly process and should enable us to read the object code of a VAX assembly program. Such knowledge, as mentioned earlier, can greatly aid debugging.

Like most assemblers, the MACRO Assembler need not know what the starting address of the object program will be when loaded in memory for execution. It assumes a starting address of zero, and addresses within a program are generated relative to this beginning address. Thus the location counter (LC) is initialized to zero at the beginning of assembly. It is then incremented by the size of the object code generated for each statement in the program. Since the basic unit on the VAX is the byte, the LC is incremented by the size of the statement in bytes. In the following, we look first at determining the size of statements and later at the process of generating object code.

When a directive is encountered in a source statement, it is looked up in the directive table. If it is found there, a branch takes place to a corresponding routine that processes the directive. For storage allocation directives, the routines determine the size of storage to be reserved according to the following:

1. Data Storage Directives

$$\text{Size} = \text{number of operands in operand field} * \begin{cases} 1 \text{ for } .\text{BYTE} \\ 2 \text{ for } .\text{WORD} \\ 4 \text{ for } .\text{LONG or} \\ \qquad\qquad .\text{ADDRESS} \\ 8 \text{ for } .\text{QUAD} \\ 16 \text{ for } .\text{OCTA} \end{cases}$$

As an example, for

```
.WORD    200,15,-175
```

size = 3*2 = 6 bytes.

2. Block Storage Allocation Directives

$$\text{Size} = \text{value in operand field} * \begin{cases} 1 \text{ for } .\text{BLKB} \\ 2 \text{ for } .\text{BLKW} \\ 4 \text{ for } .\text{BLKL or } .\text{BLKA} \\ 8 \text{ for } .\text{BLKQ} \\ 16 \text{ for } .\text{BLKO} \end{cases}$$

As an example, for

```
.BLKL    5
```

size = 5*4 = 20 bytes.

3. ASCII Character Storage Directives
   For .ASCII, size = number of characters in string (not including the delimiters)
   For .ASCIC, size = number of characters + 1.

As mentioned earlier, some directives do not generate object code; thus LC is not altered for such directives. Furthermore, direct-assignment statements do not generate any object code; rather, the symbol defined in a direct-assignment statement is simply entered in the symbol table together with its value, and no other action is taken.

Recall from Chapter 5 that the size of the object code generated for an instruction statement is determined by the size of the op code plus the number of bytes necessary to hold complete information about all the operands. Thus the size depends on the particular instruction mnemonic, the number of operands in the statement, and the addressing modes specified with the operands. In the next section we use four of the VAX-11 addressing modes in a program to illustrate the assembly process. For easy reference we summarize the object codes of these four modes in Table 7.1.

Assembling a MACRO Program

We are now ready to assemble a MACRO program. The assembly process will be illustrated by first determining the address of every label and every statement in the program, thus generating the symbol table. Then we shall generate the object code of the program.

Symbol Table Generation

As seen earlier, the address of every user-defined symbol, together with the symbol, is entered in the symbol table. The address of the symbol is the value of the location counter at the time the symbol is encountered. We will determine the value of the location counter at every statement for the simple program that follows.

LC(HEX)	SIZE	LINE(DEC)			
0	3	1	NUMS:	.BYTE	5,13,-10
3	2	2	SUM:	.BLKW	1
5	2	3		.ENTRY	SIMPLE,0
7	2	4		CLRL	R2
9	2	5		CLRL	R4
B	4	6		MOVAL	NUMS,R6
F	3	7	LOOP:	ADDB	(R6),R4
12	2	8		INCL	R6
14	2	9		INCL	R2
16	3	10		CMPL	#3,R2
19	2	11		BGTR	LOOP
1B	4	12		MOVW	R4,SUM
1F	9	13		$EXIT_S	
28		14		.END	SIMPLE

The program adds the three bytes beginning at address NUMS and stores the result in word SUM. The columns labeled LINE, SIZE, and LC show the line number, the size in bytes, and the beginning address of the corresponding statement, respectively.

We shall look briefly at determining the values in the SIZE and LC columns. For simplicity, the program has been chosen so that all displacements are byte displacements.

Line 1: At the start of assembly, LC is initialized to 0; thus the value (or address) of NUMS is 0. This statement causes 3 bytes to be reserved and initialized to the values specified; hence its size is 3 bytes, and LC is incremented by 3.

Table 7.1 Object Codes for the Four Addressing Modes

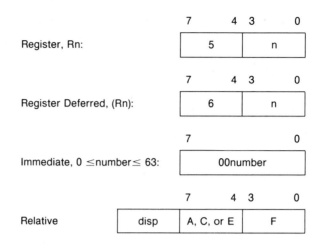

Line 2: At the start of assembling this statement LC is 3; thus, the value of SUM is 3. This directive requests reserving 1 word (2 bytes); hence the size of this statement is 2 bytes, and LC is incremented to 5.

Line 3: LC is now 5; thus the value of SIMPLE is 5. The .ENTRY directive causes the assembler to reserve 2 bytes; hence LC is incremented to 7. The two bytes reserved by .ENTRY are used as a mask for the registers to be saved, if any. In this example, and in main programs in general, no registers are saved. The .ENTRY of a procedure might specify some registers to be saved, however.

Line 4: The size of this statement is 2 bytes: 1 byte for the op code of CLRL, and 1 byte for the object code of R2. LC is incremented to 9.

Line 5: As in Line 4, LC is incremented to B.

Line 6: The op code of MOVAL is 1 byte. NUMS has a byte displacement; hence its object code is 2 bytes. R6 translates into 1 byte. Therefore, LC is incremented by 4.

Line 7: LC is F; thus the value of LOOP is F. The size of the statement is 3 bytes, and LC is incremented to 12.

Lines 8–12: Determining the size of these statements should now be straightforward.

Line 13: The system macro $EXIT_S will be expanded at assembly time. The statements in the body of the macro will be assembled much as for any other statement. The total size of these statements is 9 bytes; hence LC is incremented to 28.

Line 14: The .END directive simply signifies to the assembler the end of the program and does not generate any object code. The assembler, however, does leave in the object program information indicating that SIMPLE is the start of execution address.

The symbol table is built as the values of the symbols are determined. The symbol table for this program looks like this:

Symbol	Value
LOOP	F
NUMS	0
SIMPLE	5
SUM	3

The table is shown sorted alphabetically, as most assemblers display it in the listing file.

So far we have given the impression that the LC is incremented by the size of a statement after the entire statement is scanned and its size is determined. Although this may be the case with many assemblers, the MACRO Assembler increments the LC *as* the statement is scanned (compare this with incrementing the PC during the execution of an instruction, as described in Chapter 5). Thus, for example, in Line 1, when the character 5 is scanned, LC is incremented to 1; and when 13 is scanned, LC is incremented to 2. Then when −10 is scanned, LC is incremented to 3. As another example, when in Line 4 CLRL is scanned, LC is incremented to 8; then when R2 is scanned, LC is incremented to 9. This observation is essential for understanding object code generation by the MACRO Assembler.

Object Code Generation

We now generate (hand assemble) the object code for the foregoing program. The source statements and the object codes printed to the left of the statements are as follows. Note that the assembled bytes are listed from right to left, following the VAX-11 convention. The columns labeled LINE and LC are the same as in the previous example. The column labeled OP CODE shows the 1-byte op code of the corresponding instruction mnemonic. To the left of this column are shown a number of bytes for the object codes of the operands.

BYTE	BYTE	BYTE	OP CODE	LC	LINE			
F6	0D	05		0	1	NUMS:	.BYTE	5,13,-10
	00	00		3	2	SUM:	.BLKW	1
	00	00		5	3		.ENTRY	SIMPLE,0
		52	D4	7	4		CLRL	R2
		54	D4	9	5		CLRL	R4
56	F2	AF	DE	B	6		MOVAL	NUMS,R6
	54	66	80	F	7	LOOP:	ADDB	(R6),R4
		56	D6	12	8		INCL	R6
		52	D6	14	9		INCL	R2
	52	03	D1	16	10		CMPL	#3,R2
		F4	14	19	11		BGTR	LOOP
E4	AF	54	B0	1B	12		MOVW	R4,SUM
				1F	13		$EXIT_S	
				28	14		.END	SIMPLE

Line 1: The object code depicts the binary equivalents of the numbers in the operand field.

Line 2: Two bytes are reserved by this statement that are initialized by the assembler to 0.[3]

Line 3: The 2 bytes reserved by the .ENTRY hold information about the mask following the program name. The mask in this example is 0 (that is, no registers are to be saved); and the two bytes are initialized to 0. It should be clear that program execution starts at the program name plus 2, which in this example is address SIMPLE+2.

Line 4: The op code of CLRL is D4, and the object code of R2 is 52.

Line 5: Similar to Line 4.

Line 6: The op code of MOVAL is DE. The first operand in this statement is specified in relative mode; thus the first byte generated for NUMS is xF, where x can be A, C, or E, depending on the distance of NUMS from the LC. When encountering a direct mode operand, the LC is incremented by two: one for xF and the other for a presumed byte displacement. In this example, when the displacement of NUMS is to be determined, LC is equal to E. Hence the displacement of NUMS, whose address is 0, is:

$$0 - E = -E$$

or, using radix complement, F2. Therefore, the first byte is AF and the second byte is F2.

Had the displacement turned out to be a word displacement (that

---

[3]This is not what is actually shown in the listing file. See the next subsection.

is, more than $+127$ or -128 bytes away from LC), then the following would have to be updated:

1. LC would be incremented by 1.
2. The displacement would occupy 2 bytes.
3. x would be C instead of A.

Of course, the displacement would have to be recalculated as the distance from the updated LC. Similarly, if the displacement turned out to be a longword displacement, similar corrections would have to be made.

The last byte on this line is the object code of R6.

Lines 7–10: Determining the object code for these statements is straightforward.

Line 11: The op code of BGTR is 14. The displacement of LOOP is

$$F - 1B = -C$$

where F is the address of LOOP and 1B is the contents of LC, which is pointing to the instruction following the BGTR instruction. In radix complement, the displacement is F4.

Line 12: The op code of MOVW is B0. The object code of R4 is 54. The displacement of SUM is

$$3 - 1F = -1C \text{ or } E4$$

which is a byte displacement.

Line 13: The object code of system macros, as well as of user-defined macros, is not displayed unless requested (see Chapter 8 for requesting display of macro expansion).

Line 14: The .END directive does not generate any object code.

The Listing

An actual listing from the MACRO Assembler for the foregoing program (with comments added) is shown in Figure 7.1. The first column to the left of the source code shows the line numbers, and the second column shows the values of the location counter. The next column shows the op codes for the instruction mnemonics; for directive statements, this column shows the contents of the first byte

```
            F6 0D 05    0000     1  NUMS:   .BYTE   5,13,-10    ;NUMBERS TO BE ADDED
            00000005    0003     2  SUM:    .BLKW   1           ;WORD TO HOLD SUM
                 0000   0005     3          .ENTRY  SIMPLE,0    ;
                52 D4   0007     4          CLRL    R2          ;R2 IS LOOP COUNTER
                54 D4   0009     5          CLRL    R4          ;R4 IS ACCUMULATOR
         56 F2 AF DE    000B     6          MOVAL   NUMS,R6     ;POINT TO ARRAY NUMS
         54 66 80       000F     7  LOOP:   ADDB    (R6),R4     ;ADD ITH ELEMENT TO ACC
            56 D6       0012     8          INCL    R6          ;POINT TO NEXT ELEMENT
            52 D6       0014     9          INCL    R2          ;INCREMENT LOOP COUNTER
         52 03 D1       0016    10          CMPL    #3,R2       ;HAVE ALL NUMBERS BEEN ADDED?
            F4 14       0019    11          BGTR    LOOP        ;NO
      E4 AF 54 B0       001B    12          MOVW    R4,SUM      ;YES: STORE RESULT IN SUM
                        001F    13          $EXIT_S             ;
                        0028    14          .END    SIMPLE      ;
```

Symbol table

```
LOOP      0000000F  R      01
NUMS      00000000  R      01
SIMPLE    00000005  RG     01
SUM       00000003  R      01
SYS$EXIT  ********  GX     01
```

Figure 7.1 Listing and symbol table

reserved by the directive. The remaining columns show the rest of the object code.

One difference between the object code shown in the listing and the object code we generated previously should be pointed out. At Line 2 the listing shows the number 00000005 instead of the number 0000 shown in the hand-assembled code. This number is the address of the next statement (at Line 3). The object code that is loaded in main memory for execution, however, will have 2 bytes for the statement at Line 2 initialized to 0.

In general, for a block storage directive the assembler does not write zero bytes to the object file. Instead it writes the address of the statement following the directive statement together with some other information that indicates that a number of bytes are to be initialized to zero. Then at load time the memory locations corresponding to these bytes will be initialized. This scheme is used to save space in the object file.

Shown with the listing in Figure 7.1 is the symbol table generated by the MACRO Assembler. The values listed next to the symbols are the addresses of the symbols. The symbol SYS$EXIT shown in the table is a symbolic name within the system macro $EXIT_S; as for any symbol defined externally to the program, a string of asterisks is printed next to this symbol. Also shown with the symbol table are letters describing attributes of the symbols. The letters are:

R for *relocatable.*

G for *global.*

X for *external.*

(See previous chapter for these terms.) Note that the symbol SIMPLE has a *global* attribute. It is necessary for the program name to be global so that the operating system knows where the program is to start executing. Note also that the symbol SYS$EXIT is labeled *external,* since it is defined outside our program. Finally, the last column shown in the symbol table lists the *program section* in which the symbol appears. Our program example consists of one program section.

7.5 The Two-Pass Assembler

In the previous section we saw how the symbol table is built and the object code is generated. Although building the symbol table and generating the object code could have been done simultaneously for the program in that example, the MACRO Assembler, like most assemblers, performs this in two steps. In the first step the symbol table is constructed, and in the second the object code is generated. The reason for this can be seen in the following discussion. Consider these modifications in the program of the previous section, where a simple change in the logic is introduced at lines 11 and 12:

```
LINE

  7     LOOP:    ADDB    (R6),R4
  8              INCL    R6
  9              INCL    R2
 10              CMPL    #3,R2
 11              BLEQ    EXIT
 12              BRB     LOOP
 13     EXIT:    MOVW    R4,SUM
 14              $EXIT_S
 15              .END    START
```

Obviously, the displacement of EXIT at Line 11 cannot be determined until the label EXIT at Line 13 is encountered. In general, the object code of a user-defined symbol cannot be generated until the symbol is defined (that is, until it is encountered in the label field of a statement.) Most assemblers allow a symbol to be referenced before it is defined. References to such symbols are called *forward references.*

Except for forward references, the symbol table and the object code can be generated simultaneously. In fact, some assemblers do just that, leaving vacant bytes in the object code for a forward reference and filling in these bytes when the symbol is defined. To do this it is necessary to record the yet undefined symbols and the addresses of the vacant bytes to be filled. Such assemblers generate the object code by one scan, or one pass, over the source code and are called *one-pass assemblers.* Note the complexity and the overhead involved in keeping track of every forward reference.

The most straightforward way to deal with the problem of forward references is to scan the source program twice. In the first scan the addresses of all user-defined symbols are determined and entered in the symbol table. In the second scan the object code is generated using the addresses collected in the symbol table. Most assemblers use this method of going over the source program in two passes. Such assemblers are called *two-pass assemblers.* MACRO is a two-pass assembler.

For some assemblers, one problem in determining displacements remains: To generate the symbol table, the assembler must determine the size of every statement. To determine the size, however, the displacement of every symbol in the statement should be known. For symbols that have not been defined, this may not be possible. One way around this problem is to make assumptions about the displacement of the yet undefined symbols. Recall from Chapter 5 that the MACRO Assembler assumes different displacements for a yet undefined symbol depending on the addressing mode used with the symbol. Recall also that MACRO permits overriding the assumed displacements by using one of the displacement length specifiers B͡, W͡, or L͡.

With this background, the reader should be able to follow the flowcharts in Figures 7.2 and 7.3. These flowcharts describe some of the highlights of the two passes of the MACRO Assembler. Although the flowcharts are greatly simplified, they do illustrate the logical steps of the assembly process.

The First Pass

The purpose of the first pass is to build the symbol table. This pass begins by setting the location counter to zero. Then a line from the source program is read. The line is scanned from left to right, character by character, until the first nonblank character is found. If this character is a semicolon, the rest of the line is discarded and the next line is read; otherwise, scanning of the line continues. If the line contains a label, the symbol table is searched to determine if the label has been defined previously. If not, then the label is assigned the current value of the location counter and entered in the symbol table. If the label has already been defined, then an error indicating multiple definition of a label will result.

Whether or not the source statement has a label, the operator field of the statement is then examined. The operator is first inspected to determine whether it is a macro name. This is done by searching a table, *macro table*, that contains the names of all macros defined in the program. If a match is found, then the macro is expanded into its body. Otherwise the first character of the operator field is compared to a period. If it is a period, the directive table is searched to determine whether the field contains a legal directive. If the operator field does not begin with a period, then the op code table is searched.[4]

Finally, the operand field of the source statement is scanned to determine the size of storage to be reserved, and the value of the location counter is updated.

This sequence is repeated for each source line. When the .END directive is encountered, the symbol table is sorted in lexicographical order, the first pass is terminated, and the second pass is started.

---

[4]Note that this order of searching the tables allows a directive name or an instruction mnemonic to be redefined as a macro name. This will be clarified in Chapter 8.

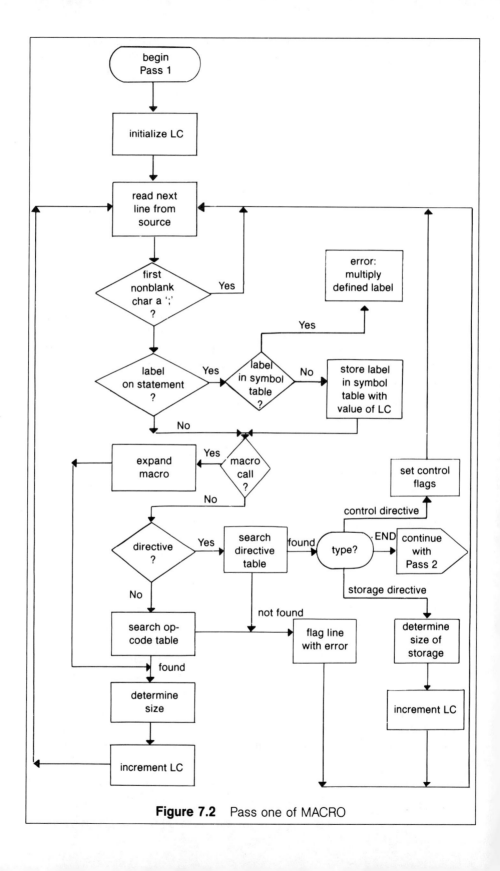

Figure 7.2 Pass one of MACRO

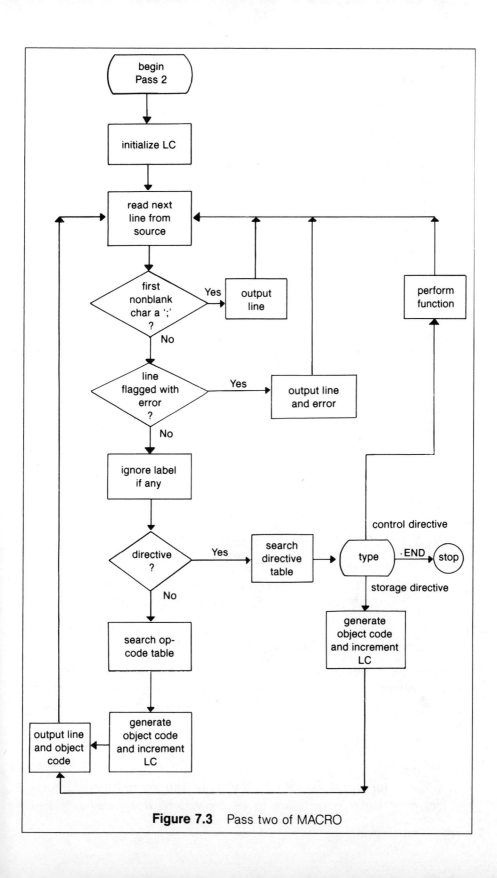

Figure 7.3 Pass two of MACRO

The Second Pass

The purpose of the second pass is to generate the object code. In addition, this pass generates the listing if one is requested. The second pass begins by initializing the location counter to zero. Then, as in the first pass, the source program is read line by line; every line that is not a comment or flagged with an error is scanned character by character. During this pass, however, the label field is ignored. The characters in the operator field of the statement are once again collected, and tests are made to determine the contents of the field. The operand field is then scanned to complete the object code generation, using the symbol table to determine the values of symbolic operand specifiers. Finally, the object code of the statement is output to the object file. When the .END is encountered, the assembly process is completed.

If a listing is requested, this pass composes a listing line for each source statement, consisting of the source text, the line number, the current value of he location counter, and the hexadecimal representation of the object code. The listing line is then output to the listing file.

As mentioned earlier, the listing file will also contain diagnostic messages for any errors detected during the assembly process. Typical errors checked by an assembler are:

1. Improper syntax.
2. Illegal characters in symbol.
3. Multiple definition of a label.
4. Referenced but undefined symbol.
5. Too few operands.
6. Too many operands.
7. Branch destination out of range.

The *VAX-11 MACRO User's Guide* contains a complete list of errors that may be generated by the MACRO Assembler.

7.6 Linking and Loading

Linking refers to the process of generating a final object program that is in machine-executable form. *Loading* refers to the process of placing the final object program in main memory prior to its execution.

Linking

In some computer systems the output of the assembler is a final object program that is ready to be loaded in main memory and executed. In other systems, however, the object code generated by the assembler requires further processing before it is ready for execution. This step is performed by a program called the *linker*.

To understand the need for linking, consider, for example, the program of Figure 7.1. In that program the system macro $EXIT_S performs a call to a system procedure named SYS$EXIT that is defined externally to the program. At assembly time, when $EXIT_S is expanded, the address of SYS$EXIT is not known. Therefore, the object code generated by the assembler for this program is not complete: the address of SYS$EXIT must first be determined. It is the job of the linker to determine this address and generate the final object code.

One might argue that the assembler could have performed the function of the linker in the foregoing example. This is true; indeed, as previously mentioned, some assemblers do this. The need for a linker, however, goes beyond the determination of addresses of external symbols: A linker is needed to link separately assembled programs and subroutines.

As an example, consider the program in Figure 7.4, where the program of Figure 7.1 has been divided into a procedure and a main program (each is contained in a file and assembled separately). In addition to determining the addresses of the external symbols ADD_NUMS and SYS$EXIT in the main program, the object codes of the main program and the procedure must be combined into a single object program. The job of the linker is to combine the two object codes.

In general, the input to the linker consists of object programs (also called *object modules*) of a main program and a number of subprograms. The subprograms may be defined by the user and contained in separate files, or they may be system routines included in the system's library. The output of the linker is an object program that is free of all external symbols and is ready to be loaded in memory and executed. The output of the linker is commonly referred to as *load module;* on the VAX-11 it is called *image file.*

For the linker to resolve external references and complete the load module, the assembler must leave behind information about external symbols and the instructions that reference them. On the VAX-11 this information is left by MACRO in the object file. MACRO flags the object code of external symbols in the listing with an apostrophe (see Figure 7.4b, Line 7).

Loading

The load module is commonly written by the linker on a disk file, where it is held until it is to be run. At that time it is read from disk

```
                0054   0000    1              .ENTRY   ADD_NUMS,^M<R2,R4,R6>
     56    04 AC  D0   0002    2              MOVL     4(AP),R6
     52    08 AC  D0   0006    3              MOVL     8(AP),R2
           54  66 80   000A    4  LOOP:       ADDB     (R6),R4
              56  D6   000D    5              INCL     R6
              52  D7   000F    6              DECL     R2
              F7  14   0011    7              BGTR     LOOP
  0C BC  54  B0        0013    8              MOVW     R4,@12(AP)
              04       0017    9              RET
                       0018   10              .END


Symbol table

ADD_NUMS            00000000 RG     01
LOOP                0000000A R      01

                                    (a)



           F6 0D 05   0000    1  NUMS:       .BYTE    5,13,-10
           00000005   0003    2  SUM:        .BLKW    1
                0000  0005    3              .ENTRY   MAIN,0
        F9 AF    DF   0007    4              PUSHAL   SUM
           03    DD   000A    5              PUSHL    #3
        F1 AF    9F   000C    6              PUSHAB   NUMS
  00000000'EF  03 FB  000F    7              CALLS    #3,ADD_NUMS
                      0016    8              $EXIT_S
                      001F    9              .END     MAIN


Symbol table

ADD_NUMS            ******** X      01
MAIN                00000005 RG     01
NUMS                00000000 R      01
SUM                 00000003 R      01
SYS$EXIT            ******** GX     01

                                    (b)
```

Figure 7.4 Program to illustrate the need for linking: (a) listing of procedure; (b) listing of main program

and physically placed in main memory. This final step is performed by a program called the *loader*.[5]

In some (small) computer systems the loader merely copies the load module as it is in main memory (such a loader is called *absolute loader*). In such systems the addresses in the load module coincide with the physical addresses the program occupies in memory. Obviously, for absolute loading the assembler (or linker) must know the starting address in memory at which the program is to be loaded. This scheme may be used in a computer system that runs one program at a time.

In computer systems in which several programs exist in main memory at the same time, the physcial starting address of a program is not known until load time. Therefore, addresses in the load mod-

---

[5]Under the VAX VMS, the loader is invoked by the RUN command.

```
00F60D05
DF000000
03DDF9AF
FBF1AF9F
0009EF03
01DD0000
409F01FB
54800001
04ACD000
08ACD056
54668052
52D756D6
54B0F714
00040CBC
```

Figure 7.5   The program of Figure 7.4 as it appears in main memory

ule are configured relative to the beginning of the program (which is usually assumed to be zero). Later on, relative addresses are modified to correspond to the physical addresses the program occupies in main memory. The process of modifying addresses is known as *relocation.*

In some systems relocation is performed at load time: The loader obtains from the operating system the starting physical address for where the program is to reside in memory; then, as the program is loaded, the loader adds this starting address to every relative address in the program. Note that, since both addresses and data in the load module are all binary strings, the linker must leave behind information so that the loader can distinguish between what is to be modified and what is not. This information is usually left in the load module together with the object code.

On the VAX-11, since symbolic addresses are translated into displacements, they are not affected by loading. Figure 7.5 shows the image file of the program in Figure 7.4 as loaded in main memory.[6] This figure is an actual "dump" of main memory using the VAX-11 debugger (see Appendix D).

7.7 Summary

An assembler translates a source code in assembly language into an object code in machine language. The major data structures used in an assembler include an op code table, a directive table, a symbol table, and a location counter. Whereas the op code and directive tables are fixed for a given assembler, the contents of the symbol

---

[6] This image file is produced by the command LINK MAIN+ADD, where MAIN is the file name of the main program and ADD is the file name of the procedure. Had the command been LINK ADD+MAIN, the procedure would have appeared on top of the main program.

table are generated individually for every program being assembled. To accommodate forward referencing, most assemblers are constructed as two-pass assemblers. This means that the source code is scanned twice to complete the assembling process. In the first pass the symbol table is constructed, and in the second pass the object code is generated.

To allow separately assembled program modules to run as a unit, a linker is used to reconcile the addresses of externally defined symbols. The linker uses the object codes produced by the assembler as inputs and generates a copy of executable code. The executable code is placed in the memory of the computer by a loader before it is run. A loader adjusts the relocatable addresses in the executable code to absolute addresses based on the location of the memory where the program is stored.

EXERCISES

1. Show the assembly code that corresponds to the instructions in the object code given below.

Address	Contents	Address	Contents
300	D4	307	51
301	50	308	62
302	90	309	80
303	65	30A	05
304	56	30B	55
305	C1	30C	97
306	60	30D	68

2. For the following program segment:
   a. Generate the symbol table.
   b. Generate the object code.

```
LIST:   .BYTE   5,16,-7,0
TEMP:   .LONG   0
BUF:    .BLKW   2
;
        .ENTRY  START,^M<>
        CLRL    R6
        ADDL    #3,R6
LOOP:   MOVB    LIST[R6],R8
        MOVB    R8,BUF[R6]
        DECL    R6
        BGEQ    LOOP
        MOVL    LIST,R8
        MOVL    R8,BUF
        $EXIT_S R0
        .END    START
```

3. For the following program:
  a. Generate the symbol table.
  b. Generate the object code.
  c. What does the program do?

```
TABLE:    .BYTE     32,20,-18,0
MAX:      .BLKW     1
;
          .ENTRY    MAIN,0
          CLRL      R5
          MOVAB     TABLE,R2
          MOVL      R2,R3
LOOP:     INCL      R3
          INCL      R5
          CMPL      #4,R5
          BLEQ      EXIT
          CMPB      (R2),(R3)
          BGTR      LOOP
          MOVL      R3,R2
          BRB       LOOP
EXIT:     MOVB      (R2),MAX
          .END
```

4. Complete the following partial listing of a program:

	00000006	0000	1	.BLKW
	001A	0006	2	.WORD
	14 20	0008	3	.BYTE
	00 DD	000A	4	
		000C	5;	
	0000	000C	6	.ENTRY
	55 D4	000E	7	
52 F5 AF	9E	0010	8	
53	52 D0	0014	9	
	53 D6	0017	10	
	55 D6	0019	11	
55	04 D1	001B	12	
	0A 15	001E	13	
63	62 91	0020	14	
	F2 14	0023	15	
52	53 D0	0025	16	
	ED 11	0028	17	
D2 AF	62 90	002A	18	
		002E	19	.END

```
              Symbol Table
AGAIN               00000025 R      01
BEGIN               0000000E R      01
EXIT                0000002A R      01
FIND_MAX            0000000C RG     01
HIGH                00000000 R      01
LIST                0000000A R      01
LOOP                00000017 R      01
NEXT                0000001B R      01
TABLE               00000008 R      01
```

5. In Exercises 5 and 6 you are to write a simplified fixed-format, two-pass assembler for the VAX-11. Exercise 5 is to be the first pass. The format of your assembler instructions is:

Columns

1–8	label	(if any)
9–16	operator	
17–24	operand 1	
25–32	operand 2	(if any)
33–40	operand 3	(if any)
41–72	comments	(if any)

Each instruction is exactly 72 characters long. Each label, op code, directive, and operand is exactly 8 characters long. For example, the label LOOP would appear as LOOPbbbb every place it is used.

Construct the symbol table and print it in the order it was constructed; then sort it in lexicographical order and print it again. The labels should be printed in ASCII and the locations in hexadecimal.

The only operators that you must treat are:

.BLKx	ADDx	CMPx	BGTR
.BYTE	SUBx	TSTx	BRB
.WORD	ADDx3	BEQU	
.LONG	SUBx3	BNEQ	
.END	MOVx	BLSS	

x = B, W, or L

The only addressing modes are those of Chapter 4: register, register deferred, immediate, and direct. There are no address expressions in the operand field (A is all right, but A+1 is not allowed). A directive can have at most one operand. All direct operands are assumed to be byte displacement (AF).

Your program should detect the following types of errors: (1) multiply defined symbol, (2) illegal op code, (3) illegal directive, (4) incorrect number of operands.

6. Complete the two-pass assembler started in Exercise 5. The completed assembler is to generate a listing file and a symbol table.

The output of your assembler must be similar to the output of the MACRO Assembler. The object code of a statement must be printed next to the statement. For this, you may want to use a data structure, LINE, that holds the statement and its line number, the current value of the LC, and the object code of the statement. LINE can then be printed on the listing file by $PUT. (The value of LC and the object code must be printed in hexadecimal.)

In addition to the errors given in Exercise 5, pass 2 of your assembler should also check for undefined symbols. You may print an error message following the statement that contains the error, or you may print all the error messages at the end of the listing file. In the latter case, you must give the line number of the erroneous statement.

The input to your assembler is a source assembly program that will be contained in a file. Your assembler needs to read this file twice. For this you should close the file after the first time and open it again before reading it the second time. For example, the following sequence of RMS I/O macro calls allows reading the input file more than once:

```
INFAB:  $FAB      ...
INRAB:  ....
           .
           .
           .
        $CREATE   FAB=OUTFAB
        $CONNECT  RAB=OUTRAB
OPEN:   $OPEN     FAB=INFAB
        $CONNECT  RAB=INRAB
           .
           .
           .
LOOP:   $GET      RAB=INRAB
        BLBC      R0,DONE
           .
           .
           .
        BRB       LOOP
           .
           .
           .
DONE:   $CLOSE    FAB=INFAB
           .
           .
           .
        BRW       OPEN        Branches to open the input
           .                  file again, so that when $GET
           .                  is called the next time it will
           .                  read from the beginning of the file
        $CLOSE    FAB=OUTFAB
```

7. Modify the assembler of Exercises 5 and 6 to write the object code to an object file. Then write a program that reads the object file and loads the object code in an area of memory. The program is then to branch to the entry point of the object code (perhaps by a BSBW instruction). After the object code is executed, control is to transfer back to the calling program (perhaps by a RSB instruction, which, of course, would require that the assembler be modified to accept RSB).

Chapter 8

Macros and Conditional Assembly

IN CHAPTER 3 we introduced the basic concept of a macro, and in Chapter 4 we used system macros (such as $OPEN, $CONNECT, and $GET) to perform input and output. System macros are provided by the manufacturer to perform common functions needed by programmers; the programmer uses a system macro by calling it with a specified format (looked up in a manual) without needing to know its internal workings. In this chapter we learn how to write and use macros of our own design. The concepts presented apply to macros in general, but we will use the VAX-11 MACRO language for examples.

In addition to macros, we present two facilities normally provided together with macros: *conditional assembly* and *repeat blocks*. Conditional assembly allows the programmer to include or exclude a segment of code in the source program during the assembly process. A repeat block enables a programmer to instruct the assembler to repeat a segment of code a number of times in succession.

Not all assemblers provide macro capabilities. Obviously, the VAX-11 MACRO Assembler does; the name of this assembler is coined because of this capability. In general, assemblers with macro capabilities are referred to as *macro assemblers*.

8.1 Macros

Assembly language programmers frequently need to repeat similar segments of code at various sites in a program. In such cases the segment of code can be defined as a macro; then, during the assembly time, wherever the name of the macro appears in the program, the assembler replaces the name by the statements within the macro. This replacement is termed *macro expansion*.

To add flexibility and generality to macros, most assemblers allow macros to have (dummy) parameters. When invoking a macro, the programmer specifies corresponding arguments to replace the parameters in the macro. This causes the assembler to generate different code for different invocations of the macro.

Macro Definitions and Macro Calls

A macro definition consists of the following parts:

1. A directive that declares the beginning of the macro.
2. The name of the macro.
3. Parameters, if any.
4. A collection of assembly statements, referred to as the *body* of the macro.
5. A directive that declares the end of the macro.

A macro is invoked by an assembly language statement that specifies the name of the macro in the operator field, and a list of arguments, corresponding to the parameters of the macro, in the operand field. Such a statement is referred to as a *macro call* or a *macro instruction*.

Macro Expansion

Expanding a macro call into the macro body involves conceptually simple text substitution. When the assembler encounters a macro definition, it enters the macro name in the *macro name table* and saves the macro body for later use. When the assembler encounters a macro instruction, it replaces the instruction by the macro body, substituting the specified arguments for the corresponding parameters.

Normally the parameters and the arguments have a one-to-one positional correspondence. That is, the first argument corresponds to the first parameter, the second argument corresponds to the second parameter, and so on. Some assemblers, however, allow this positional correspondence to be altered, as we shall see for the VAX-11 MACRO Assembler.

A symbol that is specified as an argument will be substituted for every occurrence of the corresponding parameter in the macro body. This substitution is a string substitution wherein the name of the symbol, *not* its value, is passed to the macro. This point will be made clearer when we look at examples of macros.

Macros versus Subprograms

A macro is similar to a subprogram in that it assigns a name to a sequence of statements. There are, however, several important differences between a macro and a subprogram:

1. A macro is invoked at *assembly time.* A subprogram is invoked at *execution time.*
2. When a macro is invoked, the *assembler* substitutes the macro body for the macro call. When a subprogram is invoked, the computer *hardware* transfers control to the beginning of the subprogram; upon completion, the hardware transfers control back to the calling program.
3. There are as many copies of the macro body in the object code as there are calls to the macro. There is only one copy of the subprogram in the object code, regardless of the number of calls to the subprogram.

Figures 8.1a and b compare the macro and the subprogram mechanisms schematically.

The aforementioned differences should be remembered when deciding whether to implement a segment of code as a subprogram or as a macro. The macro mechanism may result in an expanded program that requires much more memory space than the subprogram mechanism. On the other hand, the macro mechanism does not require the overhead that the subprogram mechanism requires, such as passing parameters and executing the call and return instructions. Furthermore, as we shall see in the next section, the parameter-passing facilities that are usually provided with macros can offer capabilities beyond those provided by subprograms.

8.2 The VAX-11 Macro Facility

In this section we look at the way macros are defined and called in a MACRO program. In addition, we present several features provided by the MACRO Assembler that add generality to and simplify macro writing.

For the VAX-11 MACRO, parameters in the macro definition are referred to as *formal arguments,* and the arguments in the macro call are referred to as *actual arguments.* Hence we shall use these terms in the rest of this chapter.

The general format of a macro definition is

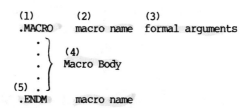

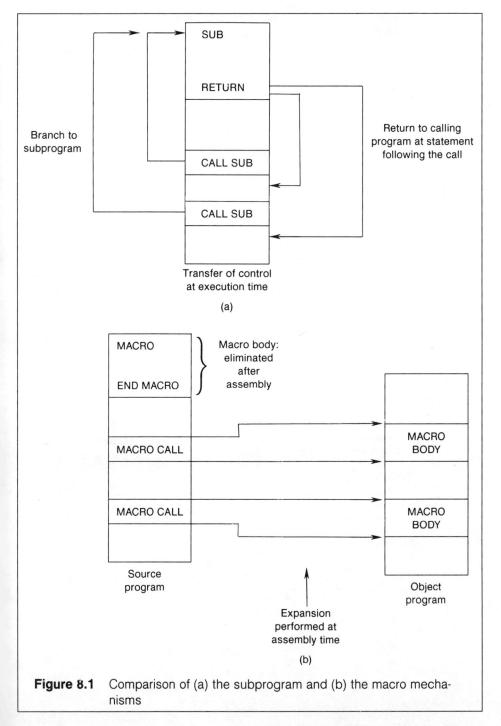

Figure 8.1 Comparison of (a) the subprogram and (b) the macro mechanisms

1. The directive .MACRO begins the definition of the macro.
2. The macro name is a user-defined symbol that should conform to the rules described in Section 4.1 for creating labels. The macro name appears in the operand field of the .MACRO statement and can be separated from the formal arguments by a blank, a comma, or a horizontal tab character.
3. The formal arguments list is a list of symbols that should also conform to the rules of Section 4.1.[1] The symbols can be separated from each other by commas, blanks, or tabs.
4. The macro body consists of assembly language statements. It can contain any statement, including macro calls to other macros. The macro body may also contain the definition of another macro within it. Such macros are referred to as *nested macros.* In fact, a macro can contain a macro call to itself. Such macros are called *recursive macros,* in analogy with recursive subprograms.
5. The .ENDM directive denotes the end of the macro definition. The macro name following .ENDM is optional but, if present, must match the name of the macro to be terminated. It is recommended that the macro name be specified with .ENDM for readability, particularly in the case of nested macros.

A macro must be completely defined prior to its first call. The general format of a macro call is

```
           (1)            (2)
Label:     macro-name     actual-arguments
```

1. The macro name appears in the operator field and is separated from the actual arguments by a blank or a horizontal tab character.
2. The list of actual arguments is a list of symbols or expressions that corresponds to the list of formal arguments in the macro definition. The actual arguments can be separated by commas, blanks, or tabs.

We now look at an example of defining and using a simple macro. Assume that in a program we frequently need to clear registers R2, R4, R5, and R6. A macro to clear these registers can be defined as follows:

---

[1] Actually, the reserved names R0–R12, AP, FP, SP, and PC can be used as macro names and formal arguments; but their use should be strongly discouraged.

```
.MACRO    CLEAR_REGS
CLRL      R2              ;CLEAR R2
CLRQ      R4              ;CLEAR R4 AND R5
CLRL      R6              ;CLEAR R6
.ENDM     CLEAR_REGS
```

Once this is done, macro calls in the program, such as

```
CLEAR_REGS
       .

       .

       .
CLEAR_REGS
```

are expanded at assembly time into the macro body to generate the code

```
CLRL    R2     ;CLEAR R2
CLRQ    R4     ;CLEAR R4 AND R5
CLRL    R6     ;CLEAR R6
   .

   .

   .
CLRL    R2     ;CLEAR R2
CLRQ    R4     ;CLEAR R4 AND R5
CLRL    R6     ;CLEAR R6
```

If a different set of registers is to be cleared at different sites in the program, then a macro with formal arguments can be defined to clear any set of, say, three registers, as follows:

```
.MACRO    CLEAR_3_LONG    ARG1,ARG2,ARG3
CLRL      ARG1
CLRL      ARG2
CLRL      ARG3
.ENDM     CLEAR_3_LONG
```

Thus, if registers R0, R1, R2 are to be cleared, then the macro call

```
CLEAR_3_LONG    R0,R1,R2
```

will be expanded into

```
CLRL    R0
CLRL    R1
CLRL    R2
```

If R2, R3, R5 are to be cleared, then

```
CLEAR_3_LONG     R2,R3,R5
```

will be expanded into

```
CLRL    R2
CLRL    R3
CLRL    R5
```

The foregoing macro can actually be used to clear any three long-words. For example, if X, Y, and Z are the names of three memory locations, the macro call

```
CLEAR_3_LONG     X,Y,Z
```

will generate the instructions

```
CLRL    X
CLRL    Y
CLRL    Z
```

which clears the three longwords at locations X, Y, and Z.

Note that the foregoing macro names, CLEAR_REGS and CLEAR _3_LONG, can be looked at as *instruction mnemonics* that extend the basic assembly instructions. In this way macros can be used to create an extended instruction set.

To illustrate the point made earlier about string substitution of actual arguments for formal arguments, consider the macro call

```
CLEAR_3_LONG     X-4,X,X+4
```

The call will generate the code

```
CLRL    X-4
CLRL    X
CLRL    X+4
```

The text string of the first actual argument, $X-4$ (not its value), is substituted for the first formal argument. A similar process is done for the remaining arguments. String substitution will be clarified further by the next example.

The operator field of a statement within a macro can also be designated as a formal argument. For example, a macro to clear a set of operands whose data type is determined by the macro call can be defined as follows:

```
.MACRO     CLEAR ARG1,ARG2,ARG3,CLR
CLR        ARG1
CLR        ARG2
CLR        ARG3
.ENDM      CLEAR
```

Then macro calls such as

```
CLEAR      R2,R3,R4,CLRL
             .
             .
             .
CLEAR      X,Y,Z,CLRW
```

will be expanded into

```
CLRL       R2
CLRL       R3
CLRL       R4
             .
             .
             .
CLRW       X
CLRW       Y
CLRW       Z
```

Macros can also be used to declare data structures. For example, assume that a data structure that consists of a number of directives is to be repeated frequently in a program. A macro for the structure can be defined as follows:

```
.MACRO     STRUCTURE    ARG1,ARG2,ARG3
.BYTE      ARG1
.BLKL      ARG2
.BLKW      ARG3
.ENDM      STRUCTURE
```

Then the macro calls

```
STRUCTURE     -10,15,5
                .
                .
STRUCTURE     ^X20,SIZE,SIZE
```

will be expanded into

```
          .BYTE    -10
          .BLKL    15
          .BLKW    5
            .
            .
            .
          .BYTE    ^X20
          .BLKL    SIZE
          .BLKW    SIZE
```

It must be mentioned that macro expansions are not printed in the assembly listing unless requested. The directives .SHOW and .NOSHOW can be specified to display or suppress macro expansions in the listing selectively. .SHOW and .NOSHOW can also be used, with arguments, to include or suppress macro definitions, as well as other source text, in the listing.

Labels within Macro Definitions

Care must be taken when labels are used in the body of a macro because the labels will be duplicated at every invocation of the macro. To illustrate, consider the following macro that clears a buffer of a certain size:

```
          .MACRO   CLEAR_BUFFER    BUFFER,SIZE
          CLRL     R1
CLEAR:    CLRB     BUFFER[R1]
          INCL     R1
          CMPL     R1,SIZE
          BLSS     CLEAR
          .ENDM    CLEAR_BUFFER
```

The macro call

```
          CLEAR_BUFFER INBUF,BUFSIZE
```

will be expanded into

```
          CLRL     R1
CLEAR:    CLRB     INBUF[R1]
          INCL     R1
          CMPL     R1,BUFSIZE
          BLSS     CLEAR
```

If the foregoing macro is invoked at another site in the program by

```
          CLEAR_BUFFER    A,#40
```

the call will be expanded into

```
        CLRL    R1
CLEAR:  CLRB    A[R1]
        INCL    R1
        CMPL    R1,#40
        BLSS    CLEAR
```

Thus the label CLEAR will be redefined, causing a multiply-defined-symbol error.

Obviously one way around the foregoing problem is to declare the labels in a macro as arguments:

```
        .MACRO  CLEAR_BUFFER    BUFFER,SIZE,CLEAR
        CLRL    R1
CLEAR:  CLRB    BUFFER[R1]
        INCL    R1
        CMPL    R1,SIZE
        BLSS    CLEAR
        .ENDM   CLEAR_BUFFER
```

Then when the macro is called, different labels can be specified for different invocations of the macro:

```
        CLEAR_BUFFER    INBUF,BUFSIZE,CLEAR1
            .
            .
            .
        CLEAR_BUFFER    A,#40,CLEAR2
```

Another way to handle labels within macro definitions is to let the assembler generate different labels for different invocations of the macro. This is done by specifying the label as a formal argument and placing a question mark (?) in front of this formal argument. As an example, the macro CLEAR_BUFFER can be defined as follows:

```
        .MACRO  CLEAR_BUFFER    BUFFER,SIZE,?CLEAR
        CLRL    R1
CLEAR:  CLRB    BUFFER[R1]
        INCL    R1
        CMPL    R1,SIZE
        BLSS    CLEAR
        .ENDM   CLEAR_BUFFER
```

Then the macro can be called with only the first two arguments specified; and when the macro is expanded, the assembler will generate a unique label for every call. The labels generated are of the form $n\$$, where n is an integer. Such labels are called *local labels*.[2] Local labels generated within a macro start at 30000$ and range up to 65535$. Using this facility, if CLEAR__BUFFER is invoked twice

```
        CLEAR__BUFFER   INBUF,BUFSIZE
            .
            .
            .
        CLEAR__BUFFER   A,#40
```

the resulting code is

```
        CLRL    R1
30000$: CLRB    INBUF[R1]
        INCL    R1
        CMPL    R1,BUFSIZE
        BLSS    30000$
            .
            .
            .
        CLRL    R1
30001$: CLRB    A[R1]
        INCL    R1
        CMPL    R1,#40
        BLSS    30001$
```

The programmer can still specify an actual argument to correspond to a formal argument that is preceded by a question mark. In this case the assembler substitutes the actual argument specified in the call for the formal argument.

Keyword Arguments

So far we have required the actual arguments to correspond to the formal arguments in number and position. This requirement can become tedious when the number of arguments is large and only a few arguments need to change from one call to another. For this reason, some assemblers allow default values to be specified for arguments. The default values will be substituted for the formal

---

[2]Local labels can also be used anywhere in a program, but their use should be discouraged in favor of more indicative symbolic names to contribute to the readability of the program. They may, however, be convenient to use for branch destinations in small loops. If a local label is introduced by a programmer, then n should be between 1 and 29999. Also, a local label is known only within the block in which it is defined, where a block is delimited by two user-defined labels.

arguments when a macro call does not specify corresponding actual arguments.

The MACRO Assembler allows the specification of default values for arguments. Such values are specified in the macro heading as follows:

formal-argument = default-value

Formal arguments specified in this manner are referred to as *keyword arguments*.

To illustrate the use of default values, consider the following macro with keyword arguments:

```
.MACRO    CLEAR_FLAGS    ARG1=FLAG1,ARG2=FLAG2,-
                         ARG3=FLAG3,CLR=CLRB
CLR       ARG1
CLR       ARG2
CLR       ARG3
.ENDM     CLEAR_FLAGS
```

This macro can be called by

```
CLEAR_FLAGS
```

which will be expanded into

```
CLRB      FLAG1
CLRB      FLAG2
CLRB      FLAG3
```

or it can be called by

```
CLEAR_FLAGS    FLAG4
```

which will be expanded into

```
CLRB      FLAG4
CLRB      FLAG2
CLRB      FLAG3
```

If it is desired to clear FLAG1, FLAG2, and FLAG4, then the first two default values need not be specified, and the macro call

```
CLEAR_FLAGS    ,,FLAG4
```

can be used, which will be expanded into

```
        CLRB    FLAG1
        CLRB    FLAG2
        CLRB    FLAG4
```

The two commas in the foregoing macro call are necessary.

An alternative to specifying actual arguments in a macro call to a macro with keyword arguments is to supply the actual arguments in the format

keyword = actual-argument

where *keyword* must be the same as the keyword of the formal argument name specified in the macro definition. Using this format, the macro call can specify any number of arguments in any order. For example, the macro CLEAR_FLAGS can be called with

```
        CLEAR_FLAGS    ARG3=FLAG4,ARG1=FLAG0
```

which will be expanded into

```
        CLRB    FLAG0
        CLRB    FLAG2
        CLRB    FLAG4
```

As a final example, the macro call

```
        CLEAR_FLAGS    ARG1=R2,ARG2=R3,ARG3=R4,CLR=CLRL
```

will generate

```
        CLRL    R2
        CLRL    R3
        CLRL    R4
```

Keyword arguments are useful when the number of arguments is large. Note that the I/O system macros of Chapter 4 use keyword arguments.

Finally, in this section we observe that no special symbol is used to distinguish a macro statement from other assembly statements. Thus at assembly time the nature of a symbol in the operator field of a statement is determined by the assembler only after searching through the tables of the assembler. MACRO searches the macro name table first. If the symbol is not in that table, then it searches the directive table or the op code table, depending on whether the symbol begins with a period or not. This search order implies that instruction mnemonics and directives can be redefined as macros.

8.3 Conditional Assembly

Conditional assembly is a facility for instructing the assembler to assemble or ignore certain blocks of code in a program, depending on certain conditions. Such blocks are referred to as *conditional blocks,* and they are normally used within macros.

The format of a conditional block in MACRO is:

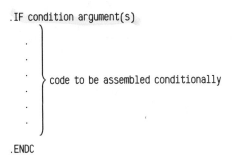

```
.IF condition argument(s)

      .
      .
      .  } code to be assembled conditionally
      .
      .
      .

.ENDC
```

The .IF directive begins the definition of the block. The .ENDC directive terminates the definition of the block. The statements within the block will be assembled if the condition of the argument(s) specified in the .IF statement is satisfied. Some of the conditions that can be tested for are:

```
EQUAL           (EQ)    Argument is equal to 0
NOT_EQUAL       (NE)    Argument is not equal to 0
GREATER         (GT)    Argument is greater than 0
GREATER_EQUAL   (GE)    Argument is greater or equal to 0
LESS_EQUAL      (LE)    Argument is less than or equal to 0
LESS_THAN       (LT)    Argument is less than 0
BLANK           (B)     Argument is blank
NOT_BLANK       (NB)    Argument is not blank
IDENTICAL       (IDN)   Arguments are identical
DIFFERENT       (DIF)   Arguments are different
```

Either the long form of the condition or the abbreviated form (shown within parentheses) can be used. Other conditions that can be tested for, as well as other forms of the .IF directive, are given in the *VAX-11 MACRO Language Reference Manual.*

The following should be observed when using the aforementioned conditions:

1. IDENTICAL and DIFFERENT require two arguments, and the rest require one argument.
2. BLANK, NOT_BLANK, IDENTICAL, and DIFFERENT test the arguments as character strings; but the others test the numeri-

cal value of an argument. (Remember that the numerical value of a label is the address that the label represents.)

Note that BLANK, NOT_BLANK, IDENTICAL, and DIFFERENT are useful only within a macro. The others may be useful anywhere in a program.

A conditional block can contain any assembly statements, including other conditional blocks. The expansion of such nested conditional blocks starts at the outermost .IF and proceeds inward. Whenever a .IF statement whose condition is not satisfied is encountered, all the statements between the .IF and its matching .ENDC are skipped.

To illustrate the use of conditional assembly, we consider a simple example of a macro that pushes the contents of two longwords on the user stack if a certain flag is equal to 0. Otherwise it pushes the contents of four longwords.

```
.MACRO    PUSH    A,B,C,D
PUSHL     A
PUSHL     B
.IF NE FLAG
      PUSHL    C
      PUSHL    D
.ENDC
.ENDM    PUSH
```

When called with the statements

```
FLAG=1
          PUSH    R1,R2,R3,R4
```

the foregoing macro generates the instructions

```
          PUSHL    R1
          PUSHL    R2
          PUSHL    R3
          PUSHL    R4
```

and when called with the statements

```
FLAG=0
          PUSH    X,Y
```

the macro generates the instructions

```
          PUSHL    X
          PUSHL    Y
```

Note that in the second call the last two arguments of the macro, C and D, are not needed; hence they can be absent or left blank in the call.

Macro PUSH in the foregoing can be made to push one or more longwords on the stack by testing for absent arguments, as follows:

```
.MACRO    PUSH    A,B,C,D
PUSHL     A
.IF  NB  B
     PUSHL    B
.ENDC
.IF  NB  C
     PUSHL    C
.ENDC
.IF  NB  D
     PUSHL    D
.ENDC
```

Now, if the macro is called by

```
PUSH    R5
```

then only R5 will be pushed, since the actual arguments corresponding to the formal arguments B, C, and D are absent in the macro call. Similarly,

```
PUSH    R5,R6
```

will push R5 and R6 only.

As another example of conditional assembly, consider the following macro, which swaps the contents of two longwords, using R0 for temporary storage.

```
.MACRO    SWAP    A,B
MOVL      A,R0
MOVL      B,A
MOVL      R0,B
.ENDM     SWAP
```

If SWAP is called with identical arguments, as in

```
SWAP    X,X
```

there is no need to generate any code. The foregoing macro can be modified to generate code only if the actual arguments are different, as follows:

```
.MACRO    SWAP    A,B
.IF  DIF   A,B
       MOVL    A,R0
       MOVL    B,A
       MOVL    R0,B
.ENDC
.ENDM    SWAP
```

This macro tests the two character strings that are passed to it as actual arguments; if they are different, then the statements between .IF and .ENDC are assembled when the macro is expanded. Otherwise the statements are skipped.

As a final example on conditional assembly, we write a recursive macro that raises the contents of a longword to a certain integer power N (N $\geq$ 0). The longword and the power are passed to the macro as arguments, and the result will be returned in a third longword argument.

```
.MACRO    POWER    X,N,Y
.IF  GT  N              ; is N > 0
COUNT=COUNT+1
       .IF  EQ  COUNT-1
          MOVL    X,Y
       .ENDC
       .IF  LT  COUNT-N
          MULL    X,Y
          POWER   X,N,Y
       .ENDC
.ENDC
.IF  EQ  N
       MOVL    #1,Y
.ENDC
.ENDM POWER
```

This macro can then be called, for example, with the statements

```
COUNT=0
       POWER    R1,5,R2
```

to generate the code for computing the contents of R1 raised to the power 5; the result will be returned in R2.

8.4 Repeat Blocks

Occasionally a program contains successive repetitions of identical or almost identical copies of the same code sequence. The directive .REPEAT (or .RPT) is useful in such cases. It requests that the assembler duplicates the code sequence, thus saving the programmer work.

The general format of a repeat block is

```
.REPEAT expression

        ⎫
  .     ⎬  code to be repeated
        ⎭

.ENDR
```

which repeats the code enclosed a number of times as specified by the expression. For example, the following repeat block reserves 100 bytes and initializes each byte to 1.[3]

```
.REPEAT    100
.BYTE      1
.ENDR
```

The block will be expanded by the assembler into

```
.BYTE    1  ⎫
.BYTE    1  ⎬
.BYTE    1  ⎬   100 times
         .  ⎬
         .  ⎬
         .  ⎬
.BYTE    1  ⎭
```

As another example, assume that an array, LIST, is to be filled with the ASCII code of the characters *a* through *z*. A repeat block to do this can be coded as follows:

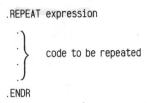

```
CHAR= A/a/
LIST:    .REPEAT    26 times
         .BYTE      CHAR
CHAR=CHAR+1
.ENDR
```

_____

[3] MACRO allows the .BYTE directive (as well as .WORD and .LONG) to specify the number of times a value in the operand field is to be repeated. Thus

```
.BYTE    1[100]
```

will have the same effect as the aforementioned repeat block. The square brackets are required syntax, and the number within the brackets is the repetition factor.

The block will be expanded into

```
LIST:     .BYTE     CHAR
CHAR=CHAR+1
          .BYTE     CHAR
CHAR=CHAR+1
          .BYTE     CHAR
CHAR=CHAR+1
          .BYTE     CHAR


                      .
                      .
                      .


CHAR=CHAR+1
          .BYTE     CHAR
CHAR=CHAR+1
          .BYTE     CHAR
```

Note that in addition to saving the programmer work, the repeat block facility saves disk space for the source file.

The expansion of a repeat block is not shown in the listing unless requested. The directives .SHOW and .NOSHOW can be used to list portions of a repeat block selectively, in a similar manner to listing macros.

Another useful repeat facility is the *indefinite repeat block*, whose general format is:

```
.IRP     symbol,<list of arguments>

         .
         .                  code to be repeated
         .
         .
         .

.ENDR
```

Indefinite repeat allows a list of arguments to be specified. The arguments must be enclosed by angle brackets and separated from each other by commas, blanks, or tab characters. The block of code is repeated once for each argument in the list. Each time the block is repeated, *symbol* is replaced by successive actual arguments from the argument list. For example, the following indefinite repeat block

```
.IRP     S,<A,B,C,D>
PUSHL    S
.ENDR
```

will generate the code

```
PUSHL    A
PUSHL    B
PUSHL    C
PUSHL    D
```

8.5 Other VAX-11 Macro Facilities

In this section we present additional macro facilities provided by the VAX-11 assembler, namely: argument concatenation, numeric arguments, and string arguments.

Argument Concatenation

Formal arguments within a macro can be concatenated with other text to form new symbols for different actual arguments passed to the macro. The concatenation operator is the apostrophe ('). For example, consider the following macro:

```
.MACRO    SWAP     A,B,TYPE
MOV'TYPE   A,R0
MOV'TYPE   B,A
MOV'TYPE   R0,B
.ENDM     SWAP
```

The text MOV will be concatenated with the actual argument (corresponding to TYPE) that is passed to macro SWAP. Thus this macro exchanges two arguments of any type (byte, word, longword, quadword, or octaword). If called by

```
SWAP    X,Y,W
```

the macro generates

```
MOVW    X,R0
MOVW    Y,X
MOVW    R0,Y
```

and if called by

```
SWAP    X,Y,Q
```

it generates

```
MOVQ    X,R0
MOVQ    Y,X
MOVQ    R0,Y
```

The concatenation operator can also follow a formal argument in the macro body. If a formal argument is followed by an apostrophe, the text after the apostrophe is concatenated with the actual argument passed to the macro. Finally, if two arguments are to be concatenated; then the two arguments must be separated by two consecutive apostrophes.

Passing Numeric Values as Arguments

So far we have seen that the name of a symbol (the character string) that is specified as an actual argument is substituted for the corresponding formal argument. (This is a result of the string substitution employed in the macro expansion.) If the numeric value of a symbol is to be substituted, a backslash (\) must be inserted in front of the symbol in the macro call. The assembler then passes the characters representing the decimal value of the symbol to the macro. As an example, the following macro generates a different label for different values of the actual arguments:

```
              .MACRO   TEMP      VALUE
LABEL'VALUE:  .BLKW    VALUE
              .ENDM    TEMP
```

The call to TEMP

```
   SIZE=5
           TEMP    \SIZE
```

generates

```
   LABEL5:   .BLKW    5
```

and the call

```
   SIZE=10
           TEMP    \SIZE
generates
   LABEL10:  .BLKW    10
```

Passing Strings as Arguments

If a character string that is to be passed as an actual argument contains separator characters such as blanks or semicolons, it must be delimited by a pair of angle brackets (< >). Consider the following macro, which converts an ASCII string into an ASCIC string.

```
.MACRO    ASC_ASCC    STRING
.ASCIC    /STRING/
.ENDM     ASC_ASCC
```

If this macro is to be called with a string argument, such as INPUT DATA (which contains a separator, a blank), the string must be enclosed by angle brackets; otherwise, INPUT and DATA would be interpreted by the assembler as two arguments. The following statements show some valid calls to the macro

```
ASC_ASCC    <INPUT DATA>
ASC_ASCC    HEADING
ASC_ASCC    VALID;STRING
```

In the last call only VALID is passed; the rest is interpreted as a comment.

If a string to be passed as an argument contains angle brackets, then a circumflex (^) that initiates the string should be used. The assembler interprets the character following the circumflex as a delimiter. For example, the macro

```
.MACRO    ENTRY    ROUTINE,MASK=^/M<R2,R3,R4,R5>/
.ENTRY    ROUTINE,MASK
.ENDM     ENTRY
```

can be called by

```
ENTRY    PROC
```

to generate

```
.ENTRY    PROC,^M<R2,R3,R4,R5>
```

or by

```
ENTRY    MAIN,^'M<>'
```

to generate

```
.ENTRY    MAIN,^M<>
```

Now we write a macro that uses the facilities of this section. The macro creates a data structure that contains the last name, first name, and social security number of a subject (such as a student or an employee). Each invocation of the macro generates an identical data structure, but each structure with a unique label and unique comments.

```
        .MACRO    STRUCTURE    SUBJECT, NUMBER, LAST_NAME,FIRST_NAME-
                               SOCIAL_SECURITY,DELIM
SUBJECT"NUMBER:                     DELIM DATA STRUCTURE FOR SUBJECT"NUMBER
        .BLKB     LAST_NAME
        .BLKB     FIRST_NAME
        .BLKB     SOCIAL_SECURITY
        .ENDM     STRUCTURE
```

To generate a structure for every subject (say, student) in a group of subjects, macro STRUCTURE can be included in a repeat block as follows:

```
LAST=12                      ;LENGTH IN BYTES OF LAST NAME,
FIRST=8                      ;...FIRST NAME, AND
SS=11                        ;...SOCIAL SECURITY
SUBJECTS=100                 ;NUMBER OF SUBJECTS
;
NUMBER=0
        .REPEAT   SUBJECTS
NUMBER=NUMBER+1
        STRUCTURE STUDENT,\NUMBER,\LAST,\FIRST,\SS,<;>
        .ENDR
```

The expansion of macro STRUCTURE for NUMBER=1 and NUMBER=2 is:

```
STUDENT1:                    ;DATA STRUCTURE FOR STUDENT1
        .BLKB     12
        .BLKB     8
        .BLKB     11
STUDENT2:
        .BLKB     12          ;DATA STRUCTURE FOR STUDENT2
        .BLKB     8
        .BLKB     11
```

For easy reference to the data structures generated in the foregoing example, a segment of code that stores the addresses STUDENT1, STUDENT2, and so on in a list of addresses may be written as follows:

```
        .MACRO    SUBJECT_ADDRESSES  SUBJECT,NUMBER
        .ADDRESS  SUBJECT''NUMBER
        .ENDM     SUBJECT_ADDRESSES
                         .
                         .
                         .
NUMBER=0
LIST:   .REPEAT   SUBJECTS
NUMBER=NUMBER+1
        SUBJECT_ADDRESSES STUDENT,\NUMBER
        .ENDR
```

```
        .MACRO   STRUCTURE   SUBJECT,NUMBER,LAST_NAME,FIRST_NAME,-
                             SOCIAL_SECURITY,DELIM
SUBJECT''NUMBER:
        .BLKB    LAST_NAME          DELIM DATA STRUCTURE FOR SUBJECT''NUMBER
        .BLKB    FIRST_NAME
        .BLKB    SOCIAL_SECURITY
        .ENDM    STRUCTURE
;
;
        .MACRO    SUBJECT_ADDRESSES  SUBJECT,NUMBER
        .ADDRESS  SUBJECT''NUMBER
        .ENDM     SUBJECT_ADDRESSES
;
;
LAST=12                               ;LENGTH IN BYTES OF LAST NAME,
FIRST=8                               ;...FIRST NAME, AND
SS=11                                 ;...AND SOCIAL SECURITY
SUBJECTS=100                          ;NUMBER OF SUBJECTS
;
;
NUMBER=0
        .REPEAT   SUBJECTS
NUMBER=NUMBER+1
        STRUCTURE STUDENT,\NUMBER,\LAST,\FIRST,\SS,<;>
        .ENDR
;
;
NUMBER=0
LIST:   .REPEAT   SUBJECTS
NUMBER=NUMBER+1
        SUBJECT_ADDRESSES STUDENT,\NUMBER
        .ENDR
;
;
NAME:   .BLKB     12                  ;LAST NAME OF A STUDENT TO BE
                                      ;...SEARCHED FOR
;                                     ;
;                                     ;
        .ENTRY    SEARCH,0            ;
        MOVAL     LIST,R6             ;R6 POINTS TO LIST OF ADDRESSES
        MOVAL     LIST+<4*SUBJECTS>,R8 ;R8 POINTS JUST BEYOND THE LIST
NEXT:   CMPC3     #LAST,NAME,@(R6)    ;IS THERE A MATCH?
        BEQL      FOUND               ;   YES
        ADDL      #4,R6               ;   NO: POINT TO NEXT ELEMENT IN LIST
        CMPL      R6,R8               ;IS IT THE END OF THE LIST?
        BLSS      NEXT                ;   NO: CONTINUE SEARCHING
              .                       ;   YES
              .                       ;
              .                       ;
FOUND:        .                       ;
              .                       ;
```

Figure 8.2 A program segment that illustrates the use of macros

Note the saving in coding and in disk space for the source file.

Figure 8.2 illustrates the use of the aforementioned two macros, STRUCTURE and SUBJECT_ADDRESSES, in a program. The program searches the last names in the list of students for a match with a last name contained in NAME. Note the use of the displacement deferred mode in the instruction labeled NEXT; since the displacement in this instance is zero, it need not be included explicitly.

8.6 Summary

Like a subprogram, a macro allows a programmer to use an instruction sequence in many places in a program by specifying the name of the macro. Unlike subprograms, however, the macros are actually expanded and inserted in place everywhere they are called during assembly time. As a result, the object code contains as many copies of a macro as the number of times it is called in the program. Conditional assembly is a feature of the assembler that allows it to include or skip a block of code in a program during assembly time depending on the result of a test. By using conditional assembly, a programmer can often make a program adapt to the local environment and consequently increase its versatility. Repeat blocks enable a programmer to generate identical or nearly identical copies of the same code sequence in a program.

EXERCISES

1. a. Write a macro that finds the absolute value of a longword. The macro is to be called with the longword as an argument, and it is to return the absolute value in a different argument.

    b. Show a macro call to the macro in Exercise 1a to find the absolute value of a memory location LOC. Also show the expansion of the macro following the call.

2. a. Write a macro that clears a buffer to all zeroes. The macro expects as arguments the buffer address; the buffer type (byte, word, or longword); and the buffer size (in bytes, words, or longwords depending on the buffer type).

    b. Show the expansion of the macro in Exercise 2a when called to clear a buffer, BUFB, of size 50 bytes.

    c. Repeat Exercise 2b for a buffer, BUFL, of size 100 longwords.

3. a. Write a macro that exchanges the contents of any two longwords. The exchange is to take place only if the first longword is greater than the second.

    b. Show a macro call to the macro in Exercise 3a that, possibly, exchanges the contents of two memory locations, LOC1 and LOC2. Also show the expansion of the macro following the call.

    c. Show a macro call to the macro in Exercise 3a that, possibly, exchanges the contents of two registers. Also show the expansion of the macro following the call.

4. a. Write a macro that copies an array of longwords into another. The macro expects as arguments the addresses of the arrays and their size.

b. Show the expansion of the macro in Exercise 4a for a call to copy an array A of size 10 longwords into an array B.

5. **a.** Write a macro that exchanges the contents of two arrays of long-words. The address of the arrays and their size are to be passed as arguments to the macro.

b. Show a macro call to the macro in Exercise 5a to exchange two arrays of size 50 longwords. Also show the expansion of the macro following the call.

6. An array is to contain the consecutive numbers 100 through 130. The first byte of the array is to have the symbolic address TABLE. Declare this array using a repeat block.

7. Initialize the contents of R0 through R10 to the numbers 0 through 10, respectively. Use an indefinite repeat block.

8. Repeat Exercise 7 using a repeat block.

9. Complete the program of Figure 8.2 to perform the following:
   a. Read in a list of records for 20 students.
   b. Prompt the user to enter the last name of a student.
   c. Print the records of all students whose last names match the name entered. If a match is not found, then print an appropriate message.

10. Write a program that reads a list of records where each record contains information about a person's:

    name (last name followed by first name separated by at least one blank)
    address
    height
    weight
    age

    The program is then to sort the list alphabetically by last name and print the sorted list. Use macros similar to those used in the program of Figure 8.2 to construct the data structures.

Chapter 9

Advanced Data Types

UP TO now we have used only a few elementary data types (or formats). We are familiar with binary integers stored as bytes, words, and longwords. We have also stored alphanumeric text as ASCII strings. These few data types taken together are only the tip of the iceberg, however. There are a number of other formats that are important in understanding the full range of computer-coded data.

For engineering and scientific computations, real numbers are stored in *floating-point* formats. The VAX-11 has four such formats: longword, quadword, and two longer formats. The MACRO assembler also provides for short floating-point literals.

On most modern computers, decimal integer (base 10) data can be stored in several ways. Algebraic signs may by placed in the last byte along with the low-order digit to form *zoned* or *overpunched* numeric strings. Decimal digits are sometimes packed two to the byte to form a *packed decimal* string. Decimal strings can also be *edited*, which means, for instance, changing the string 1234567 into the string $12,345.67. Machine instructions are often provided for performing decimal arithmetic and editing of these data types. Generally speaking, floating point is the arithmetic of science, packed decimal is the arithmetic of business, and integer binary is the arithmetic of program control.

Nonnumeric data also come in various formats that have not yet been discussed. Bit strings that start in the middle of one byte and end in the middle of another can sometimes be used as a data type. Logically related pieces of data such as the *fields* of a customer's purchase order can be grouped into a *record* and inserted into a *queue.* Newer computers sometimes have instructions for inserting and deleting from such queues. As we shall see, the VAX-11 accommodates all the aforementioned data types and has instructions for converting data from one type to another, as well as instructions for operating on each type. We now examine these formats and instructions in detail.

9.1 Floating-Point Representations and Arithmetic

So far we have seen only integer data types and integer arithmetic instructions. These instructions can be used to perform calculations that involve decimal fractions. Suppose, for example, we have the decimal numbers 1234 and -167. We can think of these as 12.34 and -1.67 without "telling" the computer. In adding, the decimal point does not have to be known to the computer. It adds two integers, and the programmer can keep track of the decimal points. Although this would be easy enough in this example, it is not so easy in the following calculation:

$$(2.61 + 0.1726 \times 384.5)/(0.0527 - 3 \times 0.685)$$

In this calculation, it is not easy to determine the number of bytes required to hold the answer, let alone keep track of the decimal point location at each stage of the computation. An even greater problem is that the actual data are usually not known at the time the program is being written. Even the range of each data item may not be sharply defined. All we might know is that the form of the computation is:

$$(a + bc)/(d - ef)$$

where the variable a ranges from 1 to 10, the variable b ranges from 0.0001 to 0.1, and so forth.

Such calculations are more common in engineering and science than in business. Some computers are not aimed at the scientific market and do not provide data types and instructions that ease the programming for these calculations. The VAX-11 does, of course. Floating-point formats provide data types for large sets of real numbers. Typically, a floating-point number x can be in the range

$$10^{-38} < x < 10^{38}$$

and can have seven or eight decimal significant figures in single precision and fifteen or sixteen significant figures in double precision. In newer computers one is likely to find a spectrum of floating-point formats with several different precision levels. Floating-point data items of a particular format require a fixed number of bytes for storage. The user can pick from the lengths provided the format best suited to the specific calculation. Floating-point computations are usually performed in binary with much internal parallelism; hence they are relatively fast.

If the result of a floating-point computation cannot be contained in the given data type, the result is truncated or rounded to a value that can be so contained. The error involved in this process is called *roundoff* (even in machines which do not round). Typically, computers do not round automatically, whereas calculators do. Rounding requires a second pass through the adder, since rounding may propagate through the whole number. This would slow the computation considerably and is often not necessary. Besides, each manufacturer wants to achieve as fast an add time as possible. Some manufactures have introduced various devices for partial rounding (that is, sometimes they do, sometimes they do not), but these devices are not considered here.

To perform a floating-point computation, a number must first be converted to binary. This in itself may involve an error in the case of fractions. (Those unfamiliar with the details of number conversions should consult Appendix A.) The binary number is then stored in one of the floating-point formats. The computations involving the numbers may create roundoff error, and the conversion of the results to a specific decimal format may introduce more error. Normally all such errors are reasonably small and quite acceptable to the engineer or scientist (but not to the accountant). In some cases rounding errors can be disastrously large. Such cases require specialists and are not treated here.

Normalized Floating-Point Numbers

A floating-point number consists of a binary fraction f, also called the *mantissa*, and a binary integer exponent e. Mathematically, the number is equal to

$$f \times 2^e$$

If the fraction is greater than or equal to 0.5 and less than 1.0 in absolute value, then the floating-point number is said to be *normalized*, or in normal form. The following numbers are in normal form.

$$(.11000000 \times 10^{10})_2 = 3_{10}$$
$$(.10000000 \times 10^{-10})_2 = 0.125_{10}$$
$$(-.10100000 \times 10^{101})_2 = -20_{10}$$

In the foregoing examples, the left side of the equality is given in binary. In the first example, the fraction is the binary number

.11000000; the base or radix is binary 10 (that is, 2); and the exponent is binary 10 (again, 2). In decimal the fraction is 0.75 or ¾, the base is 2, and the exponent is 2. Thus the number is ¾ × 4. The decimal equivalent of each number is given on the right.

The following numbers are not in normal form.

$$(1.1000000 \times 10^{01})_2 = 3_{10}$$
$$(.01000000 \times 10^{-01})_2 = 0.125_{10}$$
$$(-.00101000 \times 10^{111})_2 = -20_{10}$$

For a fraction to be normalized, it cannot have any nonzero bits to the left of the binary point (or else it would be greater than 1); and the first bit to the right of the binary point must be 1 (or else it would be less than 0.5). It is necessary to store only the fraction and the exponent, since the base is always implied—for example, 2 on the VAX-11. Some computers, such as the IBM System/370 and its succesors, use 16 for the base. Others use base 10, although newer computers seldom do.

Both the fraction and the exponent have algebraic signs. Either can be positive or negative; hence both signs must be stored. It is not convenient, however, for the computer to deal with signed exponents. In multiplying two floating-point numbers, the exponents must be added. In adding two numbers, the exponents must be compared and the mantissas aligned accordingly. The comparison operation is simpler and faster if the exponents are unsigned integers. Thus a *biased* exponent is often used where the true exponent is scaled and is always positive. On the VAX-11 an exponent is scaled by adding 128 to it. Thus a stored exponent of 128 is interpreted as a mathematical exponent of 0. An exponent of 129 is interpreted as a mathematical exponent of 1, an exponent of 127 is interpreted as -1, and so forth. Exponents are stored as 8-bit binary integers. Thus a mathematical exponent of 1 is stored as 10000001, an exponent of 0 is stored as 10000000, and an exponent of -1 is 01111111. The largest exponent possible is 11111111 or decimal 127, and the smallest is 00000000 or decimal -128. Thus floating-point numbers are limited to the range 2^{127} down to 2^{-128}. This is approximately equal to the decimal range $10^{\pm 38}$ given earlier.

Floating-Point Arithmetic

We now need to see in some detail how arithmetic is performed on floating-point data. We will use a simplified, hypothetical floating-point system for illustration.

For convenience, we will write a floating-point number in the notation (f, e), where f is the binary fraction and e is the binary integer exponent biased as previously. Also for simplicity, we will assume that all mantissas are 8 bits long. On a real computer the mantissa would normally be longer. In this system the number 3_{10} would be represented as (.11000000,10000010), and the number $.125_{10}$ would be represented as (.10000000,01111110).We consider the problems of adding and multiplying these two numbers.

In order to add two floating-point numbers, the exponents must be the same. The first order of business is to compare the two exponents and see which is larger. In this case, 10000010 is larger than 01111110. The fraction of the smaller number is then shifted one place to the right, and the exponent is incremented by one. This produces (.01000000,01111111). The number is, of course, no longer in normal form. As we know, the process of shifting is equivalent to multiplying or dividing by 2. Hence, we have divided the fraction by 2 and, at the same time, increased the exponent by 1. Thus the value of the number is unchanged. The rightmost bit of the fraction is lost in this process. In this case it was 0, so no damage was done. In other cases, a small error, called a *rounding error,* occurs as a result of the shift.

On comparing exponents again, 01111111 is still the smaller. Hence we repeat the shifting. The number .125 successively takes on the forms

    (.10000000,01111110)
    (.01000000,01111111)
    (.00100000,10000000)
    (.00010000,10000001)
    (.00001000,10000010)

Now the exponents are the same; hence the fractions can be added. We get .11001000 for the fraction of the sum. Fortunately, in this case the fraction for the sum is normalized; hence its exponent is also 10000010. If the fraction of the sum had been more than or equal to 1, say 1.00010000, then it would have been necessary to normalize the sum. We would have shifted it right and added 1 to the exponent of the sum. If it had been less than 0.5, say .00100000, we would have shifted it left two places and subtracted 2 from the exponent.

In summary, the addition operations are:

1. Compare exponents.
2. Shift the fraction of the number with the smaller exponent to the right until the exponents are the same.
3. Add the fractions.
4. Normalize the sum if required.

Multiplication is easier: we simply multiply the fractions and add the exponents. In multiplying two 8-bit fractions that are normalized, we get a 16-bit fraction as the product in which either the most significant bit or the second most significant bit is 1. Since the two fractions are less than 1, the product is also less than 1. Also, since the two fractions are greater than or equal to 0.5, the product is greater than or equal to 0.25. If there is a 1 in the first position, then the product is already normalized. If there is a 0, the fraction must be shifted left by one position and the exponent decreased by 1.

In adding the exponents, the bias is added twice. To offset, we must subtract 10000000 from the sum. Finally, we save only the leading 8 bits of the product. In our example we get

.11000000 × .10000000 = .0110000000000000
10000010 + 01111110 − 10000000 = 100000000 − 10000000 = 10000000

or, after normalization, (.11000000,01111111).

In summary:

1. Multiply the fractions.
2. Add the exponents; then subtract the extra bias (10000000).
3. Normalize the result.
4. Truncate the product fraction to eight places.

The reader might enjoy speculating on the details of floating-point subtraction and division.

Single-Precision and Double-Precision Formats

The usual floating-point format on the VAX-11 is 32 bits long. The bits are numbered from 0 to 31, from right to left as usual. This format is called the F-format. Numbers in the F-format are represented as 8 hex nibbles. This representation causes some peculiar results. For instance, the F-format representation for the number 1 is 00004080. The representation for 10 is 00004220, and the representation for .1 rounded to best accuracy is CCCD3ECC. To understand how this happens, we must examine the format in more detail.

Schematically, the F-format is the following:

31	16	15	14	7	6	0
fraction (low bits)		s	exponent		fraction	

This schema is more meaningful if read left to right as follows:

15	14	exponent	7	6	fraction	0
s		exponent			fraction	
fraction (low bits)						

Since the first bit of a normalized fraction must be 1, it is not explicitly stored. The sign bit (bit 15) is the sign of the fraction.

Let us now follow the steps in deciding how the decimal number 10 would be stored in F-format. First we convert to binary, which gives us 1010. We must now express 1010 as a normalized fraction and exponent

$$1010 = .1010 \times 10^{100}$$

Thus the fraction is .1010, and the exponent is 100. We now bias the exponent to obtain 10000100, and we omit the leading 1 in the fraction. In F-format, then, we get:

31	16	15	14	7	6	0
0000000000000000		0	10000100		0100000	

Looking at the 32 bits together, we have

00000000000000000100001000100000

In groups of four we have

0000 0000 0000 0000 0100 0010 0010 0000

In hex nibble notation, this is 00004220, as given previously.

The MACRO assembler recognizes hex constants by the prefix ^X. The aforementioned number can be stored in a longword by coding:

```
TEN:    .LONG   ^X00004220   ; or simply ^X4220
```

Equivalently, it can be stored by the directive

```
TEN:    .FLOAT  10
```

The double or D-format is a quadword floating-point format, referred to as *double precision*. Bits 0 through 31 are the same as in F-format, and the first bit of the fraction is omitted as before. The second bit of the fraction goes in bit 6, the third in bit 5, and so forth. The eighth bit of the fraction goes in bit 0. In F-format, bits 9 through 24 of the fraction are stored in bits 31, 30, . . . 16. In D-format the mantissa is longer by 32 bits. Bits 25–40 of the fraction are stored in bits 47, 46, . . . 32, and bits 41–56 are stored in 63, 62, . . . 48. Schematically, we have:

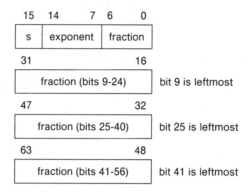

The number ten given here, when stored in D-format, would simply contain an extra longword of zeros.

31		16	15	14	7	6	0
0000000000000000			0	10000100		0100000	

63		32
00000000000000000000000000000000		

The following section of MACRO assembly code shows the assembled form of several floating point values in both F and D formats.

```
          00004220 0000   1 F_NOS:  .FLOAT  10
          00004080 0004   2         .FLOAT   1
          CCCD3ECC 0008   3         .FLOAT  .1
          D70A3D23 000C   4         .FLOAT  .01
00000000  00004220 0010   5 D_NOS:  .DOUBLE 10
00000000  00004080 0018   6         .DOUBLE  1
CCCDCCCC  CCCC3ECC 0020   7         .DOUBLE .1
A3D73D70  D70A3D23 0028   8         .DOUBLE .01
```

Besides the F and D floating formats, there are also the G and H floating formats, which we do not cover here except for mentioning that they provide more precision or larger range. Interested readers should consult the *VAX Architecture Handbook*.

Floating-Point Instructions

All the VAX-11 generic arithmetic mnemonics—ADD, SUB, MUL, and DIV, as well as CLR, MOV, TST, and CVT (CVT or convert is covered in Section 9.2)—can be suffixed with F, D, G, or H to form floating-point arithmetic instructions. As we have seen, floating-point constants can be stored in F-format with the .FLOAT directive. An alternative directive is .F_FLOATING. D format constants can be stored with .DOUBLE and .D_FLOATING.

Floating literals can also be formed by the prefix F. In this case the assembler uses literal mode if possible. Bits 7 and 6 of the first and only byte of the assembled operand must be 0. Bits 5–0 are mapped into bits 9–4 of a fictitious F-format number whose other bits are assumed to be 0 except for the exponent bias in bit 14. Only a few numbers can be so represented (64 of them, in fact). The numbers are given in the *VAX Architecture Handbook*. They include 1, 2, 4, 8, 16, 32, 64, 5, 6, 7, 8, 9, 10, and 0.5. For example, the literal F10 (or ˆF10.0, ˆF10., and so on) is stored as:

Internally, in the ALU, this literal is expanded into F format. Schematically, the following bits marked by * show where the bits are inserted. Bit 14 of the internal F format is set to 1.

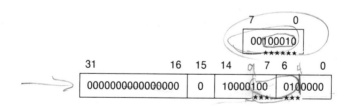

If a value is required that is not available in literal mode, the assembler uses relative mode, and a full F formatted constant is used.

We now use some of these floating instructions and directives in the following program segment, which computes the average of five floating-point numbers in F format.

The ADDF instruction is indexed by R6. The effective address is LIST plus four times the contents of R6. If this had been an ADDD instruction, eight times the contents of R6 would have been added. The literal, #ˆF5.0, in the DIVF instruction could have been coded simply #5.0 or #5, since F-format is the implied context.

```
LIST:      .FLOAT     25.7,-143781.964,382.,435.7,22367.45
             .
             .
             .
           MOVL       #4,R6            ;INDICES LIST[4],...,LIST[0]
           CLRL       R7               ;ACCESSED IN DESCENDING ORDER.
LOOP:      ADDF       LIST[R6],R7      ;ACCUMULATED IN R7
           SOBGEQ     R6,LOOP          ;TEST FOR >= 0, LOOP IF TRUE
           DIVF       #^F5.0,R7        ;AVERAGE LEFT IN R7
             .
             .
             .
```

There are two VAX-11 instructions for evaluating floating-point polynomials, POLYF and POLYD. Let us evaluate the polynomial

$$2.1x^3 - 6.82x^2 + .04x - 21.824$$

at $x = -62.9$ using F-format. The following program segment performs this task.

```
TABLE:     .FLOAT     2.1,-6.82,.04,-21.824
X    :     .FLOAT     -62.9
ANS  :     .BLKL      1
             .
             .
             .
           POLYF      X,#3,TABLE   ; EVALUATE A POLYNOMIAL
                                   ; AT X. IT IS OF DEGREE 3
                                   ; AND ITS COEFFICIENTS ARE
                                   ; STORED IN F FORMAT STARTING
                                   ; AT LOCATION TABLE.
           MOVL       R0,ANS       ; MOVE THE COMPUTED ANSWER
                                   ; FROM R0 TO LOCATION ANS.
```

POLYF returns the answer in R0, and POLYD returns the answer in R0 and R1.

The foregoing program segment in D-format would be:

```
TABLE:     .DOUBLE    2.1,-6.82,.04,-21.824
X    :     .DOUBLE    -62.9
ANS  :     .BLKQ      1
             .
             .
             .
           POLYD      X,#3,TABLE   ; EVALUATE A POLYNOMIAL
                                   ; AT X. IT IS OF DEGREE 3
                                   ; AND ITS COEFFICIENTS ARE
                                   ; STORED IN F FORMAT STARTING
                                   ; AT LOCATION TABLE.
           MOVQ       R0,ANS       ; MOVE THE COMPUTED ANSWER
                                   ; FROM R0 AND R1 TO LOCATION ANS.
```

Table 9.1 shows some of the most important floating-point instructions, including some of the instructions for converting integer longwords to and from floating point:

Table 9.1 Floating-Point Instructions

Mnemonic	Operand(s)	Effect	Instruction
ADDF2	src,dst	(dst)←(dst)+(src)	Add F-format
ADDF3	src1,src2,dst	(dst)←(src2)+(src1)	Add F-format
ADDD2	src,dst	(dst)←(dst)+(src)	Add D-format
ADDD3	src1,src2,dst	(dst)←(src2)+(src1)	Add D-format
CVTFL	src,dst	(dst)←trunc(src)	Convert F-Longword
CVTDL	src,dst	(dst)←trunc(src)	Convert D-Longword
CVTLF	src,dst	(dst)←F-float(src)	Convert Longword-F
CVTLD	src,dst	(dst)←D-float(src)	Convert Longword-D
CVTRFL	src,dst	(dst)←round(src)	Convert F-Longword
CVTRDL	src,dst	(dst)←round(src)	Convert D-Longword
DIVF2	src,dst	(dst)←(dst)/(src)	Divide F-format
DIVF3	src1,src2,dst	(dst)←(src2)/(src1)	Divide F-format
DIVD2	src,dst	(dst)←(dst)/(src)	Divide D-format
DIVD3	src1,src2,dst	(dst)←(src2)/(src1)	Divide D-format
MNEGF	src,dst	(dst)← −(src)	Move Neg F-format
MNEGD	src,dst	(dst)← −(src)	Move Neg D-format
MOVAF	src,dst	dst←src	Move Address F-format
MOVAD	src,dst	dst←src	Move Address D-format
MOVF	src,dst	(dst)←(src)	Move F-format
MOVD	src,dst	(dst)←(src)	Move D-format
MULF2	src,dst	(dst)←(dst)·(src)	Multiply F-format
MULF3	src1,src2,dst	(dst)←(src2)·(src1)	Multiply F-format
MULD2	src,dst	(dst)←(dst)·(src)	Multiply D-format
MULD3	src1,src2,dst	(dst)←(src2)·(src1)	Multiply D-format
SUBF2	src,dst	(dst)←(dst)−(src)	Subtract F-format
SUBF3	src1,src2,dst	(dst)←(src2)−(src1)	Subtract F-format
SUBD2	src,dst	(dst)←(dst)−(src)	Subtract D-format
SUBD3	src1,src2,dst	(dst)←(src2)−(src1)	Subtract D-format

9.2 Decimal Representations and Arithmetic

Decimal integer arithmetic is as important in the world of business as floating-point arithmetic is in the world of science. Its main advantages are that it requires no number system conversions and allows for variable length integer arithmetic; thus rounding errors can be avoided. (As we shall see, there is a limit of 31 digits on such calculations, but this will handle most business transactions.) Both criteria are important in business calculations, whereas speed of computation is not as important. In fact, computing is usually only a small part of the time requirements of business applications. File management and I/0 consume the bulk of the total run time. Any general-purpose computer must provide arithmetic capabilities for both scientific and business markets.

On the VAX-11, integers can be represented in 18 different formats. As mentioned earlier, we are familiar with binary integers stored as bytes, words, longwords, quadwords, and octawords. Since each binary format can be signed or unsigned, ten different data types (each representing a different range of integers) are allowed. Integers can also be stored as ASCII strings with leading sign byte of + (ASCII 2B), space (ASCII 20), or − (ASCII 2D). This format is called *leading separate numeric.* In addition, there are two ASCII formats that insert the sign in the byte with the last digit. These are called the *zoned* and the *overpunched* numeric formats. Together they are referred to as *trailing* numeric formats. Integers can also be stored as *packed demical* strings (one format) and as floating-point data (four formats). In this section we examine each of these decimal formats in turn.

Leading Separate and Trailing Numeric Formats

If we store the number −167 in ASCII, we get

BYTE-3	BYTE-2	BYTE-1	BYTE-0
37	36	31	2D

Here 2D in BYTE-0 represents the two hex nibbles 00101101, and similarly for the other bytes. This representation is straightforward and easily understandable. The leading separate format is essentially the same as ASCII format. In leading separate format, however, there must be a sign byte; it is not optional. Hence 167 must be stored in 4 bytes, the first (byte 0) being either an ASCII + or an ASCII space. If we wish to store 167 as an ASCII string of 3 bytes (that is, no sign byte) we can of course do so, but we cannot use any of the instructions that operate on leading separate data.

In contrast to the foregoing, when one stores −167 in zoned format, the minus sign shares the byte with the 7. In this byte, the leftmost hex nibble is coded as 7 instead of 3. (Remember that an ASCII 7 is 37.) Hence, in zoned format, −167 is

BYTE-2	BYTE-1	BYTE-0
77	36	31

The positive number 167 becomes

BYTE-2	BYTE-1	BYTE-0
37	36	31

Thus the ASCII string 167 is the same as the zoned format. In this format, a positive sign does not affect the last byte. In other words, the sign is stored in the left nibble of the last byte: 3 for plus and 7 for minus. Since 3 is the left nibble of ASCII numeric data, there is no difference.

In overpunched format, −167 requires three bytes of storage, and the minus shares the byte with the 7 just as in the zoned format; but the byte that contains the minus and the 7 is coded P (ASCII 50). Punched cards use a code called the Hollerith code. In this code the letter P is encoded as two punches, one in the minus row (second row from the top of the card) and one in the 7's row (tenth row from the top: the rows are + − 0 1 2 3 4 5 6 7 8 9). In this code, G (rows + and 7) is a +7. The ASCII code for G is 47. The overpunch code is a carryover from earlier times, when businesses used punched cards for their accounting files. Credits were overpunched with a minus, and debits were overpunched with a plus. Hence in this code we have

BYTE-2	BYTE-1	BYTE-0	
50	36	31	(−167)
47	36	31	(+167)
7B	36	31	(+160, Hollerith + and 0 becomes 7B)
7D	36	31	(−160, Hollerith − and 0 becomes 7D)

In order to understand this code in its entirety, the reader must understand the Hollerith code. This particular format is not important enough to pursue further here, however.

Table 9.2 shows the representation of the least significant digit and sign for the zoned and the overpunch formats. The length of each of these data types is defined as the number of digits in the number, not the number of bytes required to store it. This means that the length of −167 is 3 even if it is stored in leading separate numeric format. The largest length allowed for these types is 31; the smallest is 0. The value of a string of length 0 is 0. In leading separate format the string requires a byte for a sign (+, SP, or −) but in zoned or overpunched format no memory at all is required for length 0.

Packed Decimal

Decimal numbers can also be stored in packed decimal form. In storing −167 in one of the ASCII formats, we use one byte for each digit. Thus the 1 is stored as 00110001. Clearly, 4 bits, or one hex nibble, will suffice to store a single decimal digit. Thus in a single byte we can store both the 1 and the 6. In the second byte we can

Table 9.2 Least Significant Digit, Zoned, and Overpunch Formats (ASCII)

Digit	Zoned	Overpunch
0	0	{
1	1	A
2	2	B
3	3	C
4	4	D
5	5	E
6	6	F
7	7	G
8	8	H
9	9	I
−0	p	}
−1	q	J
−2	r	K
−3	s	L
−4	t	M
−5	u	N
−6	v	O
−7	w	P
−8	x	Q
−9	y	R

store the 7, along with a single nibble code for the minus. By convention, a minus is stored as a hex D or B, and a plus is stored as a hex C, A, E, or F. For compatibility with other hardware, the C is preferred for plus and the D for minus. Hence, −167 becomes

BYTE-1	BYTE-0
7D	16

Since −167 has three digits plus a sign, there are four characters to be stored, which fit nicely into 2 bytes. For an odd number of characters, we pad with a leading 0. Thus to store 1234 in packed decimal, we need three bytes.

BYTE-2	BYTE-1	BYTE-0
4C	23	01

The length of a packed decimal string is measured by its number of digits, not by the number of bytes required to store it. Thus the length of −167 is 3, and the length of 1234 is 4. The maximum allowable length for the packed decimal data type is 31, as in the case of the other numeric decimal formats. A packed decimal string

Table 9.3 Packed Decimal Instructions

Mnemonic	Operand(s)	Effect	Instruction
ADDP4	for 4 operands:	(dst)←(dst)+(src)	Add Packed
ADDP6	srclength,src,	(dst)←(src2)+(src1)	Add Packed
SUBP4	dstlength,dst	(dst)←(dst)−(src)	Sub Packed
SUBP6	for 6 operands: src1length,src1, src2length,src2, dstlength,dst	(dst)←(src2)−(src1)	Sub Packed
DIVP	(6 operands only)	(dst)←(src2)/(src1)	Div Packed
MULP	(6 operands only)	(dst)←(src2)·(src1)	Mul Packed

of length 0 requires one byte of storage in which the hex nibbles are 0C.

Packed decimal arithmetic is serial and variable length in nature. Two packed decimal numbers are added one byte at a time, right to left. The destination field should be long enough to receive the result. We defer an example of packed decimal arithmetic to the next section, where it is convenient to exhibit a program that combines type conversion with packed decimal arithmetic. Table 9.3 is a short table of packed decimal instructions.

Instructions for Conversion, Arithmetic, and Editing

We first consider the problem of converting two ASCII leading separate numeric strings to packed decimal, adding them, and converting the result back to leading separate numeric. Let the two given values be 1234 and −167, as previously. The following program segment performs the required task.

```
A:       .ASCII   /+1234/                     ; LEADING SEPARATE
B:       .ASCII   /-167/                      ; LEADING SEPARATE
A_PAK:   .BLKB    3                           ; ROOM FOR PACKED
B_PAK:   .BLKB    2                           ; ROOM FOR PACKED
C_PAK:   .BLKB    3                           ; ROOM FOR PACKED
C:       .BLKB    6                           ; ROOM FOR RESULT
         CVTSP    #4,A,#4,A_PAK                ; CONVERT A
         CVTSP    #3,B,#3,B_PAK                ; CONVERT B
         ADDP6    #4,A_PAK,#3,B_PAK,#4,C_PAK   ; ADD
         CVTPS    #4,C_PAK,#4,C                ; CONVERT C
```

All the convert instruction mnemonics in the VAX-11 start with the generic CVT. This is followed by a letter representing the source field and another for the destination field. There are no fewer than fifty different convert instructions. We have already seen some of the convert instructions that apply to floating-point data items. Some of the others are:

CVTSP	separate to packed
CVTPS	packed to separate
CVTPL	packed to longword
CVTLP	longword to packed

Note that these instructions use R0–R3. The ADDP6 instruction previously given uses R0–R5. In the case of the CVTSP instruction, four operands are required: source length, source address, destination length, and destination address. Note that in converting A to A_PAK, the length of both fields is 4; but only 3 bytes have been reserved for A_PAK. All the convert instructions are given in Appendix C, but we will see some more later in this chapter.

On the VAX-11 the only decimal arithmetic supplied is that for the packed decimal format. Since data originally enter (and finally leave) the computer in ASCII (leading separate, zoned, or overpunched), they must be converted to packed decimal or binary integer or floating point for computation. Financial and other numeric business data are usually converted to packed decimal for computing. The ADDP instruction is available in two forms: ADDP4 and ADDP6. The first has four arguments: source length, source address, destination length, and destination address. The 6-format form allows for the sum to be stored in a separate field in the same fashion as other VAX-11 ADD instructions.

Rather than converting the packed decimal result back to signed separate numeric or some other character format for output, the result can be edited and converted to ASCII with a single instruction. The EDITPC instruction is designed to insert currency signs, commas, periods, and so on. It also will suppress leading zeros and float the currency sign or the algebraic sign to the right as the leading zeroes are being suppressed.

Suppose, for example, we need a subroutine to compute the amount field in a check. Suppose the amount field is enclosed in a box that is ten characters long. If the amount is 1234567, then it is to be printed as $12,345.67. Counting the punctuation characters, there are exactly ten characters for the box. If the amount is 0000123, however, we wish to print $*****1.23 instead of $00,001.23 or $, 1.23. These last two formats do not look good; also, the asterisks protect the check from later alterations. The following table shows various amount fields and the required edited output.

Amount	Edited Appearance	
1234567	$12,345.67	
0123456	$*1,234.56	
0012345	$***123.45	(not $**,123.45)
0001234	$****12.34	
0000123	$*****1.23	
0000012	$******.12	
0000001	$******.01	(not $******.*1)
0000000	**********	(not $******.00)

The EDITPC (edit packed to character) instruction requires four parameters: source length, source address, pattern address, and destination. The source field is, of course, of packed decimal type. The pattern address points to what might be called the first instruction in a pattern program. These pattern instructions are pseudo-instructions and are listed in the *VAX Architecture Handbook.* The destination is specified by an address only, since its length is implied by the pattern.

The following procedure illustrates the computation of the check amount box. The routine requires two arguments: the packed decimal source address (at @4(AP)) and the destination address (at @8(AP)).

```
          .ENTRY          FILL_AMT_BOX,0
          EDITPC          #7,@4(AP),PATTERN,@8(AP)
          RET
PATTERN:
          EO$LOAD_FILL    /*/     ; SET FILL CHAR TO *
          EO$SET_SIGNIF           ; DO NOT FILL YET
          EO$INSERT       /$/     ; PUT IN THE $
          EO$CLEAR_SIGNIF         ; START FILLING
          EO$MOVE         2       ; MOVE 2 DIGITS OR FILL
          EO$INSERT       /,/     ; INSERT OR FILL
          EO$MOVE         3       ; MOVE 3 DIGITS OR FILL
          EO$SET_SIGNIF           ; STOP FILLING
          EO$INSERT       /./     ; INSERT .
          EO$MOVE         2       ; MOVE 2 DIGITS
          EO$BLANK_ZERO           ; TOTAL FILL IF 0
          EO$END
          .END
```

This pattern builds the output as follows:

1. The load fill instruction places an asterisk in a special register called the *fill register.* This character replaces leading zeros and any punctuation that occurs before the first significant digit. The replacement occurs only if another register, the *significance register,* is cleared.

2. The set significance instruction sets the register so that fill

does not occur. This allows us to insert the $ with the next instruction.

3. Significance is then cleared to allow fill with asterisks.
4. We now move the first two digits from the source to the destination. Leading zeros are replaced with asterisks.
5. Next the comma is moved. It is replaced by an asterisk if no significant digit has yet occurred.
6. The next three digits from the source are moved or filled.
7. Filling is now stopped. We do not wish asterisks to be inserted to the right of the decimal.
8. The decimal and the last two source digits are placed in the destination.
9. If the source was zero, the whole destination field is replaced with asterisks (including the $).

The source field should be packed decimal. If, through program error, it is not, then the edit instruction cannot function properly. The foregoing program does not check the input. Even if the input is in proper format, the program does not check to see if the data are negative. The reader might be interested in considering how these problems can be handled. At this point the reader should have some idea of how this might be programmed.

9.3 Bit Strings and Operations

A variable length bit field is specified by three parameters. We will designate these parameters P (position), S (size), and B (base address). If P = 21, S = 6, and B = 00001234, we are referring to a 6-bit field, the low-order bit of which is 21 bits beyond the low-order bit of address 00001234. The following figure shows such a 6-bit field containing six binary 1s surrounded by binary 0s.

Address	Contents
00001234	00000000
00001235	00000000
00001236	11100000
00001237	00000111
00001238	00000000

Bit 0 of the field is in bit 5 of address 00001236, and bit 5 of the field is in bit 2 of address 00001237. The P parameter is stored as a signed longword. Hence the starting bit position can be quite a distance from the base bit in either direction. The size, however, is stored in a single byte and is further restricted to the values 0–32.

The VAX-11 normally treats these bit strings as signed integers in 2's complement notation. The high-order bit is the sign. A variable bit string can be extracted from its location and placed in the low-order bits of a longword with the extract instruction EXTV. The sign bit is extended in the high-order bits of the longword if the size is less than 32. In the foregoing example, suppose that address 00001234 is symbolically represented by the label BASE. The instruction

```
EXTV      #21,#6,BASE,X ; EXTEND THE VARIABLE BIT STRING WHICH
                        ; STARTS 21 BITS AFTER BIT 0 OF BASE
                        ; AND WHICH IS 6 BITS LONG INTO THE
                        ; LONGWORD STARTING AT X.
```

creates a longword of binary ones in addresses X through X + 3. The instruction EXTZV does not sign extend. Binary 0s are placed in the leading bits of the receiving longword.

Variable length bit strings can be created by the insert instruction INSV. The reverse of the foregoing EXTV instruction is

```
INSV X, #21, #6, BASE
```

In inserting such a string, care must be taken if the sign of the number is to be preserved. The first bit must be a binary 1 if the number is negative and a binary 0 if the number is positive. For instance, in the foregoing INSV instruction, suppose the longword X were to contain AAAAAAAA (hex). Then the low-order 6 bits would be 101010, and these would be inserted into the variable bit string. If this string were later extended with an EXTV, the result would be FFFFFFEA, or decimal -14. In other words, 101010 is 6-bit 2's complement form for decimal -14. As a second example, suppose that X in the foregoing INSV instruction were to contain 55555555(hex). Then the low-order 6 bits would be 010101. If these were later extended, the result would be 00000015 (that is, 010101 is a binary 21_{10}).

Bit strings are useful for packing data in bytes. For instance, the BCD code is a 6-bit alphanumeric code. Thus four BCD characters can be packed into three VAX-11 bytes. Schematically we might pack the characters as follows:

```
11111122
22223333
33444444
```

Where 111111 represents the bits in which the first character is stored, and so forth. In order to use such information on the VAX-

11, we must first unpack it into 4 bytes, as follows:

```
00111111
00222222
00333333
00444444
```

Then we must convert the code byte by byte into ASCII. There is a translate instruction for this purpose that we will consider shortly.

The following subroutine unpacks four 6-bit characters at label A through A+2 and stores them at B through B+3.

```
EXTRACT: EXTZV   #2,#6,A,R6       ;FIRST 6 BITS TO R6
         MOVB    R6,B             ;NO SIGN EXTENTION
         EXTZV   #0,#6,A+2,R6     ;LAST 6 BITS TO R6
         MOVB    R6,B+3           ;THEN TO B+3
         MOVB    A+1,R7           ;USE R7 TO
         INSV    A,#8,#2,R7       ;ASSEMBLE SECOND 6 BITS
         EXTZV   #4,#6,R7,R6      ;EXTRACT IN R6
         MOVB    R6,B+1           ;MOVE EXTRACTED BYTE TO B+1
         MOVB    A+2,R7           ;ASSEMBLE THIRD 6 BITS
         INSV    A+1,#8,#4,R7     ;SIMILARLY
         EXTZV   #6,#6,R7,R6
         MOVB    R6,B+2
         RSB                      ;RETURN
```

The translate instruction is MOVTC: move translated characters. The source string is given by a length and an address. Translation takes place via a translation table (See Figure 9.1). Each byte in the source string is interpreted as an unsigned binary integer and is thus in the range 0–255. The table must be 256 bytes long. Each byte in

```
TABLE:  .ASCII  /                /
        .ASCII  /                /
        .ASCII  /                /
        .ASCII  /                /
        .ASCII  /           .<(+ /
        .ASCII  /&        !$*);^/
        .ASCII  *-/       ,%_>?*
        .ASCII  /         :#@'="/
        .ASCII  / abcdefghi      /
        .ASCII  / jklmnopqr      /
        .ASCII  /  stuvwxyz      /
        .ASCII  /                /
        .ASCII  /[ABCDEFGHI      /
        .ASCII  /]JKLMNOPQR      /
        .ASCII  /  STUVWXYZ      /
        .ASCII  /0123456789      /
EBUF:   .BLKB   80               ;EBCDIC INPUT BUFFER
ABUF:   .BLK    80               ;ASCII OUTPUT BUFFER
          .
          .
          .
        MOVTC   #80,EBUF,#0,TABLE,#80,ABUF
```

Figure 9.1 Translation table

the source string is replaced in the destination string by its offset in the table. If the source string and destination string are of different lengths, a fill character is inserted in the extra high-order bytes of the destination. The program segment shown in Figure 9.1 translates an 80-character buffer containing EBCDIC characters (not BCD) into ASCII.

9.4 Lists and Queues

A *queue* is a data structure consisting of nodes and links. The nodes contain user data, and the links order the nodes from first to last. The first node in a queue is called the HEAD of the queue, and the last node is called the TAIL. On the VAX-11, queues are doubly linked. The forward link, FLINK, of the HEAD gives the address of the next node, and so forth, until the TAIL is reached. The backward link, BLINK, of the TAIL gives the address of the next to the last node, and so forth, to the HEAD. We say that the link points to the next node. Schematically, we have

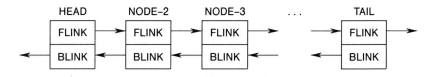

In addition to the foregoing, each node normally has a data area. The data area can be stored immediately following or preceding the links, or it may be stored in separate memory addresses. In the latter case, a longword will normally be stored with the links that contain the address of the data area.

In the preceding diagram, the TAIL FLINK is pointing to nothing, as is the HEAD BLINK. On the VAX-11 there is a separate HEADER for the queue. The HEADER contains only a FLINK and a BLINK, which point to the HEAD and TAIL, respectively. The TAIL FLINK and the HEAD BLINK point to the HEADER. The address of the HEADER is the address of the queue.

An empty queue contains only a HEADER, whose links point to itself. If a queue has only one node, it is both the HEAD and the TAIL.

If the nodes of a queue were stored in consecutive locations of memory, then there would be little need for the links. The notion of a data structure that is scattered throughout memory and that is linked together arose in connection with applications in which the amount of data changed dynamically. With the stack mechanism of the VAX-11, one can allocate or deallocate memory as needed during the execution of a program. This leaves portions of memory free when they are not needed and is thus a more efficient way to manage data storage.

Thus, if we have a queue and wish to add to a new node at the HEAD or delete a node at the TAIL, we can do so. We simply push the new node on the stack and adjust the HEADER links, the links for the new node, and the links of the old HEAD. To delete we simply mark the node in some fashion and adjust the HEADER BLINK and the FLINK of the next to last node. Later the space occupied by the deleted node can be reclaimed by the program for a new node by saving the address.

Any data structure that is connected by links is called a *list*. If the links of one node only point to the preceeding and/or succeeding node, the list is called a *linear list*. A stack is a linear list in which nodes are added and deleted (pushed and popped) on a last in, first out basis (LIFO). The user stack of the VAX-11 works on a LIFO basis, as we have seen, but no links are required. Stacks implemented by user's programs often use links. Queues usually work on a first in, first out (FIFO) basis. Nodes enter as the new HEAD and work their way to the TAIL. On the VAX-11, however, nodes may be added anywhere in the queue. A node is added by the INSQUE instruction. For instance,

        INSQUE A,B

adds a node whose two longword links start at label A after the node (or HEADER) whose links reside at label B. This instruction causes the VAX-11 to store the proper addresses in the links at A and to adjust the addresses in the links at B and the old node that used to follow B. Before the INSQUE instruction, the portion of the queue involved is linked as follows:

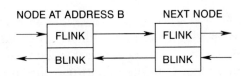

Also, before the INSQUE, the node at A is simply two contiguous longwords whose contents (whether they are link addresses or not) are not important. After the INSQUE, the affected part of the queue is connected as follows:

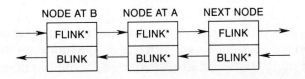

The four link addresses marked with asterisks are the ones changed by the INSQUE instruction. Similarly, a node can be deleted by the REMQUE instruction. REMQUE requires two operands: the first is the address of the node to be deleted, and the second receives the address of this deleted node. The instruction adjusts the addresses of the neighboring nodes in a similar manner to INSQUE.

To illustrate the operation of a queue, we consider the problem of finding a given record or node in a queue. In this example, each node consists of four longwords. The first two are the two links FLINK and BLINK. The third contains the key for which we are to search, and the last contains the address of the data record corresponding to the key. We assume that the key we want is stored in a longword labeled S_ARG. The queue HEADER is labeled H.

```
            MOVAL    H,R6            ; MOVE QUEUE ADDRESS TO R6
            MOVL     R6,R7           ; AND R7
LOOP:       CMPL     8(R6),S_ARG     ; LOOK FOR KEY
            BEQL     FOUND           ; 12(R6) CONTAINS REQUIRED ADDRESS
            MOVL     (R6),R6         ; ADVANCE TO NEXT NODE
            CMPL     R6,R7           ; HAVE WE RETURNED TO THE HEADER ?
            BNEQ     LOOP
NOT_THERE:                          ; HERE IF KEY NOT FOUND
              .
              .
              .
```

Had it been desired to delete the node where a match was found, REMQUE could be used:

```
    REMQUE    (R6),R0
```

R0 will contain the address of the deleted node.

9.5 Summary

In this chapter we studied a variety of data types that are supported by the VAX-11 as well as most other mid-to large-scale computers. We learned to understand and use floating-point and decimal data. We also were introduced to bit strings and queues.

Floating-point formats provide data types for large sets of real numbers. The usual floating-point format on the VAX-11 is called the F-format. Numbers in this format are represented as 8 hex nibbles. The double or D-format is a quadword floating-point format. All the VAX-11 generic arithmetic mnemonics—ADD, SUB, MUL, and DIV, as well as CLR, MOV, TST, and CVT—can be suffixed with F, D, G, or H to form floating-point arithmetic instructions. Floating-point constants can be stored with the .FLOAT and .DOUBLE directives. Floating literals can also be formed by the prefix ^F. There are two VAX-11 instructions for evaluating floating-point polynomials, POLYF and POLYD.

Decimal integer arithmetic is as important in the world of business as floating-point arithmetic is in the world of science. The leading separate format is essentially the same as ASCII format; but there must be a sign byte. The overpunch code is a carryover from earlier times, when businesses used punched cards for their accounting files. The length of each of these data types is defined as the number of digits in the number, not the number of bytes required to store it.

Decimal numbers can also be stored in packed decimal form, two digits per byte. On the VAX-11, the only decimal arithmetic supplied is that for the packed decimal format.

All the convert instruction mnemonics in the VAX-11 start with the generic CVT. This is followed by a letter representing the source field and another for the destination field.

The EDITPC instruction is designed to insert currency signs, commas, periods, and so on. It also will suppress leading zeroes and float the currency sign or the algebraic sign to the right as the leading zeroes are being suppressed.

A variable-length bit field is specified by three parameters: P (position), S (size), and B (base address). A variable bit string can be extracted from its location and placed in the low-order bits of a longword with the extract instruction EXTV. The reverse of the EXTV instruction is the INSV instruction. Bit strings are useful for packing data in bytes.

A queue is a data structure consisting of nodes and links. The nodes contain user data, and the links order the nodes from first to last. The first node in a queue is called the HEAD of the queue, and the last node is called the TAIL. On the VAX-11, queues are doubly linked. A node is added to a queue by the INSQUE instruction and deleted by the REMQUE instruction.

EXERCISES

1. What values are stored in the following F-format numbers: 00003F80, 0000447A, 000042C8, 0000C1A0? Do the four answers have anything in common? What?

2. Convert the following into F-format: 26.8, −26.8, 1000, .001.

3. Write an assembly program that will do Exercise 2 for you. Do your answers agree with MACRO's answers?

4. Show the hex nibble notation for the number 3121 in each of the following data types: word, leading separate, packed decimal, F format.

5. How many bytes are required to store the number -123456 in packed decimal? Why?

6. Who uses packed decimal? Who uses F-format? Who uses bytes, words, and longwords?

7. Modify the edit program of Section 9.2 to check the data for errors in data type and algebraic sign.

8. Write a general procedure that will check protect an amount up to $99,999,999,999.99.

9. Write a set of general procedures that will insert and delete records in (from) a queue. Also include a procedure for moving to the next node in the queue.

Chapter 10

Input/Output
Programming

CHAPTER 4 presented the rudiments of Record Management Services (RMS). This system, along with System Services (SS), performs all I/O functions for the VMS Operating System. All high-level languages supported by VMS (FORTRAN, COBOL, Pascal, and so on) have I/O statements of some type. The compiler for each of these languages translates its I/O statements into calls to appropriate RMS or SS routines. Hence the I/O software for the system is centralized and thus uniform from one compiler to the next.

The assembly language programmer can call RMS directly. He can also call some functions of SS directly and, with special privilege, can call all SS facilities. Also with special privilege, he can bypass both RMS and SS and perform I/O at the basic hardware instruction level. (Normally only experienced systems programmers would be allowed to do this.)

In this chapter we study I/O programming in enough detail for the novice programmer to learn to perform many normal tasks required of an applications programmer or a beginning systems programmer. We first examine the various levels of I/O programming in general and then concentrate on RMS. We are already somewhat familiar with the macros: \$FAB, \$RAB, \$CREATE, \$OPEN, \$CONNECT, \$GET, \$PUT, and \$CLOSE. In order to write programs that effectively manage the user terminal interactively, create print files on the printer, and process sequential files on disk, we need a deeper understanding of RMS. We shall also look briefly at *relative* and *indexed sequential* files.

10.1 Levels of Input/Output Programming

On the VAX-11 there are four distinct levels of I/O programming:

  1. The VAX-11 hardware I/O instructions.

2. The SS macros and related facilities.
3. The RMS macros and related facilities.
4. High-level language I/O facilities.

Each level depends on the previous level. If one codes a call to RMS, then RMS in turn calls SS one or more times to perform the required function. As one progresses from level 1 to level 4, through more and more layers of software, more is done for the user. In this chapter we discuss only level 3 in enough depth for the reader to write functioning programs. It is instructive to survey the other levels for perspective, however. We shall introduce a number of technical terms (which are italicized) without detailed definition. The reader will be able to understand the terms in a general sense from the context. This is sufficient for the purposes of this book.

Level 1 is tedious and time-consuming. At this level the software provides no file or record facilities. Terminal I/O, for instance, is performed one character at a time. The carriage return and line feed characters must be examined for the program to determine when a line of input is complete.

Programs written at this level are called *device drivers.* Writing a device driver is a complex task reserved for systems programmers. Detailed knowledge of the internal workings of the VMS operating system and of VAX-11 system support hardware is required. For instance, the VAX-11 hardware supports four programming modes: *user, supervisor, executive* and *kernel.* The normal progammer runs in user mode.

The DCL command language interpreter runs in supervisory mode. RMS runs in executive mode, and SS runs in kernel mode along with the drivers. Each mode has special privileges. Portions of memory reserved for I/O registers are off limits to the less privileged modes. A VAX-11 I/O instruction is simply a MOVL to or from one of these addresses in kernel mode.

The VAX-11 hardware also recognizes 31 *interrupt priority levels* (IPL), where level 1 is the lowest IPL and 31 the highest. Each process scheduled for execution has an (initial) IPL. The IPL is stored in the PSL and can be modified only if the process has sufficient privilege. I/O devices and other devices such as the *hardware timer* can issue *interrupts.* The level of the interrupt depends on the device. When the system services the interrupt, it looks for a process whose IPL is the same in a queue of waiting processes.

The VMS system utilizes a set of conventions for these IPLs that a device driver must observe. When the driver is called, it must perform as much of its task as possible at the lower priority levels. Only a few instructions can be executed at device priority levels, which are normally in the lower 20s. I/O is often started with two or three instructions at level 31; then priority is immediately reduced to device level.

Once I/O is started, the driver must wait for completion of the operation. The system suspends execution of the driver and services another process. The driver must wait for an interrupt. On completion of the I/O operation, the device issues an interrupt at its device interrupt level. The system then starts the driver again at the point at which it was suspended. The driver must then do as little as is necessary to check the I/O status. The driver must quickly lower the priority to *fork level* (normally level 8) and exit to wait for a fork level interrupt. Interrupt levels above 15 are reserved for hardware and those below 16 for software. Eventually the *fork processor* will return control to the driver to perform less sensitive I/O checking. Priority is then successively reduced in one or more succeeding waits and interrupts.

An I/O driver programmer must know not only the details of the particular device but also the details of its connection to the computer. For instance, to output a character to a terminal, the programmer must first know that the terminal is connected to a unit called UNIBUS* (buses were discussed in Chapter 2) via an interface board—for example, the DZ11. He must then know that this particular board uses two *interrupt vectors* per device and that these vectors are 8 bytes each. He must know the interrupt vector UNIBUS addresses as well as the *control status register* (CSR) address for this device, and so on. Many instructions are required to input or output a single character. Few people program at this level, however.

System services were written essentially to avoid the hardware level. Even systems programmers seldom go below level 2. At this level the software incorporates the notion of the *record*. I/O is line at a time or, equivalently, record at a time. The notion of a *file* appears only implicitly. At the SS level the user can address disk sectors by their hardware disk addresses (physical I/O privilege required), by their relative position on the disk (logical I/O privilege required), or by their relative position with respect to the beginning block of the file (virtual I/O privilege required).

RMS is the standard or normal level for assembly programmers. In RMS, files and records are described as they appear in an application. Hence at this level one deals with a file that is organized *se-*

---

*UNIBUS is a trademark of Digital Equipment Corporation.

quentially or *randomly*. The records are *fixed length* or *variable length.* Header and trailer *labels* are checked automatically for each file. Tape files need not end with the first reel. Physical records are deblocked into logical records automatically, and so forth. Since we concentrate on RMS in this chapter, we will learn how many of these facilities are evoked.

Levels 1, 2, and 3 treat all I/O data as character strings. Data enter the computer originally coded only in ASCII. If integers or floating-point numbers are required, the programmer must write or use a conversion routine. I/O statements in high-level languages, in addition to all the aforementioned services, also normally perform conversion to the proper data types. Computer scientists need to understand each level in order to appreciate fully the tasks required of the compilers and operating systems. Such a full understanding is beyond the scope of this book. We will, however, make a start with RMS.

10.2 An Overview of RMS Input/Output Macros

When one uses the $FAB macro to define a file, the MACRO assembler responds by reserving a block of 68 bytes, which are divided into 28 fields. Each field is either a byte, a word, or a longword in length. The length of each field and its relative position in the FAB are predefined by RMS. Some of the fields can be initialized by the user; others are used only by RMS. Each field has a *keyword name*, a *field size*, and an *offset*. We will use only nine of these fields:

Keyword Name	Field Size	Offset	Description
ALQ	longword	FAB$L_ALQ	Allocation quantity
BKS	byte	FAB$B_BKS	Bucket size
FAC	byte	FAB$B_FAC	File access method
FOP	longword	FAB$L_FOP	File options
FSZ	byte	FAB$B_FSZ	Fixed control size
MRS	word	FAB$W_MRS	Maximum record size
ORG	byte	FAB$B_ORG	File organization
RAT	byte	FAB$B_RAT	Record attributes
RFM	byte	FAB$B_RFM	Record format

The following $FAB initializes some of these fields.

```
DISK_FILE:
        $FAB    FNM=<MYFILE.DAT>,ALQ=200,FAC=<PUT>,FOP=<TEF>,MRS=125,-
                ORG=SEQ,RAT=CR,RFM=FIX
```

Each field that the user wishes to initialize appears as an operand. In this example there are eight operands. They all have the form of a keyword followed by an equal sign and then by the value of the field. Sometimes the value is a numeric quantity and sometimes an address; sometimes it is a file name and sometimes a symbol. Since the operands are defined by their keywords, they can appear in any order in the $FAB. On the other hand, their actual order in the file access block is predefined.

In the foregoing example the first operand defines the file name (FNM). Unlike the other keywords, FNM is not a field in the FAB. In fact, it is a shorthand way of defining two FAB fields: FNA (file specification string address) and FNS (file specification string size). The string of characters between the angled brackets is stored outside the FAB. The string address and size are stored in the FAB. In this case the file name is MYFILE, and the file type is DAT (the normal type for a data file).

The keyword ALQ allocates 200 disk blocks to the file (each disk block is 512 characters long), and the FAC keyword tells RMS that the present program is going to use $PUT for this file. If it were going to use both $GET and $PUT, the proper definition of the field would be FAC=<GET,PUT> or FAC=<PUT,GET>. FOP tells RMS that the user wishes to give back unused disk blocks whenever a $CLOSE is issued. Hence, RMS first reserves 200 blocks (ALQ) and then uses them little by little on each $PUT (FAC) and gives back any that are left when $CLOSE is issued (FOP). The value TEF for FOP means truncate at end of file. It can be used only for sequential files. MRS says that the maximum record size is 125 bytes. ORG says that this is a sequential file. RAT declares that if this file is printed or typed, then each record should be followed by an RMS-supplied carriage return and line feed. Again, only sequential files can be printed or typed. RFM says that the records are fixed length. Hence, from the MRS parameter, all the records are 125 characters long.

For fixed-length records, RMS appends 1 (7 for indexed files) extra character of control information per record. Hence 126 characters are stored on disk. For sequential files, records are packed into blocks on disk. Since blocks are 512 characters long and (in this example) records use 126 bytes, the first four records (504 characters) and the first 8 characters of the fifth record are placed in the first block on disk. The second block contains the other 118 characters of the fifth record, all of records six through eight, the first 16 characters of the ninth record, and so on.

In actuality, data must be written to disk, a block at a time. RMS makes the actual storage of the data transparent to the user, however. When the user says $PUT, RMS dutifully accepts the 125 characters in the user's buffer (RBF) and transfers them to its own buffer. When a whole block is complete in its buffer (or buffers), it issues a command (via SS) to write to disk. When the user says $CLOSE, it takes care to write out the partial contents of its last buffer, if any. The user can thus think of a file in which each record is 125 characters long and each $PUT (or $GET) accesses the next record.

The macro $RAB defines a record access block (RAB) that consists of 63 bytes divided into 26 fields, of which we will discuss only 12.

Keyword Name	Field Size	Offset	Description
FAB	longword	RAB$L_FAB	FAB address
KBF	longword	RAB$L_KBF	Key buffer address
KRF	byte	RAB$B_KRF	Key of reference
KSZ	byte	RAB$B_KSZ	Key buffer size
PBF	longword	RAB$L_PBF	Prompt buffer address
PSZ	byte	RAB$B_PSZ	Prompt buffer size
RAC	byte	RAB$B_RAC	Record access mode
RBF	longword	RAB$L_RBF	Record buffer address
ROP	longword	RAB$L_ROP	Record options
RSZ	word	RAB$W_RSZ	Record buffer size
UBF	longword	RAB$L_UBF	User buffer address
USZ	word	RAB$W_USZ	User buffer size

Of these 12 parameters, 8 are concerned with buffers. Each RAB contains information on three buffers: a user's buffer (for input), a record buffer (for output), and either a key buffer (for random access on disk) or a prompt buffer (for terminal prompts). Each buffer is specified by an address and a length. For instance, the user's buffer address is specified by the UBF field and the length (size) by USZ. The $GET macro uses this buffer for data input. Similarly, the $PUT macro outputs the RBF buffer of length RSZ. If the RAB is associated with an input file so that $GET service is the only service required that involves buffers, then the only buffer parameters that must be defined are UBF and USZ. Similarly, if the RAB is associated with an output file that requires only $PUT service, then only RBF and RSZ are required.

An input file from the user terminal may also use the prompt buffer, and a relative file or an indexed sequential file on disk may need a key buffer (if access is to be random). The prompt buffer address (PBF) and the key buffer address (KBF) occupy the same field in the RAB since there is no chance that they would be used simultaneously in a single RAB. Similarly, PSZ and KSZ are really the same location in the RAB.

The following RAB initializes some of these fields.

```
DISK_RECORD:
        $RAB    FAB=DISK_FILE,RAC=SEQ,RBF=BUFF_OUT,RSZ=100
```

BUFF_OUT must also be defined. This would normally be accomplished by a directive such as .BLKB. Since we have learned that it is not good programming practice to have constants such as 100 scattered throughout our program, the following sequence of statements is better:

```
BUFF_SIZE=100
DISK_RECORD:
        $RAB    FAB=DISK_FILE,RAC=SEQ,RBF=BUFF_OUT,RSZ=BUFF-SIZE
BUFF-OUT:
        .BLKB   BUFF_SIZE
```

The keyword FAB in this example associates this RAB with the FAB labeled DISK_FILE defined earlier. The parameter RAC in this example says that records are to be accessed sequentially. Notice that in the FAB we have ORG=SEQ, and in the RAB we have RAC= SEQ. In other words, we have a file that is organized sequentially in which the records are to be accessed sequentially. There is a difference in the organization of a file and the access method. Indeed, if a sequential file is composed of fixed-length records, RMS allows the file to be accessed by key (randomly). Similarly, relative files and indexed sequential files can be accessed either sequentially or by key. If the user does not initialize the RAC field, RMS assumes sequential access as the default. If the user says that access is by key, then the key buffer must be set to the correct key before each $GET or $PUT. We defer discussion of random access to Section 10.6

Both $FAB and $RAB do their work at assembly time. Each field is initialized to the required setting before the program starts execution. If the user wishes to change a field dynamically while his program is executing, he can do so. The offsets represent predefined addresses for RMS. For example, in the foregoing RAB, the RBF field has been set to the address of BUFF_OUT. Suppose we wish to change this address to BUFF_2. From the preceding table, we know that RBF is a longword. The address of this longword is DISK_RECORD+RAB$L_RBF. In other words, the address is the address of the RAB plus the offset. Hence to change the address, we simply code

```
        MOVAL   BUFF_2,DISK_RECORD+RAB$L_RBF
```

Notice that all the RAB offsets are of the form RAB$X_KKK, where X is B for byte, W for word, or L for longword; and KKK is the keyword name. The FAB offsets are named similarly. The fields of the FABs and RABs can also be changed dynamically at run time by the macros $FAB_STORE and $RAB_STORE, but we will not discuss these macros here.

The macros $OPEN, $CREATE, $CONNECT, $GET, $PUT, and $CLOSE all act during program execution. We are already somewhat familiar with them. Normally the programmer should check for errors when issuing these macros. On completion of each of these macros, RMS returns a completion code in R0. An even number means that something abnormal or unusual happened, and an odd number means that the macro executed normally. Hence testing for error can be done with the BLBC instruction, or testing for normality can be done with BLBS. For example:

```
        $CREATE     FAB=DISK_FAB
        BLBC        R0,CREATE_ERR
        $CONNECT    RAB=DISK_RECORD
        BLBC        R0,CONNECT_ERR
        $PUT        RAB=DISK_RECORD
        BLBC        R0,PUT_ERR
              .
              .
              .
CREATE_ERR:
              .
              .
              .
CONNECT_ERR:
              .
              .
              .
PUT_ERR:
              .
              .
              .
```

If the user desires to make full-fledged procedures out of CREATE_ERR, CONNECT_ERR, and so on, then the macros are coded

```
        $CREATE     FAB=DISK_FAB,ERR=CREATE_ERR
```

In this case the label CREATE_ERR should be an .ENTRY or .WORD directive. A frame is stored into the stack in the usual manner for a VAX-11 procedure call, and control is passed to the procedure. The procedure can be assembled with the rest of the user's program, or it can be assembled separately.

The error procedures (or labels) must determine the nature of the error. On a $GET, for example, the "error" might be a legitimate read error. On the other hand, it might be only an end of file. Hence, the designation *error procedure* is misleading. RMS returns an even number in R0 in all cases in which the service does not accomplish its normal task. The normal task for a $GET is to get a record, but many things can prevent this from happening. The following table shows some of the codes that can be returned in R0 as the result of a $GET. The table lists the actual hex value returned along with predefined direct assignment symbols that the user can use. The symbols are known as *completion status code* symbols. A complete discussion of all these codes is beyond the scope of this chapter. The approximately 200 such codes are listed in Appendix A of the *RMS Reference Manual.* Each service, such as $GET, uses only a subset of these codes.

Symbolic Value	Hex Value	Severity	Description
RMS$_DNR	00018272	error	Device not ready
RMS$_EOF	0001827A	error	End of file
RMS$_KBF	0001858C	severe	Invalid key buffer address
RMS$_KRF	0001859C	severe	Invalid key of reference
RMS$_RER	0001C0F4	severe	Read error
RMS$_RNF	000182B2	error	Record not found
RMS$_RTB	000181A8	warning	Record too big for UBF
RMS$_CONTROLY	00010611	success	Input terminated by cntl Y
RMS$_NORMAL	00010001	success	Normal completion

The user can test for end of file, for example, as follows:

```
CMPL    R0,#RMS$_EOF
BEQL    EOF_ROUTINE
```

The severity of the return code is only a suggestion to the programmer. A severe error usually calls for immediate termination of the program. An error can usually be handled by the program, and a warning may or may not be important.

In the following sections we will discuss the FAB and RAB fields that we have not yet covered, as well as examine some of the others in more detail. We will also consider the run time macros in more detail as we use them.

10.3 Interactive Terminal Input/Output

In using the VAX interactively, the user terminal is both an input device and an output device. The keyboard supplies input, and the CRT provides output. RMS associates a file with the input device and a file with the output device. The lines of input from the terminal (that is, all the characters typed between successive carriage returns) form the records of the input file; and all the characters displayed on a line of the CRT (with some wraparound allowed) form the records of the output file. On disk, files are given names by the user; but on the terminal, the input file has been assigned the name SYS$INPUT and the output file has been assigned the name SYS$OUTPUT by RMS. Suppose that we wish to read input records from the terminal and that each record is to be 30 characters long. We can code this as follows:

```
BUFF_SIZE=30
TERM_IN_FAB:
        $FAB    FNM=<SYS$INPUT>,RAT=CR
TERM_IN_RAB:
        $RAB    FAB=TERM_IN_FAB,UBF=BUFF,USZ=BUFF_SIZE
BUFF:   .BLKB   BUFF_SIZE
```

After issuing $OPEN and $CONNECT for this file, the programmer can then issue $GET for each line of input. The $GET suspends the program until the user types in a line of data (ending with a carriage return, which is not transmitted to BUFF). There are several possibilities:

1. The user types in fewer than 30 characters.
2. The user types in exactly 30 characters.
3. The user types in more than 30 characters.
4. The user refuses to type in anything.

Cases 1 and 2 are considered normal. In case 3, RMS accepts the first 30 characters, places them in BUFF, and then returns RMS$_RTB in R0. The other characters are lost to the user. In all cases, RMS returns the exact number of characters read in the RSZ field of the RAB. It also sets the RBF field to the address of BUFF. The user can then test these fields to see the address of the last record and its length. Also, if the user follows the $GET with a $PUT, the record will be echoed back to the CRT (even though there is no file for SYS$OUTPUT).

In case 4 the program will wait forever. There are provisions in RMS for setting a time-out period for terminal input. Indeed, there is a time-out field in the RAB. If this period is exceeded, RMS returns a code in R0. We will not go into this feature here, however.

Specifically, the $GET performs all the following functions when input is read from the terminal:

1. First, the ROP (record options) field is checked to see if the user specified ROP=PMT (prompt). If so, the prompt buffer (PBF) of size PSZ is displayed on the CRT. In this case the cursor is left sitting at the first space after the prompt.
2. The input is read into the UBF address up to USZ characters. If more than USZ characters are in the line, a warning code is returned in R0.

3. The address and length of the input are deposited in the RBF and RSZ fields.

The first function is a special feature of the SYS$INPUT file. We are now ready to look at a complete program that uses the terminal. This program uses many of the concepts, instructions, and data types introduced in the previous chapters. By now the reader should be ready to read nontrivial VAX assembly programs. The program is intended to be self-documented. Just by looking at the comments and the code, you should be able to understand what it does.

Terminal Input, Prompt, and Echo

```
        .TITLE  SOC_SEC_READ
        .SBTTL  READS SS_PER_RECORD (3 IN THIS EXAMPLE) S S NOS PER RECORD
        .IDENT  /SSREAD/
;
;THIS PROGRAM READS ONE OR MORE SOCIAL SECURITY NUMBERS PER INPUT LINE
;FROM THE TERMINAL, CONVERTS THEM INTO BINARY LONGWORDS AND STORES THEM
;IN A TABLE. EACH SS NUMBER IS SS_SIZE DIGITS LONG. THE USER MUST TYPE
;IN A SPACE AND THEN THE FIRST NUMBER, ANOTHER SPACE AND THEN THE NEXT
;NUMBER, ETC. IF SS_PER_RECORD = 3 AND SS_SIZE = 9 FOR EXAMPLE, EACH
;INPUT LINE MUST BE EXACTLY 30 CHARACTERS LONG. EXAMPLE:
;_123456789_987654321_111111111*   (_ MEANS SPACE AND * MEANS CR )
;THE FOLLOWING 5 STATEMENTS DEFINE PROGRAM PARAMETERS
;
BUFF_SIZE = 30
TABLE_SIZE = 100
SS_SIZE = 9
PROMPT_SIZE = 12
SS_PER_RECORD = 3
        .PSECT  TABLE,WRT,NOEXE                    ;DATA PROGRAM SECTION
;
;INPUT COMES FROM THE TERMINAL. OUTPUT CONSISTS OF PROMPTS TO THE USER,
;ECHOING OF THE INPUT DATA IN THE SAME FORMAT AS IT WAS INPUT AND
;MESSAGES INDICATING TABLE OVERFLOW IF IT OCCURS AND END OF EXECUTION.


INFAB:  $FAB   FNM=SYS$INPUT,RAT=CR               ;INPUT FILE FROM TERMINAL
INRAB:  $RAB   FAB=INFAB,UBF=BIN,USZ=BUFF_SIZE-   ;ALSO DOES PROMPTS TO
               PBF=PMSG,PSZ=PROMPT_SIZE,ROP=PMT   ;USER AND OUTPUT
;
;INPUT BUFFER (AS WELL AS OUTPUT BUFFER) IS BIN. SS NUMBERS ARE STORED AS
;A TABLE OF LONGWORDS IN TABLE.
;
BIN:    .BLKB   BUFF_SIZE
TABLE:  .BLKL   TABLE_SIZE
;
;SS NUMBERS ARE CONVERTED FROM ASCII INTO PACKED DECIMAL (INTERMEDIATE)
;AND THEN INTO BINARY LONGWORDS. PACKED IS A TEMPORARY HOLDING LOCATION.
;THE USER SIGNALS WHEN TO STOP BY TYPING IN E AS THE FIRST CHARACTER
;AFTER THE LAST SS NUMBER.
;
PACKED: .BLKB   5
LAST:    .ASCII /E/
;
```

```
;THERE ARE THREE OUTPUT MESSAGES, PMSG (NORMAL PROMPT), FMSG (END OF RUN),
;AND EMSG (ERROR ON TABLE OVERFLOW). PMSG IS THE PROMPT BUFFER AND IS
;OUTPUT EACH TIME A $GET IS EXECUTED. FMSG AND EMSG ARE OUTPUT AS NEEDED.
;THEY MUST BE MOVED TO THE (OUTPUT) BUFFER BIN AND THEN WRITTEN WITH A
;$PUT MACRO.
;IN THIS EXAMPLE, THE SIZES OF THE PROMPT BUFFER AND THE OUTPUT BUFFER ARE
;EQUAL TO PROMPT_SIZE. HENCE, BEFORE ISSUING A $PUT THE RSZ FIELD OF THE
;RAB, INRAB, MUST BE SET TO THIS VALUE
;
PMSG:   .ASCII  /TYPE IN REC./

FMSG:   .ASCII  / FINISHED  /
EMSG:   .ASCII  /TABLE FULL  /
;
;EXECUTABLE INSTRUCTIONS FOLLOW. R2 AND R3 ARE SAVED BECAUSE OF THE
;CONVERT INSTRUCTIONS
;
        .PSECT  SSREAD,NOWRT,EXE
BEGIN:  .ENTRY  SSREAD,0
        $OPEN   FAB=INFAB                   ;INITIALIZE TERMINAL FILE
        $CONNECT RAB=INRAB
;
;THE NEXT INSTRUCTION INITIALIZES R9 TO ZERO. R9 IS USED TO COUNT THE
;SS NUMBERS AS THEY ARE READ. IT IS ALSO USED TO CHECK FOR TABLE OVERFLOW.
;
        CLRL    R9
;
;LOOPB IS THE BIG LOOP. IT IS EXECUTED ONCE FOR EACH INPUT RECORD.
;R10 KEEPS TRACK OF WHICH SS NUMBER IN THE RECORD IS BEING PROCESSED.
;R11 POINTS TO THE ADDRESS OF THAT SS NUMBER. (I.E. R10 = INDEX,
;AND R11 = ADDRESS.)
;
LOOPB:  MOVL    #SS_PER_RECORD,R10
        MOVAL   BIN,R11
        $GET    RAB=INRAB                   ;FETCH DATA AND
        $PUT    RAB=INRAB                   ;ECHO DATA BACK
;
;LOOPL IS THE LITTLE LOOP. IT IS EXECUTED ONCE FOR EACH SS NUMBER. LOOPL
;IS EXECUTED SS_PER_RECORD TIMES FOR EACH EXECUTION OF LOOPB
;
LOOPL:  CMPB    (R11),LAST                          ;TEST FOR END (E)
        BEQL    FIN
        CVTSP   #SS_SIZE,(R11),#SS_SIZE,PACKED      ;CONVERT ASCII TO BINARY
        CVTPL   #SS_SIZE,PACKED,TABLE[R9]
        ADDL    #SS_SIZE+1,R11                      ;ADJUST INDICES FOR NEXT
        INCL    R9                                  ;SS NUMBER
        CMPL    #TABLE_SIZE,R9
        BLEQ    FULL
        SOBGTR  R10,LOOPL
        BRB     LOOPB
FULL:   MOVC3   #PROMPT_SIZE,EMSG,BIN               ;TABLE OVERFLOW EXIT
        MOVW    #PROMPT_SIZE,INRAB+RAB$W_RSZ
        $PUT    RAB=INRAB
        CLRL    R2                                  ;SET R2 TO INDICATE ERR
        BRB     FINL
FIN:    MOVC3   #PROMPT_SIZE,FMSG,BIN               ;NORMAL EXIT
        MOVW    #PROMPT_SIZE,INRAB+RAB$W_RSZ        ;SET OUTPUT LENGTH
        $PUT    RAB=INRAB
        MOVL    #1,R2                               ;SET R2 TO NORMAL
FINL:   $CLOSE  FAB=INFAB                           ;COMPLETION STATUS
        MOVL    R2,R0                               ;LEFT IN R0

        RET
        .END    BEGIN
```

We did not check for I/O errors in this program. If something were to go wrong during a $GET or $PUT or one of the other I/O macros, RMS would post a return code in R0, but we would not know it because we did not check for it. Unfortunately, such checking, when done properly, requires many instructions; hence we have omitted it here. The foregoing program can be run as a stand-alone program or as a procedure by deleting the operand BEGIN from the .END directive.

Terminal Output

If the user wishes to use the terminal for both input and output and the output is not just an echo check of the input plus occasional messages, it is convenient to declare FABs and RABs for both SYS$INPUT and SYS$OUTPUT. Since $GET destroys the contents of both the RBF and RSZ fields (which are used by $PUT) it may be cumbersome to initialize them before each $PUT. If both files are declared by the user, then SYS$OUTPUT has its own FAB and RAB. Hence $GET does not destroy the record buffer fields of the output file. We saw an example of this in Chapter 4.

10.4 Line Printer Output

Most VAX systems have an on-line printer that is used for final output of data in hard copy form. The assembly language programmer may or may not access this printer during execution of the program. He may choose to output results to disk and then, after termination of the program, use the DCL command PRINT. In doing this, the programmer is *spooling* his output for later printing. When the PRINT is issued, the operating system spools the output again. That is, the user's file is copied to another file in the print queue. The user is then notified how the output is identified. The identification technique is local to the computer center being used. If the user wishes to output directly to the print queue, he can do so with the file name SYS$PRINT. In either case, the RAT (record attribute) field of the FAB is important. If the user specifies RAT=CR, the records of the file will be printed one after another on lines of the printer. Most printers used on the VAX have room for 132 characters per line. RAT=CR makes no provisions for controlling the vertical positioning of the printer. The user cannot skip to the top of the next page, double space, or overprint. If the user wishes to improve the appearance of his output, RMS provides two methods, which we now discuss.

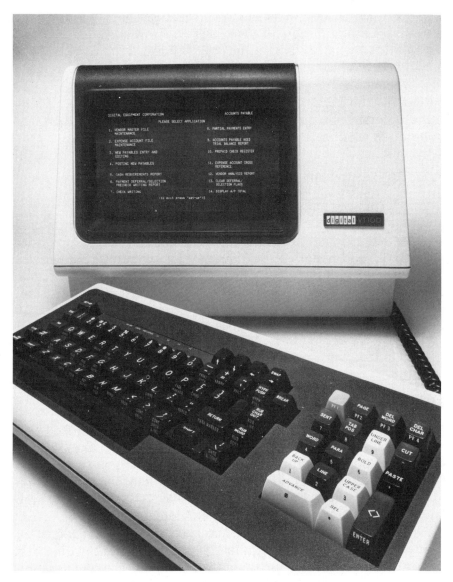

Figure 10.1 VT100 terminal and keyboard layouts

FORTRAN Carriage Control

RAT=FTN tells RMS that the user is supplying vertical carriage control characters via the FORTRAN conventions. In this method the first character of the output buffer (RBF) is not printed. Instead, it tells RMS the type of vertical spacing that is required before the line is printed. The following table lists the carriage control characters.

ASCII	Hex	Description
SP	20	Single space: line feed (LF), print, carriage return (CR).
0	30	Double space: LF, LF, print, CR.
1	31	New page: form feed (FF), print, CR.
+	28	Overprint: print, CR.
$	24	Prompt: LF, print.
NULL	00	No carriage control: print.

Any other character in the control position is treated as though it were a blank (SP).

Print File Carriage Control

RAT=PRN indicates to RMS that the user has adopted the print file format. To explain this format, it should first be mentioned that RMS recognizes three different record formats: fixed length records, variable length records, and variable length with fixed control records. The FAB field RFM specifies the record form, RFM=FIX, RFM=VAR, or RFM=VFC. As we have seen, RMS appends an extra byte to each fixed length record as it is put to disk (seven extra bytes for indexed files). The extra byte essentially says "this record is of fixed length." The length can be determined by the MRS (maximum record size) field. For variable-length records, 3 extra bytes are written with the record (9 for indexed files). The first says that the record is of variable length. The next two (the next word) give the length, which is copied from the RSZ field of the RAB. The user writes variable-length records simply by setting the RBF and RSZ fields of the RAB and then issuing a $PUT.

In creating a file of VFC records, the user must specify both the maximum record size (MRS) and the fixed control area size, FSZ. In VFC records, MRS refers only to the variable part. Thus if the two FAB fields were coded FSZ=10,MRS=80, RMS would interpret this to mean that all records in this file have a 10-byte fixed-length part followed by a variable-length part of up to 80 characters.

VFC records are popular with the various system components of VMS, in particular for print files. A *print file* is a file of VFC records in which the first 2 bytes of the fixed control area are used to control printing. The first byte gives print control that is to be exercised before the record is printed, and the second gives print control that is to be performed after the record is printed.

If either of these bytes contains a binary integer in the range 00–7F hex, then that many LF, CR combinations precede (or follow) the printing of the variable part. If either byte contains 80–9F, then the low-order seven bits contain one of the ASCII control characters, and that control character is transmitted to the output device (which can be either the printer or another device if the user wishes) before or after the data. Thus if the first byte were to contain 89, then the low-order 7 bits would be 0001001, which is the 7-bit ASCII code for HT (horizontal tab). This character would be transmitted before the data (variable) part of the record. Presumably this character would cause the output device to advance horizontally to the next tab. If the output device has no horizontal tabs, then the transmitted character is usually printed as a blank (SP).

Other values in these bytes are either reserved or are too advanced to discuss here. Beginning programmers might well be advised to avoid RAT=PRN unless the output must be printed on a preprinted form. In this case, these bytes can be used to count lines in order to insert output at the proper coordinates of the form.

10.5 Sequential Files on Disk

By now the reader should understand the basics of writing assembly programs that use sequential files. Two areas have not been discussed, however. The first is estimating the time required to use disk files, and the second is understanding the difference between using RMS to create a new file and using RMS to access an old file.

The programmer is often asked to estimate the time requirements of his program. Often the amount of disk activity is either the dominating factor or an important one. In order to make such estimates, the programmer must have a rudimentary understanding of the physical characteristics of disks.

Physical Characteristics of Disk

As we have seen, on the VAX-11 data are stored on disk in *sectors* or *blocks*. Each block is 512 characters long. These blocks are stored one after the other along the circumference of a circle on the disk that has the disk spindle as its center. Between each two blocks is a vacant space on the circumference. The arrangement is thus similar to the storage of a tune on a phonograph record. The circumference is called a *track*. Hence blocks are stored on concentric disk tracks. The number of blocks per track, as well as the number of tracks per disk surface, varies with the type of disk. Other manufacturers, notably IBM, make disks in which each track is one continuous recordable medium so that there is no concept of a sector.

The number of sectors per track is a constant despite the fact that the inner tracks have less linear distance than the outer tracks. This means that data are packed more tightly near the center of the disk.

Several disk platters loaded on a common spindle form a *disk pack*. Most disk units have user-mountable and removable packs; a few, however, mainly older units, have packs that cannot be removed. If the pack has n platters, then there are $2n$ disk surfaces. The user has access to $2n-1$ of these surfaces, the other being reserved for the hardware. The disks are accessed by a set of read-write heads that can be positioned between the platters, one head for each surface. In older disks these heads could be moved independently, so that while one head was at an outer track of one surface, another could be at an inner track of another surface. This proved to be costly and error-prone. In most newer disks the heads all move together in lock-step. Hence all are positioned to read tracks that are at a common radius from the spindle. Because the moving of the heads is time-consuming, it is convenient to organize disk files into *cylinders* of information. Thus when a sequential file is written to disk, the first few records are written to a track on a single surface. When this track is filled, writing continues on another track of another surface in the same cylinder so that the heads need not be moved. When the cylinder is full, all the heads are moved simultaneously to the next cylinder.

In order to read a record at random, the heads must be moved to the proper cylinder. This is called *seek* time. Then the disk must wait for the proper sector to pass under the appropriate head. This is called *rotational delay* or *latency*. Once the sector is properly positioned, data can be transferred quite rapidly.

We now look at the physical characteristics of two popular disk units that are used on the VAX-11.

Disk Attribute	RM03	RP06
Number of platters	3	10
Number of user surfaces	5	19
Number of tracks per surface	823	815
Number of sectors per track	32	22
Number of bytes per pack	67M	176M
Speed of rotation (RPM)	3600	3600
Rotational delay (½ revolution, MS)	8.3	8.3
Seek time (average, MS)	30	28
Transfer rate (bytes per sec.)	1200K	806K

Figure 10.2 depicts the physical properties of disks discussed here.

We can now estimate the time required for disk access. Let us consider a typical but simple problem. Suppose we have a program that creates a sequential file. The file consists of 5,000 fixed-length records. Each record is 150 characters long. How long will it take to create the file?

Since the records are fixed length and the organization is sequential, RMS requires 151 characters per record. Hence each block will hold 3.39 records. Thus 5,000/3.39 or approximately 1,475 blocks must be written. Each write involves both seek time and rotational delay. Remember that the VAX-11 is a multiprogrammed computer.

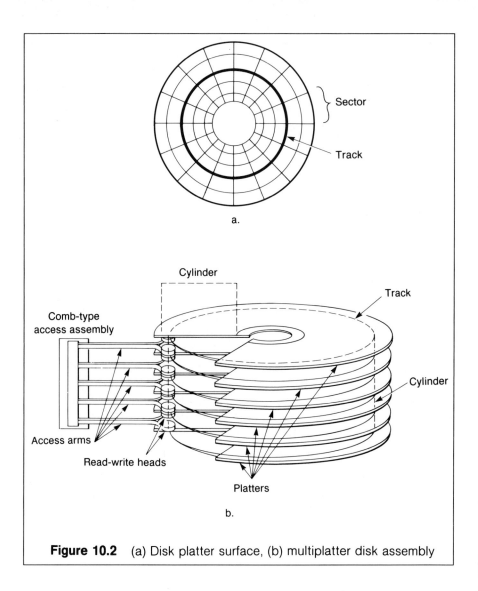

Sector

Track

a.

Cylinder

Track

Comb-type
access assembly

Cylinder

Access arms

Read-write heads

Platters

b.

Figure 10.2 (a) Disk platter surface, (b) multiplatter disk assembly

Many users are using the disk simultaneously. Thus between consecutive writes of one user's program, the disk heads must be moved for other programs. For simplicity and safety, let us say that the number of writes is 1,500. Then we have, using the RM03 disk,

$$1,500 \times (30 + 8.3) = 57,450 \text{ MS} = 57.5 \text{ sec.}$$

We must transmit $151 \times 5,000$ or 755,000 characters to disk. The actual transfer requires only $755/1200$ or .63 sec. Hence the job will take only one minute of disk time to write the file.

The designators RM03 and RP06 are DEC designators. Other manufacturers produce compatible units.

Creating a Sequential File

In creating a sequential file the user must specify the FAB and RAB fields. If the fields are not specified, defaults are used in a few cases; but in others, an error results. Sometimes the defaults may not be to the user's advantage. The following table specifies which fields (in the authors' opinion) should be set before one issues a $CREATE. These fields can be set in the $FAB and $RAB or they can be set by using the offsets. The table also lists the defaults.

FAB Fields		RAB Fields	
Field	*Default*	*Field*	*Default*
ALQ	locally defined	FAB	none—field is required
FAC	none	RAC	SEQ
FNM	none—field is required		
FSZ	required for VFC records		
MRS	none		
ORG	SEQ		
RAT	none		
RFM	UDF (undefined)		

In addition, the RBF and RSZ fields must be set before the first $PUT, and the UBF and USZ fields must be set before the first $GET.

Using a Sequential File

In writing a program that uses a sequential file that has already been created, it is not necessary to repeat the fields that were used at creation time. Here the only field required for $FAB is FNM, and the only fields required for $RAB are the buffer fields and RAC if access is not to be sequential. We will not discuss random access of sequential files; we only indicate that it is allowed.

10.6 Overview of Relative and Indexed Files

There are some limitations if one chooses to access a sequential file randomly. One cannot delete a record from the middle of the file or add a new record to the middle. Sequential files are not organized for dynamic updating, but RMS supplies two organization methods that are. ORG=REL declares a relative file, and ORG=IDX declares an indexed file. This latter organization is also referred to as indexed sequential. The relative file organization is the simpler of the two and the faster in terms of access time. In fact, each time an indexed file is accessed on disk, two (or more) accesses are required: one or more for the *index tree* and another for the record.

We now discuss these two file organizations in enough depth that the reader should be able to see the advantages and disadvantages of each. The reader should also get a general idea of when to use one of these organizations and when to use the other.

Relative Files

The records of a relative file are stored in *cells* on disk. The records may be fixed length, variable length, or variable with fixed control; but the cells in which they are stored are always fixed length. Hence it is easy to waste disk space in this file organization. If the records are variable length with only a few long records and many short ones, all cells will be equal in length to the largest record (MRS). The cells are numbered 1, 2, 3 . . . n for each relative file. Thus the cell number does not represent the actual address on disk or the relative position of the cell on the disk. Instead it represents the relative position of the cell in the file. As noted earlier, this is called *virtual I/O*.

Each cell can be either empty or occupied. If the user specifies ORG=REL in the FAB and RAC=SEQ in the RAB (that is, a relative file that is accessed sequentially) then the first $PUT stores the RBF field in cell 1, the second $PUT stores into cell 2, and so on. On the other hand, if the user specifies RAC=KEY, then storage can proceed randomly. In this case a key buffer address (KBF) and size (KSZ) must also be specified in the RAB. Relative files always require the key buffer to be a longword. Hence one must always code KSZ=4 for relative files. To store a given cell, one simply places the cell number in the key buffer and then issues $PUT. To retrieve a record, one sets the key buffer and issues $GET. One deletes with $DELETE and updates with $UPDATE. The services required must be specified in the FAB. If one plans to get, put, delete, and update (that is, change an occupied cell) all in the same program, he should specify FAC=<GET,PUT,DEL,UPD>.

Cells are not packed on disk the way records are in sequential files. Instead, cells are not allowed to cross *bucket* boundaries. The programmer specifies the bucket size in terms of disk sectors. For instance, the FAB parameter BKS=1 specifies that a bucket is one block. Hence if cells are 151 characters long, there will be three cells to a block. The other bytes of the block will be unused. This makes the procedures of finding cells and updating cells faster. If BKS=2, then each disk access is done two blocks at a time, and a cell may straddle the two blocks. Thus relative files provide for a trade-off between ease of access and efficiency of storage.

Indexed Sequential Files

Let us now consider the problem of creating and later using a file that contains information on the employees of a company. Employees are to be identified by their social security numbers. After the file has been created, it will be necessary to retrieve an employee's record given only his or her social security number. Occasionally it will be necessary to retrieve someone's record given only his name. What must we do in the program that creates this file?

If we select the relative organization, we have the problem of deciding which cell number should be used for each employee. Later we will have the problem of translating a social security number or a name into a cell number. We have many techniques at our disposal if we know how to use them.

We can build a table of social security numbers versus cell numbers. We can search this table linearly, or we can sort it and do a binary search. Instead, we can invent a *hashing* function that maps social security numbers into cell numbers. Since there are more social security numbers than cell numbers, this mapping cannot be one to one. We must resolve possible *collisions*. Alternatively, we can develop some type of data structure to locate the proper cell. We can use a tree structure of some type and write a tree search procedure.

Indexed files save us the trouble of doing any of these procedures. With indexed files, RMS will handle this problem for us. We must pay a price, of course; indexed files are slower because of the extra overhead.

In indexed files the key or keys are part of the record. The key is not a separate cell number. The length of the key can be any size the user wishes. There can also be more than one key. There must be one key that is called the primary key, but there can be many alternative keys. In this example the employee's social security number would be the primary key, and the employee's name would be the secondary key. To access the file either by key or sequentially, the user must specify the *key of reference* in the KRF field of the RAB. The primary key is 0, the first alternative is 1, and so on.

Now suppose that we choose to create the file sequentially by primary key. In the FAB we specify ORG=IDX. In the RAB we specify RAC=SEQ and KRF=0. We omit the particulars of how keys are defined. In this method of creating the file, the records must be put in order by social security number. If we declared RAC=KEY, the order would not matter.

Later, if we wanted to access the file by name, we would specify RAC=KEY, KRF=1, KBF=KBUFF, KSZ=KBUFF_SIZE. We would then insert a name in the KBF buffer and issue $GET. If instead we said RAC=SEQ, KRF=1, then no key buffer would be needed. Each $GET would produce the next name in order. In other words, an index file can be considered to be in order by all keys simultaneously. The user gives the key of reference, and the order desired is evoked. This is called *inverting* the file. By using the offsets, the KRF can be changed dynamically, as can the RAC. Suppose we declared KRF=1 and RAC=KEY. In the key buffer we insert "SMITH"; then we say $GET. RMS will get the first SMITH it finds. This record then becomes the *current record.* Now suppose we change KRF to 0 and RAC to SEQ. (One needs to know the symbolic predefined direct assignment symbol for RAC=SEQ in order to do this.) The next $GET will produce that employee whose social security number follows SMITH's social security number.

Indexed files are complicated to explain in all their details. Here we have presented only an introduction.

10.7 Summary

In this chapter we have learned RMS in enough detail to manipulate the user terminal interactively, to print quality output files, and to create and maintain sequential files on disk. We have also looked briefly at relative and indexed files.

The $FAB macro defines a file access block of 68 bytes, which are divided into 28 fields. The length of each field and its relative position in the FAB are predefined by RMS. Each field has a *keyword name,* a *field size,* and an *offset.* These fields can be initialized by the $FAB or changed dynamically by the $FAB-STORE macro or by using predefined offset values. Similarly, $RAB defines a record access block, which consists of 63 bytes divided into 26 fields.

Normally the programmer should check for errors when issuing RMS macros. On completion of each macro, RMS returns a completion code in R0. An even number means that something abnormal or unusual happened, and an odd number means that the macro executed normally.

In using the VAX interactively, the user terminal is both an input device and an output device. Its input file has been assigned the name SYS$INPUT, and the output file has been assigned the name SYS$OUTPUT by RMS. If the user wishes to use the terminal for both input and output, it is sometimes convenient to declare FABs and RABs for both SYS$INPUT and SYS$OUTPUT.

Most VAX systems have an on-line printer that is used for final output of data in hard copy form. Its associated file is named SYS-$PRINT. RMS provides three methods for controlling the print carriage: CR, FTN, and PRN.

The programmer is often asked to estimate the time requirements of his program, and often the amount of disk activity is the dominating factor. Hence this chapter presented the physical characteristics of disks, such as platters, surfaces, heads, sectors, cylinders, rotational delay, seek time, and buckets.

RMS supplies two organization methods for random access: ORG=REL declares a relative file, and ORG=IDX declares an indexed file. The relative file organization is the simpler of the two and the faster in terms of access time. The advantages and disadvantages of each were presented in some depth.

EXERCISES

1. Write an assembly program with RMS that prompts the user with WHAT IS YOUR NAME? After the user types in his name—say, JOHN—the computer is to respond with PLEASED TO MEET YOU JOHN. Use only SYS$INPUT.

2. Write an assembly program to print the English alphabet using RAT=FTN. First output the two characters $A (2441 hex) with $PUT. Then output NULL and B (0042) through NULL and Y in a loop. Finally output + and Z.

3. How much disk time is required on the RM03 to print a sequential file of 7,000 records when each record is 115 characters long?

4. Suppose we wish to create a relative file of 8,000 fixed-length records of length 200 each. We wish to pick a bucket size that utilizes 90 percent or more of the disk space assigned. What is a good bucket size? What is the minimum ALQ that can be used with this bucket size?

5. Make a table of the advantages and disadvantages of each of the three types of files available with RMS.

6. Write a general procedure that will convert a sequential file into a relative one. Store the file in successive cells. Pass all required parameters via CALLS.

Appendix A

Number Representations
and Arithmetic

TO DEAL with computers at the assembly language level, one should be familiar with a variety of number representations. It is particularly important to understand the binary, octal, and hexadecimal number systems and to be able to convert numbers from the decimal system to these systems and back.

For those unfamiliar with such concepts, this appendix introduces these number representations and the more general notion of positional representation using an artibrary base (or radix). We also introduce the notion of complements and complement arithmetic. It is convenient to start by reviewing the notion of *number* and the various classes of numbers we will deal with.

A.1 Numbers

The computer scientist's conception of *number* must be somewhat more sophisticated than that of the layman. Programmers and analysts must deal with engineers, scientists, mathematicians, accountants, and others whose business requires extensive use of numbers. Different types of numbers require different internal computer representations. Hence it is advisable to review various categories of numbers that will be important in this respect.

We will deal with the following classes of numbers:

Natural Numbers: 1, 2, 3, 4, . . . These are also called counting numbers and are the basis of elementary arithmetic.

Integers: . . . -4, -3, -2, -1, 0, 1, 2, 3, 4, . . . These extend the notion of natural numbers. The positive integers can also be written $+1$, $+2$, . . .

Rational Numbers: All numbers of the form a/b, where a is an integer and b is a natural number. From the user's point of view, computers deal with rational numbers, or fractions, in decimal form. Hence

    1/2 = 0.5
    1/4 = 0.25
    2/5 = 0.4

Some fractions cannot be precisely represented in this form. For instance,

    1/3 = .3333333333 . . .
    1/7 = .1428571428571428 . . .

The decimal representation of a fraction, however, always has a repeating pattern, such as the sequence 142857 in $1/7$. Conversely, any decimal representation that ends in a repeating pattern, including 00000 . . . , can be converted into a fraction.

Irrational Numbers: These are all decimal representations that do not terminate in a repeating pattern. They include

    $\sqrt{2}$ = 1.414214 . . .
    π = 3.141592653589 . . .
    e = 2.7182818 . . .

In dealing with rational or irrational numbers, we often approximate the number by rounding it to some fixed number of digits. We also usually represent very "large" and "small" numbers—numbers with many digits to the left of the decimal point or many leading zeroes to the right of the decimal point—in *scientific notation.* For example,

    0.12345×10^{12} = 123450000000.
    0.12345×10^{-12} = .00000000000012345

Real Numbers: The union of all the aforementioned sets of numbers forms the set of real numbers.

Complex numbers of the form $a + ib$ where a and b are real and $i = \sqrt{-1}$ are also important in scientific computing but will not be treated in this appendix.

Computationally, it is common practice to recognize and distinguish only two sets of numbers: integers and reals. A computer can, of course, represent only finite subsets of these two sets. Integer computations are called fixed-point arithmetic, and real computations are called floating-point arithmetic. Most computers provide separate facilities for both types of computation. The VAX-11 provides for several types of integer representation and several types of real, or floating representation.

A.2 Positional Number Representation

We know that, in the decimal number system that we normally use, the symbolic string 3,185 stands for a number. We also know that this string is a shorthand notation for

$$3 \times 1{,}000 + 1 \times 100 + 8 \times 10 + 5 \times 1$$

In other words, the 3 means 3,000 because it is in the fourth position to the left of the decimal point. Similarly, the 8 means 80 because it is in the second position. Any system for representing numbers on the basis of the position of a symbol (or digit) in a string is called a *positional number system*.

Not all systems for representing numbers are positional. For instance, consider the Roman numeral LXXIV. This stands for the number 74. L means 50. X means 10 and is repeated to give 50 + 10 + 10. I stands for 1, and V stands for 5; I before V, however, means "subtract 1 from 5."

We often fail to appreciate the subtlety of our system of representing numbers and its associated expressive and computational power. For instance, try writing 2,347,681 as a Roman numeral, or try multiplying MCMLXXXII times LXXIV.

The Decimal System

The number 3,185 mentioned earlier can also be thought of as

$$3 \times 10^3 + 1 \times 10^1 + 8 \times 10^3 + 5 \times 10^0$$

That is, 5 times the zero power of 10, 8 times the first power of 10, and so forth. This interpretation shows us clearly the role that 10 plays in our usual way of representing numbers. Each position represents a different power of 10. Hence we call our system the *decimal* system, with 10 as the *base* or *radix* of the system. Fractions can be interpreted similarly. Thus:

$$0.682 = 6 \times 10^{-1} + 8 \times 10^{-2} + 2 \times 10^{-3}$$

There are ten digits in the decimal system: 0, 1, 2, 3, 4, 5, 6, 7, 8, and 9. Each position must be filled with one of these ten digits. It is no coincidence that the number of digits is equal to the base of the system. Suppose we only had nine digits—say, 0, 1, 2, 3, 4, 5, 6, 7, and 8. How could we represent 9? We could not. Anything in the unit's position would be too small, and anything in the ten's position would be too large. On the other hand, suppose we had eleven digits—say, 0, 1, 2, 3, 4, 5, 6, 7, 8, 9, and A, where A stands for 10. Then the number 20 could be represented in two ways, namely 20 and 1A. In order to achieve a representation that is both complete and unique, the number of digits must equal the base.

There does not appear to be any logical reason that our culture selected 10 for the base of its number system. It is widely thought to be related to the number of fingers we have. The decimal system is not the only positional number system, however. Other systems have been used and studied throughout the history of arithmetic. Some of these have become especially important with the invention of the computer.

Other Number Systems

In this section we present three number systems that are important to computer users: binary, octal, and hexadecimal. All these systems are positional number systems.

Since in the decimal system each position represents a power of 10, it seems reasonable that in the binary system each position represents a power of 2. Note the parallel rationale. There can be only two digits in this system, denoted by 0 and 1. Hence the string 101, interpreted as a binary number, means:

$$1 \times 2^2 + 0 \times 2^1 + 1 \times 2^0 = 4 + 0 + 1 = 5$$

Note that the process of interpreting the binary value 101 by the foregoing equations is also, in fact, a method of converting binary to decimal, which we consider in more detail in the next section. We count in binary as follows: 1, 10, 11, 100, 101, 110, 111, 1000, . . . Binary numbers rapidly become extremely long, so it is easy to understand why this system is not popular for human use. Computers, on the other hand, can store zeroes and ones readily. Hence binary is widely used as the system for internal computer representation.

In order to avoid confusion over whether 101 means one hundred and one or five, we often write the base of the system in decimal as a subscript. We can then write the equality:

$$101_2 = 5_{10}$$

When the base is clear from the context, we follow standard convention and omit the subscript.

Fractions can also be represented in binary:

$$0.101 = 1\times2^{-1} + 0\times2^{-2} + 1\times2^{-3} = .5 + 0 + .125 = .625$$

In this case, the point is called the *binary point* instead of the decimal point.

In the octal number system, the positions represent powers of 8. This system uses the digits 0, 1, 2, 3, 4, 5, 6, and 7. Hence the octal number 721 is equal to the decimal number

$$7\times8^2 + 2\times8^1 + 1\times8^0 = 465$$

Fractions use negative powers of 8. The octal number 0.21, interpreted in decimal, is:

$$2\times8^{-1} + 1\times8^{-2} = .25 + .015625 = .265625$$

The hexadecimal number system uses 16 as its base and has the digits 0, 1, 2, 3, 4, 5, 6, 7, 8, 9, A, B, C, D, E, and F. The letters A through F represent the numbers 10 through 15, respectively. Hence the hexadecimal number A0F in decimal is

$$10\times16^2 + 0\times16^1 + 15\times16^0 = 2575$$

The hexadecimal fraction 0.A in decimal is

$$10\times16^{-1} = 10/16 = .625$$

In general, computers do not represent numbers in octal or hexadecimal (hex for short). As we shall see, however, both octal and hex serve as shorthand methods for expressing binary numbers.

We have seen that some fractions cannot be represented precisely as decimal fractions. Similarly, some fractions cannot be represented exactly in binary or octal or hex. In fact, many fractions that can be represented exactly in decimal cannot be represented exactly in binary. For instance:

$$0.5_{10} = 0.1_2 \text{ exactly}$$

but

$$0.05_{10} = 0.00001100110011001100\ldots_2$$

The converse is not true. All binary fractions are exactly representable as decimal fractions. This is easily seen since

$$2^{-p} = (10/5)^{-p} = (5/10)^p = 5^p/10^p$$

Hence,

$$1/2 = 5/10$$
$$1/4 = 25/100$$
$$1/8 = 125/1000$$

and so on.

A fraction is exactly representable in decimal if and only if its denominator in reduced form is the product of a power of 2 and a power of 5. A fraction is exactly representable in binary if and only if its denominator in reduced form is a power of 2.

We can now generalize the notion of number systems. Let r be any counting number greater than 1. Let $c_1, c_2, \ldots c_r$ be a set of r distinct digits. Let p_i be an arbitrary member of this set for $i = n$, $n-1, n-2, \ldots 2, 1, 0, -1, \ldots -m$. Then

$$p_n p_{n-1} p_{n-2} \cdots p_1 p_0 \cdot p_{-1} \cdots p_{-m}$$

stands for

$$p_n \times r^n + p_{n-1} \times r^{n-1} + \ldots + p_0 \times r^0 + \ldots + p_{-m} \times r^{-m}$$

Here r is the radix or base of the system.

Conversion among Number Systems

We must be able not only to understand these new number systems but also to convert from and to decimal notation. Let us start with an example in which we convert from decimal to binary. Suppose we have the number 38. In binary (powers of 2) this number is clearly equal to $32 + 4 + 2$, or

$$1 \times 2^5 + 0 \times 2^4 + 0 \times 2^3 + 1 \times 2^2 + 1 \times 2^1 + 0 \times 2^0 = 100110$$

If we divide 100110 by 2, we get 10011. In other words, when we divide a binary number by 2, it moves the binary point one position to the left in the same way that dividing a decimal number by 10 moves the decimal point. If we now divide 10011 by 2, we get 1001.1, or 1001 with a remainder of 1. If we then divide 1001 by 2, we get 100 with a remainder of 1. Continuing in this manner, we observe the following:

Dividend	Quotient	Remainder
100110	10011	0
10011	1001	1
1001	100	1
100	10	0
10	1	0
1	0	1

In other words, if we successively divide a binary number by 2, then the remainders are the successive binary digits of the number. Note that the first remainder is the units position, the second remainder is the two's position and so forth. The same results hold if the number is given in decimal, since the remainder must be 0 or 1.

Dividend	Quotient	Remainder
38	19	0
19	9	1
9	4	1
4	2	0
2	1	0
1	0	1

We stop when a quotient of 0 is obtained, and we read the resulting binary number from bottom to top.

The mathematical justification for this algorithm is as follows. The number 38 is equal to some unknown binary integer of the form $32a + 16b + 8c + 4d + 2e + 1f$. The letters a, b, c, d, e, and f are the unknown coefficients. Each is either 0 or 1 and must be determined. On dividing by 2, we have

$$38/2 = 19 = 16a + 8b + 4c + 2d + 1e + f/2$$

Clearly, f cannot be 1. If it were, the right-hand side would not be an integer and hence could not equal 19. Thus f is 0. Substituting 0 for f, we now have an equation involving only a, b, c, d, and e, which can be solved for in turn.

To convert from decimal to octal, we successively divide by 8. For example, let us convert 385 to octal.

Dividend	Quotient	Remainder
385	48	1
48	6	0
6	0	6

Hence the resulting octal number is 601. Finally, let us convert 240 from decimal to hex. We divide by 16.

Dividend	Quotient	Remainder
240	15	0
15	0	F

The resulting hex value is F0.

Conversion of decimal fractions into binary requires successive multiplication by 2. For instance, the decimal fraction 0.625 is equal to the binary fraction 0.101:

$$6 \times 10^{-1} + 2 \times 10^{-2} + 5 \times 10^{-3} = 2^{-1} + 2^{-3}$$

If we multiply 0.101 by 2, we get 1.01. The integer part was the binary digit in the one-halves position, and the fractional part is 0.01. Multiplying by 2 again, we get 0.1. The integer part was the digit in the one-quarters position, and so forth. In tabular form we have:

Multiplicand	Integer Part	Fraction
0.101	1	.01
0.01	0	.1
0.1	1	.0

We stop when we achieve a fraction of 0, and we read the binary fraction from top to bottom (not bottom to top). In decimal we have

Multiplicand	Integer Part	Fraction
0.625	1	.25
0.25	0	.5
0.5	1	.0

The mathematical justification is similar to the integer case. The decimal fraction 0.625 is equal to some unknown binary fraction of the form:

$$a \times 2^{-1} + b \times 2^{-2} + c \times 2^{-3} + \ldots$$

The unknown coefficients $a, b, c, \ldots$ must be either 0 or 1, as before. On multiplication by 2, we have:

$$1.25 = a + b \times 2^{-1} + c \times 2^{-2} + \ldots$$

Clearly, a must be 1. If it were 0, the right-hand side of the foregoing equation would be a pure fraction. Thus we are left with

$$0.25 = b \times 2^{-1} + c \times 2^{-2} + \ldots$$

Multiplying by 2 again, we solve for *b,* and so forth. The procedure for converting decimal fractions to binary, unlike the integer procedure, may never terminate in a 0 fraction. Hence one may have to stop when enough binary positions have been computed. For example:

Multiplicand	Integer part	Fraction
0.05	0	.1
0.1	0	.2
0.2	0	.4
0.4	0	.8
0.8	1	.6
0.6	1	.2
0.2	0	.4
0.4	0	.8
0.8	1	.6

The resulting binary fraction is .00001100110011001100 . . .

Let us now convert 0.625 to octal. We successively multiply by 8:

Multiplicand	Integer Part	Fraction
0.625	5	.0

That is all. The octal value is 0.5 (⅝). Finally, we convert 0.71875 to hex.

Multiplicand	Integer Part	Fraction
0.71875	B	.5
0.5	8	.0

The hex value is 0.B8.

In order to convert a decimal number that has both an integer part and a fractional part, we first convert the integer part by successive division, then the fractional part by successive multiplication.

We now consider the reverse problem: conversion from binary, octal, or hex to decimal. This is easy since the positions represent powers of the base. For instance, consider the binary number 1011.01. The meaning of this representation is $8 + 2 + 1 + 0.25$; hence the decimal value is 11.25.

For computational purposes, the integer part can be nested into successive multiply-add cycles. Suppose we want to convert the octal number 721 to decimal. We compute

$$(7 \times 8 + 2) \times 8 + 1$$

Similarly, the fractional part can be computed by successive divide-add cycles. Thus 0.524 octal becomes:

$$((4/8 + 2)/8 + 5)/8$$

Note that the digits are used in reverse order and that there is a division at the end.

We now consider conversion between binary, octal, and hex. Note that an unknown binary number of the form

$$32a + 16b + 8c + 4d + 2e + 1f + g/2 + h/4$$

where a through h are binary digits (either 0 or 1) can be written

$$(4a + 2b + c)8 + (4d + 2e + 1f)1 + (4g + 2h + 0)/8$$

Each of the expressions in parentheses is in the range 0–7. Hence octal can be converted to binary by simply converting each octal digit into three binary digits:

$$721.45_8 = 111010001.100101_2$$

Thus 7 becomes 111 (binary 7), 2 becomes 010 (binary 2), and so forth. Also, binary can be converted to octal by grouping the binary digits into groups of three, starting at the binary point:

$$10110.01_2 = 010110.010_2 = 26.2_8$$

To convert hex to binary, each hex digit becomes four binary digits. The hex digit 0 becomes 0000, 1 becomes 0001, 2 becomes 0010, and so forth to F, which becomes 1111. Thus 4D.5 in hex becomes 01001101.0101 or, omitting the leading 0, 1001101.0101. Binary becomes hex by grouping binary digits by four starting at the binary point. Hence, 10100.11 becomes 14.C.

The reason conversion between these three number systems is so easy is that 8 is 2 cubed and 16 is 2 to the fourth power.

A.3 Arithmetic in Binary and Hexadecimal

The VAX-11, like most contemporary computers, performs its basic arithmetic in binary. Hence we need to know something about binary arithmetic. Hex arithmetic is also important since hex numbers are just binary numbers rewritten as groups of four. Octal arithmetic is also just binary arithmetic in groups of three; most analysts, however, mimic the binary arithmetic of the computer by doing hex arithmetic. Computer printouts that show the actual contents of memory most often use hex. Thus if the number 10110110 is stored in the computer, the printout will read B6 (1011 0110). In general, older computers mimicked binary by octal, and newer ones do so by hex. Older computers stored data in 6-bit binary "bytes." These 6 bits (digits) could thus be represented as 2 octal "nibbles." The VAX-11 uses 8-bit bytes so that the data can be given as 2 hex nibbles. (More is said about bits, nibbles, and bytes in Chapter 2.)

We first consider the problem of adding in binary. In each binary position there is either the digit 0 or the digit 1. Clearly $0 + 0 = 0$, $0 + 1 = 1$, $1 + 0 = 1$, and $1 + 1 = 10$ or 0 with a carry of 1 into the next higher position. Thus in adding each position, we will have the two digits plus a possible carry. The largest number we will have to deal with in any given position is thus $1 + 1 + 1 = 11$ (binary 3), or 1 with a carry of 1. Let us add 111101 to 11001. Schematically we have:

Carry	111 1
Augend	111101
Addend	11001
Sum	1010110

Clearly, binary addition is much easier than decimal addition. One can also infer that binary arithmetic is easier to implement electronically than decimal and that it is very fast by comparison.

In binary subtraction, one may have to borrow 2 from the next higher position in the same way that one borrows 10 in the decimal system. For example, to subtract 11100 from 1001101, we have:

Borrow	1
Minuend	1001101
Subtrahend	11100
Difference	110001

If a binary number is multiplied by 0, the product is 0. If it is multiplied by 1, the product is the original number. To perform binary multiplication in general, we again mimic what we do in decimal: single-digit multiplies followed by staged additions. Let us multiply 101 by 110:

Multiplicand	101
Multiplier	110
	000
	101
	101
Product	11110

Binary division is seldom needed, so we leave it as an exercise for the reader to divide in binary.

We add and multiply in decimal by first memorizing tables. We know that 9 + 8 gives 7 with a carry of 1 because we have memorized this fact, which we use in addition. In binary, the corresponding tables are quite simple. In hex, the tables are bigger than in decimal. For instance, A + B (10 plus 11) gives 5 with a carry of 1(16). A×B gives E (14) with a carry of 6 (96). In hex addition, a carry occurs if and only if the sum of two digits is 16 or greater. For example:

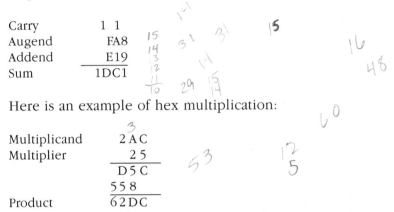

Carry	1 1
Augend	FA8
Addend	E19
Sum	1DC1

Here is an example of hex multiplication:

Multiplicand	2 A C
Multiplier	2 5
	D 5 C
	5 5 8
Product	6 2 DC

Some calculators have the ability to perform arithmetic in hex and octal.

A.4 Representations of Negative Numbers

All the foregoing examples have dealt with positive numbers. Of course, one can express negative numbers in binary, hex, or any other system by prefixing a minus sign to the number, just as in decimal. The usual rules of signed-number arithmetic apply unchanged. Computers may or may not represent negative numbers in this fashion. We now examine three alternative methods in which negative numbers are represented.

Signed Magnitude

We are used to dealing with numbers as quantities of variable length. Hence we use four digits to represent 2,658, but only one digit to represent 6. We can, of course, represent 6 as four digits—namely, 0006—but since leading zeroes do nothing for us, we leave them out. The hardware of computers, however, normally requires all numbers in a given range to have the same number of digits.

Suppose we have a computer that stores numbers as 8 bits. We could then store 0 as 00000000 and 1 as 00000001. In this way we could count to 11111111, or binary 255. In other words, we could store the integers 0–255 only. If we wish to store negative numbers, we could instead use the first bit from the left for a sign. This bit is called the most significant bit (MSB). Suppose we let 0 stand for + and 1 for −. If we were to do this, then 1 would still be 00000001 but −1 would be 10000001. The largest positive number would then be 01111111 (127), and the smallest negative number would be 11111111 (−127.) There would be two zeroes, +0 and −0, given by 00000000 and 10000000. Some computers represent integers in this way, which is analogous to the way we normally handle signed numbers. This representation is called *signed magnitude*. The VAX-11, like most new computers, does not use it for integer representation or arithmetic, as we shall see in Section A.5.

2's Complement

We continue to restrict our attention to integers that are represented by 8 bits. In 2's complement notation, positive numbers are represented in the same way as signed magnitude. Thus we still have the numbers 0–127 represented as 00000000–01111111. Negative numbers, however, are represented by subtracting their positive counterpart from 100000000 (that is, 1 followed by eight zeroes). Thus −1 becomes 100000000 − 00000001 = 11111111. Since all positive numbers have a 0 in the leftmost bit, the subtraction ensures that all negative numbers have a 1 in the leftmost bit. The number −126 is represented as 100000000 − 01111110 = 10000010. Also −127 is given by 10000001. Counting down further, 10000000 can serve as a representation of −128. With this choice, there is no problem of double representation of 0 (+0 and −0) as in signed magnitude representation. Thus in 2's complement notation we can represent the range [−128, 127]. If all numbers were represented as 16 bits, we would have the range [−32768, 32767]. If all numbers were represented as 32 bits, our range would be plus or minus 2 billion, approximately, with one more negative integer than positive.

The VAX-11 represents integers in each of these three ranges. There are separate instructions to deal with each range; hence in a single program the user can use all three as needed. There are, in addition, some cases in which 64-bit or even 128-bit integers are allowed.

Let us now represent −5 in 8-bit 2's complement notation. We subtract +5 or 00000101 from 100000000.

$$
\begin{array}{ll}
100000000 & (\,2^8\,) \\
\underline{00000101} & (\,5\,) \\
11111011 & (2^8 - 5)
\end{array}
$$

1's Complement

Some computers use 1's complement notation. Here the positive numbers are still the same as before, and the negative numbers are formed by replacing all 1s by 0s and all 0s by 1s in their positive counterpart. Thus for 8-bit numbers, -1 is given by 11111110. For such integers, this is the same as subtracting the number from 11111111. Zero can be represented by either 00000000 or 11111111. Since the 2's complement is formed by subtracting the number from 100000000 ($11111111+1$), it follows that the 2's complement of a number can be formed by adding 1 to the 1's complement of the number.

In the decimal number system there is a 9's complement and a 10's complement, the decimal counterparts to the 1's complement and the 2's complement of the binary system. In general, for any radix there is the *radix complement* and the *diminished radix complement*. It is an interesting exercise for the reader to experiment with these complements.

A.5 Complement Arithmetic

Why do computers such as the VAX-11 represent negative numbers in these complement forms? The answer has to do with subtraction. A subtrahend can be subtracted from a minuend by adding the 2's complement of the subtrahend to the minuend and discarding the high-order bit (the ninth bit for 8-bit integers) of the sum if it is not 0. The subtraction can also be accomplished by adding the 1's complement (and then adding 1 in some cases) and ignoring the possibly nonzero high-order bit.

Most computers today use the 2's complement. In general, 1's complement addition requires more time than 2's complement addition. It does take more time, however, to find the 2's complement of a number than the 1's complement. Normally the 2's complement is produced by first finding the 1's complement by reversing the 0,1 pattern and then using the arithmetic facilities of the computer (that is, the adder, in the ALU) to add 1 to the result.

The hardware combination of an adder and a complementer in effect allow for subtraction.

2's Complement Arithmetic

Let us subtract 5 from 18 in 8-bit, 2's complement notation:

$$18_{10} = 00010010_2$$
$$-5_{10} = 11111011_2$$
$$100001101$$

If we add these two numbers, we get the 9-bit sum 100001101. Ignoring the high-order bit, we have 00001101 or decimal 13.

The mathematics behind this algorithm is clear. The number -5 is actually represented by $2^8 - 5$ (an 8-bit quantity). The sum is $2^8 - 5 + 18$ (a 9-bit quantity). Discarding the high-order bit is the same as eliminating 2^8 from the result.

Now let us subtract a positive 5 from a negative 18.

$$-18 = 11101110$$
$$- 5 = 11111011$$

Here we get the 9-bit sum 111101001. Ignoring the high-order bit, we have 11101001, or -23 in decimal. Mathematically, we have added $2^8 - 18$ and $2^8 - 5$ and produced $2^9 - 23$ (a nine-place sum). If we ignore the high-order position, the sum becomes $2^9 - 23 - 2^8$, or simply $2^8 - 23$. In other words, all numbers in the range $[-128, 127]$ can be added with the same algorithm; there is no reason to distinguish positive numbers from negative ones. In signed magnitude form, we must check the numbers we are adding to see if they have the same sign. If not, the computer usually complements and adds. If the result is negative, it must recomplement the answer. All this is time-consuming and clearly less desirable.

In 2's complement notation, if one must subtract one positive number from another, a complement must be taken; but it is never necessary to recomplement.

1's Complement Arithmetic

If we subtract 5 from 18 in 1's complement arithmetic, we get

$$18 = 00010010$$
$$- 5 = \underline{11111010} \qquad [(2^8 - 1) - 5]_{10}$$
$$100001100 \qquad [(2^8 - 1) + 13]_{10}$$
$$\underline{00000001} \qquad [\text{ at this point 1 must be added}]$$
$$100001101 \qquad [(2^8) + 13]_{10}$$
$$00001101 = 13_{10}$$

Note that $2^8 - 1$ in decimal is 11111111 in binary. Similarly, if we subtract 5 from -18, we get

$$-18 = 11101101 \qquad [(2^8 - 1) - 18]_{10}$$
$$- 5 = \underline{11111010} \qquad [(2^8 - 1) - 5]_{10}$$
$$111100111 \qquad [(2^9 - 2) - 23]_{10}$$
$$\underline{00000001} \qquad [\text{again 1 must be added}]$$
$$111101000 \qquad [(2^9 - 1) - 23]_{10}$$
$$11101000 \qquad [(2^8 - 1) - 23]_{10}$$
$$ = -23 \text{ in 1's complement notation}$$

Let us now subtract 18 from 5.

$$5 = 00000101 \; [5]$$
$$-18 = \underline{11101101} \; [(2^8 - 1) - 18]_{10}$$
$$11110010 \; [(2^8 - 1) - 13]_{10}$$

Here it was not necessary to add 1. In general, the question of whether or not it is necessary to add 1 can be answered very easily. If, in adding the numbers, a 1 is lost by a carry out of the high-order position, then a 1 must be added to the low-order position. In other words, if the high-order position carries into the low-order position, the result turns out to be correct.

The problem of double representation of 0 exists in 1's complement arithmetic, as mentioned before. Let us add 1 and -1

$$1 = 00000001$$
$$-1 = \underline{11111110}$$
$$11111111$$

Overflow

In dealing with numbers in the range $[-128, 127]$, it is possible to add two of them that sum to a number not in the range. Restricting our attention to 2's complement arithmetic, we consider some cases in which this can happen. Suppose, for instance, we wanted to add 64 to 64. We would have:

```
01000000
01000000
```

On adding, we would produce 10000000, or -128. Recall that the leftmost bit is special; hence in adding two numbers in this range we must be cautious. If in adding two numbers of the same sign we produce a number of different sign, then the result is not in range, and we say that an *overflow* has occurred. As an example of negative number addition, let us return to the foregoing example of -5 and -18:

```
11111011
11101110
```

The sum is 111101001 or, ignoring the high-order ninth bit, 11101001, which is the correct representation for -23 decimal. Here there was a carry into the sign bit, but there was also a carry out of the sign bit. Thus the result is of the same sign, and no overflow has occurred. Two's complement overflow detection can also be summarized by the following set of rules:

1. If there is no carry into or out of the sign bit, the result is valid.
2. If there is a carry both into and out of the sign bit, the result is valid.
3. If there is a carry into the sign bit or a carry out of the sign bit but not both, the result is not valid, and an overflow has occurred.

A.6 Logical Operations on Binary Numbers

In assembly language programming, it is sometimes necessary or convenient to perform logical operations on binary numbers. The most commonly used logical operations are the AND operation, the OR operation, and the NOT operation. These operations are called *logical operations* since they are the main object of study in elementary logic courses.

The AND of two single bits can be viewed as follows: if the first number (which must be either 0 or 1) is 1 *and* the second (which must also be 0 or 1) is also 1, then the result is 1. If either the first number or the second or both are 0, however, then the result is 0. We can express this mathematically by introducing the AND operator($\cdot$).

$$1 \cdot 1 = 1$$
$$1 \cdot 0 = 0$$
$$0 \cdot 1 = 0$$
$$0 \cdot 0 = 0$$

This operator, like the multiplication operator $\times$, requires two operands, one written before the operator and one after. Such an operator is called a *binary operator* because it has *two* operands. An operator that has only one operand (such as $-$ for negation) is called a *unary* operator. Note that -5 can be interpreted as "the number minus five" or as "the unary negation operator operating on (plus) five".

It is sometimes convenient to summarize the results of logical operators in tabular form:

$\cdot$	0	1
0	0	0
1	0	1

This table is called the *truth table* of the($\cdot$)operator. The left and right operands form the top row and left column of the table, and the results are listed in the corresponding row and column.

The formula $a \cdot b$ is called a *logical* or *Boolean expression* and is read *a* AND *b*. We can think of it as meaning: if *a* is true (or equivalently if *a* is 1, if *a* is a closed circuit, if *a* is the positive pole of a magnet, and so on) and if *b* is true, then the *proposition a·b* is true.

The AND of two binary integers of fixed length, say 8 bits, is just the AND of each position. Hence:

$$10110110 \cdot 00110111 = 00110110$$

The inclusive OR of two single-bit binary numbers is: if either number is 1 (either *or* both), then the result is 1; otherwise (if both are 0), the result is 0. The NOT of a single-bit binary number is the 1's complement of that number. The NOT operator is thus a unary operator. Let us represent OR by + and NOT by ~. Then:

$$\tilde{\ }1 = 0$$
$$1 + 0 = 1$$
$$(\tilde{\ }0) + 0 = 1$$
$$\tilde{\ }(0 + 1 \cdot 0) = 1$$

If more than one logical operator appears in a Boolean expression, ~ is performed first, then ·, and then +, from left to right. Parentheses can be used in the usual way to control the order of computation and change the normal hierarchy. Thus:

$$1+1 \cdot 0 = 1, \text{ but } (1+1) \cdot 0 = 0.$$

In many respects, · is like multiplication, + is like addition, and ~ is like a unary minus sign.

The OR and NOT of binary integers of fixed length is computed position by position, just like the AND.

$$11110000 + 10101010 = 11111010$$
$$\tilde{\ }11110000 = 00001111$$

In the OR operation, the first operand is sometimes thought of as a *mask*. In the foregoing example, the mask 11110000 can be thought of as follows: set the first 4 bits of the second operand to 1, and leave the rest alone. Thus the OR operator is sometimes referred to as the *bit set* operator. Similarly, in an AND operation, the NOT of the first operand can be viewed as a bit clear mask:

$$11110000 \cdot 10101010 = (\tilde{\ }00001111) \cdot 10101010 = 10100000$$

In other words, clear the right four bits.

One last logical operator should be mentioned. The exclusive OR of two single-bit binary numbers results in 1 if and only if exactly one of them is 1. This operator is often referred to as XOR and thus has as its truth table:

XOR	0	1
0	0	1
1	1	0

The VAX-11 has instructions for bit setting, bit clearing, complementing (not-ing), and exclusive or-ing.

EXERCISES

In Exercises 1–4, carry out your results to four digits to the right of the radix point of the number system into which you are converting. In order to compute the answer to the best four places, it may be necessary to compute five places and round back to four. How does one round five places to four in decimal? By analogy, how does one round in binary, octal, and hex?

1. Convert the following numbers into their decimal equivalent:
   a. 106.04_8
   b. $A1B.F12_{16}$
   c. 120.212_3
   d. 01100101111.101101_2
   e. $A1B.34_{12}$

2. Convert to octal and hexadecimal:
   a. 368_{10}
   b. 2351.62_{10}

3. Convert accordingly:
   a. $263.75_{10} = ?_2$
   b. $2310.103_4 = ?_2$
   c. $3F6.AC_{16} = ?_8$

4. Fill in the following table in the boxes that have not been crossed out.

DECIMAL	HEX	OCTAL	BINARY	BASE 7
768				
.768				XXXXXXXXX
	F27			XXXXXXXXX
	F.27		XXXXXXXXXX	
		777		
			1011.101	XXXXXXXXX
				62
-1000				
-10.01			XXXXXXXXXX	XXXXXXXXX
	-F.F			XXXXXXXXX
		-1.1		

5. Perform the following using binary arithmetic

    a. 010111011 + 11000110 =

    b. 01010010 − 1001000 =

    c. 01010001 − 00110111 =

    d. 101111.10 × 11111.01 =

    e. 11011001.11 / 0110.1 =

6. List the first 40 nonnegative integers in the base 5 system.

7. Given the following data in 16-bit 2's complement form with high-order sign bit, what are the decimal integer values of these numbers?

0	1010101010000000	_____
0	0000001111111111	_____
1	1111111111100000	_____
1	0000000000000001	_____
1	0000000000000000	_____

8. Express each of the 16-bit binary strings of problem 7 as 4 hex nibbles.

0101	0101	0100	0000
0010	0001	1111	1111
1111	1111	1110	0000

9. What is the largest positive integer that can be expressed in 15 bits plus high-order sign?_____ (Give the result in decimal.) What is the smallest (most negative) integer that can be expressed in 15 bits, 2's complement, plus high-order sign bit?_____ Are these two numbers equal in magnitude? If not, why not?

10. Perform the given binary operation on the operands A and B in the given base (for example, A + B in base 8 arithmetic).

A	B	OPERATOR	BASE
3647031	2156254	+	8
D5E3026	262BA93	+	16
3C528E2	592FF3F	+	16
637257	254324	−	8
9A3FE06	7FD9EB1	−	16
A0B1	22C3	×	16
7777	1007	×	8
64	A	/	16

11. Perform the following arithmetic in binary with 2's complement arithmetic. First write each number as a 15-bit binary number plus sign in the high-order bit. Use 2's complement for negative numbers. Discard carries out of the high-order bit. State whether overflow occurs or not.

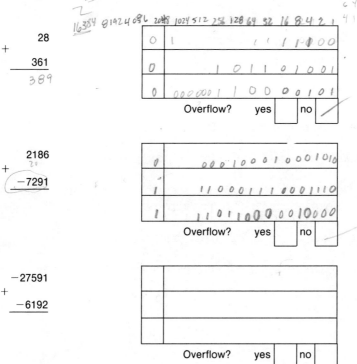

$\begin{array}{r} 28 \\ + \quad 361 \\ \hline 389 \end{array}$

$\begin{array}{r} 2186 \\ + \quad -7291 \\ \hline \end{array}$

$\begin{array}{r} -27591 \\ + \quad -6192 \\ \hline \end{array}$

Overflow?   yes   no

(Continued)

9759

$$-32767$$
$$\underline{-\qquad 1}$$

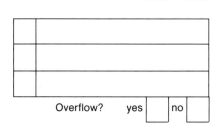

I	0 0 0 0 0 0

Overflow?   yes ☐   no ☐

$$-1$$
$$\underline{+\qquad -1}$$

Overflow?   yes ☐   no ☐

12. Consider a 2's complement machine that stores integers using 6 bits only. Perform the operation A + B as it would be performed internally by such a machine.

	A	B
a.	22	9 ⊐ ＼＼＼＼＼
b.	−9	−7 ≈
c.	−1	7 ／
d.	25	16
e.	21	−21
f.	−16	−16
g.	16	16
h.	−21	−12

13. Repeat Exercise 12 for A − B.

14. Repeat Exercises 12 and 13 for a 1's complement machine.

15. What is the range of integers representable in a sign magnitude machine using 3 bits? 4 bits? 8 bits? Generalize your result to *n* bits.

+3, -3 7, -7 127, -127

16. Repeat Exercise 15 for 2's complement machine. 8 bits   127, -128
                                                                    7 -8
                                                                    3, -3

17. Repeat Exercise 15 for a 1's complement machine.

Appendix B

Entering, Editing, and Executing a MACRO Program

THIS APPENDIX describes procedures for creating and executing a MACRO program interactively from a terminal. In addition, it describes a subset of the DCL (Digital Command Language) commands for communicating with the operating system. All commands are described as supported by the VMS (virtual memory system) version 3.0.

In the following,

$\boxed{\text{ret}}$: carriage return key

$\boxed{\text{esc}}$: escape key

$\boxed{\text{del}}$: delete key (on some terminals this key is labeled RUBOUT)

$\boxed{\text{ctrl/u}}$: hold control key down and enter u

file-spec : file specification. Has the format

   filename.filetype

where filename is one to nine alphanumeric characters, and filetype is one to three alphanumeric characters. The .filetype is optional but strongly recommended. If you specify a filetype, it is recommended that you use the default filetype MAR for an assembly file and DAT for a data file.

Note: A period at the end of filename is always part of the file name. Thus even if you use filename only in your file spec, your file will be named filename. on disk, and this is how you refer to the file.

B.1 Login

The procedure by which you access the system from a terminal and identify yourself to the system is called login. To login, enter

 .

System returns with

Username: ← enter your username then (ret)

Password: ← enter your password then (ret)

System returns with the prompt ($).

When the $ prompt is displayed, the system is said to be at the DCL level. While at this level, you can create a program, edit a program, execute a program, and so on.

B.2 Entering a Program

One way to enter and create a program is to use the editor. The editor is a system's program that enables you to type in strings of text (such as lines of code) and modify the text if needed. The VAX-11 has several editors; in the following we describe the SOS editor supported by most VAX installations.[1]

Next to $, enter

EDIT/SOS file-spec (ret)

System returns with the number 00100. (This is the number of the first line in your file.) You are now in the *input mode*. Enter your program giving (ret) at the end of every line.

While in the input mode, you can make corrections only on the line you are currently typing. For corrections,

(del)   deletes the last character entered

(ctrl/u)   deletes the current line

These are also the keys for deletions at any time during your terminal session.

---

[1] The complete SOS editor is described in the *VAX-11 SOS Text Editing Reference Manual*. A screen-oriented editor is also available under VMS; it is described in the *EDT Editor Manual*.

When you finish entering your program, enter

System returns with the prompt (*). You are now in the *edit mode*. While in this mode, you can edit your program or exit the editor and return to the DCL level. Before you proceed, however, you should save your program—that is, make a permanent copy of it on disk. To save your program enter one of the commands:

W (ret)   (save current file and remain in edit mode).

E (ret)   (save current file and return to DCL level).

B.3 Editing a Preexisting File

If you exited the editor and later want to edit your file, then next to $ enter

    EDIT/SOS file-spec (ret)

System returns with (*). You can now enter any editing command. A partial list of the editing commands follows. Note that:

1. Every command must be terminated by a (ret).
2. In editing a file, there is a pointer that always points to the *current line*. You can display the current line by the command

    P. (ret)

3. The pointer to the current line is moved following a command, normally to the last line processed. If a command fails, then the current line is unchanged. Also, the D (delete) command leaves current line undefined; in this case you can reposition the current line by some other command.

Command	*Function*
P.	Print current line.
P300	Print line 300.
P100:500	Print lines 100 through 500.
P.:300	Print current line through 300.
P300!10	Print 10 lines starting with line 300.

Command	Function
P	Print the next 16 lines starting with current line.
P^	Print first line.
P*	Print last line.
P.:*	Print all lines between current line and last line.
(ret)	Print next line.
(esc)	Print previous line.
.200	Set current line pointer to line 200.
..−5	Set current line pointer to current line minus 5 lines.
Fstring (esc)	Starting at the line after the current line, find the first line that contains string.
Sstring₁ (esc) string₂ (esc)	Starting with the current line, find the first line that contains $string_1$ and substitute all occurrences of $string_1$ in that line by $string_2$.
Sstring₁ (esc) string₂ (esc) 300:800	Substitute all occurrences of $string_1$ in lines 300 thru 800 by $string_2$.
D.	Delete current line.
D300	Delete line 300.
Dargument	(The delete command can have arguments similar to those for the print command.)
R.	Replace current line by a new line (input new line following line number given by system).
R300	Replace line 300.
R*	Replace last line by new lines; enter (esc) after last line you enter.
Rargument	(The replace command can have arguments similar to those for the print command.)
I.	Insert a new line following current line.
I300	Insert a new line following line 300.
I300,5	Insert new lines following line 300; increment new lines by 5; enter (esc) after last line you enter.
C800,200:600	Copy lines 200 through 600 following line 800.

Command	Function
C.,200:600	Copy lines 200 through 600 following current line.
C900=file-spec,100:500	Following line 900 of the current file, copy lines 100 through 500 from another file specified by file-spec.
T800,300:700	Transfer lines 300 through 700 from their place and insert them following line 800.
N	ReNumber the lines in the file in increments of 100.
Nn	ReNumber the lines in increments of n.
W	Save current file and do not exit the editor.
E	End the editing session, save the current file, and return to DCL level.
EQ	End the editing session, do *not* save the current file, and return to the DCL level.

It is advisable while you are entering a program to save your file by the W command every so often (perhaps every 10 minutes or so). When the system returns to the editor, use the I. command to return to the input mode and continue entering your program. It is also advisable to save from time to time while editing your program. SOS has two options to perform automatic file saving while in the edit mode or the input mode. Both options are requested while in the edit mode—that is, when (*) is displayed: Next to * enter one of the following:

/SAVE:20   Perform automatic file saving after every 20 edit-mode commands that modify the file.

/ISAVE:20   Perform automatic file saving after every 20 lines added in input mode.

Refer to the *VAX-11 Text Editing Reference Manual* for more commands and for other modes of operations of the SOS editor.

B.4 DCL Commands

In this section we present some of the VMS commands that are used frequently. We first introduce the concept of version numbers supported by VMS.

Version Numbers of Files

During a terminal session, several versions of a file may be created by the system. A version number is a number that is appended to the file-spec (for example, file-spec;1). When you create a file (for example, with the editor), the system assigns the file the version number 1. When you edit the file and then save it, the system automatically creates a new version and increments the version number by 1. New versions are also created when you assemble, compile, or link a file.

In most cases you need not be concerned with the version numbers of a file (the default value for input is the highest existing version number, and for output is the highest number plus 1). You can, however, access any version of a file by specifying the version number. For example:

EDIT/SOS file-spec;3 (ret)

File Commands

Command	Function
Command	*Function*
DIR	Display all file names in directory (The directory is a file that contains the names of all user's files).
DIR/SIZE	Display all file names in directory together with the sizes of the files.
DIR file-spec	Display all versions of file-spec.
PRINT file-spec	Print file on a printer (system returns with job *nnn*, where *nnn* is the job number).
TYPE file-spec	Display the contents of file on the terminal.
COPY file-spec$_1$ file-spec$_2$	Make a copy of file-spec$_1$ into file-spec$_2$.
RENAME file-spec$_1$ file-spec$_2$	Change the name of file-spec$_1$ to file-spec$_2$.
DELETE file-spec;1	Delete version 1 of file.
DELETE file-spec;*	Delete all versions of file.
PURGE file-spec	Delete all versions except most recent one.
PURGE/KEEP=2 file-spec	Delete all versions except the two most recent.
PURGE	Delete all files of all types except the most recent version of each file.
DIFF file-spec$_1$ file-spec$_2$	Find differences between file-spec$_1$ and file-spec$_2$.

Miscellaneous

HELP command	Display information about a certain command (PRINT, EDIT, COPY, and so on).
(ctrl/c) or (ctrl/y)	Terminate command in progress.

While a large amount of output is being displayed on a terminal, you may wish to suspend the output temporarily and look at it:

(ctrl/s)	Suspend output in progress.
(ctrl/q)	Resume output suspended by (ctrl/s).

Most commands on VMS can be abbreviated to the first four or fewer characters. Refer to the *VAX-11 Command Language User's Guide* for the abbreviations, for more options on the foregoing commands, and for more commands.

B.5 Assembling, Linking, and Running a Program

In order to run a MACRO program on the VAX-11, the program must first be assembled, then linked, then run.

Assembling the Program

Once your assembly program is created and edited, you are ready to assemble it. To assemble a source program contained in a file, enter the DCL command

MACRO/LIST file-spec (ret)

The MACRO command assembles a program and produces the object code. The object code will be contained in a file with the same file name as the file name of your source program, but with the file type OBJ. The /LIST qualifier produces a listing of the source program. The listing, together with the errors (if any), will be contained in a file with the same file name as the file name of your source program but with the file type LIS. The /LIST qualifier is optional.

After the MACRO command is executed, if the assembly is successful (that is, no errors), the system displays the $ prompt and waits for the next command. If there are errors in the source program, the system displays diagnostic messages on the terminal. If you cannot easily identify the errors, obtain a hard copy of the listing by:

PRINT filename.LIS (ret)　　　(print listing on the printer)

Or, on a hard copy terminal, enter

TYPE filename.LIS (ret)　　　(print listing on the terminal)

Study the errors in the listing, correct them using the editor, and repeat the foregoing MACRO command. Once your program assembles without errors, you are ready to link the object code.

Linking the Object Module

At the DCL level, enter

LINK filename.OBJ (ret)

This LINK command links the object code of your program to the system's library procedures needed and generates a file, the *executable image file*. The image file will be contained in a file with the same file name as the file name of your source program but with the file type EXE. If the LINK command does not complete successfully, the linker displays error messages on the terminal. Error messages generated by the linker are caused by errors in the source program. Study the errors, correct them using the editor, and repeat the MACRO and LINK commands.

Running the Program

After your program is linked successfully, it is ready to be run. At the DCL level, enter

RUN filename.EXE (ret)

If your program specified disk files for input and output, the program will do its I/O on those files; and at the end the system returns with the $ prompt. (If there are run-time errors, they will be displayed on the terminal.)

If your program specified SYS$INPUT as the input file (that is, if it specified the terminal as the input device), then you supply the data from the terminal while the program is executing. The program will stop for data every time it reaches an input statement. Of course, data must be supplied in the order that your input statements occur in your program. If your program tests for an end of file (eof), then you must supply eof indicator at the end of your data; (ctrl/z) signifies eof.

Alternatively, you can request the system to equate a data file with SYS$INPUT so that your program will read from the data file instead of from the terminal. For this you must have first created a data file, say IN.DAT, and then:

1. Prior to running the program, enter the DCL command

```
ASSIGN IN.DAT SYS$INPUT
```

2. Immediately after running the program, enter

```
DEASSIGN SYS$INPUT
```

Similarly, you can request the system to equate an output disk file with SYS$OUTPUT so that your program will write its output to the specified file instead of to the terminal. For this, assuming you wish to name the file OUT.DAT:

1. Prior to running the program enter

```
ASSIGN OUT.DAT SYS$OUTPUT
```

2. Immediately after running the program enter

```
DEASSIGN SYS$OUTPUT
```

B.6 Logout

When you are finished using the computer, enter

```
LOGOUT (ret)
```

It is important to log out at the end of a terminal session. Shutting your terminal off does not cause the system to log you out automatically. If you do not log out properly, another user can later turn the terminal on and access your files, since your login will still be active.

Appendix C

VAX-11 Instruction Set

C.1 Operand Specifier Notation Legend

THE STANDARD notation for operand specifiers is:

<name> . <access type> <data type>

where:

1. Name is a suggestive name for the operand in the context of the instruction. It is the capitalized name of a register or block for implied operands.

2. Access type is a letter denoting the operand specifier access type.

   a—Calculate the effective address of the specified operand. Address is returned in a pointer which is the actual instruction operand. Context of address calculation is given by <data type>.

   b—No operand reference. Operand specifier is branch displacement. Size of branch displacement is given by <data type>.

   m—operand is modified (both read and written)

   r—operand is read only

   v—if not "Rn", same as a. If "Rn", R[n + 1] R[n]

---

w—operand is written only

3. Data type is a letter denoting the data type of the operand

b—byte

d—D_floating

f—F_floating

g—G_floating

h—H_floating

l—longword

o—octaword

q—quadword

v—field (used only on implied operands)

w—word

x—first data type specified by instruction

y—second data type specified by instruction

*—multiple longwords (used only on implied operands)

4. Implied operands—that is, locations that are accessed by the instruction, but not specified in an operand—are denoted in enclosing brackets, [ ].

C.2 Condition Codes Legend

* = conditionally cleared set

— = not affected

0 = cleared

1 = set

Table C.1   Instruction Set (Listed in Alphabetic Order of Mnemonics)

OP	Mnemonic	Description	Arguments	N	Z	V	C
9D	ACBB	Add compare and branch byte	limit.rb, add.rb, index.mb, displ.bw	•	•	•	–
6F	ACBD	Add compare and branch double	limit.rd, add.rd, index.md, displ.bw	•	•	•	–
4F	ACBF	Add compare and branch floating	limit.rf, add.rf, index.mf, displ.bw	•	•	•	–
4FFD	ACBG	Add, compare and branch G_floatfloating	limit.rg, add.rg index.mg, displ.bw	•	•	•	–
6FFD	ACBH	Add, compare and branch H_floatfloating	limit.rh, add.rh, index.mh, displ.bw	•	•	•	–
F1	ACBL	Add compare and branch long	limit.rl, add.rl, index.ml, displ.bw	•	•	•	–
3D	ACBW	Add compare and branch word	limit.rw, add.rw, index.mw, displ.bw	•	•	•	–
58	ADAWI	Add aligned word interlocked	add.rw, sum.mw	•	•	•	•
80	ADDB2	Add byte 2-operand	add.rb, sum.mb	•	•	•	•
81	ADDB3	Add byte 3-operand	add1.rb, add2.rb, sum.wb	•	•	•	0
60	ADDD2	Add double 2-operand	add.rd, sum.md	•	•	•	0
61	ADDD3	Add double 3-operand	add1.rd, add2.rd, sum.wd	•	•	•	0
40	ADDF2	Add floating 2-operand	add.rf, sum.mf	•	•	•	0
41	ADDF3	Add floating 3-operand	add1.rf, add2.rf, sum.wf	•	•	•	0
40FD	ADDG2	Add G_floating 2 operand	add.rg, sum.mg	•	•	•	0
41FD	ADDG3	Add G_floating 3 operand	addl.rg, add2.rg, sum.wg	•	•	•	0
60FD	ADDH2	Add H_floating 2 operand	add.rh, sum.wh	•	•	•	0
61FD	ADDH3	Add H_floating 3 operand	addl.rh, add2.rh, sum.wh	•	•	•	0
C0	ADDL2	Add long 2-operand	add.rl, sum.ml	•	•	•	•
C1	ADDL3	Add long 3-operand	add1.rl, add2.rl, sum.wl	•	•	•	0
20	ADDP4	Add packed 4-operand	addlen.rw, addaddr.ab, sumlen.rw, sumaddr.ab, [R0-3.wl]	•	•	•	0
21	ADDP6	Add packed 6-operand	add1len.rw, add1addr.ab, add2len.rw, add2addr.ab, sumlen.rw, sumaddr.ab, [R0-5.wl]	•	•	•	0
A0	ADDW2	Add word 2-operand	add.rw, sum.mw	•	•	•	•
A1	ADDW3	Add word 3-operand	add1.rw, add2.rw, sum.ww	•	•	•	0
D8	ADWC	Add with carry	add.rl, sum.ml	•	•	•	•
F3	AOBLEQ	Add one and branch on less or equal	limit.rl, index.ml, displ.bb	•	•	•	–
F2	AOBLSS	Add one and branch on less	limit.rl, index.ml, displ.bb	•	•	•	–
78	ASHL	Arithmetic shift long	count.rb, src.rl, dst.wl	•	•	•	0
F8	ASHP	Arithmetic shift and round packed	count.rb, srclen.rw, srcaddr.ab, round.rb, dstlen.rw, dstaddr.ab, [R0-3.wl]	•	•	•	0
79	ASHQ	Arithmetic shift quad	count.rb, src.rq, dst.wq	•	•	•	0
E1	BBC	Branch on bit clear	pos.rl, base.vb, displ.bb, [field.rv]	–	–	–	–
E5	BBCC	Branch on bit clear and clear	pos.rl, base.vb, displ.bb, [field.mv]	–	–	–	–
E7	BBCCI	Branch on bit clear and clear interlocked	pos.rl, base.vb. displ.bb. [field.mv]	–	–	–	–
E3	BBCS	Branch on bit clear and set	pos.rl, base.vb, displ.bb, [field.mv]	–	–	–	–
E0	BBS	Branch on bit set	pos.rl, base.vb, displ.bb. [field.rv]	–	–	–	–
E4	BBSC	Branch on bit set and clear	pos.rl, base.vb, displ.bb, [field.mv]	–	–	–	–
E2	BBSS	Branch on bit set and set	pos.rl, base.vb, displ.bb, [field.mv]	–	–	–	–
E6	BBSSI	Branch on bit set and set interlocked	pos.rl, base.vb, displ.bb, [field.mv]	–	–	–	–
1E	BCC	Branch on carry clear	displ.bb	–	–	–	–
1F	BCS	Branch on carry set	displ.bb	–	–	–	–
13	BEQL	Branch on equal	displ.bb	–	–	–	–
13	BEQLU	Branch on equal unsigned	displ.bb	–	–	–	–
18	BGEQ	Branch on greater or equal	displ.bb	–	–	–	–
1E	BGEQU	Branch on greater or equal unsigned	displ.bb	–	–	–	–

Table C.1 Instruction Set *(Continued)*

OP	Mnemonic	Description	Arguments	N	Z	V	C
				Cond. Codes			
14	BGTR	Branch on greater	displ.bb	–	–	–	–
1A	BGTRU	Branch on greater unsigned	displ.bb	–	–	–	–
8A	BICB2	Bit clear byte 2-operand	mask.rb, dst.mb	•	•	0	–
8B	BICB3	Bit clear byte 3-operand	mask.rb, src.rb, dst.wb	•	•	0	–
CA	BICL2	Bit clear long 2-operand	mask.rl, dst.ml	•	•	0	–
CB	BICL3	Bit clear long 3-operand	mask.rl, src.rl, dst.wl	•	•	0	–
B9	BICPSW	Bit clear processor status word	mask.rw	•	•	•	•
AA	BICW2	Bit clear word 2-operand	mask.rw, dst.mw	•	•	0	–
AB	BICW3	Bit clear word 3-operand	mask.rw, src.rw, dst.ww	•	•	0	–
88	BISB2	Bit set byte 2-operand	mask.rb, dst.mb	•	•	0	–
89	BISB3	Bit set byte 3-operand	mask.rb, src.rb, dst.wb	•	•	0	–
C8	BISL2	Bit set long 2-operand	mask.rl, dst.ml	•	•	0	–
C9	BISL3	Bit set long 3-operand	mask.rl, src.rl, dst.wl	•	•	0	–
B8	BISPSW	Bit set processor status word	mask.rw	•	•	•	•
A8	BISW2	Bit set word 2-operand	mask.rw, dst.mw	•	•	0	–
A9	BISW3	Bit set word 3-operand	mask.rw, src.rw, dst.ww	•	•	0	–
93	BITB	Bit test byte	mask.rb, src.rb	•	•	0	–
D3	BITL	Bit test long	mask.rl, src.rl	•	•	0	–
B3	BITW	Bit test word	mask.rw, src.rw	•	•	0	–
E9	BLBC	Branch on low bit clear	src.rl, displ.bb	–	–	–	–
E8	BLBS	Branch on low bit set	src.rl, displ.bb	–	–	–	–
15	BLEQ	Branch on less or equal	displ.bb	–	–	–	–
1B	BLEQU	Branch on less or equal unsigned	displ.bb	–	–	–	–
19	BLSS	Branch on less	displ.bb	–	–	–	–
1F	BLSSU	Branch on less unsigned	displ.bb	–	–	–	–
12	BNEQ	Branch on not equal	displ.bb	–	–	–	–
12	BNEQU	Branch on not equal unsigned	displ.bb	–	–	–	–
03	BPT	Break point fault	[–(KSP).w']	0	0	0	0
11	BRB	Branch with byte displacement	displ.bb	–	–	–	–
31	BRW	Branch with word displacement	displ.bw	–	–	–	–
10	BSBB	Branch to subroutine with byte displacement	displ.bb, [–(SP).wl]	–	–	–	–
30	BSBW	Branch to subroutine with word displacement	displ.bw, [–(SP).wl]	–	–	–	–
FDFF	BUGL	Bugcheck longword	message.il	–	–	–	–
FEFF	BUGW	Bugcheck word	message.iw	–	–	–	–
1C	BVC	Branch on overflow clear	displ.bb	–	–	–	–
1D	BVS	Branch on overflow set	displ.bb	–	–	–	–
FA	CALLG	Call with general argument list	arglist.ab, dst.ab, [–(SP).w']	0	0	0	0
FB	CALLS	Call with argument list on stack	numarg.rl, dst.ab, [–(SP).w']	0	0	0	0
8F	CASEB	Case byte	selector.rb, base.rb, limit.rb, displ.bw-list	•	•	0	•
CF	CASEL	Case long	selector.rl, base.rl, limit.rl, displ.bw-list	•	•	0	•
AF	CASEW	Case word	selector.rw, base.rw, limit.rw, displ.bw-list	•	•	0	•
BD	CHME	Change mode to executive	param.rw, [–(ySP).w'] y = MINU(E. PSL*current-mode*)	0	0	0	0
BC	CHMK	Change mode to kernal	param.rw, [–(KSP).w']	0	0	0	0
BE	CHMS	Change mode to supervisor	param.rw, [–(ySP).w'] y = MINU(S, PSL*current-mode*)	0	0	0	0
BF	CHMU	Change mode to user	param.rw, [–(SP).w']	0	0	0	0
94	CLRB	Clear byte	dst.wb	0	1	0	–

(Continued)

Table C.1   Instruction Set *(Continued)*

OP	Mnemonic	Description	Arguments	Cond. Codes N	Z	V	C
7C	CLRD	Clear double	dst.wd	0	1	0	–
D4	CLRF	Clear floating	dst.wf	0	1	0	–
7C	CLRG	Clear G_floatfloating	dist.wg	0	1	0	–
7CFD	CLRH	Clear H_floatfloating	dist.wh	0	1	0	–
D4	CLRL	Clear long	dst.wl	0	1	0	–
7CFD	CLRO	Clear octaword	dist.wo	0	1	0	–
7C	CLRQ	Clear quad	dst.wq	0	1	0	–
B4	CLRW	Clear word	dst.ww	0	1	0	–
91	CMPB	Compare byte	src1.rb, src2.rb	•	•	0	•
29	CMPC3	Compare character 3-operand	len.rw, src1addr.ab, src2addr.ab, [R0-3.wl]	•	•	0	•
2D	CMPC5	Compare character 5-operand	src1len.rw, src1addr.ab, fill.rb, src2len.rw, src2addr.ab, [R0-3.wl]	•	•	0	•
71	CMPD	Compare double	src1.rd, src2.rd	•	•	0	0
51	CMPF	Compare floating	src1.rf, src2, rf	•	•	0	0
51FD	CMPG	Compare G_floating	src1.rg, src2.rg	•	•	0	0
71FD	CMPH	Compare H_floating	src1.rh, scr2.rh	•	•	0	0
D1	CMPL	Compare long	src1.rl, src2.rl	•	•	0	•
35	CMPP3	Compare packed 3-operand	len.rw, src1addr.ab, src2addr.ab, [R0-3.wl]	•	•	0	0
37	CMPP4	Compare packed 4-operand	src1len.rw, src1addr.ab, src2len.rw, src2addr.ab, [R0-3.wl]	•	•	0	0
EC	CMPV	Compare field	pos.rl, size.rb, base.vb, [field.rv], src.rl	•	•	0	•
B1	CMPW	Compare word	src1.rw, src2.rw	•	•	0	•
ED	CMPZV	Compare zero-extended field	pos.rl, size.rb, base.vb, [field.rv], src.rl	•	•	0	•
0B	CRC	Calculate cyclic redundancy check	tbl.ab, initialcrc.rl, strlen.rw, stream.ab, [R0-5.wl], dst.wl	•	•	0	–
6C	CVTBD	Convert byte to double	src.rb, dst.wd	•	•	•	0
4C	CVTBF	Convert byte to floating	src.rb, dst.wf	•	•	•	0
4CFD	CVTBG	Convert byte to G_floating	src.rb, dst.wg	•	•	•	0
6CFD	CVTBH	Convert byte to H_floating	src.rb, dst.wh	•	•	•	0
98	CVTBL	Convert byte to long	src.rb, dst.wl	•	•	•	0
99	CVTBW	Convert byte to word	src.rb, dst.ww	•	•	•	0
68	CVTDB	Convert double to byte	src.rd, dst.wb	•	•	•	0
76	CVTDF	Convert double to floating	src.rd, dst.wf	•	•	•	0
32FD	CVTDH	Convert D_floating to H_floating	src.rd, dst.wh	•	•	•	0
6A	CVTDL	Convert double to long	src.rd, dst.wl	•	•	•	0
69	CVTDW	Convert double to word	src.rd, dst.ww	•	•	•	0
48	CVTFB	Convert floating to byte	src.rf, dst.wb	•	•	•	0
56	CVTFD	Convert floating to double	src.rf, dst.wd	•	•	•	0
99FD	CVTFG	Convert F_floating to G_floating	src.rf, dst.wg	•	•	•	0
98FD	CVTFH	Convert F_floating to H_floating	src.rf, dst.wh	•	•	•	0
4A	CVTFL	Convert floating to long	src.rf, dst.wl	•	•	•	0
49	CVTFW	Convert floating to word	src.rf, dst.ww	•	•	•	0
48FD	CVTGB	Convert G_floating to byte	src.rg, dst.wb	•	•	•	0
33FD	CVTGF	Convert G_floating to F_floating	src.rg, dst.wf	•	•	•	0
56FD	CVTGH	Convert G_floating to H_floating	src.rg, dst.wh	•	•	•	0
4AFD	CVTGL	Convert G_floating to longword	src.rg, dst.wl	•	•	•	0
49FD	CVTGW	Convert G_floating to word	src.rg, dst.ww	•	•	•	0
68FD	CVTHB	Convert H_floating to byte	src.rh, dst.wb	•	•	•	0
F7FD	CVTHD	Convert H_floating to D_floating	src.rh, dst.wd	•	•	•	0
F6FD	CVTHF	Convert H_floating to F_floating	src.rh, dst.wf	•	•	•	0

Table C.1   Instruction Set *(Continued)*

OP	Mnemonic	Description	Arguments	N	Z	V	C
76FD	CVTHG	Convert H_floating to G_floating	src.rh, dst.wg	•	•	•	0
6AFD	CVTHL	Convert H_floating to longword	src.rh, dst.wl	•	•	•	0
69FD	CVTHW	Convert H_floating to word	src.rl, dst.ww				
F6	CVTLB	Convert long to byte	src.rl, dst.wb	•	•	•	0
6E	CVTLD	Convert long to double	src.rl, dst.wd	•	•	•	0
4E	CVTLF	Convert long to floating	src.rl, dst.wf	•	•	•	0
4EFD	CVTLG	Convert longword to G_floating	src.rl, dst.wg	•	•	•	0
6EFD	CVTLH	Convert longword to H_floating	src.rl, dst.wh	•	•	•	0
F9	CVTLP	Convert long to packed	src.rl, dstlen.rw, dstaddr.ab, [R0-3.wl]	•	•	•	0
F7	CVTLW	Convert long to word	src.rl, dst.ww	•	•	•	0
36	CVTPL	Convert packed to long	srclen.rw, srcaddr.ab, [R0-3.wl], dst.wl	•	•	•	0
08	CVTPS	Convert packed to leading separate	srclen.rw, srcaddr.ab, dstlen.rw, dstaddr.ab, [R0-3.wl]	•	•	•	0
24	CVTPT	Convert packed to trailing	srclen.rw, srcaddr.ab, tbladdr.ab, dstlen.rw, dstaddr.ab, [R0-3, wl]	•	•	•	0
6B	CVTRDL	Convert rounded double to long	src.rd, dst.wl	•	•	•	0
4B	CVTRFL	Convert rounded floating to long	src.rf, dst.wl	•	•	•	0
4BFD	CVTRGL	Convert rounded G_floating to longword	src.rg, dst.wl	•	•	•	0
6BFD	CVTRHL	Convert rounded H_floating to longword	src.rh, dst.wl	•	•	•	0
09	CVTSP	Convert leading separate to packed	srclen.rw, srcaddr.ab, dstlen.rw, dstaddr.ab, [R0-3.wl]	•	•	•	0
26	CVTTP	Convert trailing to packed	srclen.rw, srcaddr.ab, tbladdr.ab, dstlen.rw, dstaddr.ab, [R0-3.wl]	•	•	•	0
33	CVTWB	Convert word to byte	src.rw, dst.wb	•	•	•	0
6D	CVTWD	Convert word to double	src.rw, dst.wd	•	•	•	0
4D	CVTWF	Convert word to floating	src.rw, dst.wf	•	•	•	0
4DFD	CVTWG	Convert word to G_floating	src.rw, dst.wg	•	•	•	0
6DFD	CVTWH	Convert word to H_floating	src.rw, dst.wh	•	•	•	0
32	CVTWL	Convert word to long	src.rw, dst.wl	•	•	•	0
97	DECB	Decrement byte	dif.mb	•	•	•	•
D7	DECL	Decrement long	dif.ml	•	•	•	•
B7	DECW	Decrement word	dif.mw	•	•	•	•
86	DIVB2	Divide byte 2-operand	divr.rb, quo.mb	•	•	•	0
87	DIVB3	Divide byte 3-operand	divr.rb, divd.rb, quo.wb	•	•	•	0
66	DIVD2	Divide double 2-operand	divr.rd, quo.md	•	•	•	0
67	DIVD3	Divide double 3-operand	divr.rd, divd.rd, quo.wd	•	•	•	0
46	DIVF2	Divide floating 2-operand	divr.rf, quo.mf	•	•	•	0
47	DIVF3	Divide floating 3-operand	divr.rf, divd.rf, quo.wf	•	•	•	0
46FD	DIVG2	Divide G_floating 2-Operand	divr.rg, quo.mg	•	•	•	0
47FD	DIVG3	Divide G_floating 3-Operand	divr.rg, divd.rg, quo.wg	•	•	•	0
66FD	DIVH2	Divide H_floating 2-Operand	divr.rh, quo.mh	•	•	•	0
67FD	DIVH3	Divide H_floating 3-Operand	divr.rh, divd.rh, quo.wh	•	•	•	0
C6	DIVL2	Divide long 2-operand	divr.rl, quo.ml	•	•	•	0
C7	DIVL3	Divide long 3-operand	divr.rl, divd.rl, quo.wl	•	•	•	0
27	DIVP	Divide packed	divrlen.rw, divraddr.ab, divdlen.rw, divdaddr.ab, quolen.rw, quoaddr.ab, [R0-5.wl, — 16(SP): — 1(SP).wb]	•	•	•	0
A6	DIVW2	Divide word 2-operand	divr.rw, quo.mw	•	•	•	0

(Continued)

Table C.1 Instruction Set (Continued)

OP	Mnemonic	Description	Arguments	N	Z	V	C
A7	DIVW3	Divide word 3-operand	divr.rw, divd.rw, quo.ww	•	•	•	0
38	EDITPC	Edit packed to character string	srclen.rw, srcaddr.ab, pattern.ab, dstaddr.ab, [R0-5.wl]	•	•	•	•
7B	EDIV	Extended divide	divr.rl, divd.rq, quo.wl, rem.wl	•	•	•	0
74	EMODD	Extended modulus double	mulr.rd, mulrx.rb, muld.rd, int.wl, fract.wd	•	•	•	0
54	EMODF	Extended modulus floating	mulr.rf, mulrx.rb, muld.rf, int.wl fract.wf	•	•	•	0
54FD	EMODG	Extended modulus G_floating	mulr.rg, mulrx.rw, muld.rg, int.wl, fract.wg	•	•	•	0
74FD	EMODH	Extended modulus H_floating	mulr.rh, mulrx.rb muld.rh, int.wl, fract.wh	•	•	•	0
7A	EMUL	Extended multiply	mulr.rl, muld.rl, add.rl, prod.wq	•	•	0	0
EE	EXTV	Extract field	pos.rl, size.rb, base.vb, [field.rv], dst.wl	•	•	0	–
EF	EXTZV	Extract zero-extended field	pos.rl, size.rb, base.vb, [field.rv], dst.wl	•	•	0	–
EB	FFC	Find first clear bit	startpos.rl, size.rb, base.vb, [field.rv], findpos.wl	0	•	0	0
EA	FFS	Find first set bit	startpos.rl, size.rb, base.vb, [field.rv], findpos.wl	0	•	0	0
00	HALT	Halt (Kernel Mode only)	[–(KSP).w*]	•	•	•	•
96	INCB	Increment byte	sum.mb	•	•	•	•
D6	INCL	Increment long	sum.ml	•	•	•	•
B6	INCW	Increment word	sum.mw	•	•	•	•
0A	INDEX	Index calculation	subscript.rl, low.rl, high.rl, size.rl, entry.rl, addr.wl	•	•	0	0
5C	INSQHI	Insert into queue head, Interlocked	entry.ab, header ag	·0	•	0	•
5D	INSQTI	Insert into queue tail, Interlocked	entry.ab, header.aq	0	•	0	•
0E	INSQUE	Insert into queue	entry.ab, addr.wl	•	•	0	•
F0	INSV	Insert field	src.rl, pos.rl, size.rb, base.vb, [field.wv]	–	–	–	–
17	JMP	Jump	dst.ab	–	–	–	–
16	JSB	Jump to subroutine	dst.ab, [–(SP)+.wl]	–	–	–	–
06	LDPCTX	Load process context (only legal on interrupt stack)	[PCB.r*, –(KSP).w*]	–	–	–	–
3A	LOCC	Locate character	char.rb, len.rw, addr.ab, [R0-1.wl]	0	•	0	0
39	MATCHC	Match characters	len1.rw, addr1.ab, len2.rw, addr2.ab, [R0-3.wl]	0	•	0	0
92	MCOMB	Move complemented byte	src.rb, dst.wb	•	•	0	–
D2	MCOML	Move complemented long	src.rl, dst.wl	•	•	0	–
B2	MCOMW	Move complemented word	src.rw, dst.ww	•	•	0	–
DB	MFPR	Move from processor register (Kernel Mode only)	procreg.rl, dst.wl	•	•	0	–
8E	MNEGB	Move negated byte	src.rb, dst.wb	•	•	•	•
72	MNEGD	Move negated double	src.rd, dst.wd	•	•	0	0
52	MNEGF	Move negated floating	src.rf, dst.wf	•	•	0	0
52FD	MNEGG	Move negated G_floating	src.rg, dst.wg	•	•	0	0
72FD	MNEGH	Move negated H_floating	src.rh, dst.wh	•	•	0	0
CE	MNEGL	Move negated long	src.rl, dst.wl	•	•	•	•
AE	MNEGW	Move negated word	src.rw, dst.ww	•	•	•	•
9E	MOVAB	Move address of byte	src.ab, dst.wl	•	•	0	–
7E	MOVAD	Move address of double	src.aq, dst.wl	•	•	0	–
DE	MOVAF	Move address of floating	src.al, dst.wl	•	•	0	–

Table C.1   Instruction Set (Continued)

OP	Mnemonic	Description	Arguments	N	Z	V	C
7E	MOVAG	Move address of G_floating	src.ag, dst.wl	·	·	0	-
7EFD	MOVAH	Move address of H_floating	src.ah, dst.wl	·	·	0	-
DE	MOVAL	Move address of long	src.al, dst.wl	·	·	0	-
7EFD	MOVAO	Move address of octaword	src.ro, dst.wl	·	·	0	-
7E	MOVAQ	Move address of quad	src.aq, dst.wl	·	·	0	-
3E	MOVAW	Move address of word	src.aw, dst.wl	·	·	0	-
90	MOVB	Move byte	src.rb, dst.wb	·	·	0	-
28	MOVC3	Move character 3-operand	len.rw, srcaddr.ab, dstaddr.ab, [R0-5.wl]	0	1	0	0
2C	MOVC5	Move character 5-operand	srclen.rw, srcaddr.ab, fill.rb, dstlen.rw, dstaddr.ab, [R0-5.wl]	·	·	0	·
70	MOVD	Move double	src.rd, dst.wd	·	·	0	-
50	MOVF	Move floating	src.rf, dst.wf	·	·	0	-
50FD	MOVG	Move G_floating	src.rg, dst.wg	·	·	0	-
70FD	MOVH	Move H_floating	src.rh, dst.wh	·	·	0	-
D0	MOVL	Move long	src.rl, dst.wl	·	·	0	-
7DFD	MOVO	Move Octaword	src.ro, dst.wo	·	·	0	-
34	MOVP	Move packed	len.rw, srcaddr.ab, dstaddr.ab, [R0-3.wl]	·	·	0	-
DC	MOVPSL	Move processor status longword	dst.wl	-	-	-	-
7D	MOVQ	Move quad	src.rq, dst.wq	·	·	0	-
2E	MOVTUC	Move translated characters	srclen.rw, srcaddr.ab, fill.rb, tbladdr.ab, dstlen.rw, dstaddr.ab, [R0-5.wl]	·	·	0	·
2F	MOVTUC	Move translated until character	srclen.rw, srcaddr.ab, escape.rb, tbladdr.ab, dstlen.rw, dstaddr.ab, [R0-5.wl]	·	·	·	·
B0	MOVW	Move word	src.rw, dst.ww	·	·	0	-
9A	MOVZBL	Move zero-extended byte to long	src.rb, dst.wl	0	·	0	-
9B	MOVZBW	Move zero-extended byte to word	src.rb, dst.ww	0	·	0	-
3C	MOVZWL	Move zero-extended word to long	src.rw, dst.wl	0	·	0	-
DA	MTPR	Move to processor register (Kernel Mode only)	src.rl, procreg.rl	·	·	0	-
84	MULB2	Multiply byte 2-operand	mulr.rb, prod.mb	·	·	·	0
85	MULB3	Multply byte 3-operand	mulr.rb, muld.rb, prod.wb	·	·	·	0
64	MULD2	Multiply double 2-operand	mulr.rd, prod.md	·	·	·	0
65	MULD3	Multiply double 3-operand	mulr.rd, muld.rd, prod.wd	·	·	·	0
44	MULF2	Multiply floating 2-operand	mulr.rf, prod.mf	·	·	·	0
45	MULF3	Multiply floating 3-operand	mulr.rf, muld.rf, prod.wf	·	·	·	0
44FD	MULG2	Multiply G_floating 2-Operand	mulr.rg, prod.mg	·	·	·	0
45FD	MULG3	Multiply G_floating 3-Operand	mulr.rg, muld.rg, prod.wg	·	·	·	0
64FD	MULH2	Multiply H_floating 2-Operand	mulr.rh, prod.mh	·	·	·	0
65FD	MULH3	Multiply H_floating 3-Operand	mulr.rh, ul.rh, prod.wh	·	·	·	0
C4	MULL2	Multiply long 2-operand	mulr.rl, prod.ml	·	·	·	0
C5	MULL3	Multiply long 3-operand	mulr.rl, muld.rl, prod.wl	·	·	·	0
25	MULP	Multiply packed	mulrlen.rw, mulradr.ab, muldlen.rw, muldadr.ab, prodlen.rw, prodadr.ab, [R0-5.wl]	·	·	·	0
A4	MULW2	Multiply word 2-operand	mulr.rw, prod.mw	·	·	·	0
A5	MULW3	Multiply word 3-operand	mulr.rw, muld.rw, prod.ww	·	·	·	0
01	NOP	No operation		-	-	-	-
75	POLYD	Evaluate polynomial double	arg.rd, degree.rw, tbladdr.ab, [R0-5.wl]	·	·	·	0

(Continued)

Table C.1 Instruction Set (Continued)

OP	Mnemonic	Description	Arguments	N	Z	V	C
55	POLYF	Evaluate polynomial floating	arg.rf, degree.rw, tbladdr.ab, [R0-3.wl]	•	•	•	0
55FD	POLYG	Polynomial evaluation G_floating	arg.rg, degree.rw, tbladdr.ab	•	•	•	0
75FD	POLYH	Polynomial evaluation H_floating	arg.rh, degree.rw, tbladdr.ab	•	•	•	0
BA	POPR	Pop registers	mask.rw, [(SP)+.r*]	–	–	–	–
0C	PROBER	Probe read access	mode.rb, len.rw, base.ab	0	•	0	–
0D	PROBEW	Probe write access	mode.rb, len.rw, base.ab	0	•	0	–
9F	PUSHAB	Push address of byte	src.ab, [—(SP).wl]	•	•	0	–
7F	PUSHAD	Push address of double	src.aq, [—(SP).wl]	•	•	0	–
DF	PUSHAF	Push address of floating	src.al, [—(SP).wl]	•	•	0	–
7F	PUSHAG	Push Address of G_floating	src.ag	•	•	0	–
7FFD	PUSHAH	Push address of H_floating	src.ah	•	•	0	–
DF	PUSHAL	Push address of long	src.al, [—(SP).wl]	•	•	0	–
7FFD	PUSHAO	Push address of octaword	src.ah	•	•	0	–
7F	PUSHAQ	Push address of quad	src.aq, [—(SP).wl]	•	•	0	–
3F	PUSHAW	Push address of word	src.aw, [—(SP).wl]	•	•	0	–
DD	PUSHL	Push long	src.rl, [—(SP).wl]	•	•	0	–
BB	PUSHR	Push registers	mask.rw, [—(SP).w*]	–	–	–	–
02	REI	Return from exception or interrupt	[(SP)+.r*]	•	•	•	•
5E	REMQHI	Remove from queue head, Interlocked	header.ag, addr.wl	0	•	•	•
5F	REMQTI	Remove from queue tail, Interlocked	header.ag, addr.wl	0	•	•	•
0F	REMQUE	Remove from queue	entry.ab, addr.wl	•	•	•	•
04	RET	Return from procedure	[(SP)+.r*]	•	•	•	•
9C	ROTL	Rotate long	count.rb, src.rl, dst.wl	•	•	0	–
05	RSB	Return from subroutine	[(SP)+.rl]	–	–	–	–
D9	SBWC	Subtract with carry	sub.rl, dif.ml	•	•	•	•
2A	SCANC	Scan for character	len.rw, addr.ab, tbladdr.ab, mask.rb, [R0-3.wl]	0	•	0	0
3B	SKPC	Skip character	char.rb, len.rw, addr.ab, [R0-1.wl]	0	•	0	0
F4	SOBGEQ	Subtract one and branch on greater or equal	index.ml, displ.bb	•	•	•	–
F5	SOBGTR	Subtract one and branch on greater	index.ml, displ.bb	•	•	•	–
2B	SPANC	Span characters	len.rw, addr.ab, tbladdr.ab, mask.rb, [R0-3.wl]	0	•	0	0
82	SUBB2	Subtract byte 2-operand	sub.rb, dif.mb	•	•	•	•
83	SUBB3	Subtract byte 3-operand	sub.rb, min.rb, dif.wb	•	•	•	0
62	SUBD2	Subtract double 2-operand	sub.rd, dif.md	•	•	•	0
63	SUBD3	Subtract double 3-operand	sub.rd, min.rd, dif.wd	•	•	•	0
42	SUBF2	Subtract floating 2-operand	sub.rf, dif.mf	•	•	•	0
43	SUBF3	Subtract floating 3-operand	sub.rf, min.rf, dif.wf	•	•	•	0
42FD	SUBG2	Subtract G_floating 2-Operand	sub.rg, dif.mg	•	•	•	0
43FD	SUBG3	Subtract G_floating 3-Operand	sub.rg, min.rg, dif.wg	•	•	•	0
62FD	SUBH2	Subtract H_floating 2-Operand	sub.rh, dif.mh	•	•	•	0
63FD	SUBH3	Subtract H_floating 3-Operand	sub.rh, min.rh, dif.wh	•	•	•	0
C2	SUBL2	Subtract long 2-operand	sub.rl, dif.ml	•	•	•	•
C3	SUBL3	Subtract long 3-operand	sub.rl, min.rl, dif.wl	•	•	•	0
22	SUBP4	Subtract packed 4-operand	sublen.rw, subaddr.ab, diflen.rw, difaddr.ab, [R0-3.wl]	•	•	•	0
23	SUBP6	Subtract packed 6-operand	sublen.rw, subaddr.ab, minlen.rw, minaddr.ab, diflen.rw, difaddr.ab, [R0-5.wl]	•	•	•	0
A2	SUBW2	Subtract word 2-operand	sub.rw, dif.mw	•	•	•	•
A3	SUBW3	Subtract word 3-operand	sub.rw, min.rw, dif.ww	•	•	•	0

306   VAX-11 INSTRUCTION SET

Table C.1 Instruction Set *(Continued)*

OP	Mnemonic	Description	Arguments	N	Z	V	C
07	SVPCTX	Save process context (Kernel Mode only)	[(SP)+.r*, —(KSP).w*]	–	–	–	–
95	TSTB	Test byte	src.rb	·	·	0	0
73	TSTD	Test double	src.rd	·	·	0	0
53	TSTF	Test floating	src.rf	·	·	0	0
53FD	TSTG	Test G_floating	src.rg	·	·	0	0
73FD	TSTH	Test H_floating	src.rh	·	·	0	0
D5	TSTL	Test long	src.rl	·	·	0	0
B5	TSTW	Test word	src.rw	·	·	0	0
FC	XFC	Extended function call	user defined operands	0	0	0	0
8C	XORB2	Exclusive OR byte 2-operand	mask.rb, dst.mb	·	·	0	–
8D	XORB3	Exclusive OR byte 3-operand	mask.rb, src.rb, dst.wb	·	·	0	–
CC	XORL2	Exclusive OR long 2-operand	mask.rl, dst.ml	·	·	0	–
CD	XORL3	Exclusive OR long 3-operand	mask.rl, src.rl, dst.wl	·	·	0	–
AC	XORW2	Exclusive OR word 2-operand	mask.rw, dst.mw	·	·	0	–
AD	XORW3	Exclusive OR word 3-operand	mask.rw, src.rw, dst.ww	·	·	0	–

Table C.2 Instruction Set (Listed in numerical order of the op codes)

Op Code	Mnemonic	Op Code	Mnemonic	Op Code	Mnemonic	Op Code	Mnemonic
00	HALT	17	JMP	2E	MOVTC	47	DIVF3
01	NOP	18	BGEQ	2F	MOVTUC	48	CVTFB
02	REI	19	BLSS	30	BSBW	49	CVTFW
03	BPT	1A	BGTRU	31	BRW	4A	CVTFL
04	RET	1B	BLEQU	32	CVTWL	4B	CVTRFL
05	RSB	1C	BVC	33	CVTWB	4C	CVTBF
06	LDPCTX	1D	BVS	34	MOVP	4D	CVTWF
07	SVPCTX	1E	BCC,	35	CMPP3	4E	CVTLF
08	CVTPS		BGEQU	36	CVTPL	4F	ACBF
09	CVTSP	1F	BCS,	37	CMPP4	50	MOVF
0A	INDEX		BLSSU	38	EDITPC	51	CMPF
0B	CRC	20	ADDP4	39	MATCHC	52	MNEGF
0C	PROBER	21	ADDP6	3A	LOCC	53	TSTF
0D	PROBEW	22	SUBP4	3B	SKPC	54	EMODF
0E	INSQUE	23	SUBP6	3C	MOVZWL	55	POLYF
0F	REMQUE	24	CVTPT	3D	ACBW	56	CVTFD
10	BSBB	25	MULP	3E	MOVAW	57	reserved
11	BRB	26	CVTTP	3F	PUSHAW,	58	ADAWI
12	BNEQ,	27	DIVP	40	ADDF2	59	reserved
	BNEQU	28	MOVC3	41	ADDF3	5A	reserved
13	BEQL,	29	CMPC3	42	SUBF2	5B	reserved
	BEQLU	2A	SCANC	43	SUBF3	5C	INSQHI
14	BGTR	2B	SPANC	44	MULF2	5D	INSQTI
15	BLEQ	2C	MOVC5	45	MULF3	5E	REMQHI
16	JSB	2D	CMPC5	46	DIVF2	5F	REMQTI

Table C.2   Instruction Set *(Continued)*

Op Code	Mnemonic	Op Code	Mnemonic	Op Code	Mnemonic	Op Code	Mnemonic
60	ADDD2	8B	BICB3	BC	CHMK	EA	FFS
61	ADDD3	8C	XORB2	BD	CHME	EB	FFC
62	SUBD2	8D	XORB3	BE	CHMS	EC	CMPV
63	SUBD3	8E	MNEGB	BF	CHMU	ED	CMPZV
64	MULD2	8F	CASEB	C0	ADDL2	EE	EXTV
65	MULD3	90	MOVB	C1	ADDL3	EF	EXTZV
66	DIVD2	91	CMPB	C2	SUBL2	F0	INSV
67	DIVD3	92	MCOMB	C3	SUBL3	F1	ACBL
68	CVTDB	93	BITB	C4	MULL2	F2	AOBLSS
69	CVTDW	94	CLRB	C5	MULL3	F3	AOBLEQ
6A	CVTDL	95	TSTB	C6	DIVL2	F4	SOBGEQ
6B	CVTRDL	96	INCB	C7	DIVL3	F5	SOBGTR
6C	CVTBD	97	DECB	C8	BISL2	F6	CVTLB
6D	CVTWD	98	CVTBL	C9	BISL3	F7	CVTLW
6E	CVTLD	99	CVTBW	CA	BICL2	F8	ASHP
6F	ACBD	9A	MOVZBL	CB	BICL3	F9	CVTLP
70	MOVD	9B	MOVZBW	CC	XORL2	FA	CALLG
71	CMPD	9C	ROTL	CD	XORL3	FB	CALLS
72	MNEGD	9D	ACBB	CE	MNEGL	FC	XFC
73	TSTD	9E	MOVAB	CF	CASEL	32FD	CVTDH
74	EMODD	9F	PUSHAB	D0	MOVL	33FD	CVTGF
75	POLYD	A0	ADDW2	D1	CMPL	40FD	ADDG2
76	CVTDF	A1	ADDW3	D2	MCOML	41FD	ADDG3
77	reserved	A2	SUBW2	D3	BITL	42FD	SUBG2
78	ASHL	A3	SUBW3	D4	CLRF,	43FD	SUBG3
79	ASHQ	A4	MULW2		CLRL	44FD	MULG2
7A	EMUL	A5	MULW3	D5	TSTL	45FD	MULG3
7B	EDIV	A6	DIVW2	D6	INCL	46FD	DIVG2
7C	CLRD,	A7	DIVW3	D7	DECL	47FD	DIVG3
	CLRG,	A8	BISW2	D8	ADWC	48FD	CVTGB
	CLRQ	A9	BISW3	D9	SBWC	49FD	CVTGW
7D	MOVQ	AA	BICW2	DA	MTPR	4AFD	CVTGL
7E	MOVAD,	AB	BICW3	DB	MFPR	4BFD	CVTRGL
	MOVAG,	AC	XORW2	DC	MOVPSL	4CFD	CVTBG
	MOVAQ	AD	XORW3	DD	PUSHL	4DFD	CUTWG
7F	PUSHAD	AE	MNEGW	DE	MOVAF,	4EFD	CVTLG
	PUSHAG	AF	CASEW		MOVAL	4FFD	ACBG
	PUSHAO	B0	MOVW	DF	PUSHAF,	50FD	MOVG
80	ADDB2	B1	CMPW		PUSHAL	51FD	CMPG
81	ADDB3	B2	MCOMW	E0	BBS	52FD	MNEGG
82	SUBB2	B3	BITW	E1	BBC	53FD	TSTG
83	SUBB3	B4	CLRW	E2	BBSS	54FD	EMODG
84	MULB2	B5	TSTW	E3	BBCS	55FD	POLYG
85	MULB3	B6	INCW	E4	BBSC	56FD	CVTGH
86	DIVB2	B7	DECW	E5	BBCC	60FD	ADDH2
87	DIVB3	B8	BISPSW	E6	BBSSI	61FD	ADDH3
88	BISB2	B9	BICPSW	E7	BBCCI	62FD	SUBH2
89	BISB3	BA	POPR	E8	BLBS	63FD	SUBH3
8A	BICB2	BB	PUSHR	E9	BLBC	64FD	MULH2

Table C.2 Instruction Set *(Continued)*

Op Code	Mnemonic	Op Code	Mnemonic	Op Code	Mnemonic	Op Code	Mnemonic
65FD	MULH3	6DFD	CVTWH	75FD	POLYH		PUSHAO
66FD	DIVH2	6EFD	CVTLH	76FD	CVTHG	98FD	CVTFH
67FD	DIVH3	6FFD	ACBH	7CFD	CLRH,	99FD	CVTFG
68FD	CVTHB	70FD	MOVH		CLRO	F6FD	CVTHF
69FD	CVTHW	71FD	CMPH	7DFD	MOVO	F7FD	CVTHD
6AFD	CVTHL	72FD	MNEGH	7EFD	MOVAH,	FDFF	BUGL
6BFD	C\'TRHL	73FD	TSTH		MOVAO	FE	reserved
6CFD	CVTBH	74FD	EMODH	7FFD	PUSHAH,	FEFF	BUGW

Appendix D

ASCII Character Set

Table D.1 Hexadecimal-ASCII Conversion

HEX Code	ASCII Char	HEX Code	ASCII Char	HEX Code	ASCII Char	HEX Code	ASCII Char
00	NUL	20	SP	40	@	60	\
01	SOH	21	!	41	A	61	a
02	STX	22	' '	42	B	62	b
03	ETX	23	#	43	C	63	c
04	EOT	24	$	44	D	64	d
05	ENQ	25	%	45	E	65	e
06	ACK	26	&	46	F	66	f
07	BEL	27	'	47	G	67	g
08	BS	28	(	48	H	68	h
09	HT	29	)	49	I	69	i
0A	LF	2A	*	4A	J	6A	j
0B	VT	2B	+	4B	K	6B	k
0C	FF	2C	,	4C	L	6C	l
0D	CR	2D	–	4D	M	6D	m
0E	SO	2E	.	4E	N	6E	n
0F	SI	2F	/	4F	O	6F	o
10	DLE	30	0	50	P	70	p
11	DC1	31	1	51	Q	71	q
12	DC2	32	2	52	R	72	r
13	DC3	33	3	53	S	73	s
14	DC4	34	4	54	T	74	t
15	NAK	35	5	55	U	75	u
16	SYN	36	6	56	V	76	v
17	ETB	37	7	57	W	77	w
18	CAN	38	8	58	X	78	x
19	EM	39	9	59	Y	79	y
1A	SUB	3A	:	5A	Z	7A	z
1B	ESC	3B	;	5B	[	7B	{
1C	FS	3C	<	5C	\	7C		
1D	GS	3D	=	5D	]	7D	}
1E	RS	3E	>	5E	^	7E	~
1F	US	3F	?	5F	–	7F	DEL

Table D.2   ASCII Character Definitions

NUL	Null	DLE	Data Link Escape
SOH	Start of Heading	DC1	Device Control 1
STX	Start of Text	DC2	Device Control 2
ETX	End of Text	DC3	Device Control 3
EOT	End of Transmission	DC4	Device Control 4
ENQ	Enquiry	NAK	Negative Acknowledge
ACK	Acknowledge	SYN	Synchronous Idle
BEL	Bell	ETB	End of Transmission Block
BS	Backspace	CAN	Cancel
HT	Horizontal Tabulation	EM	End of Medium
LF	Line Feed	SUB	Substitute
VT	Vertical Tabulation	ESC	ESCAPE
FF	Form Feed	FS	File Separator
CR	Carriage Return	GS	Group Separator
SO	Shift Out	RS	Record Separator
SI	Shift In	US	Unit Separator
SP	Space	DEL	Delete

Appendix E

The VAX-11 Symbolic Debugger

A *debugger* is a program that enables you to monitor the execution of your program. Using a debugger, you can request that your program stop its execution at a certain point in the program; then you can examine the contents of memory locations (variables and instructions) to determine whether they are the desired contents. This is very helpful in debugging a program.

Typically, using a debugger you can do the following:

1. Examine contents of memory locations as well as registers.
2. Set breakpoints. A *breakpoint* is the address of an instruction where execution of your program is suspended just before executing that instruction. At a breakpoint the debugger gains control, and you can examine contents of any memory location as well as any register.
3. Set watchpoints. A *watchpoint* is the address of a location that is specified to determine when an instruction modifies that location. Your program stops if an instruction modifies a watchpoint, and the debugger gains control immediately after that instruction is executed. This allows you to determine if a location is being incorrectly modified.
4. Single step through your program—that is, execute one instruction at a time.
5. Evaluate expressions and perform arithmetic; that is, the debugger can be used as a calculator.

When a debugger allows inspection of the contents of memory locations by specifying their symbolic names, it is referred to as a *symbolic debugger*. For this, the debugger must maintain a table for the symbols in the program. This table is prepared at assembly time and at link time by appropriate qualifiers to the assemble and link commands.

To prepare for a debugging session on the VAX-11 under the VMS

312

operating system, assemble your MACRO program with the command:

```
MACRO/LIST/■DEBUG file-spec
```

Then link your object program with the command:

```
LINK/DEBUG file-spec
```

The /LIST qualifier in the MACRO command is not required, but the listing file is helpful in a debugging session.

At run time (when you enter the RUN command), the debugger gains control first. The following message is displayed:

```
VAX-11 DEBUG Version 3.0-5
%DEBUG-I-INITIAL, language is MACRO, module set to '.MAIN.'
```

After this message, the debugger prompts you for a command. The prompt has the form:

```
DBG>
```

When this prompt is displayed, you can enter any debugger command. For example, you can set breakpoints, set watchpoints, examine memory locations, and so on.

Some of the VAX-11 debugger commands follow. For a detailed description of commands and features of the debugger, refer to the *VAX-11 MACRO User's Guide* or the *VAX-11 Symbolic Debugger Reference Manual.*

By default, the VAX-11 symbolic debugger

1. Displays its output values in hexadecimal.
2. Interprets values in input commands as hexadecimal values.
3. Displays data values as longword integers.

You can change these default values:

1. By specifying qualifiers on individual commands, such as /DECIMAL, /WORD.
2. By setting the desired mode or type for the duration of your debugging session (or until the settings are superceded or canceled); for example, SET MODE DECIMAL, SET TYPE BYTE.

In the following, the term *address* can represent a symbolic address, an address expression, or a numeric address. If a numeric address is specified as a hexadecimal number that begins with a digit between A and F, the address must be preceded by the digit 0.

Some of the common VAX-11 debugger commands follow.

GO Command:

Format: GO
Function: Start or continue execution of program. Your program runs until one of the following occurs:

- A breakpoint or a watchpoint or a run-time error in your program is encountered: debugger takes control and prompts you for a command.
- An input statement to read from terminal is encountered: program waits for your input.
- The program is completed: debugger takes control.

EXIT Command:

Format: EXIT
Function: Terminate debugging session and return to DCL level.

SET BREAK Command:

Format: SET BREAK address
Function: Set breakpoint at address specified. Your program stops execution just before instruction at breakpoint is executed, and debugger takes control. At this point you can use the following EXAMINE commands to inspect contents of locations.

SET WATCH Command:

Format: SET WATCH address
Function: Set watchpoint at address specified. Your program stops execution whenever an instruction writes to a watchpoint location. The system displays address of instruction that modified the watchpoint, and debugger takes control.

EXAMINE Command:

Format	Function
EXAMINE address	Display contents of location at address.
EXAMINE address1:address2	Display contents of contiguous locations between address1 and address2.

Format	Function
EXAMINE/DECIMAL address	Display, in decimal, contents of location at address.
EXAMINE/BYTE address	Display contents of byte at address.
EXAMINE/HEX/WORD address	Display, in hexadecimal, contents of word at address.
EXAMINE/ASCII address	Display, in ASCII, contents of location at address.
EXAMINE/INSTRUCTION address	Display instruction at address.
EXAMINE	Display contents of location that is immediately after the last location displayed.

You can also display contents of registers by specifying the register names (R0–R12, AP, FP, SP, PC) in the address field of the EXAMINE command. For example:

EXAMINE R5	Display contents of register R5.
EXAMINE R10:FP	Display contents of registers R10, R11, AP, FP.

STEP Command:

The STEP command is used to execute one instruction (or a number of instructions) at a time. The program stops execution after the specified number of instructions; then debugger gains control.

Format	Function
STEP	Execute the next instruction, then stop.
STEP *n*	Execute the next *n* instructions, then stop; *n* is interpreted as a decimal number.

SET Command:

The following commands change the default mode (hex) and default type (long) to other modes and types. The new modes and types are used in the EXAMINE and DEPOSIT commands when these commands do not specify a mode or a type explicitly. The new modes and types remain in effect until changed by other commands.

Format

SET MODE DECIMAL

SET MODE HEX

SET MODE OCTAL

SET TYPE ASCII

SET TYPE BYTE

SET TYPE INSTRUCTION

SET TYPE LONG

SET TYPE WORD

Note: SET MODE changes mode of data displayed as well as data entered in debugger commands.

CANCEL Command:

Format	Function
CANCEL BREAK address	Cancel breakpoint at address.
CANCEL BREAK/ALL	Cancel all breakpoints.
CANCEL WATCH address	Cancel watchpoint at address.
CANCEL WATCH/ALL	Cancel all watchpoints.
CANCEL MODE	Restore all mode and type defaults.
CANCEL ALL	Cancel all breakpoints and watchpoints, and restore any user-set modes and types to their defaults.

SHOW Command:

Format	Function
SHOW BREAK	Display current breakpoints.
SHOW WATCH	Display current watchpoints.
SHOW MODE	Display current mode.
SHOW TYPE	Display current type.

Other Commands:

Format	Function
DEPOSIT address=value	Store value at address specified (the DEPOSIT command can have similar qualifiers to those for the EXAMINE command).
EVALUATE expression	Display value of expression (EVALUATE can have the qualifiers /DECIMAL, /HEX, /OCTAL).
HELP	Display the debugger commands.

Format	*Function*
HELP command	Display information about specified command.
	Same as EXIT command.
cntrl/c or cntrl/y	Interrupt execution of program and return to DCL level. You may now enter the DCL command DEBUG to return control to the debugger at the point your program was interrupted. This is useful if your program is executing an infinite loop that does not contain a breakpoint.

Note that the debugger can be used in languages other than MACRO, such as Pascal and FORTRAN. See the VAX-11 symbolic debugger or the corresponding language reference manual for details.

Appendix F

Linking FORTRAN and Pascal to MACRO

THIS APPENDIX is intended for users who wish to write routines (such as I/O routines) in FORTRAN or Pascal and link them to a MACRO program. The steps for linking will be illustrated by means of a simple program example consisting of a main program, an input routine, and an output routine whose functions are:

Input routine: Read in the name of a geometric figure (square or circle) and its dimension (side or radius).

Main program: Determine the area of the figure.

Output routine: Print the area.

The program uses three data types: integer, real, and character strings. We will illustrate the linking requirements for these three data types only.

F.1 Linking FORTRAN to MACRO

For the foregoing program, the input and output routines written in FORTRAN and the main program written in MACRO are shown in Figure F.1.[1]

Before we look at the steps for linking the routines to the main program, we observe the following:

- FORTRAN subroutines are implemented as VAX procedures. Therefore, they can be called by CALLG or CALLS.
- The default for an integer or a single precision real in FORTRAN is a longword. A character string occupies a number of bytes equal to the number of characters in the string.

---

[1] The details of the MACRO program of Figure F.1b may not be fully understood until chapter 6 is studied.

```
       SUBROUTINE INP(FLAG,DIM,SHAPE)
       CHARACTER *6 SHAPE
       INTEGER FLAG,DIM
       READ(5,20,END=10) SHAPE,DIM
       IF (SHAPE.EQ.'SQUARE' .OR. SHAPE.EQ.'CIRCLE')THEN
          WRITE(6,30) SHAPE,DIM
          FLAG=0
       ELSE
          WRITE(5,40) SHAPE
          FLAG=1
       END IF
       RETURN
  10   FLAG=-1
       RETURN
  20   FORMAT(A6,I5)
  30   FORMAT(' SHAPE IS A ',A6,' OF DIMENSION ',I3,' CENTIMETERS')
  40   FORMAT(' UNRECOGNIZED SHAPE: ',A6)
       END
C
C
       SUBROUTINE OUTP(AREA,SHAPE)
       CHARACTER *6 SHAPE
       REAL AREA
       WRITE(6,10)SHAPE,AREA
  10   FORMAT(' THE AREA OF THE ',A6,' IS', F8.2,' CENTIMETERS SQUARED')
       RETURN
       END
```

(a)

```
SHAPE:  .BLKB   6               ;STORAGE FOR NAME OF SHAPE
DIM:    .BLKL   1               ;STORAGE FOR DIMENSION OF SHAPE
AREA:   .BLKF   1               ;STORAGE FOR AREA OF SHAPE
FLAG:   .BLKL   1               ;FLAG=0 IF LEGAL SHAPE IS READ IN
                                ;     =1 IF ILLEGAL SHAPE IS READ IN
                                ;     =-1 ON EOF
SQUARE: .ASCII  'SQUARE'        ;
CIRCLE: .ASCII  'CIRCLE'        ;
PI:     .FLOAT  3.14            ;
;                               ;
;STRING DESCRIPTOR FOR CHARACTER STRING, SHAPE, IN FORTRAN SUBROUTINES
DESCR:                          ;
        .LONG   0               ;
        .ADDRESS SHAPE          ;
;                               ;
;ARGUMENT LIST FOR INPUT ROUTINE;
INLIST: .LONG   3               ;NUMBER OF ARGUMENTS
        .ADDRESS FLAG           ;ADDRESS OF FIRST ARGUMENT
        .ADDRESS DIM            ;ADDRESS OF SECOND ARGUMENT
        .ADDRESS DESCR          ;ADDRESS OF STRING DESCRIPTOR
;                               ;
;ARGUMENT LIST FOR OUTPUT ROUTINE
OUTLIST:.LONG   2               ;NUMBER OF ARGUMENTS
        .ADDRESS AREA           ;ADDRESS OF FIRST ARGUMENT
        .ADDRESS DESCR          ;ADDRESS OF STRING DESCRIPTOR
;                               ;
        .ENTRY  COMPUTE_AREA,0 ;
READ:   CALLG   INLIST,INP      ;READ IN A SHAPE AND ITS DIMENSION
        CMPL    FLAG,#-1        ;IS IT EOF?
        BEQL    EXIT            ; YES: EXIT PROGRAM
        CMPL    FLAG,#1         ; NO: IS SHAPE READ IN LEGAL?
        BEQL    READ            ;     NO: READ NEXT SHAPE
        MULL3   DIM,DIM,R6      ;     YES: COMPUTE SQUARE OF DIMENSION
        CVTLF   R6,R6           ;          AND CONVERT RESULT TO FLOATING
        CMPC3   #6,SHAPE,SQUARE ;IS SHAPE READ IN A SQUARE?
        BNEQ    ROUND           ; NO: MUST BE A CIRCLE
        MOVF    R6,AREA         ; YES: AREA=DIM**2 IS IN R6
        BRB     PRINT           ;      BRANCH TO OUTPUT ROUTINE
ROUND:  MULF3   PI,R6,AREA      ;COMPUTE AREA OF CIRCLE
PRINT:  CALLG   OUTLIST,OUTP    ;PRINT AREA
        BRB     READ            ;CONTINUE READING
EXIT:   $EXIT_S                 ;
        .END    COMPUTE_AREA    ;
```

(b)

Figure F.1 Program to compute the area of a geometric shape: (a) I/O
routines; (b) main program

- A MACRO program that calls a FORTRAN subroutine must construct an argument list to correspond to the parameters of the subroutine. The argument list contains the addresses of the integer and real arguments. For a character string argument, the argument list contains the address of a data structure called *string descriptor*. The string descriptor consists of two longwords; the first longword may simply contain zero, and the second longword contains the address of the character string argument. For a parameter that is an array of integers or reals, the argument list contains the beginning address of the corresponding array argument.

The first longword in the argument list contains, in the rightmost byte, the number of arguments. The following longwords contain the addresses of the arguments and the string descriptors. All addresses in the argument list must be in a one-to-one correspondence with the parameters.

To illustrate, consider the parameters of subroutine INP in Figure F.1a:

```
SUBROUTINE INP (FLAG,DIM,SHAPE)
```

The corresponding argument list, from Figure F.1a is:

```
INLIST: .LONG    3          ;NUMBER OF ARGUMENTS
        .ADDRESS FLAG        ;ADDRESS OF FIRST ARGUMENT
        .ADDRESS DIM         ;ADDRESS OF SECOND ARGUMENT
        .ADDRESS DESCR       ;ADDRESS OF STRING DESCRIPTOR
```

The last line of the foregoing defines the address of the string descriptor:

```
DESCR:  .LONG    0          ;STRING DESCRIPTOR
        .ADDRESS SHAPE       ;ADDRESS OF CHARACTER STRING
```

FLAG and DIM, which are integer parameters in the called subroutine, are declared as longwords in the calling program. SHAPE is declared as a block of 6 bytes to correspond to the string declared by CHARACTER *6 in the subroutine. Finally, subroutine INP is called by

```
        CALLG    INLIST,INP
```

Now, assuming that the two subroutines of Figure F.1 are contained in file INOUT.FOR, and that the main program is contained in file AREA.MAR, then to link them, proceed as follows:

1. Assemble the MACRO program by the command

```
MACRO AREA.MAR
```

   The object program will be in file AREA.OBJ.
2. Compile the FORTRAN subroutines by the command

```
FORTRAN INOUT.FOR
```

   The object program will be in file INOUT.OBJ (the FOR-TRAN command may be qualified with/LIST).
3. Link the two object programs by the command

```
LINK AREA.OBJ+INOUT.OBJ
```

   The image file will be in file AREA.EXE.
4. Now you can run the program by the command

```
RUN AREA.EXE
```

Had subroutines INP and OUTP been contained in two separate files, then each would be compiled separately and the three object programs linked by one LINK command.)

F.2 Linking Pascal to MACRO

The VAX-11 Pascal supports separate compilations of Pascal procedures using the concept of a MODULE. As of this writing, however, VMS does not have a "clean" method for linking Pascal procedures that reference input and output files to a MACRO program. This is because of the inability of the Pascal MODULE to prepare the input and ouput files for I/O. We have found the following method to work:

1. Declare the Pascal procedures in a main program with a null body.
2. Prior to calling the Pascal procedures, have the MACRO program call the Pascal main program (as a procedure) using a CALL instruction. The CALL instruction specifies the name of the Pascal program as the second argument; the first argument can be a null argument list. The purpose of this call is to prepare the input and output files.

3. Link the object codes of the MACRO program and the Pascal program, specifying the object file of the MACRO program first in the LINK command. The linker will give a warning because of the two entry points, one in each main program. Ignore this warning.
4. Run the program, specifying the file name of the MACRO program as the image file.

We will illustrate these steps on the program of the previous section. The input and output routines for the program, written in Pascal, are shown in Figure F.2a. The MACRO program is shown in Figure F.2b. This MACRO program is identical to the one in Figure F.1a except for the call to the Pascal main program (the call is immediately after the .ENTRY statement). This call specifies an argument list with one longword initialized to zero (a null argument list).

```
PROGRAM INOUT(INPUT,OUTPUT);
TYPE
  STRING= PACKED ARRAY[1..6] OF CHAR;

PROCEDURE INP(VAR FLAG,DIM: INTEGER; VAR SHAPE: STRING);
BEGIN
  IF EOF
     THEN FLAG:=-1
     ELSE
       BEGIN
         READLN (SHAPE,DIM);
         IF (SHAPE='SQUARE') OR (SHAPE='CIRCLE')
           THEN BEGIN
                  WRITELN (' SHAPE IS A ',SHAPE,' OF DIMENSION ',
                           DIM,' CENTIMETERS');
                  FLAG:=0
                END
           ELSE  BEGIN
                   WRITELN (' UNRECOGNIZED SHAPE: ',SHAPE);
                   FLAG:=1
                 END
       END
END;


PROCEDURE OUTP(AREA: REAL;SHAPE: STRING);
BEGIN
  WRITELN (' THE AREA OF THE ',SHAPE,' IS', AREA:8:2,
           'CENTIMETERS SQUARED')
END;

BEGIN {A NULL MAIN PROGRAM}
END.
```

                                    (a)

```
SHAPE:   .BLKB    6               ;STORAGE FOR NAME OF SHAPE
DIM:     .BLKL    1               ;STORAGE FOR DIMENSION OF SHAPE
AREA:    .BLKF    1               ;STORAGE FOR AREA OF SHAPE
FLAG:    .BLKL    1               ;FLAG=0 IF LEGAL SHAPE IS READ IN
                                  ;     =1 IF ILLEGAL SHAPE IS READ IN
                                  ;     =-1 ON EOF
SQUARE:  .ASCII   'SQUARE'        ;
CIRCLE:  .ASCII   'CIRCLE'        ;
PI:      .FLOAT   3.14            ;
;
;STRING DESCRIPTOR FOR CHARACTER STRING, SHAPE, IN PASCAL PROCEDURES
DESCR:                            ;
         .LONG    0               ;
         .ADDRESS SHAPE           ;
;
;ARGUMENT LIST FOR INPUT ROUTINE
INLIST: .LONG     3               ;NUMBER OF ARGUMENTS
         .ADDRESS FLAG            ;ADDRESS OF FIRST ARGUMENT
         .ADDRESS DIM             ;ADDRESS OF SECOND ARGUMENT
         .ADDRESS DESCR           ;ADDRESS OF STRING DESCRIPTOR
;
;ARGUMENT LIST FOR OUTPUT ROUTINE
OUTLIST:.LONG     2               ;NUMBER OF ARGUMENTS
         .ADDRESS AREA            ;ADDRESS OF FIRST ARGUMENT
         .ADDRESS DESCR           ;ADDRESS OF STRING DESCRIPTOR
;
;NULL ARGUMENT LIST FOR PASCAL PROGRAM INOUT
NULL:    .LONG    0               ;
;
         .ENTRY   COMPUTE_AREA,0   ;
         CALLG    NULL,INOUT      ;A CALL TO PROGRAM INOUT TO OPEN FILES
READ:    CALLG    INLIST,INP      ;READ IN A SHAPE AND ITS DIMENSION
         CMPL     FLAG,#-1        ;IS IT EOF?
         BEQL     EXIT            ; YES: EXIT PROGRAM
         CMPL     FLAG,#1         ; NO: IS SHAPE READ IN LEGAL?
         BEQL     READ            ;      NO: READ NEXT SHAPE
         MULL3    DIM,DIM,R6      ;      YES: COMPUTE SQUARE OF DIMENSION
         CVTLF    R6,R6           ;           AND CONVERT RESULT TO FLOATING
         CMPC3    #6,SHAPE,SQUARE ;IS SHAPE READ IN A SQUARE?
         BNEQ     ROUND           ; NO: MUST BE A CIRCLE
         MOVF     R6,AREA         ; YES: AREA=DIM**2 IS IN R6
         BRB      PRINT           ;      BRANCH TO OUTPUT ROUTINE
ROUND:   MULF3    PI,R6,AREA      ;COMPUTE AREA OF CIRCLE
PRINT:   CALLG    OUTLIST,OUTP    ;PRINT AREA
         BRB      READ            ;CONTINUE READING
EXIT:    $EXIT_S                  ;
         .END     COMPUTE_AREA    ;
```

(b)

Figure F.2 Program to compute the area of a geometric shape: (a) I/O
routines: (b) main program

Assume that the Pascal program of Figure F.2 is contained in file
INOUT.PAS and that the MACRO program is contained in file
AREA.MAR. Then to link the two programs, proceed as follows:

1. Assemble the MACRO program by

   ```
   MACRO AREA.MAR
   ```

2. Compile the Pascal program by

   ```
   PASCAL INOUT.PAS
   ```

3. Link the two object programs by

```
LINK AREA.OBJ+INOUT.OBJ
```

4. Run the program

```
RUN AREA
```

The order of the two files in the link command is important.

Glossary

Absolute address: An address mode in the MACRO assembler in which the value is a fixed constant that is not to be changed by the linker. Input/output data and control registers, for instance, have absolute addresses.

Absolute loader: A loader that places an object program as is in main memory, without address modification. For this the addresses in the object program must be actual physical addresses.

Access mode: The VAX-11 has four access modes, which are, from most privileged to least: (1) kernel (mode 0); (2) executive (mode 1); (3) supervisor (mode 2); and (4) user (mode 3). User programs are run in user mode. The command interpreter (DCL) runs in supervisor mode. Record Management Services (RMS) runs in executive mode, and System Services (SS) runs in kernel mode.

Access violation: An attempt to access an address that is not accessible by the current access mode. A usual occurrence of this violation occurs when the pound sign is erroneously omitted from a literal—for example ADDB2 2,R0 instead of ADDB2 #2,R0.

Accumulator: Any computer register that is used for the purpose of retaining the results of addition and subtraction operations. Some computers have only one accumulator; others use a bank of general-purpose registers.

Actual argument: An argument in a macro call that corresponds to a formal argument in the macro definition.

Address: A numeric value specifying the location in main memory of a given data item or instruction. Each byte of VAX-11 data has an address consisting of 32 bits. Disk units also have addresses that consist of cylinder number, track number, and sector number.

Address expression: An expression whose value is an address.

Address mode: A method of determining the address of an instructional operand. The VAX-11 has many addressing modes. In register mode, the address is the address of one of the 16 general-purpose registers. In relative mode, the address is given as a displacement from the program counter (PC). In literal mode, the address is not an address, but is (literally) the data itself.

Address space: VAX-11 addresses are 32 bits long; hence the total possible range of addresses is 0 through $2^{32} - 1$. Virtual address space includes this entire range, whereas physical address space includes only the first part of this range corresponding to the actual physical size of the memory. The assembly language programmer deals only with virtual addresses. The conversion to physical addresses is performed by the computer.

Alphanumeric character: The letters A–Z and the digits 0–9 normally form the set of alphanumeric characters. On the VAX-11 the characters $ and _ (underscore), as well as the lowercase letters, are also included in this set. Minor variations in the definition of this set occur in other computers.

Alternate key: An optional key of reference in an indexed file. This key is one of the fields in the record of the file, and the record can be retrieved on the basis of this key.

Argument: An input value to or an output value from a macro, subroutine, or procedure. Arguments can be passed by value or by address.

Argument list: The set of arguments to a procedure. On the VAX-11 an argument list is a (contiguous) table in which each entry is usually a longword. The entry may contain the address of the argument or the data, at the discretion of the assembly language programmer.

Argument pointer (AP): General register 12 of the VAX-11 (the AP) is used to point to the argument list of a procedure called by the CALLS or CALLG instruction.

Arithmetic logic unit (ALU): The hardware unit of the computer, which performs arithmetic and logical operations. The ALU often has internal registers to hold temporary or intermediate results of the operations.

ASCII: American Standard Code for Information Interchange. A set of 8-bit binary numbers (whose leading bit is usually 0, since ASCII was originally a 7-bit code) representing the alphabet (both capital and small letters); the set of numeric digits; a number of special characters (such as ! @ # $, .); and a number of unprintable control characters (such as carriage return CR, line feed LF, and the blank or space character SP).

Assembler: A computer program that translates another computer program written in a symbolic form of machine language into the numeric form of machine language that is used by the computer for program execution.

Assembly instruction: An instruction that is encoded in symbolic assembly language and that corresponds to one machine instruction.

Assembly language: A symbolic form of machine language wherein machine instructions are encoded mnemonically, and addresses and registers are referred to by names.

Assembly time: The interval of time in which an assembler performs its task. Assembly language programs must first be assembled before they can be run (executed).

Autoincrement deferred mode: A VAX-11 address mode that specifies a general-purpose register that contains the address of the instructional operand. After accessing the operand, the register is incremented by 4 (the number of bytes in an address).

Autoincrement mode: A VAX-11 address mode in which the contents of a general-purpose register are first used as an instructional operand and then incremented by the size of the operand in bytes.

Base: The radix of a positional number system. The number that is raised to the power given by the exponent in a floating-point data type.

Base operand address: The beginning address (or one less than the beginning address in some usages) of a table, array, program, or other item of contiguously stored data.

Binary: A positional number system based on the number 2. A device with two states. An event with two outcomes. An operator requiring two operands. The two binary states are usually designated 0 and 1 (true or false, T or F, on or off, and so on). Each position of a binary number is either 0 or 1.

Binary operator: Any mathematical or logical function that requires two arguments. Examples include the addition operator $a+b$, the multiplication operator $a \times b$, and the logical "AND" operator $a \cdot b$.

Binary point: The binary number system equivalent of the decimal point.

Bit: A binary state value of 0 or 1.

Block: The primary unit of disk storage. Most VAX-11 disk units store data in 512 byte blocks. A block is also called a sector. Data on magnetic tape are also stored by variable-length block or physical record.

Boolean expression: A formula involving only logical operations such as "AND", "OR," and "NOT," along with their operands.

Boundary alignment: The positioning of a data type in memory at an address that is a multiple of its length. For instance, a VAX-11 longword that requires 4 bytes is boundary-aligned if its starting address is a multiple of 4. In general, the VAX-11 does not require boundary alignment but runs faster if its data types are boundary-aligned.

Bucket: The primary unit of I/O transfer of relative and indexed files in the VAX-11 Record Management Services (RMS) system. Buckets are specified in units of disk blocks (sectors).

Bus: A hardware path for electronic signals to pass from one device to another. For instance, a bus may connect the CPU with memory.

Byte: A unit of information consisting of 8 (or 6) bits. Newer computers usually have bytes of 8 bits. There are 256 possible states for a byte. Hence one byte can store the numbers 0 through 255, or the numbers -128 through 127 in 2's complement notation, or a set of up to 255 alphanumeric characters in a character code such as ASCII or EBCDIC. The contents of a byte are usually given as two hexadecimal digits. Hence if a byte is said to contain B3, it contains 10110011.

Byte-addressable: A computer memory organization in which each byte is assigned its own unique address. The VAX-11 is byte-addressable.

Call-by-address: The method of passing a parameter to a subroutine or a procedure by specifying its address.

Call-by-reference: See Call-by-address.

Call-by-value: The method of passing a parameter to a subroutine or a procedure by specifying its value.

Call frame: A data structure pushed to the stack during execution of a CALLS or CALLG instruction. It consists of several longwords that contain information such as the contents of the PC, PSW, selected general registers, and so on. These values are restored to the given registers on execution of a RET instruction.

Cell: The space on disk into which a record can be stored in a relative file. All cells of a given relative file are of the same length, even though the records may be of variable length. At any point in time a cell either contains a record or is empty.

Central processing unit (CPU): The control unit and the arithmetic logic unit of a computer.

Character: A symbol represented in the VAX-11 by the ASCII code (see ASCII).

Character string: A contiguous set of characters in main memory, on disk or tape, on a CRT screen, and so on. In memory, a character string is identified by its starting (low-order) address and its length measured in characters.

Compiler: A program that translates another computer program written in a higher-level language into the numeric form of machine language.

Complement arithmetic: The use of complements as an alternative to signed magnitude for performing arithmetic involving both positive and negative numbers.

Conditional block: A sequence of statements that is enclosed within a .IF statement and assembled if the condition specified by the .IF statement is satisfied; otherwise the block is ignored.

Condition codes: Four bits in the processor status longword (PSL) that indicate the relative results (negative, zero, overflow, and carry) of previously executed instructions.

Console: A special computer terminal used to initiate and manage the operation of a medium-sized to large computer. The video portion of any computer terminal.

Control status register: A register used to store control information and status information regarding I/O to a given device.

Control unit (CU):   The part of a computer that fetches instructions from memory, interprets them, and executes them in sequence.

Core: The central or main memory of the computer. Although such memories are no longer usually made of magnetic cores, this term is still used.

Current record: The target record for RMS macros $UPDATE, $DELETE, and $GET (if preceeded by $FIND).

Cylinder: The set of tracks on a disk storage device that are all located at the same distance (or radius) from its spindle.

Data type: Any of the several ways of storing data on a computer. Data stored in ASCII are of data type character. Other data types are packed decimal, F-floating, byte (binary integer), word (binary integer), and so on.

Deferred addressing: Also called indirect addressing by some manufacturers. The technique of allowing an instruction operand to contain an address as its contents such that the computer uses this address as its effective operand. In performing deferred addressing, the computer must first access the address of the operand and then access the address contained there.

Device driver: A program that handles physical I/O for a given unit or device. Such programs are usually written in assembly language and must adhere to strict operating system conventions.

Direct addressing: The technique of accessing data from main memory given its memory address. The MACRO assembler allows the user to use symbols for direct memory addressing, such as ADDL A,B. The data at A are directly addressed by the symbol A. The MACRO assembler converts this address to relative mode, in which the address is specified as an offset from the address currently in the program counter (PC).

Direct assignment statement: An assembly language statement that assigns a symbolic name to a value.

Directive: A command to the assembler to perform a certain task at assembly time. (Contrast this with an instruction, which is a command to the computer hardware to perform a certain action at run time.)

Directive table: A table that lists all directives supported by an assembler, together with addresses of routines that process the directives.

Direct memory access (DMA): An I/O path to memory with its associated hardware and programming conventions designed for high-speed I/O transfer.

Disk file: A set of records stored on disk that have similar, if not identical, data formats.

Disk pack: One or more disk platters that revolve on a common spindle.

Displacement: A numerically valued offset from a given reference point (or address).

Displacement mode: A VAX-11 addressing mode in which the effective address is computed to be the sum of the contents of a general register and a displacement. If the general register is the PC, then this mode is equivalent to relative mode. The VAX-11 allows displacements to be bytes, words, or longwords.

Driver: See Device driver.

EBCDIC: Extended Binary Coded Decimal Interchange Code. A set of 8-bit binary numbers representing the alphabet (both capital and small letters); the set of numeric digits; a number of special characters (such as ! @ # $, .); and a number of unprintable control characters (such as carriage return CR, line feed LF, and the blank or space character SP). IBM computers usually use EBCDIC as their native code. DEC computers normally use ASCII (see ASCII).

EDITPC: A VAX-11 instruction that inserts punctuation such as dollar signs ($), commas (,), and periods (.) in packed decimal data while converting them to ASCII.

Effective address: The final address of an instructional operand after all modification required by paging, indexing, displacing, and other modifications required by a given addressing mode.

Entry: The memory address of an entry mask. The entry mask is immediately followed by the first executable instruction of a program or a procedure. See Entry mask.

Entry mask: A word whose bits represent the registers to be saved or restored on a procedure call or return using the instructions CALLS, CALLG, or RET.

Entry point: The address of the first executable instruction of a program or a subprogram.

Execution time: The interval of time in which the instructions of a program are carried out by the computer hardware.

Executive mode: See Access mode.

Field: A contiguous set of bytes within a record or program that together form a lexical and semantic unit. The fields of a record might be name, address, telephone number, and the like.

File: A set of records that have similar, if not identical, data formats.

File access block (FAB): A set of contiguous bytes in main memory reserved by RMS with the $FAB macro that contain information on a given file.

Fill register: A register used by the VAX-11 instruction EDITPC.

Fixed-format assembler: An assembler that requires the fields of an assembly statement to start in particular columns.

Floating point: A data type for the storage of real numbers. This data type usually consists of a mantissa (fraction) and an exponent. The value of the number is the mantissa times 2 raised to the exponent. In some machines the base is 10 or 16 instead of 2.

Fork level: An interrupt level used by device drivers.

Formal argument: An argument (or parameter) in a macro definition.

Forward reference: A label in a program that is referenced before it is defined.

Frame pointer (FP): Register R13 on the VAX-11. At any point in time the FP should contain the base address of the most recent call frame on the stack.

Free format assembler: An assembler that allows the fields of an assembly statement to start anywhere on a line.

General register: A register that can be used as an operand for a variety of functions such as integer arithmetic, floating arithmetic, or indexing. On the VAX-11 there are 16 such registers, R0–R15. R12–R15 have special hardware functions, however. R12 is the argument pointer (AP), R13 is the frame pointer (FP), R14 is the stack pointer (SP), and R15 is the program counter (PC). General registers on other computers such as the IBM 370 series have similar (but not identical) functions. For instance, the IBM 370 general registers cannot be used as operands for floating-point arithmetic.

Global: A variable or direct assignment that is defined in such a manner that it can be used in program sections other than the one in which it is declared. The addresses of such data are known to the VAX-11 linker and are supplied to other program modules during the LINK command.

Hexadecimal: The positional number system with base 16. The digits for this system are 0 through 9 and A (decimal 10) through F (decimal 15).

Image file: (or executable image file) contains the object program that is the output of the linker and is in machine-executable form—that is, ready for execution.

Immediate address: An instruction operand that contains the data themselves instead of the address of the data. On the VAX-11, small integer data items in the range 0–63 can be stored directly in the instruction. This is a form of immediate addressing that is called literal mode. Other values can be stored in the instruction in immediate mode. Hence ADD #10,R5 generates literal mode, whereas ADD #92,R5 generates immediate mode. Both modes are forms of immediate addressing.

Immediate mode: A VAX-11 addressing mode utilizing immediate addressing.

Index: A register or memory address used to count or keep track of a repetitive portion of a program or a position in a structured data type such as a table or a matrix. The VAX-11 has an index addressing mode. The instruction ADDB A[R6],R7 contains the indexed operand A[R6] in which the contents of R6 are added to the address A to form the effective address. If the operation code were ADDW (ADDL), then twice (four times) the contents of R6 would be added to A to form the effective address.

Indexed sequential: One of the three file organizations supported by RMS. Indexed files have one or more keys that are fields within the records of the file. RMS provides for random or sequential access of these files by any of its keys.

Indirect addressing: See Deferred addressing.

Instruction: See Machine instruction.

Interrupt: An event other than a branch instruction (including JMP, CASEL, CALLS, and so on) or a program exception that preempts the normal sequential execution of instructions. Interrupts are generally initiated external to the process currently executing. On the VAX-11, interrupts are classified as software interrupts, interrupt priority levels (IPL) 1–15 (15 is highest), and hardware interrupts (IPL levels 16–31).

Interrupt priority level (IPL): See Interrupt.

Kernel mode: The most privileged of four access modes in which the VAX-11 can be run. The operating system's most privileged routines, such as device drivers, execute in this mode.

Key of reference: A field in the record access block (RAB) that designates which key of an indexed file is currently being used.

Keyword argument: A formal argument in a macro definition that is specified by a name and a value. The value is used for the argument if the macro call does not specify an actual argument to correspond to the formal keyword argument. Otherwise, the specified actual argument is used.

Label: An assembly language symbolic address. The label can be either the address of an instruction or the address of an item of data. The label field is optional in a MACRO statement. If present, it is the first field of the statement and is followed by a colon (:). MACRO labels can be 1 to 31 alphanumeric characters long.

Latency: The amount of time required for a disk sector to rotate from an arbitrary position to a position that can be accessed by a disk read-write head.

Leading separate: A data type for storing signed integers as ASCII characters preceeded by an ASCII plus, minus, or blank.

Lexical scanning: The process of scanning a source program during the translation phase to determine the various elements in the statements of the program.

LIFO: Last in, first out. A typical method for queuing data.

Linker: A program that accepts as input object programs of separately assembled (or compiled) source programs and generates a single object program that is ready for execution. The linker is needed to determine addresses of externally defined symbols.

Listing: A file that is generated by an assembler (or compiler) and contains the source statements, their line numbers, their addresses, and their equivalent object code. It also contains error messages, if any, and other pertinent information about the source program.

Literal: A MACRO operand whose first character is #, which signifies that the data following are to be the operand, not the address of the operand. Literals may be decimal integers, ASCII strings, binary integers, floating point numbers, and so on. If the literal is a decimal integer in the range 0–63, then the literal causes the assembler to generate literal mode. Otherwise the assembler will generate immediate mode or relative mode, depending on the literal.

Literal mode: See Immediate mode.

Loader: A program that loads (places) an object program into main memory, possibly modifying addresses in the program to correspond to physical addresses.

Local label: A label in an assembly language program of the form $n\$$, where n is an integer. The term *local* refers to the fact that normally the label is used to be referenced from a small distance from where it is defined.

Location counter (LC): A counter maintained by an assembler for the purpose of determining the addresses of the statements being assembled. If a statement has a label, the label and its LC value are retained in the symbol table. The addresses computed in the LC are usually relative to the beginning of the program. When the program is loaded in memory for execution, the loader adjusts these addresses to reflect the actual memory addresses.

Longword: A VAX-11 information unit consisting of four 8-bit bytes. Any four contiguous bytes of VAX-11 memory can be used as a longword. The declaratives .BLKL and .LONG reserve memory in blocks of longwords and store given values in longwords, respectively.

Longword relative addressing: See Displacement mode.

Machine instruction: A basic instruction (such as ADD, MULTIPLY, BRANCH) that can be executed by the computer hardware directly.

Machine language: A numeric form of a language wherein data, instructions, addresses, and register names are encoded in their binary equivalents. Machine language is the native language of a computer and the only language the computer can execute directly. All programs must be translated into machine language before they can be executed.

Macro: A named sequence of assembly statements. At assembly time the sequence of statements is inserted in the program at every place the name is invoked. A macro definition may include parameters to be substituted with the arguments specified in the call.

MACRO: The name of the principal assembler used for assembly programming on the VAX-11 and on the PDP-11. The VAX version is sometimes referred to as MACRO32. The MACRO assembler features many facilities for defining and using macros.

Macro assembler: An assembler that has macro capabilities; that is, it allows defining and calling macros.

Macro call: An assembly statement that invokes a macro. The statement specifies the macro name and possibly actual arguments to correspond to the formal arguments of the macro.

Macro expansion: Refers to substituting a macro call by the statements of the macro, and substituting the actual arguments specified in the call for the formal arguments used within the macro.

Macro instruction: Same as Macro call.

Macro table: When a macro definition is encountered by the assembler, the macro is stored (in its source form) in an area within the assembler program. The macro table keeps the names of all macros in a program and pointers to where the macros are stored. The table is used by the assembler for macro expansion.

Main memory: That unit of a computer in which both data and programs are stored during program execution for rapid access and modification. The fastest random access storage device on a computer that is not part of the CPU. See Memory.

Mass storage device: A device capable of storing large amounts of data that must be transferred to main memory for processing. Typical mass storage devices are disks and drums.

Memory: That part of a computer that retains instructions and data needed for program execution. Main memory features fast random access of instructions and data and normally uses bipolar, MOS, or core technologies.

Memory access time: The amount of time required to fetch data from main memory into the memory buffer register (MBR).

Memory address: See Address.

Memory address register (MAR): A register that holds the memory address to be fetched or stored when reading or writing main memory.

Memory bandwidth: The maximum amount of information (in bits) that the memory unit can input or output in unit time.

Memory buffer register (MBR): A register that receives the data to be fetched or holds the data to be stored when reading or writing main memory.

Memory cycle time: The minimum time delay between the initiation of two memory operations.

Memory word: The amount of information (in bits) that can be moved into or out of main memory in one memory operation.

Mnemonic: Symbolic name chosen for a machine instruction that aids in remembering the action performed by the instruction.

Mode: A method or style of performing some operation. An addressing mode is a method of determining an address. An access mode is a set of conditions or rules in effect when running a program.

Multiprogramming system: A computer system that is capable of executing several programs simultaneously.

Nibble: The 4 high-order bits of a byte or the 4 low-order bits. Each nibble can be represented as one hexadecimal digit.

Normalized: A floating-point number whose mantissa, M, is in the range

$$0.5 \leq M < 1$$

Object module: See Object program.

Object program: A program that is the machine language equivalent of a source program, where instructions, data, register names, and so forth are translated into their binary forms.

Octal: The positional number system with base 8. The digits of this system are 0 through 7.

Octaword: A VAX-11 information unit consisting of 16 8-bit bytes. Any 16 contiguous bytes of VAX-11 memory can be used as an octaword.

Offset: See Displacement.

One-pass assembler: An assembler that generates object code in one scan of the source program.

Op code (operation code): Numeric code for representing a basic machine operation such as ADD, COMPARE, BRANCH. The computer hardware is designed to interpret the op code and execute the requested operation.

Op code table: A table that lists mnemonics of all instructions supported by an assembler together with their op codes.

Operating system: A collection of program modules that hides the complexities of the computer hardware, thus providing a hospitable interface between the user and the computer. Modern operating systems also allow several users to share the computer simultaneously.

Overflow: A condition in which the result of an instruction is too large to be contained in the given data type.

Overpunched: A VAX-11 data type used to store variable-length signed decimal integers. The digits of the number are given in ASCII except for the least significant one, which shares a byte with the algebraic sign. Similar to the zoned data type but with a different method for storing the sign.

Packed decimal: A VAX-11 data type for storing variable-length signed decimal integers two digits to the byte. The maximum length for such integers is 31 digits.

Page: A unit of virtual or physical memory equal to 512 bytes on the VAX-11. Virtual pages are stored on disk and are read into a physical memory page as needed during program execution.

Page frame: A page of physical memory.

Parity: A method of detecting data error by adding an extra bit or bits so that the total number of 1 bits in the data is an odd number (odd parity) or an even number (even parity).

Physical address: An address in physical main memory or a disk address expressed as a cylinder number, a track number, and a sector number.

Primary memory: See Main memory.

Procedure call: The execution of a VAX-11 CALLG or CALLS instruction. These instructions save the AP, FP, SP, PC, and all registers designated by the procedure mask along with program status in a call frame that is pushed onto the user stack prior to the execution of the procedure.

Processor status register: A register that contains the status of the computer at each instance of program execution. Status includes the condition codes, the interrupt priority level, the mode of execution, and so on. The VAX-11 maintains status in a processor status longword.

Program counter (PC): General register 15 on the VAX-11. The register that holds the address of each instruction executed by a program.

Program counter addressing: Any VAX-11 addressing mode in which the right nibble of the mode byte contains the hex value F signifying register 15. Program counter addressing modes include: immediate mode; absolute mode; byte (word, longword) mode; relative mode; and relative deferred.

Program section: A portion of a MACRO assembly program that begins with a .PSECT directive specifying its name and attributes and ends just before the next .PSECT containing a different name or the end of the module.

Pseudo-operation: See Directive.

Quadword: An information unit on the VAX-11 consisting of 8 bytes.

Queue: A doubly linked list data structure supported by VAX-11 hardware instructions for insertion and deletion.

Radix: The base of a number system.

Random access: The provision for access of any element of a group of objects in approximately the same time as any other element.

Random file: A file organization that allows random access of its records. See Relative file and Indexed sequential.

Record: A contiguous set of one or more fields of related data that are usually read into or written from main memory together. Records are the elements of a file. Records are sometimes blocked together for compact storage, in which case one may distinguish between a *physical record* and a *logical record*.

Record access block (RAB): A set of contiguous bytes in main memory reserved by RMS with the $RAB macro which contains information concerning the processing of records of a given file.

Recursive macro: A macro that contains a call to itself, in analogy with recursive subprograms.

Register: An element of computer memory that is designed for fast storage and retrieval and is often located in the CPU.

Register deferred mode: A VAX-11 addressing mode in which the register contains the address of the instruction operand.

Relative deferred mode: A Vax-11 addressing mode in which the relative address contains as its contents the address of the instruction operand.

Relative file: One of the three file organizations supported by VAX-11 RMS. The records of a relative file are stored in disk cells of equal size and can be accessed randomly by cell number.

Relative mode: See Displacement mode.

Relocation: The process of modifying relative addresses into physical addresses.

Repeat block: A sequence of statements enclosed within a .REPEAT statement. The block is duplicated by the assembler a number of times as specified by the .REPEAT statement.

RMS: Record Management Services, the file processing system of the VAX-11 VMS operating system.

Rotational delay: See Latency.

Run time: The interval of time during which the instructions of a program are executed by the computer hardware.

Secondary memory: Memory units such as magnetic disks, tapes, and drums that allow relatively low-cost storage of large amounts of data but that have slower access times than main memory.

Sector: See Block.

Sequential file: One of the three file organizations supported by VAX-11 RMS. The records of a sequential file are packed together on disk blocks, with block boundaries being ignored. Although such records may be accessed randomly if all records are the same size, the file is intended for sequential execution.

Signed magnitude: A method of storing signed numbers in which one bit serves as the sign, and the other bits contain the absolute value or magnitude of the number.

Significance register: One of the registers used by the EDITPC instruction.

Source program: A program whose statements are encoded in symbolic form, as opposed to numeric machine language programs.

Stack: A data type whose elements are stored and retrieved on a last in, first out (LIFO) basis. The VAX-11 features stacks that are supported by hardware instructions for insertion (pushing) and deletion (popping). Each user program has its own stack. The user stack is pointed to by the stack pointer (SP), general register 14.

Stack pointer (SP): See Stack.

Subroutine call: The execution of the VAX-11 instruction BSB or JSB. No call frame is stored. VAX-11 subroutine calls feature fast, low-overhead linkage. See Procedure call.

Supervisor mode: See Access mode.

Symbol table: A table that is built during the translation phase to store all user-defined symbols in a program and their relative addresses or values.

Track: All data stored on a single disk surface at equal radius from its center. All data stored in one line parallel to the length of a magnetic tape.

Translation phase: The time period during which a source program is translated into an object program.

Two-pass assembler: An assembler that scans a source program twice for translating it into object code. In the first pass it generates the symbol table, and in the second it generates the object code.

Unary operator: An operator that requires only one operand.

User mode: See Access mode.

User stack: See Stack.

Virtual address extension: The meaning of the abbreviation VAX.

Von Neumann machine: The classical model of computer organization involving a CPU, memory, and I/O.

Word: A VAX-11 information unit consisting of two 8-bit bytes. Any two contiguous bytes of VAX-11 memory can be used as a word. The declaratives .BLKW and .WORD reserve memory in blocks of words and store given values in words, respectively. In 2's complement notation, a word can hold an integer in the range -2^{15} to $2^{15} - 1$.

Word relative addressing: See Displacement mode.

Zoned: A VAX-11 data type used to store variable-length signed decimal integers. The digits of the number are given in ASCII except for the least significant one, which shares a byte with the algebraic sign. Similar to the overpunched data type, but with a different method for storing a sign.

References

Barron, D.W. *Assemblers and Loaders*. New York: Macdonald/Elsevier, 1969.

Calingaert, P. *Assemblers, Compilers and Program Translation*. Rockville, Md.: Computer Science Press, 1979.

Digital Equipment Corporation. *VAX-11 EDT Editor Manual AA-J726-TC*, October 1980.

———. *VAX Architecture Handbook*, 1981.

———. *VAX-11 Command Language User's Guide AA-D023C-TE,* May 1982.

———. *VAX-11 MACRO Language Reference Manual AA-D032D-TE,* May 1982.

———. *VAX-11 MACRO User's Guide AA-D033D-TE,* May 1982.

———. *VAX-11 Record Management Services Reference Manual AA-D031D-TE,* May 1982.

———. *VAX-11 SOS Text Editing Reference Manual AA-M538A-TE,* May 1982.

———. *VAX-11 Symbolic Debugger Reference Manual AA-D026D-TE,* May 1982.

———. *VAX Hardware Handbook,* 1982–1983.

———. *VAX Software Handbook,* 1982–1983.

Donovan, J.J. *System Programming*. New York: McGraw-Hill, 1972.

Gear, C.W. *Computer Organization and Programming,* 3rd ed. New York: McGraw-Hill, 1980.

Gill, A. *Machine and Assembly Language Programming of the PDP-11,* 2nd ed. Englewood Cliffs, N.J.: Prentice-Hall, 1982.

Hamacher, V.C.; Vranesic, Z.G.; and Zaky, S.G. *Computer Organization*. New York: McGraw-Hill, 1978.

Kapps, C.A., and Stafford, R.L. *Assembly Language for the PDP-11*. Boston: CBI Publishing Company, Prindle, Weber and Schmidt, 1981.

Knuth, D.E. *The Art of Computer Programming,* vol. 1: *Fundamental Algorithms*. Reading, Mass.: Addison-Wesley, 1968.

Levy, H.M., and Eckhouse, R.H., Jr. *Computer Programming and Architecture—the VAX-11.* Maynard, Mass.: Digital Press, 1980.

Madnick, S.E., and Donovan, J.J. *Operating Systems.* New York: McGraw-Hill, 1974.

Peterson, J.L. *Computer Organization and Assembly Language Programming.* New York: Academic Press, 1978.

Presser, L., and White, J.R. "Linkers and Loaders." *Computing Surveys* 4, no. 3 (September 1972): 149–168.

Rosen, S. "Electronic Computers: A Historical Survey." *Computing Surveys* 1, no. 1 (March 1969): 7–36.

Stone, H.S., ed. *Introduction to Computer Architecture*, 2nd ed. Chicago: Science Research Associates, 1980.

Stone, H.S., and Siewiorek, D.P. *Introduction to Computer Organization and Data Structures: PDP-11 Edition.* New York: McGraw-Hill, 1975.

Tuggle, S.K. *Assembler Language Programming: System/360 and 370.* Palo Alto, Calif.: SRA, 1975.

Index